P9-DHN-462

THROUGH THE LABYRINTH

ALSO BY PETER OCCHIOGROSSO

Inside Spinal Tap

Once a Catholic

WITH LARRY KING

Tell It to the King

Tell Me More

WITH FRANK ZAPPA

The Real Frank Zappa Book

THROUGH
· · · · THE · · · ·
LABYRINTH

Stories of the Search
for Spiritual Transformation
in Everyday Life

·

Peter Occhiogrosso

·

VIKING

VIKING
Published by the Penguin Group
Viking Penguin, a division of Penguin Books USA Inc.,
375 Hudson Street, New York, New York 10014, U.S.A.
Penguin Books Ltd, 27 Wrights Lane, London W8 5TZ, England
Penguin Books Australia Ltd, Ringwood, Victoria, Australia
Penguin Books Canada Ltd, 10 Alcorn Avenue, Suite 300, Toronto, Ontario, Canada M4V 3B2
Penguin Books (N.Z.) Ltd, 182–190 Wairau Road, Auckland 10, New Zealand

Penguin Books Ltd, Registered Offices: Harmondsworth, Middlesex, England

First published in 1991 by Viking Penguin, a division of Penguin Books USA Inc.

1 3 5 7 9 10 8 6 4 2

Copyright © Peter Occhiogrosso, 1991
All rights reserved

Grateful acknowledgment is made for permission to reprint excerpts from the following copyrighted works:
Visions of Glory by Barbara Grizzuti Harrison. By permission of the author.
Freedom from the Known by J. Krishnamurti. Copyright © 1969 by the Krishnamurti Foundation Trust. Reprinted by permission of HarperCollins Publishers and Krishnamurti Foundation Trust Ltd.
"Whatever Gets You Through the Night" by John Lennon. Copyright © 1974 Lenono Music. All rights administered by Sony Music Publishing, Nashville, TN. Reprinted by permission of the publisher.
The Experiment is Over by Paul Lowe. By permission of Roximillion Publications Corporation.
Nine-Headed Dragon River by Peter Matthiessen. © 1985 by the Zen Center of New York. Reprinted by permission of Shambhala Publications, Inc., Boston, MA.
Unseen Rain by Jelaluddin Rumi, translated by John Moyne and Coleman Barks. By permission of Threshold Books, Putney, VT.
The Kundalini Experience: Psychosis or Transcendence? by Lee Sannella, M.D. By permission of Integral Publishing.
Meditation in Action by Chögyam Trungpa. © 1991 by Diana Mukpo. Reprinted by permission of Shambhala Publications, Inc.

LIBRARY OF CONGRESS CATALOGING IN PUBLICATION DATA
Occhiogrosso, Peter.
Through the labyrinth : stories of the search for
spiritual transformation in everyday life / Peter Occhiogrosso.
   p. cm.
Includes bibliographical references and index.
ISBN 0–670–82993–5
1. Spiritual life. I. Title.
BL624.O287 1991
248.4—dc20   91–50156

Printed in the United States of America
Set in Meridien
Designed by Kathryn Parise

Without limiting the rights under copyright reserved above, no part of this publication may be reproduced, stored in or introduced into a retrieval system, or transmitted, in any form or by any means (electronic, mechanical, photocopying, recording or otherwise), without the prior written permission of both the copyright owner and the above publisher of this book.

TO FIN DRURY

1949—1991

This rediscovery of religion is the great intellectual, moral and spiritual adventure of our time. It is something which calls for all our energies, and involves both labour and sacrifice. But it cannot be a mass movement. The discovery has to be made by each individual for himself. Each one approaches it from a different angle and has to work out his own particular problem. Each alike is given the golden string and has to find his own way through the labyrinth.

—Dom Bede Griffiths, *The Golden String*

ACKNOWLEDGMENTS

. . .

Without question, this has been the most difficult book I have undertaken to write so far, and I couldn't have done it without the help of a series of guides who seemed to appear when I needed them most. I picked up precious insights from people I met at spiritual gatherings, workshops, and bookstores, or on the ball field or just in passing, and I'm grateful to all of them. The people whose names appear below were extremely generous with their time in helping me to understand specific spiritual disciplines and in directing me to potential interview subjects.

I am especially indebted to Howard Finkelson for his continuing elucidation of many aspects of spiritual development and his suggestions for a number of interviews that proved fruitful. Over the time I've worked on this book, Howard has become a good friend and a reliable source of knowledge which he imparts with more enthusiasm than one could imagine possible. Some of the others who helped me in my researches are, in no particular order, Anne Roberts of Mirabai Books in Woodstock, Jean Boyle of Pope John XXIII Seminary, Rabbi Burton Visotzky of Jewish Theological Seminary, Eduardo Rauch of the Melton Center, Chad Roche and Ellen Kieve of Eckankar, Michael Chender of Shambhala Training in Nova Scotia, Mantak Chia of the Healing Tao Center, Bill McBrien of Hofstra University, Stuart Krichevsky, Joby Washburn, John Leira, Gloria Stevens, Holly Beye, Jennifer Dignan, James Manuel, Laurence Morris, Hollie Clark, Enrique Fernández, Dean Taylor, Rebecca Daniels, Marybeth and Christopher Kearns-Barrett, David Adams, Jon DeRobertis, Maxine Duer, Rick Moody, Esther Katz, Deirdre Levinson, Daniel Silberberg, Roger Woolger, John Duggan, and Thomas Boland, S.J.

Larry Kessenich, my former editor at Houghton Mifflin, deserves much of the credit for helping me formulate the initial conception of the book from out of the void. Dawn Seferian, my editor at Viking, let me write the book I wanted to write.

I am thankful to Rebecca Daniels and Shayan Malkine for their faithful transcriptions of hours of recorded interviews, and for their unsolicited evaluations of my interview subjects. ("This guy is really boring and self-important. I hope you're not going to include *him*.")

Several people helped to refine the manuscript, including my manuscript editor Beena Kamlani, whose eye for detail is sharp and all-encompassing. Barbara Flanagan applied her fearless genius to a large portion of the text, and her blue pencil left only clarity in its wake. And I am grateful most of all for the careful and insightful readings and rereadings and the incisive revisions suggested by my wife, Margery, whose encouragement was a persuasive antidote to perpetual second-guessing (and who rewrote this run-on sentence).

I should add that I am also deeply appreciative of the many spiritual teachers, formal and informal, whom I met along the way and who awakened in me some awareness of my own spiritual process, such as it is. Their assistance, in the long run, was the most beneficial of all.

CONTENTS

. . .

CHAPTER 1

A Critique of
Impure Reason

. . .

Our minds have reacted so violently towards provable logical theorems and demonstrable mechanical or chemical facts that we have become incapable of metaphysical truth, and try to cast out incredible and silly lies by credible and clever ones.
—G. B. Shaw in the Preface to *Back to Methuselah*

The intellectual world that underlies contemporary secular humanism, the intellectual substructure supporting our friends and contemporaries who don't worry about God and so forth, has really been exhausted. Logical positivism has been exhausted. It's been taken as far as it can go. . . . Secular positivism is not giving anything . . . [to] ordinary people who feel lost and disoriented.
—Robert Stone, quoted in *Once a Catholic*

I always figured on bein' reasonable.
—Van Heflin in *Shane*

.

To talk about God or the life of the spirit in intellectual circles is only marginally more acceptable today than it was ten or twenty years ago. In the academic world, it has been virtually taboo for some time, although this appears to be changing slowly. During the 1960s and 1970s, you could talk about religious experience in countercultural company if you kept it mystical, preferably Oriental, and possibly in tandem with psychedelic drugs. But intellectual or not, most Amer-

icans who turned away from mainstream religion have figured, like
the doggedly determined sodbuster Joe Start played by Van Heflin in
the movie *Shane*, that being reasonable would be enough to get them
through even the most absurd of times. If recent Western civilization
has relied faithfully on one thing—despite the evidence of irrationality
implicit in two world wars and the Holocaust—it is the power of
reason, the ability to know and understand logically and scientifically.
The same reliance on reason that helped lead many Westerners away
from the traditional faiths of their parents also served to guide them
through the anxieties occasioned by the loss of that older kind of faith.
Or did it?

As several surveys taken in recent years attest, atheistic secular
humanists make up a much smaller percentage of the American population than many writers and media pundits would have us believe.
Part of the reason for that misperception may be the vehemence with
which the religious right has trumpeted the threat of encroaching
secularism (leading Judge Brevard Hand of Alabama in one landmark
case to declare secular humanism a "religion"), but such alarmist
pronouncements don't change the fact that atheists are in the distinct
minority in this country. Nonetheless, during much of the century,
secular humanism served as the major alternative world view for those
adventurous or disillusioned souls who were put off by the arbitrary
and legalistic character of Roman Catholicism and Orthodox Judaism
or by the blandness of mainline Protestantism.

Like many members of my generation, I reached a point fairly early
in life at which reason urged me to discard a system of theology that
no longer made sense to me. Maybe reason wasn't the only factor,
but it carried the load for a number of gut feelings and glandular
impulses that went counter to the laws of the Catholicism in which
I had been raised. My growing reliance on reason appeared to create
a terminal paradox, for how could I satisfy the innate urge to reverence
I had felt in childhood and still accommodate the intellectual world
that I was growing into? That world, dominated by existentialist philosophers and playwrights, among others, was vividly calling my attention to the impossibility that a universe as absurd as ours could
have been started up and kept humming by a loving God. And so
reason delivered the coup de grâce that left the very idea of structured

religious faith reeling and bleeding on the aromatic soil of late adolescence.

Many years and much internal wrangling later, I began to suspect that in my carefully reasoned rejection of belief I was actually casting out, as Shaw suggested, "the adulteration of religion," despising the reduction of vast metaphysical truths to a pious and punitive format rather than the truths themselves. I also suspected that this rejection not only didn't stand me in especially good stead, but in its ultra-rational way didn't make much sense, either. Was it really sensible to believe that one could reason scientifically around areas of existence that, as more and more scientists have begun admitting, are complex beyond all reasoning? And did it necessarily deny the existence of God to admit that the world is indeed absurd, more absurd perhaps than Ionesco and Beckett and Sartre and Camus ever imagined?

Only recently, I came across the work of a Western spiritual teacher trained in the Hindu traditions of India who voices an understanding of the essential absurdity of life from a spiritual perspective. Da Free John, who later changed his name to Da Love-Ananda and is now called Da Kalki, is one of a small but growing number of alternative teachers with worldwide followings who grew up in the United States. Born Franklin Jones in Jamaica, New York, in 1939, Da Kalki studied and practiced with a number of spiritual masters, most notably Swami Muktananda in India, before going off to teach on his own. In his 1978 book *The Enlightenment of the Whole Body**, Da writes, "Life is completely absurd. Every particle of it would move you toward some experience or other, and yet all experience conceals the ultimate message of the necessity for transcendence or freedom from experience. That one must attain freedom from something that is unnecessary to begin with is utterly absurd. Why bother with it to begin with?"

Enlightenment, to Da, consists of seeing the essential "seriousness" of experience, the false importance which we attach to all the aspects of life that must inevitably come to an end. "Self-indulgence is serious, stressful effort is serious, discipline is serious, knowledge is serious: death, sex, food; everything is completely serious. This movement or tendency to survive, to continue in independent form, is profoundly

* San Rafael, Calif.: Dawn Horse Press, 1978.

serious, and it is also absurd because it must be transcended. Enlightenment is to be restored to Divine humor, to realize that nothing is necessary. No experience is necessary. . . . We are under the incredibly absurd illusion that there is an objective world 'outside' Consciousness. There is not a shred of truth in this presumption." He goes on to explain his version of the Hindu belief that objective reality is merely an illusion based upon what he calls "a bizarre phenomenon of the brain" and is a distraction from what we must be about. Da's way of expressing the absurdity of the universe strikes me now as more radical and more profound than the essentially agnostic or atheistic expressions of the philosophers and writers who had captured my imagination as I was coming of age.

A refreshingly humanistic college biology professor of mine once likened the world of microbic life pullulating under our illuminated microscopes to "a kind of millefleur tapestry." At the time, that appealed to me as a fine interdisciplinary metaphor, mixing science and art, stirring dull students with the unexpected. In retrospect, the image takes on spiritual overtones. In greater numbers now, scientists and scientific writers such as Gary Zukav, Fritjof Capra, and David Bohm have begun finding room for God, or at least questions about God, in their cosmos. For them, as for an increasing number of artists, intellectuals, and business people who have relied primarily on their intellects to bring them sustenance and pleasure, something appears to be missing, something which they are beginning to sense may be filled only by a sense of the numinous.

Naturally, not all scientists or artists think this way. One could also argue that artists rely less on intellect than on intuition and feeling. But modern painters, musicians, writers, and filmmakers, with a few notable exceptions, seem to have resisted anything that smacked of the overtly religious, as if that might sabotage their image as freethinkers (free, that is, to contemplate any but a spiritual underpinning to life). If ambiguity and a sense of the mysterious were acceptable in their creative work, the same attitude applied to questions of life and death and the afterlife might not be welcomed by their colleagues with hearty backslaps and calls for another round of drinks. Their attitude may have sprung in part from a pejorative identification of religion with the benighted masses in need of their dose of opiate (some artists and intellectuals preferring actual opium to the metaphorical variety). Their dread of theological belief was probably also tied to a perception of religion as an authoritarian institution opposed to the free expression of art and philosophy, as established religions have often been. For similar reasons perhaps, the rejection of religion took on political overtones as well. As hostility to the spiritual realm in educated circles has abated somewhat in recent years, however, the radical Catholic left, joined by bands of activist Protestants and Jews, can take credit for holding out all along for the compatibility of political activism, intellectual integrity, and spiritual fervor.

Perhaps all religion at its core represents the triumph of intuition, irrationality, and awe in spite of intellect. Intellect may bring the nonbeliever to the threshold of belief, but it must abandon him there. The late Paul Twitchell's survey of Eastern religion, *Letters to a Chela*, describes how the masters of Mahayana Buddhism fight rational thinking by whacking or teasing their disciples, evading their questions, and using riddles called koans, highly resistant to reasonable solution. The aim of the masters, according to Twitchell, is to teach their chelas, or students, to "trust your intuition, short-circuit reflection, discard caution, and act spontaneously." That sounds like good advice for anyone navigating the transition from secular humanism to spiritual investigation. Perhaps the most common struggle for those who have set out to explore the spiritual realm is the contest of the heart to countermand the edicts of the mind and set free the soul.

A further wrinkle is added to the reason vs. intuition argument by the scholar Jacob Needleman in his review of some Eastern traditions and teachers that have taken root in the West, entitled *The New Religions* (1970). One way that many of these teachings may change our conception of religion, Needleman writes, is that "they bring the idea that our mind and the power of thought itself is wretchedly inept without exposure to a spiritual discipline." The religions from which many Westerners have broken away, either in despair or disgust, Needleman argues, have been guilty of excluding the mind from the religious process and focusing instead largely on the will (which may explain the vengeance with which reason has ousted faith in the past century or so). But Eastern religions, and Christianity and Judaism at their mystical cores, involve a training of the mind along with the will and the spirit. Far from bypassing the mind altogether, as some observers fear, Eastern religions teach that "we are chained by our subjectivity," that "choice without intellectual freedom is only impulse, the impulse of the animal," and that true intellectual freedom requires the training of the mind through spiritual discipline. Even a superficial look at the techniques of Western monasticism, Zen, or Hinduism will show how lacking in rigor the standard Western spiritual training actually is. The implication of Needleman's argument is that the rational intellect is itself flawed, incomplete, an unreliable guide. Western rationality may be good for understanding the complicated physics and mathematics required to launch a space shuttle, but does it give us the best shot at understanding ourselves and finding fulfillment? Or rather, as we are learning, are the technological advances that science has made possible actually threatening our physical existence?

Without question, the very effort of going against the tide, not only of our own imperfect rationality but of the common perception of our contemporaries that such undisciplined and limited thought is enough to carry us through, can prove a formidable challenge. In *Faith, Sex, Mystery*, the prominent theater critic and essayist Richard Gilman gives a well-wrought account of his conversion at age twenty-nine from atheistic Judaism to Catholicism and his subsequent loss of faith eight years later—or what he calls "the report of a journey to the frontier, a sojourn there and a retreat." Although his narrative has an ending that may seem contrary to the direction taken by the subjects of this book, Gilman's comments often transcend the obvious. He begins by saying that he can't be the only person in this deeply secular society ("despite the fundamentalist twitchings at the surface") who hasn't at some point at least entertained "the idea of the spiritual." "The unfashionableness of the spiritual and of religion in general in the 'brighter,' more enlightened sectors of society, the ones I professionally belong to," he goes on, "the odd, almost offensive quality of its whole vocabulary—faith, transcendence, soul, eternal life, God—all this seems to me precisely a solicitation to take it up again. For whatever is fashionable or unfashionable in such realms as these is by that token suspect."

Gilman says that "fashion is a form of tyranny as well as a sign of boredom," and that although it may be trivializing religion to talk about it in terms of fashion ("was it 'fashionable' to be religious in the Middle Ages?" he asks), nonetheless, "to examine whatever is excluded on principle by the age, or some part of it, may be idle or foolish but is surely some sort of act of freedom." I'm not sure just how many people share Gilman's willingness to consider that the way we are "carried along in matters of the psyche and the spirit by our place and time" and "held more or less firmly in tow" by those controlling factors is reason enough to break away, stand back, and have another look at spiritual possibilities. But for some Americans over the last few decades, the decision to do so was dictated by feelings so strong they could hardly be denied.

A spiritually oriented healer named Michael Hayes whom I visited in Pennsylvania told me of the crisis precipitated in his life when feelings of that sort suddenly surfaced. "My father was a mathematician and a very firm atheist," he said, "and that's how I was raised. When I started to have all kinds of spiritual feelings and experiences in my late teens, it created a great deal of conflict in me, because they went against everything that I had been taught as a child." On the basis of stories like that one and several more that appear in these pages, I have come to feel that the time is past due for a re-evaluation of the secular humanist stance. As one of the first steps in that re-evaluation, however, we need to understand exactly what we mean when we begin to discuss spirituality and spiritual experience.

CHAPTER 2

What Is Spirituality?

. . .

At last, when the pain grows unbearable . . . they must listen to the voice from within, look closely at inner experiences that they have previously ignored, and search for paths leading to a new system of belief.

—Karlfried Graf Dürckheim, *Zen and Us*

The Ways unto God are as the number of the souls of men.

—Sufi saying

.

For some people, spirituality is a complex system of religious observations and moral precepts. For others, it is an equally convoluted set of laws determining the nature and intensity of certain inner "experiences," which can be at once profoundly mystical and palpably physical—from feelings of complete unity with the Godhead to sensations of utter bliss, of energy coursing through their bodies—experiences which can lead to a state of perfected spiritual awareness often referred to as enlightenment or realization. Still others have simplified the spiritual to the essential principle of compassionate living, of treating people with awareness and decency. True spirituality probably consists of a subtle balance of all three conceptions, although the second category, mystical experiences, often sounds the most gripping. Reading descriptions of enlightenment, mystical union, satori, Oneness, or whatever term the writer chooses, I have often been struck by how powerful and yet impossibly far from my life they seem.

Moreover, I have long had the feeling that accounts of ordinary people who underwent extraordinary developments in their lives might be both more accessible and more helpful to those who feel drawn to the spiritual realm, but cannot somehow imagine leaving behind home and work and family and heading off to India or Tibet or some Trappist monastery to explore the implications of that yearning. With that in mind, I set out to ask people about the spiritually transforming moments in their lives, and as I did so, I gradually came to realize that almost any event can be experienced as spiritual, depending on the context. Coming up with a definition of spirituality and inner experiences is ultimately less useful than describing them and placing them within the setting of an entire life. Two stories— one which was told to me and one I came upon in a book—may help to make this point.

"I was an open spirit, and there I was in the middle of a war. In combat situations where there's life and death in your normal work day, there's a richness to life and a strong desire to keep living. Breathing is great and taking a shower is great. Anything you do takes on a lot more meaning and a lot more joy, and you want to keep doing that. I once went out on an operation in the middle of the night, dark as pitch, going from little island to little island with mud and water all around. And on one little island we came to, there was one tree full of fireflies. I was in a whole atmosphere of death and destruction and depression and hopelessness, and all of a sudden I saw this tree lit up brighter than most Christmas trees—from fireflies! I wanted to drop to my knees. I just stood there with my mouth open like everybody else. But I wanted to drop on my knees and pray, 'God, thanks for the sign,' you know? That helped me get through the rest of the period. It was a sign of life itself, a sign from life."

Sam "Arch" Crawford was talking about his stint in Vietnam in 1966, an experience that had clearly been a turning point not only in his life but also in his spiritual development. When he came home from Southeast Asia, he brought with him a radically different appreciation of life. "I'd been in the jungle for a number of months where you had to do what was absolutely necessary to keep everybody alive," he said. "Then I came back to New York and people were fighting over a parking place. That was a milestone for me. I said, 'These people don't know what life is about.' That's what I mean when I say that Vietnam was a spiritual experience. I felt an intensity there, a desire for life. Here people are killing themselves in bars and with drugs, doing everything to deaden the sense of life. Combat brings that sense to life: you really want to live."

On the surface, Arch Crawford is as absorbed in the material milieu of modern life as you might expect from any single man in his mid-forties who lives on the Upper East Side of Manhattan and produces his own stock market newsletter. When I interviewed him in his apartment-cum-office, strewn with copies of his newsletter, he had been riding a hot streak timing trends in the market based on a combination of technical and astrological analysis. Unlikely as that may sound, Crawford has been consistently ranked among the top ten market "timers" in the country by trade publications such as *Timer Digest*. He also follows a daily regimen of meditation aided by high-tech tape recordings, under the tutelage of a Virginia-based guru named Brother Charles, which he feels enhances both his performance and his enjoyment of life.

We were talking about the journey that had begun for him with his childhood in a Southern Methodist family in North Carolina when Crawford mentioned his progression from finding a passion for life in Vietnam to encountering death-in-life on the streets of New York. His description was so down to earth, despite the exotic, even heroic, setting, that it subtly but surely changed my understanding of what a spiritual experience could be. I got the feeling that if Arch Crawford could have a spiritual experience in the jungle battlefields of Vietnam, maybe other people could have similar experiences in their daily lives, while driving to work, raising the kids, or taking a bath. He had given me a new frame of reference for a term that had previously seemed irritatingly vague and mystifying.

But why does one event or feeling qualify as spiritual and another as profane, materialistic, ordinary? The word "spirit," which comes from the Latin for "breathing," connotes both the sense of vital force and of something invisible. And so by extension, spirituality can refer to the notion of an invisible realm that functions in human life not merely alongside visible, material reality, but also as the animating force of the physical, which is inextricably bound to it. Anyone who has ever awoken in the middle of a dream, for example, may have been left with the distinct sensation that the dream sphere is as real as or possibly more real than the waking, visible plane into which he or she has just emerged. Psychoanalysis has attempted to provide us with all sorts of rational explanations for the dream process, but has never completely succeeded in expunging the feeling that the dream state represents another distinct level of reality. Likewise, the numerous accounts of near-death experiences recorded by Raymond Moody and Barbara Harris (in *Life After Life* and *Full Circle*, respectively), would seem to confirm the reality of other planes of being occurring alongside the visible plane. In these accounts, people return to consciousness after having spent some time in a kind of spirit realm between life and afterlife that not only seems completely real to them but that in many cases also changes their perception of life once they return to the visible realm.

For my purposes, the word "spiritual" is preferable to "religious" because it is not limited to the denotation of an organized communal practice. Most of the subjects I interviewed do follow some kind of regular practice, but not all of those practices would qualify as "organized religion." Furthermore, certain Eastern systems of belief, such as Buddhism and Taoism, do not encompass an understanding of God that would be recognizable to Westerners versed in the Hebrew-Christian tradition. So, although the word "God" appears frequently in these pages, it should not be construed as the sole criterion or focal point of a spiritual life. Nor should we make the mistake of assuming that spiritually oriented people necessarily look down on the physical realm as somehow degrading or inferior. One of the things on which Eastern and Western spiritual teachers appear to agree is that, whatever the difficulties or dissatisfactions of life on the material plane, the only way to achieve salvation, or deliverance through enlightenment, is by the act of embodiment. Christians, Jews, and Muslims believe we get only one chance, whereas Hindus, Buddhists, and most Easterners presume a continuing progression through many lifetimes. Yet they all feel, as the ninth-century Hindu philosopher and saint Shankara expressed it, that having been born in a human body is one of the things for which we should daily give thanks to God.

In that vein, the focus of this book will be on people whose spiritual experiences have led them not out of the material world to some tonsured, eremitic state in a monastery atop the Himalayas, but into a deeper appreciation of the role of the spirit in daily life. I will seek to examine religion not as a jumping-off place for otherworldly mysticism, for developing psychic powers or seeking out-of-body experiences, but as a way of transforming how people live in the "real world."

If Arch Crawford's experience was a turning point in his life, it is only one of the steps that led to his current appreciation of spirituality as a part of everyday existence. The spiritual element is integrated into his being in a way that is significant to him, and yet to the outside observer, to someone paying for his skills as a market analyst and adviser, let's say, it might appear quite irrelevant. By contrast, the American author and teacher Ram Dass, who underwent an enormous transformation over the course of many years, is more obviously engaged in living a spiritual life. He writes and lectures on different aspects of spirituality, including how to maintain a personal meditation and spiritual practice. Among other things, he is notable for the way in which he has tied spirituality to the practical applications of working to ease the suffering of others, especially in the areas of illness and approaching death. Known earlier in his life as Richard Alpert, a Harvard psychologist and associate of Timothy Leary, Ram Dass has also told of a seminal transformative experience.

As he describes it in his first book, *Be Here Now*, Alpert was journeying through Tibet and India in search of enlightenment. At the time, he was deep in despair after becoming disillusioned by his roles in various "games": Harvard professor, psychedelic pioneer, spokesman for the wonders of LSD. But he was disturbed that no matter how much LSD he took, he eventually had to come down, so that his chemically induced enlightenment remained as transitory as everything else. One night during his travels, he was standing out under the stars thinking about his mother, who had died of a spleen ailment the previous year, and he felt her presence. The next day he was taken to meet an Indian guru whom he calls Maharaji, who promptly asked whether Alpert would give him the expensive Land Rover he had driven there. Alpert of course declined. Some time later, Maharaji took Alpert aside and said to him, "You were out under the stars last night. You were thinking about your mother." Alpert was impressed. Then Maharaji added matter-of-factly that Alpert's mother had died the year before because of her spleen.

Alpert had two immediate responses. "The first thing that happened," he writes, "was that my mind raced faster and faster to try to get leverage—to get a hold on what he had just done. I went through every super CIA paranoia I've ever had. 'Who is he?' 'Who does he represent?' 'Where's the button he pushes where the file appears?' and 'Why have they brought me here?' None of it would gel. It was just too impossible that this could have happened this way . . . and the whole thing was just too far out. My mind went faster and faster and faster."

Finally, he writes,

> I felt like what happens when a computer is fed an insoluble problem; the bell rings and the red light goes on and the machine stops. And my mind just gave up. It burned out its circuitry . . . its zeal to have an explanation. I needed something to get closure at the rational level and there wasn't anything. There just wasn't a place I could hide in my head about this.
>
> And at the same moment, I felt this extremely violent pain in my chest and a tremendous wrenching feeling and I started to cry. And I cried and I cried and I cried. And I wasn't happy and I wasn't sad. It was not that kind of crying. The only thing I could say was that it felt like I was home. Like the journey was over. Like I had finished.

Thereafter he found himself willing to offer Maharaji the Land Rover or anything else he wanted, although the guru instead took him on as his disciple for no fee. Maharaji *did* ask for and take a triple dose of the high-grade LSD that Alpert was carrying with him. Alpert observed the holy man the entire day, but witnessed no visible reaction. He had finally encountered someone who was able to answer his questions about LSD. Maharaji was unaffected by the massive dose of acid, Alpert reasoned, because he was already beyond it. From that point on, Alpert could let go of his attachment to seeking enlightenment through chemicals and move on to other things.

This story represents a turning point in Richard Alpert/Ram Dass's spiritual process, but again it is only one moment on a path that extends across decades. More than twenty years after these events took place, Ram Dass is still evolving and expanding his way of integrating his spiritual realizations into the world of the everyday. And so, when we speak of spiritual transformation, we are not talking about a single "experience," something that happens once and then is comfortably over and done with, leaving one permanently "enlightened." Enlightenment, as the American Zen abbot Bernard Glassman says, is an ongoing process. It has to be worked on continually. When I asked the Eastern Orthodox theologian Father Thomas Hopko whether he had experienced a spiritual transformation at some point in his life, he put it this way: "My life could be described as a series of transformations all along, or perpetual transformation."

The lives presented in this book are composed, then, of a series of transformations, some more dramatic or radical than others, but all ultimately leaving those lives changed in a crucial way. That doesn't mean that a linear trajectory applies in each case. People sometimes leave their spiritual explorations for a time or alter them permanently in ways that might seem confusing or unrecognizable to an observer, but even in those cases the aftereffects of genuine transformation continue to shape lives in unique ways. I am not concerned with only extraordinary states of being that are inaccessible to most people, or with men and women whose ways of life appear largely beyond our grasp—monks and swamis and ascetics. Aside from the experiences that the people interviewed here recount, and a willingness to reflect upon their condition as other than purely material beings, little separates most of them from the mainstream of American life. Some are involved in business and the arts; some are homemakers; some are in the healing professions; a few have become spiritual instructors. They come from the working class and the middle class; one has spent time in prison and one lives on an inheritance. They grew up in Jewish, Catholic, Protestant, agnostic, and atheistic families. And they have found new ways of seeing the world through spiritual disciplines of all descriptions, from mainstream Protestantism, Catholicism, and Judaism to Buddhism, Islam, and Hindu and New Age beliefs; and some, as Duke Ellington said of certain musicians in his orchestra, are beyond category.

The twentieth-century Russian mystic and teacher G. I. Gurdjieff spoke of the Fourth Way, by which he meant the combination of a system of intensive and precisely regulated inner work and the fulfillment of the normal obligations of everyday life. In *Gurdjieff: A Very Great Enigma*, the noted Gurdjieff scholar J. G. Bennett, after asking rhetorically what makes it possible for humanity to fulfill its cosmic duty, responds:

For those who do not know of the Fourth Way it must appear that it is best done in retirement from life. The intensification and acceleration of this work was formerly supposed to be the task of monks and recluses, withdrawn from the world, who could devote the whole of their time and energy to this action which brings about the transformation of substances. It is probably true that this was more generally the case in earlier times, when the conditions of life on the earth were much simpler than they are now. But our present-day problem is different, and Gurdjieff was well aware that there is a far more intimate interlocking of lives on the earth, due to the progress of communications and various other technological advances; so that it is no longer possible to rely mainly upon withdrawal from the world to produce the required results. Therefore, it is necessary that means should be found whereby people can increase this work in the ordinary conditions of life. And this is the so very remarkable thing about the present century, that a number of new movements have appeared in all different parts of the world, under different names, connected with all the great religions of the world, but in every case, there has been a movement towards the carrying out of one's spiritual obligations in the ordinary conditions of life.

This direction away from the old notion of the separation of spiritual and material activities (not to be confused with the separation of Church and State) is, as Bennett states, being taken by some practitioners of traditional, millennia-old religions. "People tend to make a sharp distinction between spiritual life and everyday life," the renowned Buddhist teacher Chögyam Trungpa Rinpoche notes in his book *Meditation in Action*. "They will label a man as 'worldly' or 'spiritual' and they generally make a hard and fast division between the two. So if one speaks about meditation, awareness and understanding, then the ordinary person, who has never heard of such things, obviously would not have a clue and he probably would not even be sufficiently interested to listen properly. And because of this division he finds it almost impossible to take the next step and he can never really communicate with himself or with others in this particular way."

Trungpa concludes that it is the job of modern spiritual guides "to provide some clue for the man in the street, some way of finding out, some concept that he can understand and which will still be related to his life." In this respect, Trungpa seems to agree with the Catholic theologian and former priest Eugene Kennedy, who, in the Introduction to his book *Tomorrow's Catholics/Yesterday's Church*, complains of the disservice done to religion by its mystification at the hands of writers such as Augustine and Origen (whose statement *Credo quia ineptum*—"I believe because it is impossible"—could as easily be a motto of the New Age as of Christianity). "Such notions are perpetuated in always seeking for miracles that break the laws of nature and in visions granted mostly to saints who rejected ordinary life," Kennedy says. "I sing of the everyday mystery, of the spiritual roots of such ordinary occurrences as falling in love, telling the truth, raising a child, teaching a class, forgiving each other after we have hurt each other, of surprise, and sexuality, and the radiance of existence. Of such is the kingdom of heaven, and of such homely mysteries is genuine religion made."

Judging by the comments of the people I have spoken with, a sense of the spiritual in everyday life can be as simple a thing as recognizing a content to their dreams beyond that commonly addressed by psychoanalysis. It can include a subtle sense of opening their hearts to others, or of developing an ability to see more clearly the effects of their actions on themselves and others. It can be a change in feeling and orientation which comes over them as gradually as a cloud, yet which after a period of years or decades has left them with the sense that their lives have been irrevocably altered. These subtle but significant transformations, rather than the miracles and mystical states and mind-boggling revelations that we often associate with conversion experiences, are the real essence of spiritual growth as it is understood by those who have actually experienced it. Even in cases in which events appear to depart from our accustomed picture of "normal" life, the interior changes may take place in the most mundane of contexts.

The parameters of the term "spiritual transformation" are too broad, however, to render the phrase much more than vague, encompassing both spectacular conversion experiences and the subtle levels of inchwise growth just mentioned, which take place across a span of time measured less in months or years than in decades. For that reason, I will attempt to follow these transformations over as long a period as possible in the lives of the individuals profiled here, taking into account the religious environment, if any, in which they were brought up, and their earliest spiritual impulses. Whether their experiences represent part of a growing movement toward spiritual exploration in the larger society is open to question. Yet certain facts are becoming evident, even if they have been somewhat clouded by notices in the popular press documenting apparently contradictory trends in spiritual activity. We read, for instance, that membership in organized religions is on the wane but "belief in God" has increased (bearing out Lenny Bruce's line "Every day people are straying away from the church and going back to God"); or that a shortage of qualified new clergy is causing problems for mainstream American religions, whereas New Age cults are flourishing; or that worship is burgeoning among members of a specific generation (usually that favorite of today's chart-makers, the so-called baby boomers).

Although these surveys are often at odds with each other, they do reflect a trend that is markedly different from the one operating twenty to thirty years ago, when a fascination with Eastern religion swept the American subculture. The most intriguing implication of current reports is that today's interest in spiritual affairs, whether superficial or profound, is taking place across the board. As membership in mainstream religions slowly increases, especially among those segments of the population that had previously been losing interest, involvement in less conventional creeds is also intensifying.

The point has been made (most recently by the Catholic historian Garry Wills in his book *Under God*) that America is a far more religious nation than most academics and intellectuals prefer to believe, and the evidence bears out that observation. George Gallup, Jr., and Jim Castelli, for example, find in their 1989 survey entitled *The People's Religion: American Faith in the 90's* that nine out of ten Americans say they believe in God, eight out of ten believe in a Judgment Day, eight in ten believe God still works miracles, and seven in ten believe in an afterlife, making the United States the most religious nation in the developed world (and second only to India in the percentage of respondents who said religion was "very important" in their lives). Unfortunately, much of that belief is either perfunctory, strongly linked to ethnic and social origins, or desperate, expressing a fearful need to bring an unruly and menacing world into line without stopping to examine the underlying premises of the beliefs.

The kind of spiritual life I am presenting here is more subtle and more profound than that; to begin with, it changes people's lives with irrevocable force, although it gets little media attention until a religious cult like Jonestown or a guru like Bhagwan Shree Rajneesh goes awry. The single characteristic that most clearly separates this kind of spirituality from the religion with which we are familiar is probably the sense of its being a full-time endeavor covering all aspects of one's life and being. Spiritual practice that involves only a weekly social gathering and a few token prayers is of little interest to a growing number of believers who want not mere comfort or morality but a genuine knowing, whatever the cost. Somewhere between the hard edge of Christian fundamentalism and the self-satisfaction of secular humanism, each of which in its own way seems to threaten dominance of American life at times, a whole world of spiritual growth and transformation is taking place. The purpose of this book is to present a small but representative sample of those transformative experiences.

Since there is probably no way that such a sample could be completely balanced, I have chosen the stories that were most interesting and that promised to cover as much territory as possible. Rather than try to be geographically representative, for example, I decided to stay for the most part in the Northeast and to let it serve as a microcosm for the country, partly because it's the area I know best and partly because it has a long tradition of religious tolerance and evenhandedness (well, since the Salem witch trials, anyway). Because I could not possibly have included accounts involving most of the religious sects active in America today, I arbitrarily divided possible subjects into Christian, Jewish, Islamic, Eastern, and New Age believers, and tried to get a few from each major group. I did not include certain organizations that foster an informal spirituality aimed at achieving a specific goal, such as Alcoholics Anonymous, Adult Children of Alcoholics, Narcotics Anonymous, and other twelve-step programs, because even though they are indicative in some way of the yearning and need for spiritual transformation, their focus is rather too narrow for my purposes. For reasons of space, I was not able to include detailed accounts of some areas that interest me but which are less central to American spiritual development than the ones I chose to explore, such as Arica, Christian Science, Reconstructionist Judaism, the Book of Urantia, Bahai, and many, many more. (All of the above groups should be distinguished from a whole panoply of pseudoreligions ranging from Marxism to the occult. One could further point to any number of surrogates for religion in modern life, from standard-brand psychotherapy to personality cults, from drugs and alcohol to a mania for fitness or an obsession with watching sports on television. Having worshipped at some of those altars myself, I can attest to what appears to be an innate human need to substitute *something*, however humble or grandiose, for the religious impulse. But all these are substitutes or, at best, adjuncts, not true spiritual experiences.)

Wherever necessary, I have tried to explain terms and concepts that might be unfamiliar to the general reader, and to provide a brief historical context for religious traditions outside the mainstream. In a few places, I have devoted chapters to explaining larger subjects such as meditation or the New Age. Otherwise, I've tried to stay out of my subjects' way and let them tell their own stories as directly as possible.

One thing I could not avoid, however, was a personal response of great uneasiness at much of what was said by the people I interviewed, many of the books I read in the course of doing research, and some of what went on within me as I progressed through the work. I have come to realize in all of this that spiritual awareness, when seriously engaged, is something that cannot but be upsetting. Of its very nature it shakes up the carefully constructed comforts of life and introduces an element of radical uncertainty. The labyrinth which Dom Bede Griffiths refers to in the epigraph at the start of this book as his metaphor for the spiritual path was located under the palace of King Minos at Knossos on Crete. There, according to myth, the Minotaur was kept until it was slain by Theseus. The double dilemma facing Theseus in his heroic battle with the beast, half human and half bull, was that even if the Minotaur didn't devour him, he had no guarantee of finding his way back through the maze. Of the many warnings that have been voiced about entering on the labyrinthine spiritual path, perhaps the most succinct is an old Buddhist teaching that goes something like this: "Better not to begin. But once you begin, better to finish it." I would go so far as to say that one can hardly enter even a discussion of this subject without feeling upset at many points, which is one reason that talk of genuine spirituality, as opposed to the Sunday-go-to-meeting kind, makes people so acutely uncomfortable.

Upsets, however, can be of great value and should not be ignored or brushed aside. No one should come to this process expecting a quick and satisfying answer to uncertainties. My own experience and that of almost everyone with whom I spoke indicates that the process is long, slow, and tortuous, generating more doubts than sure answers along the way. The Buddhist warning above is based on the fact that many people who begin various paths do try to turn back, often ending up more confused than when they began. And yet involvement in the process is in some sense its own reward.

One final note. The difficulty for me in working on a project of this sort over a period of years is that by the time I finish, I have inevitably come to see things in a very different way from when I started out. I am then plagued with thoughts that if I had the book to start all over again, I would go about writing it quite differently. After completing work on this book, I came to the conclusion that for all their diverse and often convoluted character, spiritual disciplines in the end ought to deal with just a few major issues: suffering and death, sex and material goods, and relationship to God and other people. Having realized this, my second-guessing nature then wanted me to rewrite the whole book from the perspective of getting people to answer the basic questions related to those issues, and forget about telling their life stories. Finally it occurred to me that, in relating their stories, everyone interviewed for this book had addressed precisely those issues in one way or another. The search for answers to those crucial questions, in fact, is what their lives are about.

CHAPTER 3

The Role of Tradition

. . .

You could compare the esoteric core of a religion to a very pure, high-octane fuel. Put it into an old Volkswagen, and the car will go like hell for a mile before it blows apart. If we're going to have a spiritual path for our culture, it needs to have levels that recognize where we are, and opens for us in stages that gradually move us upward.

—Jacob Needleman, "In the Spirit of Philosophy,"
Free Spirit, Winter–Spring 1989–90

.

Lex Hixon lives with Sheila, his wife of twenty-five years, in a lovely old wood-shingled house near the historic Wave Hill section of Riverdale, New York, not far from the end of the Broadway IRT line. The house sits on a slight promontory overlooking the Hudson, its living-room window encircled by an enormous wisteria vine almost as old as the house, which dates back to the early part of this century and which, as I approached it, seemed suffused with mystery. Since it was the middle of January, the wisteria was not in bloom, but it did bear a number of curiously shaped pods whose skin, Sheila said, is the texture of velvet. Seated in his study, Hixon looked casually resplendent in light blue flannel pajamas, white cardigan, and Birkenstock sandals, his large head framed by a mane of white hair. During the course of our interview, with the Metro-North train station and the Hudson River visible in the distance below, the daylight slowly faded to dusk and finally darkness outside.

Hixon practices Islam, the religion established in the Arabian desert in the seventh century by the Prophet Muhammad, and followed today by close to a billion Muslims throughout the world. Most of those are located in the Middle East, India, and Southeast Asia, but there are several million Muslims in the United States, a number of whom, like Hixon, belong to Sufi Orders. Sufism is a classification of Islam that is sometimes said to emphasize a mystical expression and that has often strayed far from orthodox Muslim practices, especially in the West. Hixon doesn't much like the mystical tag applied to Sufis, since he feels that Islam is mystical enough; and he considers himself an orthodox Muslim. In fact, he is a sheikh (pronounced *shake*), or spiritual leader, who presides over mosques in Mexico City, Manhattan, and Newark, New Jersey—no mean achievement for a man born fifty years ago in Los Angeles to nominally Episcopalian parents.

Among the key beliefs of Sufism is a reverence for all the world's great religions. Unlike many of their more orthodox and even fundamentalist Muslim brethren, Sufis recognize that Islam is but one of the paths to God that men and women may follow. And so it is no contradiction that Lex Hixon is also a Christian, a member in good standing of the Eastern Orthodox Church. The practice of multiple religious formats also fits in with the philosophy of Vedanta, a kind of universalist branch of Hinduism which Hixon embraces and which teaches that all religions are valid and valuable. No good Vedantist would have a problem with the fact that, in addition to those three spiritual traditions, Hixon practices meditation as part of the Gelugpa Order of Tibetan Buddhism.

Most of Hixon's teachers in the four disciplines feel that his multisectarian approach to devotion is, at best, fraught with danger, but he approaches the situation with what Da Kalki might call "Divine humor." When I asked how much time he devotes to each tradition on any given day, for instance, Hixon replied that he is like a migrant worker. "When the strawberries are in season, I'm mostly picking strawberries, and when the grapes are in season, I'm mostly picking grapes. For instance, right now Ramadan and Lent happen to be coinciding, and they will be for the next few years, which gives me a big scheduling headache." He admitted that if holding a religious lineage is defined only by its external practices, he would be in trouble, because "there is no way to do all of those practices all the time to the greatest fullness. But if holding a lineage has to do with an inner spirit, an inner knowledge, then they are compatible. It's like saying you can speak French and Chinese and German and Hebrew, and then someone asks, 'Can you speak them all at the same time, every day?' Of course not, but you can know them simultaneously and be enriched by them without pitting them against one another. You could say that mine is a general theory of relativity for religions."

If such an approach is not without its peculiar difficulties, for Hixon it represents a kind of "experiment," an attempt to see what happens when one maintains one's consciousness in distinct traditions, each of which has been widely accepted over many centuries. Whether the experiment will yield valuable spiritual data—he hasn't come to any conclusions yet—is less important than the fact that it keeps him actively engaged in the interdisciplinary dialogue that is an essential feature of the American religious landscape. And so, although Hixon may not be "typical" in any sociological sense, he is in an advantageous position not only to report firsthand on the course of four major rivers of faith, but also to evaluate the role of religion in American society in general. Besides his four practices, he holds a Ph.D. in comparative religion from Columbia University, and is gifted with a brilliant mind that is evident in the way he effortlessly interpolates ideas from one religion to another. Hixon likens his own role to that of United Nations interpreters: "You can have a UN only because of people who know how to translate between the different languages. We're just beginning to know how to translate between, say, Islam and Christianity, and that's one of the things I'm working on."

Hixon did a lot of translating in his first book, *Coming Home: The Experience of Enlightenment in Sacred Traditions*, a fascinating if occasionally arcane overview of spiritual thinkers from Heidegger and Krishnamurti to Plotinus, St. Paul, and Israel Ba'al Shem Tov, the founder of the Hasidic movement in Judaism. At the time I first read *Coming Home*, I was looking for someone who could explain and interpret the Islamic experience, and I began to think that Hixon was a prime candidate. He agreed to be interviewed and to speak openly about the often confusing subjects of Sufism, Black Muslims, Islamic fundamentalism, the Ayatollah and Salman Rushdie, among other things. I prepared myself by reading his second book, *Heart of the Koran*, a series of meditations on verses from the Islamic holy book, but I had trouble relating to it. Although the Koran is permeated with a tone of love and reverence evocative of Christianity at its most devotional, it also purveys some of that Old Testament windiness that can prove so tiresome at times. Hixon later assured me that I had at least gotten the basic point, since Islam, often mistakenly thought of as an Eastern religion, proceeds directly from Judaism and Christianity, and views itself as the final jewel in this triple crown of Western religious tradition.

So, when I met with Hixon at his home in Riverdale, I was eager to get his views on Islam, but things were not so simple. Before we could even begin, I had a problem with the tape recorder that turned out to be ridiculously elementary. As I fiddled with the various wires and plugs in my confusion and finally realized what I had done wrong, I explained the problem to Lex, but he was dismissive. "That's a good sign," he said. "It means we're already on the edge of some kind of mystery."

What was mysterious to me was that, despite my best efforts to get Hixon to talk about his spiritual evolution in biographical terms—his earliest religious impulses, first teachers, and so forth—he insisted on speaking only in general terms. As we talked, I was aware that the discussion was not at all going the way I had planned, yet I had a vague feeling (which I suppressed in my anxiety to get his history) that the things he was saying might have a deeper value than any biographical recounting. Not until I listened to the tapes the following day did I realize that he had given me a rich commentary on the place of religious practice in today's culture. He began by responding to my statement that my book would focus on the role of spirituality in everyday life rather than on monastic or esoteric experience.

"If we go back even fifty to a hundred years," Hixon said, "we'll see that what we know as the spiritual traditions, which we as modern intellectuals have become a little distanced from, *are* the world. These spiritual traditions are not only the grounds of the values by which people operate in their lives—things that surround birth, death, marriage, and livelihood—but also, in a subtler way, the very stuff and substance of our conceptuality. This includes even the way we physically perceive things, the way we look at a beautiful day or a beautiful person. So human experience is inextricably linked with the notion of a spiritual tradition and a spiritual vision. It isn't just something a culture can opt for or not opt for. Modern people have experimented with a secular approach that says, 'With science and law, we can build up our world.' But I think this was an aberration from the mature human standpoint, like saying we don't need art anymore. Religion, or the spiritual quest, is the very substance of our humanity, and there's no way to distance ourselves from it. If we reject it entirely, then we get pseudoreligions."

As previously suggested, those pseudoreligions can include political or social cults ranging from Maoism to the Ku Klux Klan. "But just as art needs criticism," Hixon continued, "spirituality needs its own form of criticism in order to keep it honest and authentic. If we don't have a critical enough view of religion, then we get fundamentalism and charlatanism and various forms of distortion. So there's no way we can ever relax as human beings. It's always a matter of vigilance and constant efforts at reminding ourselves."

By way of example, Hixon mentioned the Islamic practice of praying five times a day, which the Prophet Muhammad borrowed and expanded from the daily Office of the Christian monks whom he encountered in the Arabian desert. These can be, Hixon said, "very brief flashes of prayer. They don't have to last for more than ten minutes, although they can be elaborated by people who want to spend more time at it. But these five bursts of formal prayer every day have a tremendous power to remind people that they can never take a vacation from vigilance, from commitment to the highest values. So Islam is very strongly integrated into daily life, family life, the life of social responsibility. But it's not superior to any of the other noble traditions, which have different methods and configurations. And it doesn't call itself superior, either. The Koran states that prophets have come to every nation, bringing essentially the same message: Turn your limited life in the direction of the limitless Source of life, and submit to that. That is what I mean by human vigilance, which is not just a luxury for a few people who are especially gifted, but is the very stuff and substance of our world. The Buddhists call this mindfulness, or attention."

As Hixon sees it, Westerners would like to practice this kind of attentiveness without having a large religious superstructure and the traditions and scriptures and ceremonies that go with it. But, he insisted, you can no more have spirituality without the traditions than you can have ordinary awareness "without all the neurons in your brain functioning, all the synapses in your nervous system, all the complicated organs of your body." Spiritual awareness is the source of our values, "the inner ear which keeps us balanced as we walk through life, whether we're walking through Wall Street or through the jungles of Vietnam. This sense of balance, this inner ear of spiritual awareness, relies upon a whole complex, organic body of doctrine and practice and spiritual leadership and spiritual study."

Seen from Hixon's viewpoint, both secular humanists and religious fundamentalists are hiding behind the same fallacy. The idea that we can do away with religion is as naive to him as the notion that traditional religion should be in the driver's seat, running society at every moment. Furthermore, religion's built-in "self-critical function" that prevents the abuse of spiritual power must be complemented by our own internal sense of truth that will warn us when something seems to be going awry. "Ultimately, the spiritual truth of any teacher or tradition has to be corroborated with our own internal mechanisms," he said, "such as conscience and compassion for others and certain precious sensibilities we were given." Dangers arise when immature spiritual teachers or religious communities say we shouldn't trust ourselves because we're sinful or haven't developed the particular sensitivity that they recommend. Then we have to stand up for our own integrity, while remaining aware that we can also deceive ourselves at times. "One has deceptive thoughts or impulses, too," Hixon added. "When one is integrated into a religious tradition which is functional and benign, one has to be willing to renounce those deceptive notions and not just say, 'This is the way I see it. This is my integrity, so I should do it this way.' There has to be a subtle balance, a different kind of critical faculty employed in each instance."

"Subtle" is certainly the word for it. But as fine as some of Hixon's distinctions are, balanced and counterbalanced like the steel plates and dingleberries of a Calder mobile, they are also both self-evident and essential. To my mind, they represent the difficult kinds of things that need to be said plainly in the arena of spiritual bluster, somewhere between the hectoring gush of the fundamentalists and the cheery vagueness not only of the New Age but also of the highly accommodating mainstream churches that too often tailor their spiritual directives to fit the audience of newly religious baby boomers they hope to attract. Hixon's comments also recalled something I'd read in an interview in the Winter 1989–90 issue of *Free Spirit* with the

Jewish scholar Jacob Needleman about striking a balance between esoteric and exoteric practices of religion. "Christianity, Judaism, and Islamic belief all provide people with moral precepts," Needleman says, "ways of living meant to be obeyed by the masses." These exoteric religious practices are intended "to give balance and steadiness to our experience," not "to *transform* us, to give us *nirvana* or God-realization." He acknowledges that esoteric disciplines do exist within mainstream Western religions, but that, as many teachers have said, "the esoteric work is only for those who have been through the exoteric, and have achieved the necessary balance." What is arriving nowadays in the West, Needleman concludes, is "a lot of information about inner practice, available to people who haven't really had an *outer* practice."

I asked Hixon for his thoughts on Needleman's cautionary distinction between inner and outer practices. "I don't think it's useful to talk about opposing dimensions of a phenomenon," he said, seemingly sidestepping the question. "Take, for instance, the left brain and the right brain. I'm sure that there's some biological basis to the fact that we have very subtle, complex modes of thinking and that some of them appear to originate from one side of the brain one time, and the other side of the brain another time. But if we start thinking that we're two-sided brains, we're actually driving ourselves a little crazy. We must feel that we are integrated beings, not that impulses are coming from different places, because ultimately they're coming from the very core and root of our being. Similarly, in religion, it's wrong to separate exoteric and esoteric, or the daily disciplines from the hidden mystical teachings. That's separating something which isn't separable."

But isn't it a fact, I wondered aloud, that the mystical aspects of mainstream religions are divorced from the daily laws and practices by the institutions themselves? Christianity, for example, has a long tradition of meditation, from the early Desert Fathers through twentieth-century contemplatives like Thomas Merton and Basil Pennington, but this tradition is not taught in parochial schools or preached from the pulpit.

"There's a problem with that," Hixon replied, "because, for instance, communion is an intensely mystical practice of Christianity. In fact, it's more mystical than meditation. People have somehow forgotten that communion is a level of mysticism even more advanced than many forms of yoga and Zen in other cultures. In Islam we have a similar problem whereby people occasionally think the five-times-daily prayers are only for beginners, whereas under advanced Sufi guidance you might be repeating some of the divine names of Allah with every breath, and you might be moving and breathing certain ways. But the fact is that the prayers of Islam themselves are motion, are breath, are chanting the divine names, and have access to the most radical levels of the religion."

When a culture subtly desacralizes or demystifies certain areas of religion, possibly in an effort to control them better, then the daily dimensions of religion, which Hixon called "the most radically mystical practice," somehow get "dimmed down or concealed. And then people begin to look at it as institutionalized or, maybe, institutionalizable." But since everyone is completely different in the expression of his or her beliefs, Hixon argued, mechanical repetition runs counter to the spiritual sensibility. "Ibn el-Arabi, the great mystic from Andalusia in the twelfth century," he said, "taught very clearly that Allah or God recreates the universe every split second, and never creates it in the same way twice. This kind of heightened attention takes great effort to sustain. Sometimes cultures as well as individuals lose nerve and are not willing to try to sustain it, and so, for institutional purposes, they might try to cover over the radicalness of religion."

Going deeper into this problem, Hixon objects to the term "mysticism" being used for only certain specialized dimensions of a religious tradition. A believer who knows nothing about special meditative exercises can still be a radical mystic by virtue of his or her simple belief in God. "A Buddhist, who doesn't have the same structure of a creator God as Christians and Muslims," he said, "is still convinced that the state of complete enlightenment is possible and indeed inevitable for every living being, given enough evolution, and he is seeing this potentiality for Buddhahood even in a cat or a mosquito. This is as mystical as you want to get. In fact, human life itself is mystical beyond all imagination. How can you, sitting over there right now, just with your eyes and ears, be in such a full state of comprehension of all of these things that I'm thinking and that are emitting from my mouth as sounds? This is extraordinary beyond any kind of analysis. But we take daily conversation for granted, forgetting that maybe just two human beings communicating with each other is a sacrament. So the sacramentality of daily life is also dimmed down, not only by our cultures or institutions but, frankly, by ourselves, out of a personal laziness and egocentricity that wants to have a habitual life pattern in which we can feel comfortable."

Religion, like art, is a means that human beings use to restimulate their sense of the extraordinariness of daily experience, Hixon reasons. Hence his reluctance to separate the mystical and the mundane. Among other things, religion is the source of our commitment to justice, of our sense of beauty, and of our sense that another human being is more than just a lump of flesh. Even mankind's most secular understanding of the sanctity of life is in itself a religious sentiment. "We can't necessarily rely on a religious tradition outside of us to come in and cultivate these special sensibilities," Hixon said. "We have to take the responsibility ourselves. But the religious traditions are our greatest friends and supports in these efforts."

The balance between personal practice and communal participation within a given tradition can also be difficult to maintain. The emphasis on meditation and mystical union described in many of the books I came across in religious bookstores gives the impression that belonging to a community of believers is sometimes secondary to developing an internal mystical life—a notion that Hixon categorically rejects. "Religion is not primarily about doctrines," he said. "It's about living in religious communities. It is not about private practice at all. Privacy is some sort of modern concept of the alienated, isolated individual. This doesn't mean that one doesn't have the precincts of one's own heart to which to retire in every tradition. But working out some sort of private understanding of one's own religion that one makes up oneself and maybe attracts a few people to—that's not the way the history of religion has developed. Those peripheral developments have always occurred, but the main forces within religion have been vibrant communities, rich in depth, and not simply circling around one charismatic individual."

Although many of the world's great religions did originate around charismatic individuals—Moses, Buddha, Christ, Muhammad—Hixon is referring to the long, vital process of development, growth, and self-regulation these traditions all underwent. That is why he feels that the so-called New Age—a loose aggregate of religious and psychological groups which I will explore later—is wrongheaded in its emphasis on accelerated spiritual growth and a modest level of commitment. "Spiritual development *does* take a minimum of ten or fifteen years," he said. "You don't necessarily have to be living in a cave or washing the feet of a guru. You can be attending mass every Sunday or the mosque every Friday, but it does take many years to get any sort of maturity. Ask a concert pianist or a dancer. It's obvious that by practicing twenty minutes a day, you cannot become Nureyev."

Some of the religions that have emerged in the last fifty years or so, such as Eckankar, which calls itself a "New Age religion," advance the idea that twenty or thirty minutes a day of contemplation is a sound base for spiritual growth (although Eckankar does advise other spiritual exercises). "This is what classifies Eckankar as a part of the New Age mentality," Hixon said, "and hence, as far as I'm concerned, not really a part of the fully authentic spiritual traditions. New Age people are going to have to go back and renew themselves at the roots of tradition again and again. People will realize that you can't exist in some modern nonritual, nonceremonial mode, that you have to have that sacramental life, just as marriage is coming back in again, and people want to have singing and reading from the Scriptures. That sacramental atmosphere is as necessary to the human soul as oxygen is necessary to the human organism."

I wonder about his comparison. The resurgence of interest in the social traditions of marriage and monogamy may represent some kind of reaction against the freewheeling days of the Sexual Revolution, and its attendant dissatisfactions. But rather than signaling a return to religion, the new focus on marriage is more likely just a return swing of the pendulum, acquiring momentum from a growing fear of AIDS as much as from anything else, and is apt to be followed in time by a swing back the other way. I would argue instead that the search for a spiritual base to life is ongoing and incremental, and does not necessarily respond to blips in the curve of social fashion—which is not to say that the growing interest in both traditional and New Age religions is not connected to this ongoing human search. As Hixon himself admitted in concluding his thoughts about less traditional paths to God, "Some wonderful help can come from all different areas, because the religious person believes that everything is coming through God's will, that the divine presence is carried in everything. If someone beats you on the street, or if someone comes up and helps you when you need it, both of those things come from God as teachings. 'Wherever two or three are gathered in my name, I am there,' Jesus said in the Gospels. But he also said, 'Not everyone who calls unto me, Lord, Lord, will enter the Kingdom of Heaven.' You have to balance those things out. Christ is present everywhere, even where the most ornery, rebellious sect of Christians may be. But they may be shouting, 'Lord, Lord,' and he won't acknowledge them on the day of the Kingdom.''

It was nearly dark by the time Hixon finished his preamble. "That's a long monologue," he said. "And that's about all I have to say regarding the whole thing." Of course, it wasn't quite all. We pursued a lengthy list of topics that evening, including, at last, his personal background and his experience of Islam, and continued the dialogue in his mosque some weeks later, and again by telephone. In retrospect, the process of interviewing him seemed to replicate in some microcosmic way the difficulty outsiders face in exposing themselves to any great religion with which they are not familiar. Spiritual teachers can appear elusive, contradictory, purposefully mystifying, even vaguely threatening, and Hixon was all of that in my first encounter with him. But they can also be generous, kind, merciful, and illuminating, and Hixon was all of that, too.

I left his home that evening feeling confused and irritated, yet the more I pondered his words in the months that followed, the more I appreciated the perspective they provided for me. He had a way of mixing the esoteric and the everyday that paralleled what I was seeking to do. And I find Hixon's outlook of particular value precisely because it goes against the grain of mainstream America's attitude toward religion, and undercuts the extremes of spiritual ideology represented by atheistic secular humanism at one end of the spectrum and Christian fundamentalism at the other.

CHAPTER 4

Rachel Cowan:
The Search for Community

■   ■   ■

Organized religion deals with our epidemic of loneliness [by offering us] the opportunity to share in worship. . . . We all recite the same words in prayer, not because we all believe the same things (how could we?), but because in the process of reading together, singing together, chanting together, something truly remarkable happens. We transcend our sense of being unconnected individuals. We are lifted out of our individual isolation and transformed into a single organism, singing and rejoicing in the presence of God.

—Harold Kushner, *Who Needs God*

■

In the course of conducting research and interviews, I was struck by the disproportionate number of people on alternative spiritual paths, from Zen to Sufism, who had come from Jewish backgrounds, something for which no one has yet offered me an irrefutable explanation. The argument can be made that American Jews face a specifically modern dilemma in that, although Judaism is both ethnically based and deeply spiritual, a large number of American Jews grew up in families that were only moderately or culturally observant—keeping the holidays and some rituals, but without any vital connection to a spiritual belief system or practice. Those among them who later sought deeper levels of spiritual involvement were faced with a choice between the relative fundamentalism of Orthodox or Conservative congregations and the almost secular humanism of the Reform movement.

Especially for politically conscious men and women who grew up in the fifties or later, Orthodox and Conservative practices may have seemed unacceptably sexist and fundamentalist, whereas Reform offered an uninviting alternative perceived as perhaps too modernized, not mystical enough.

(For anyone unfamiliar with the three basic divisions of Judaism, a few brief distinctions may be helpful. The Reform movement developed in Germany in the early nineteenth century as a response to the gradual dropping of legal and political barriers against European Jews, and sought to integrate Jews into a mainstream society that was increasingly available to them politically and socially. It abbreviated the liturgy, introduced prayers and sermons in the vernacular and singing with organ accompaniment, and rendered the observance of dietary and Sabbath restrictions optional. Orthodox Jews, for their part, have insisted on retaining traditional Jewish laws and customs, as they relate not only to liturgy but also to diet and dress. They demand full submission to the authority of Halakah, the massive accretion of the written and oral laws of Judaism that include separation of the sexes during worship, and other roles for women that are at odds with social changes sought by the women's movement. Conservative Judaism began in the mid-nineteenth century as something of a counterreformation in response to the perceived excesses of the Reform movement. Conservative Jews hailed the Westernization of Judaism in the areas of education and culture, but kept the use of Hebrew in the liturgy and the observance of dietary laws and the Sabbath.)

One solution for the dilemma facing today's Jews is to explore other religions, usually outside the American mainstream. (Few, for instance, convert to mainline Protestantism.) A second route is to seek out the mystical element of Judaism through the study of the Kabbalah, an esoteric Jewish tradition that is often studied and practiced by non-Jews too. And a third resolution is to evolve a new, personal understanding of Judaism that is at once culturally rooted, spiritually oriented, and politically viable. This process is exemplified by the late Paul Cowan, the journalist, civil rights and antiwar activist, and author whose lifelong struggle to rediscover his lost heritage and forge a new Jewish identity for himself is eloquently described in his book *An Orphan in History* (1982). Descended from a long line of rabbis, Cowan's parents had become so thoroughly assimilated that he referred to them as "Jewish WASPs"; only by using his prowess as an investigative journalist was he able to uncover his real roots, both ethnic and religious.

Cowan died of leukemia in 1988, however, while this book was in the planning stages. But even as I looked around for someone with a similar experience of Jewish rediscovery, my interest became transferred to his widow, Rachel. At the age of fifty, Rachel Cowan is something of an exceptional figure in America, one of a small but growing number of women (about one hundred fifty in all) to be ordained as rabbis. She is also part of a far smaller group of rabbis, no more than a handful, who are converts to Judaism. Rachel came out of a New England Protestant family whose religion had little appeal for her, and went on to pursue a growing fascination with Judaism that culminated in her conversion and ordination.

Both Rachel and Paul came from relatively privileged backgrounds that differed in the way that old and new money are different. His father was the enormously successful producer of "The Quiz Kids" and "The $64,000 Question" and was once president of CBS-TV, and his mother was the child of the mail-order magnate Modie Spiegel; Rachel Brown's father traces his lineage back to the *Mayflower*, and her mother only slightly thereafter. The couple also shared a heritage of social consciousness passed on from their parents, who were involved in various kinds of activism, and this set them apart from their classmates at exclusive schools such as Choate and Wellesley. In his book, Paul wrote of himself and Rachel: "We were both Adlai Stevenson Democrats amid Dwight Eisenhower Republicans, dismayed by our classmates' political conservatism because our parents were such outspoken liberals." He also wrote that as a child Rachel had read *The Diary of Anne Frank* and "had developed a silent, lifelong conviction that she possessed some sort of spiritual kinship to Holocaust victims. So, though she knew very few Jews, she fought the anti-Semites who dominated her school with much more self-confidence than I was able to muster at Choate."

Paul's journey back to his Jewish roots paralleled Rachel's growing involvement in and conversion to the faith and tradition with which he was busy reconnecting. Following six years of study for the rabbinate, and less than a year after her husband died, Rachel was ordained a rabbi on New York's Upper West Side. She is not attached to a particular synagogue but serves as a spiritual counselor to a varied community in her neighborhood.

For all of Cowan's distinctions, no special aura surrounded her when we met in her apartment high atop Riverside Drive, where the wind swirled noisily outside and rattled the windowpanes as we spoke. A tall woman with sandy blond hair and wire-rimmed glasses, dressed casually in a dark green forties-style gabardine shirt and bluejeans, she bore no resemblance to any rabbi I had ever seen. Fatigued from fighting off a cold, she nonetheless brought out tea and cookies and made a stab at cleaning up the residue of the previous night's Passover seder. Then she reclined on the sofa and, against the howling wind, proceeded to lay out the course of her journey from rebellious atheist to Reform rabbi.

Rachel Cowan's parents were born in Maine, and she spent most of her early life in New England. Her mother's father owned a shoe factory in Somersworth, New Hampshire, and their family was wealthy until the Depression, when their shoe business went under and they lost all their money. Her mother grew up in Newton, Massachusetts, and became a children's librarian. Rachel's maternal grandmother, whom she credits as a major influence in several respects, was a "very devout woman, originally a Congregationalist—which is what New England small-town aristocracy was—who became Episcopalian during or after the Depression." Rachel's father, the scion of a Maine farming family, was a Rhodes Scholar who earned his Ph.D. in mathematics at Princeton and a radical leftist who supported the anti-Fascists in the Spanish Civil War. In fact, it was their mutual involvement in left-wing political activism in the late 1930s that brought Rachel's parents together.

Shortly after she was born in Princeton in 1941, Rachel and her family began a series of moves brought on by her father's work as a civilian mathematician who did systems analysis for the Navy. "Whenever we lived near my mother's mother, I would go to church with her, and to Sunday School," Rachel said. "She had wanted me to be christened, and although my mother, who was not religious, and my father, who was an atheist, didn't want me to be christened, they agreed that they would do it for her sake." They were living in Virginia, and her grandmother insisted it be done in the church where George

Washington had been christened. That was too much for Rachel's radical parents, and she was never christened. Perhaps for that reason, her grandmother imbued in her the notion of purgatory, even though her mother didn't recall that teaching as Episcopal doctrine. "I imagined purgatory being outer space," Cowan said, "and my soul like a satellite, perpetually in orbit, never able to go up or down, which was not a comforting thought."

Cowan's mother often said she wished she could believe as had *her* mother, "a very devout woman, unquestioning in her faith," but she couldn't. The religion Rachel's mother rejected involved a rather intrusive and judgmental God. She once described for Rachel having stolen an orange as a child and feeling her lips burn when she ate it, as if God were punishing her. When Rachel went to church with her grandmother, she felt very uncomfortable. "There was something about the Crucifixion that I could never accept," she said. "I never could believe the idea of Jesus being the son of God. I loved the Christ child story, but I wanted it to be Mary and Joseph's baby, not God's baby." She didn't know why, although something in her father's attitude—he found the idea that God could have a physical son absurd—may have been transmitted to her.

Rachel also hated the notion of Jesus being nailed to the Cross, especially since the Crucifixion followed so hard upon the Christmas season. That Christ is born on Christmas and is "already dead by Easter seemed very brutal to me, and I didn't want to get involved in caring about that. But when we weren't with my grandmother, it didn't come up anyway. My father was very rational and I inherited from him the idea that being a religious person meant that you weren't strong enough to support yourself." To his mind, religion was not so much the opiate of the masses as a crutch for the weak, and for Rachel, that was a persuasive antireligious argument.

Nevertheless, Rachel's parents had what she considered "very good values," living as they did in a Virginia socialist community called Tauxmont, near Washington, D.C., that was integrated at a time when segregation was still the norm in the South. Tauxmont was made up of people who had come to work there during the New Deal, bought land cooperatively, and divided it up. It was the kind of egalitarian place where Rachel felt "free to roam around." Because the surrounding public schools were segregated, she was sent for two years to a progressive private school called Burgundy Farms, and enjoyed "a very nurturing, progressive, child-centered childhood in Virginia." However, the family continued to move seemingly every other year. When her father took a teaching position at MIT, they settled in Newton in a mixed community with "many Jewish children. We had a Hanukkah-Christmas play and I learned Hanukkah songs at the time, but didn't think much about it."

By fourth grade, the family had moved to England, where Rachel went to a Church of England girls' school. "I was very adaptable, and learned all those hymns," she said. "We knelt on the floor every morning, and I didn't mind it at all. Even though the theology didn't make sense, I liked the ritual of it. I always liked ritual a lot." (This attraction to ritual and the attachment to a larger spiritual community that it implied may have grown out of her family's continual uprooting, but in any case appears to have been a constant in her life. When she was in college and working in the civil rights movement, her maternal grandmother told her about an ancestor who, while serving as governor of the colony of New Hampshire, saved some Quaker women who were being persecuted. "She was convinced that I'd inherited this quality of justice from that ancestor," Cowan said. "That gave me a sense of having a heritage, but the only way I could express that in New England would be to join the Daughters of the American Revolution, a racist, sexist, anti-Semitic organization which I would never want to be part of. So there was nothing I could do about it.")

Back in America again, Rachel was in fifth grade when her father applied to work for the Israeli government designing the port system of Haifa. The family sold their house, got the necessary inoculations, and learned a good deal about Israel, but her father was denied a security clearance. The year was 1952, and his prior left-wing activism was enough to make him suspect. "That really hurt," Cowan said. Instead, her father took a job with a private consulting firm in Cambridge, Massachusetts, and they moved to Wellesley, which Cowan characterized as an "uptight, WASP, Republican, insurance industry-dominated suburb. It was a major culture shock moving there from the pro-integrationist, Democratic, socialist, egalitarian community we'd been living in."

The social context of Wellesley required belonging to a church of some sort, and Rachel's parents joined the Unitarian Church because it had the most liberal congregation and an intellectual tradition with which they identified. Rachel became active in Sunday School and the youth group, and later taught Sunday School. In her thirteenth summer, she went to a Quaker camp in Vermont and found the services amenable. She liked the Quaker meditations, but more than that she liked the ritual, just as she had enjoyed the Burgundy Farms celebration of the Jewish harvest feast of Sukkot. "Everybody brought harvest fruits and we sang harvest songs," she said. "I liked when we did something that conveyed an idea about a time or place. It was seasonal, but also somewhat spiritual. You brought fruits, but they were going to hungry people. You appreciated what you had, but you also thought of others."

Wellesley was an inimical place, featuring "a lot of genteel, WASP anti-Semitism, very right wing. Being an intellectual girl on the top track at school was not a socially desirable thing." Besides that, Rachel's family life lacked any connection to a meaningful tradition. "Christmas was the tree and presents," she said. "Easter was Easter eggs and ham, and Thanksgiving was a family dinner, but we didn't even visit relatives. These were rootless holidays, with no extended family, and I always wanted them to be more." At least the Unitarian Church had a midnight service on Christmas Eve, and "a beautiful Christmas service. The Easter service had lovely music, and I remember how beautiful the church looked. It was a moment when you stopped and stepped out of what was ordinary about your life and—although I wouldn't have used the word then—you sanctified a time and space."

Cowan's work in the Unitarian Sunday School was considerably less sanctified. She taught that Moses had learned monotheism from the Egyptian pharaoh Akhenaton, and that the Red Sea was really the Reed Sea, a marsh that was easily crossed without divine intervention. "It was a totally naturalist interpretation of Exodus," she said. "I don't know who developed the curriculum or taught us how to teach Sunday School." For the next three summers Rachel was back at the Quaker camp, and once again found the experience of silent meditation "very meaningful." The practice at the camp was to have meetings every morning. In good weather, the meetings were held on the dock; on Sundays, in a spot in the meadow, where the campers sat in a circle. "If someone was moved to speak, they would speak, and then we'd conclude with a couple of songs. The testimonies usually had an underlying Christian message: 'I am moved to think about the beauty of the mountains,' or 'I think about the poverty in the world.' They were about something terrible in the world plus something lucky we had to share. I loved that meditation time. They didn't give us any techniques. We just sat there in silence for twenty minutes on weekdays, and an hour on Sunday."

At Bryn Mawr College, Cowan majored in sociology, and took one elective course on the New Testament. If she had any interest in religion then, she didn't act on it. By her own account, she "never did one formal or informal religious thing, except going to camp. It never occurred to me to do anything religious in an organized way. I never thought of anything as spiritual or religious." What spiritual impulses she had came from nature, beginning the summer she worked at the Quaker camp as a nature counselor. "In the woods," she said, "I always felt there must be a God because, Look at this butterfly! This sunset is too awesome to be just a meaningless natural phenomenon. It was at that level of theology. Even in the Quaker meetings, I didn't develop that into any kind of idea. It was just a feeling that I never had in my daily life in the city."

Graduating in 1963, and infused with her parents' social conscience, she went to Cambridge, Maryland, to work in the civil rights movement. Being part of the movement was exhilarating. "Every night in the church there was a freedom rally that gave you a sense that a community of people could change the world and make it better," she said. That summer she met Paul Cowan, who was also involved in the movement. In *An Orphan in History*, he recorded his first impression of Rachel as "the kind of preppy I'd been avoiding . . . an earnest blond social worker who felt enough guilt about racism to try to combat it for a single summer of a life that was destined to be safe and untroubled." Their romance didn't begin to take shape until they unexpectedly shared a long drive from Cambridge to the University of Chicago, where they had both enrolled in graduate school.

"We didn't know each other very well in Cambridge," Cowan said. "Paul was a journalist who wrote speeches for the leader of the movement, and I was tutoring black kids who were going to integrate white schools. But we discovered we were both enrolled in graduate school in Chicago, so we drove out together, and we fell in love on the way, just stopping for coffee and talking." They had agreed to travel in separate cars but to stop for a coffee break at a Howard Johnson's along the way. The breaks continued at each Howard Johnson's they passed, and progressed to two- and three-hour conversations that revealed a growing attraction.

"The night before we arrived in Chicago," she continued, "we stopped for dinner at a hamburger joint in Benton Harbor, Michigan, and Paul said, 'Well, it's sunset. I'm going to eat a cheeseburger and then I'm not going to eat for twenty-four hours.' I asked, 'Why not?' He said, 'It's Yom Kippur. Jews don't eat on Yom Kippur.' " He hadn't yet discovered that they also go to synagogue and stop traveling, as Jewish law commands. "I asked, 'Why not?' And he said, 'I'm not sure, but I think it's solidarity with Israel.'

"I was strongly attracted to somebody who would fast for twenty-four hours for some spiritual idea, so I said, 'Great. I feel solidarity with Israel, so I'll fast too.' About four hours later we got to Chicago and went to his sister's place. At this time Paul knew zilch about Judaism. He had been very clear in telling me during our trip that the reason he had been in Cambridge was that, as a Jew, he had a responsibility to the Holocaust victims to make sure that nothing like that could ever happen to anyone here. It struck me that he had a Jewish reason for being there. I had a 'good' person's reason for being there, but I couldn't say I was there as a Christian or Unitarian or Quaker. Anyway, when we got to his sister Holly's apartment, she said, 'I'm going to get something to eat.'

" 'What do you mean?' Paul said. 'It's Yom Kippur. We can't eat for twenty-four hours.' And Holly said, 'Yom Kippur's not until next week.' It's amazing that somebody who was Jewish wouldn't know this major date. But it impressed me that being Jewish meant enough to him that he had dropped out of school and gone to Israel, which was a very important experience for him. That interested me, and was one reason I was attracted to him."

The following summer, they went to Mississippi together to work in the civil rights movement. Once again, Paul felt it was his responsibility as a Jew. "What would he tell his grandchildren if he hadn't been there?" Cowan said. "I lived with a black woman and went to church with her, church clearly being very powerful for the people there, although it didn't grab me. It had so obviously come from the

Southern black culture. I could hear the ministers speaking 'Glory be in the name of Jesus Christ,' but I never felt that that was why I was there. I had no sense of any religious basis for the strong values I held. I was risking my life for those values, so they were clearly significant, but they were very much my parents' values. And they were political values, not religious ones."

When Paul and Rachel decided to marry in June 1965, their shared confusion about religion came to the fore. He didn't know a rabbi, and she didn't know a minister, but her uncle played poker with the chaplain of Smith College, so something was arranged. She chose to be married in New England on her uncle's farm, because those were her roots. The wedding was held outside under a huge tree. "Reverend Harold Anderson, the Smith chaplain, was black, which was a plus," she said. "We asked him not to mention Jesus, and he agreed. I read from Albert Camus and Paul read from James Agee." The music was by Bob Dylan and Vivaldi. At the end, Paul broke a glass and the minister said, "*Shalom.*" "It was the beginning of the era of hippie weddings," Cowan said, "and it expressed who we were, which was also typical of Paul's influence on me. I grew up thinking there were right ways and wrong ways to do things. You didn't create your own way. But Paul was a very creative and enterprising person. He said, 'We can really do the wedding this way.' "

They went to Israel on their honeymoon because Paul had been invited to take part in a panel of the American Jewish Congress Dialogue between American and Israeli Jewish youth. Driving through Galilee, Rachel found that all her images were of Jesus. "I seemed to see him coming along the path, not because I believed in Christ, but because it looked like all the pictures I'd ever seen." The trip wasn't much fun for her, though, because they weren't used to being tourists. And, as an intermarried couple, they were unwelcome in Israel. For the first time, she met Jews who were prejudiced against Christians, and she took it personally. "I felt rejected. We also met terrific people with whom we became friends, but it didn't make me want to go back there or be part of a Jewish world in America. If this was the Jewish world, then who needs it?"

Paul got his draft notice while they were on their honeymoon, and they elected to sign up for the Peace Corps instead. They went to Ecuador for a year and a half, and to Rachel it was merely "a very

Catholic country," a place where she could see how organized religion oppressed people while reinforcing feudal structures. Worse than that was the anti-Semitism they encountered among the Peace Corps volunteers, the same "ignorant WASP anti-Semitism" Rachel had encountered in high school. The Cowans came to feel that they were being used as public relations for the United States, became disillusioned, then were almost kicked out for protesting.

When they returned to the States, they moved to Washington, D.C. Rachel was pregnant and was working on the Poor People's Campaign, while Paul was writing a book about his experiences in the civil rights movement and the Peace Corps, which was later published as *The Making of an Un-American*. When their daughter Lisa was born in 1968, they moved to Riverside Drive in New York. There Rachel started writing free lance and remained involved in political work and the antiwar movement, but she still hadn't found a base in any religious community. They often went to her parents' in Boston on Christmas Eve and then, on Christmas Day, to New York, where Paul's parents always gave a lavish Christmas party. "They had a huge apartment on Park Avenue, a huge Christmas tree, and a huge party," Cowan said. "Paul's mother was a highly organized German Jewish woman, and every year under the tree she placed a cloth with each kid's initial on it. No sooner did they open each present than the paper wrapping would be in the wastebasket, and a list would be made of who gave it to them. It was very mechanical. My family had few traditions, but at least at Christmas you made the cookies and the Christmas tree decorations yourself, you cooked the dinner yourself, and only one person at a time opened a present. It was the old New England way of doing it."

Paul's family were completely assimilated, yet Christmas wasn't a holiday that had any resonance in their cultural history. "They were just doing it because Americans did it," Cowan said. "For Paul, what mattered was that he had a Jewish identity expressed in relation to the Holocaust and Israel. He'd been to Israel, and he'd read a lot of Jewish novels. He loved *Call It Sleep* by Harold Roth, and all of Saul Bellow. But his life was in his value system, the conscious motivation for his political action."

Their son Matt was born in 1970, and the family's holidays together were usually split between Jewish and Christian observances, Passover seders and Easter egg hunts. One Christmas Eve in the year that, as Rachel put it, the United States "bombed the hospitals in Hanoi," Rachel and Paul had a group of alarmed writers over to their place to decide what their response would be to the new bombing campaign, although Rachel was aware she still hadn't decorated the tree. When the writers finally left, she wrapped the presents. "I remember," she said, "thinking about Christmas: Why is it that you end up completely exhausted, with all these presents? We had not yet begun to do anything about Hanukkah. I had a sense that Christmas worked when you were a little kid, but it didn't work for me now. I found it unpleasant to have a Christmas tree with nothing larger attached to it than the need to put a big pile of presents under it."

What might have been a confusing issue of whether to raise the children Christian or Jewish, however, was breached without a question. "I don't think we entertained it," Cowan said, "because we assumed they'd be going on civil rights and peace marches and they'd have black friends. They'd have as much as possible of everything, and they'd learn about being Jewish and being Christian and maybe Muslim. The idea was to express the faith that we were all brothers and we all worked for peace."

The next year, Rachel became involved in a parents' co-op day-care center. The teacher was her friend Jerry Raik, who told the kids the Hanukkah story, to their delight. The story celebrates the struggle of the Jewish Maccabees against the Syrian Hellenes, and the Miracle of the Lights, when the Hasmonean Jews returned to the temple to find that the Greeks had defiled all the oil except for one cruse. Although it was enough to keep the candelabrum burning for only one night, they were able to keep it burning for eight nights. Rachel thought, Why not invite Jerry to come and tell the story at their place? The ensuing Hanukkah party was a big success, which they repeated every year. Another acquaintance, Arthur Waskow, had organized something called a Freedom Seder, a politicized version of the traditional Jewish Passover dinner, for which he wrote a Haggadah in English. The Haggadah, or liturgy for the Passover seder service, usually consists of an account of the Egyptian bondage of the Jews and a thanksgiving to God for their deliverance, interspersed with traditional rituals, stories, Psalms, and songs. Waskow's Haggadah, called *Freedom Seder for Passover*, was a self-consciously modern variant that incorporated the values of the sixties. For instance, guests were urged to sing the old Union hymn "Solidarity Forever": "Solidarity forever, for the movement makes us strong." The Freedom Seder was held at the Chase Manhattan Bank, which Rachel and her friends considered "one of the ten plagues." She was attracted to the idea that a religious event could be combined with political sentiments. Another time when, as often happens, Easter and Passover overlapped, Waskow held a Freedom Seder with a sunrise service and Easter egg hunt that impressed Rachel. She wanted to start doing "Jewish things" in her house, concerned that, if their children grew up to know as little about Judaism as Paul knew, "it would be a horrible waste of a history. It was a crime not to know where you came from, because it was so clear to me where I came from. It seemed they ought to have an equal sense of their roots. And I felt that every tradition we added was to the good, because it gave life more ritual and tradition, which I valued. So we started having seders at home."

Around that time, Paul had begun to find great power in the idea that religious conviction motivated people to burn draft cards, take risks, and turn spiritual ideas into political statements. He had no sense of how a Jew would do that, other than the occasional Freedom Seder. But he was moved by Catholics like Daniel and Philip Berrigan, priests who were frequently arrested for their antiwar protests. Rachel didn't share his enthusiasm, since Christian metaphors had never appealed to her. "They worship plaster saints and gory bodies on crosses," she said. "So I was not moved to become Catholic—which in some sense Paul was."

But after the massacre of Israeli Olympic athletes in Munich in 1972, Paul began to notice that most non-Jews weren't very upset about it, that they seemed to have more sympathy for the Palestinians than for the Israelis. "That was a dividing point in his life," Cowan said. "He began to hear a lot of the speeches people were making 'in the name of Jesus Christ,' and he said, 'That's not why I'm doing this. I'd better find out why I am.' " As a secular humanist, Rachel felt no such need. She did want her kids to have more of a sense of history, though, so Paul's need to find out where he came from as a Jew and her need to create a traditional base for the family worked together.

One event that helped to shape Rachel's spiritual development was taking the children to a party for the feast of Purim in 1973. Purim celebrates the time, recounted in the Old Testament Book of Esther, when the Jews were saved from slaughter by the intercession of Queen Esther. The cousin and adopted daughter of a Jew named Mordecai, Esther had been chosen by the Persian king Ahasuerus from all the virgins in his kingdom to be queen. When the king's adviser, the sinister Haman, subsequently proposed to eradicate all the Jews because of Mordecai's refusal to bow down to him, only Esther's intervention saved the day. Their fortunes were reversed: Haman was hanged by the king, Mordecai ascended to a position of high power, and the Jews were allowed to arm and defend themselves, and they prevailed against those who sought to destroy them.

"I didn't know anything much about Purim," Cowan said, "but if it was a ritual, it sounded good to me." At the Purim party, held at the New York Havurah on 98th Street, a puppet play told the story of Esther, Haman, and Mordecai. A Havurah, from the Hebrew word for "fellowship," is a group that meets informally to celebrate the Jewish holidays and discuss the issues of the day from a Jewish perspective. The play turned out to be very frightening to three-year-old Matt, who came running over to Rachel and said, "Ma, Haman's not going to kill me, is he? I'm just half-Jewish." Her response was to reassure him by agreeing with his evaluation. "But what does that mean to a kid to say he's just half something," she thought, "or to feel his Jewish half might be killed? I figured he'd better find out what Jews live for, not just what they're killed for." With some friends, she started a school sponsored by the Havurah that met once a week to teach Judaism to their children, but the woman who helped organize it insisted that the parents get involved. "Every week a parent had to teach along with the teacher, so we had to talk about who we were and what we wanted to teach our kids. I took full part in those discussions, but I didn't understand a lot of the baggage the other parents were bringing to them. I didn't know what an ambivalent thing Jewish identity is."

In the chaotic atmosphere of those times, during which many of the Cowans' friends were getting divorced, their kids seemed to need some kind of reassurance, something to anchor them. They asked if Paul and Rachel would promise not to get divorced. But how do you make a promise like that seem reasonable to a child? They felt that a Friday night dinner together every week would be a reassuring ritual.

They didn't know much about the Jewish observance of Shabbat, or Sabbath, but on their honeymoon in Israel they had spent Shabbat with a religious couple and remembered it as a very peaceful occasion. Derived from the Hebrew word for "rest," Shabbat traditionally begins at sundown on Friday and lasts until the first three stars appear in the evening sky on Saturday. During that time, observant Jews do not work, travel other than on foot, or use the telephone, among other things.

The notion of a personal prayer life seemed to be of considerably less interest to Rachel then. Back in high school, when each day began with the Lord's Prayer, she had abstained. "To me it was an important principle not to say the Lord's Prayer," she said. "I didn't believe it and didn't think that we should be required to do it. I didn't think they could force you to pray at a certain time, so I used to knit socks for my boyfriends during those prayers." Since Paul died, however, she thinks more often about what prayer is. Sometimes it's as simple as going to synagogue and saying, "God, I'm here, where are you?" She likes the sense that prayer can be both individual and communal. And she always liked that there were no hymn numbers on the synagogue walls. "Even though a lot of the service was in Hebrew," she said, "there were meditations on atonement and repentance, which are the themes of Rosh Hashannah and Yom Kippur. They didn't expect you to say, 'Oh, I'm evil, but I'll turn over a new leaf and be good.' It was a sense of process, that we'd all rather do things differently, but we can't change overnight. Yom Kippur was a time to reflect on how nobody else can atone for you, and you need to work this out yourself. One quotation from a Hasidic rabbi named Susya stood out especially: 'When I die, no one is going to ask me why I wasn't Moses. They're going to ask me why I wasn't Susya.' That hit me like lightning, the thought that I spend so much time trying to be somebody I'm not, and why can't I just think about being me?"

Through the Havurah school, Rachel began to learn more about Judaism, growing into it without any urgency. "Conversion means you're walking down the road and Boom! lightning strikes, and then you have faith," she said. "But nobody was pressing me to convert." The family now observed both Hanukkah and Christmas, although without all the traditions she remembered from her childhood. Her mother's great-aunt Anne Carroll Moore was the first children's librarian in America and had started the Children's Reading Room in the New York Public Library. Moore had a wooden doll named Nicholas, and wherever she went she told stories and people gave Nicholas presents. When she came to the Brown house every year on St. Nicholas Eve, December 5, with Nicholas and all his treasures, Rachel and her brothers and sisters took out all their Christmas books. "Auntie Carroll would always give us a new book, and since she knew children's literature, it was always a wonderful book."

Much as Rachel loved such rituals, she was unable to recreate them for her own children at Christmas. She and Paul didn't go to church or "contextualize it in any meaningful way." To complicate matters, if they were to make Hanukkah seem equally important to the kids, they would have to make sure that the Hanukkah presents were as good as the Christmas presents. Instead of celebrating what they cared about, she and Paul put most of their energy into "thinking about presents." It was "too much work," and Rachel found it draining, beginning with eating matzoh on Passover Friday night. She once took matzoh to her mother's house on Easter. (By then her mother had stopped buying ham and started serving chicken.) "She had a plate of hot cross buns, and I had a box of matzoh. I was thinking, It's Passover, and I'm not supposed to eat leavened bread. But here are these hot cross buns, which are my childhood. Finally I took one. That was a moment of decision that told me I was not yet ready to give up certain things."

The juxtaposition of hot cross buns and matzoh is probably more than just a culinary coincidence. As the unleavened bread the ancient Hebrews ate during their flight from Egyptian captivity, matzoh holds a high place in Jewish ritual. Meanwhile, the authors of a book entitled *Lindow Man—The Life and Death of a Druid Prince** have traced the Lenten hot cross bun (originally baked only on Good Friday) to a partially burned barley griddle cake traditionally eaten by sacrificial victims of the Druid priests of the Celts. That may be somewhat speculative, but it makes the point that the Jews were not the only people to intermingle culture and diet with religious rites.

Paul's parents died in a fire in 1976, an event which, apart from

---

* Anne Ross and Don Robins, *Lindow Man—The Life and Death of a Druid Prince: The Story of an Archaeological Sensation* (New York: Simon & Schuster, 1990).

its inherent tragedy, jolted Rachel into an awareness of her own mortality. She thought with urgency, "My God, their lives are all over. What is my life now? What do I want to do with it? What does it mean?" Suddenly the religious questions she used to think about in junior high school, Quaker camp, or Sunday School began to come back to her, and she had nobody to discuss them with. "It never occurred to me to find an Episcopal minister," she said, "or go to a Unitarian Church, or back to St. John the Divine, a place that Paul had liked but I hadn't." Instead, she began to be much more interested in Judaism.

As Cowan became increasingly involved in thinking about "Jewish things," she didn't consider converting because she still didn't feel she was religious. "To be a secular Jew you don't need to convert," she said. "You just need to live on the Upper West Side in New York." For the holiday of Shavuot, which celebrates the giving of the Torah to Moses on Mount Sinai, she went on a retreat with the Havurah and wound up in a discussion of sexism in the Old Testament. The tradition of Shavuot is to stay up all night studying, but Rachel was too sleepy. When she awoke the next morning to find everybody else outside praying, she was struck by her distance from a group of people praying in an ancient language. "I can never become this," she thought. "I don't know this language. I don't have this history." Those genetic Jews in their prayer shawls seemed too deeply rooted in a certain sacred place that she could never become part of. "I went off walking in the woods, where I saw a beautiful Brewster's warbler and I thought, This is my temple, out here in the woods."

Nevertheless, she continued her studies in Judaism, and in the summer of 1979 went to Israel with Paul and the kids to study solar energy as part of her job with the Scientists' Institute for Public Information, an organization investigating alternative energy sources. One Saturday they went to the Wailing Wall to pray, and Rachel was horrified to see the women crowded into one little section, separate from the men. "How on earth could I convert?" she thought. "This religion was sexist from so far back. I can't possibly do this." She burst into tears and fled, but a friend who lived in Israel later took her aside and said to her, "That's not where God is. You don't need to worry about the Wall. It's a place that Israelis have constructed as a national religious space, but it's not a holy space." Cowan acknowledges that few Jews agree with him. "Many people find it a very holy place. But I didn't see how a place that's so sexist could be holy. The way women who tried to pray there have been treated is more about politics than about God."

Cowan now feels that the separation of the sexes probably has more to do with Mideast customs than with the Jewish religion. In any case, she had already started thinking about converting before she went to Israel. A rabbi friend told her she might as well have an Orthodox conversion, because then nobody would ever question it. But after talking to the most progressive Orthodox rabbis she knew, Cowan discovered that they each had a different problem with her. "My kids weren't converting, or I wasn't going to take on all the mitzvot," she said, using the Hebrew term for laws or commandments. "Or I didn't belong to an Orthodox synagogue. I always ended up feeling bad. All I wanted to do was be Jewish, and yet there were all these obstacles. Finally, I realized that I wasn't an Orthodox Jew, and it was perfectly all right not to be an Orthodox Jew. If I were converted by rabbis who were friends of mine and who celebrated Judaism the way I did, they wouldn't have a problem with it and neither would I."

One of the turning points in her progress came during a small Torah study group that met in Jerry Raik's apartment at 111th Street and Broadway. Looking out a window that faced the Cathedral of St. John the Divine, Cowan caught herself thinking about how little she related to it. "It was my grandmother's spiritual home," she said, "but it's not mine. But, I thought, this living room is, and this Torah really is. This is where I belong. It was one of those moments that I have come to accept as moments of knowledge. To call them moments of revelation makes them sound more public or dramatic than they are. They're shifts of consciousness when all of a sudden something seems true that didn't seem true before. What seemed true to me at that point was that I really was Jewish, and that this was the path. However problematic it was, I knew it was *my* path."

Problematic it proved to be. After all, what did Jews mean when they talked about conversion? She could find very little written on the subject, and nobody she talked to knew much about it. She was told that since Jews believe that a Christian is just as entitled to share in the world to come as the Jews are, there is no theological basis in

Judaism for conversion. Rachel didn't like the idea of the mitzvot, either, which seemed to imply, on the other hand, that there was something wrong with not being Jewish, or with her parents or how she'd been raised. Finally, she talked to an international authority on the Talmud, Rabbi Adin Steinsaltz, and told him of the problems she was having with conversion. He felt that the real metaphor for conversion was marriage. When you married somebody, you didn't give up your identity, but you entered into an intense relationship. Then you grew together, building on the base that you brought to the marriage. That seemed feasible to Rachel. "And so, having worked through the problems of sexism, authenticity, Orthodoxy, and metaphor, it all came together, and I decided to convert," she said. "It was very important that I do it myself, not for Paul but for me. I couldn't convert until it was clear to me that Judaism had paths that led to truths I wanted and needed. But I was also thinking about God's reality. When you grow up believing that to be religious is to have a crutch, that's a secular religion in its own right. My conversion was not from Christianity to Judaism, but from secularism to being religious. And Judaism was the path I chose to do that."

Cowan converted in 1980. The formal requirements for conversion include a period of study and meeting with three rabbis. During these meetings, she discussed why she was making this decision, what was involved, and to what sort of Jewish practice she would commit herself. The rabbis wanted to know, for instance, if she understood about anti-Semitism and what the consequences might be. Finally, she was taken to the mikvah, a small tile pool about eight feet by eight and four feet deep, in which she was to immerse herself completely. A rabbi stood outside the door while Cowan went in, removed her clothes, and immersed herself. A woman called the "mikvah lady" made sure that she was totally immersed, that every piece of hair had gone under. After doing this and saying two blessings, she was converted.

As part of her conversion studies, Cowan had taken a course at Jewish Theological Seminary taught by a professor named Neil Gilman, who had been influenced by the Jewish theologians Abraham Heschel and Martin Buber and who talked in terms of religious existentialism. To Cowan, the idea that one could make an existential religious commitment was stunning. "It wasn't as if you had to prove that God existed before you could accept God's reality, but you could lead your life *as if*. From that, many things flow: a life of prayer, a life of spiritual discipline, a community tradition. But again, that could be a somewhat empty intellectual idea." She did, however, have a couple of experiences that she chose to interpret as revelatory. One happened while she was walking on Broadway and saw the sun on a bunch of flowers in a Korean fruit stand. "It was a lot like those summer-camp butterfly experiences," she said, "although it wasn't that there must be a God if this is beautiful. But it somehow meant God is real. My professor at rabbinical school, Eugene Borowitz, talked about such a moment being like a footprint in the sand. When you describe the experience it doesn't sound compelling to anybody else, but the footprint is there: you have been changed. Wolfe Kelman, a rabbi who was one of my most important teachers, called them 'moments of faith.' I had always assumed that a genuinely religious person sustained faith on that high level constantly, but he said, 'No, no. It's more like you have moments.' "

Kelman's remarks echo what Bernard Glassman said about his Zen enlightenment experiences, or some Christian theologians' belief that what is really remarkable about mystical experiences is how rare they are. This is one of those points on which disparate wisdom traditions can agree: the moment of faith, enlightenment, satori, or illumination may come or it may not. But if it does, it is usually surrounded by days, weeks, and years of quotidian practice, perhaps of darkness and doubt. Kelman's term reminded Cowan of the humanistic psychologist Abraham Maslow's phrase "peak experiences." But what enables one to connect those moments, those peaks, and to have a life in between them? "That's what religious discipline is, in a way," she said. "You don't often learn of other people's spiritual journeys, so you don't know whether what's happening to you is just some idiosyncratic event." But the discipline provides a context for those events.

Cowan had another "moment of faith," although she wasn't sure if it occurred just before waking up or deep in a dream. "It was an experience of intensely powerful light," she said, "more intense than anything I'd ever imagined. I felt so happy. I felt that God is real. I don't know if it was a dream or not, but it doesn't matter, because it made me feel that this relationship exists. I exist now in relationship with God. Before Paul died, it wasn't as hard a relationship. Ever since he first got sick, it's been a very hard relationship, but I have never doubted that it's a real one."

Paul was diagnosed with leukemia in 1987, and died a year later. He spent six months of the year before his death in the hospital because chemotherapy treatments following a bone-marrow transplant had disarmed his immune system. Rachel lived a lot of that time with him in the hospital, and there she experienced for the first time being an intimate part of the life of somebody facing death. "Not that we talked about death very much," she said. "We always focused on the odds that he would live." But she was constantly aware of "the fragility of being on the boundary between life and death." It was a merging of borders which she related to the merging that occurs during those times "when prayer opens you up. Occasionally it also seemed like the point where, when you make love and it's absolutely sensational, you lose your boundary and you join. Sometimes prayer is a bursting through your narrow constraint into the divine, universal, transcendent, something at a different level. It's not the same as sex, but like it. Here Paul was on the boundary between life and death, and I felt that this very fragile boundary had something in common with those experiences. And I thought, Why would living on the margin of death be like sex?" It was another time when she wondered whether "anybody else ever thought that, or if that was a weird thing to think."

Cowan had not come across any definitive Jewish teachings about death or any indication of where Judaism fits within the two poles of traditional afterlife beliefs: the reincarnation scenario of the Eastern religions and the "heavenly journey" of Christianity and Islam. "I found rituals helpful, but the teachings were not particularly helpful, partly because there are so many," she said. "There's a certain modern, particularly Reform idea that we live in the works we leave behind, in the memory of others. In Judaism they say of somebody who has died, 'May his memory be for a blessing.' About six months before Paul died, but while he was very sick, the fifteen-month-old son of my friends Ken and Doris died. The only idea I can get any comfort from is a mystical Jewish idea that souls start in the perfection of the limitless and then come down to earth. To get back, they must perfect themselves again through manifestations in various lives. So I always think of my friend's son that he must have needed to do just a little more work, and after fifteen months he was done and he could go back."

On an intellectual plane Cowan does not believe "that God caused Paul to be sick or to die," but she has trouble understanding why his death is so troubling to her. "It's just that in the face of a death like that, you struggle to reattach any meaning to life," she said. The question became whether she could reaffirm and reconnect with her relationship to God. "I've been doing that, and I've had some very profound moments feeling that reconnection, but on top of so much pain it's not easy."

For one thing, she learned that the conventional wisdom which says that spiritual life is automatically a help in times of crisis is not necessarily accurate. "It's so untrue," she said. "People said to me, 'Your faith must have been such a comfort to you through all this.' My mother made the same sort of supposition about my grandmother, and I don't know if it was true of her, either. I'm sure that we posited, on her behalf, a lot more solidity in her faith than she herself experienced. There are steps of grief, and you go through them all. For instance, I do a lot of crying in synagogue. The idea of Passover coming again this year without him was unbearable." On the other hand, she does feel that religion is "a gift, a resource, an insight," and she has been helped by being in the community. "I look around and see people who survived the Holocaust, and I know that if they survived that, I can survive this. I see Ken and Doris who lost their son, and they're still here. There is a community of people who know life is tough and yet it has meaning."

At first Cowan had trouble saying Kaddish, the traditional Jewish prayer for the dead, which is to be said daily for the month following the death of a spouse. "You go to synagogue every day and say this prayer that doesn't mention death," she said. "It's all about praising God for his wonderful powers, and you're thinking, Why am I sitting here praising him, after what happened? The tension of doing that every day means that occasionally you leap ahead, and although you may take a few steps back, you're still further along. So you have a halting journey through the first year of the healing process." In fact, when the month was up, Cowan continued to say Kaddish because she "wasn't ready to stop yet. In grief you're self-absorbed, so this brings you constantly into dialogue with something outside yourself that is transcendent. There are days you rebel against that and you can't say Kaddish, and other days when you can affirm it."

Cowan now sees grieving as a paradoxical process by which a tragic event makes a believer question her belief, and at the same time the belief system and rituals tease the believer back to reality from her despairing state. And that is the value of being in touch with a spiritual tradition. You can avail yourself of the wisdom which has been built up over thousands of years. "When you do the traditional Haggadah at Passover, a lot of it is irrelevant and dated, but if that's the core, then you can add things," she said. "If we had taken Arthur Wascow's Freedom Seder as our Haggadah, it would be totally out of date now because it had a very limited political focus. We couldn't do anything with it, since it spoke only to that moment. The traditional Haggadah speaks to today because it's so basic and so old. For centuries, Jews have been in dialogue with it, as their times have dictated their needs."

She considers herself lucky to be tied into a tradition, because many of her friends, in contrast, "regard religion as something which they reject if it's not there the minute they need it. Maybe somebody dies and they want it to be there for them. They wish they could pray, and then they walk into synagogue and they are wordless." This is precisely what spiritual teachers across the board have emphasized: Whether you think of religion as merely, in Marx's phrase, "a haven in a heartless world," or as a fountain of the most profound mystical enlightenment, it doesn't work unless you also treat it as a daily practice. One priest in my old parish church often spoke disparagingly of Catholics who set foot inside a church only three times in their lives: when they were "hatched, matched, and dispatched." That sounded like pious hype at the time, but after listening to people describe what has worked for them over many years, I can see it now in a different light.

Cowan is disturbed by the trend toward rootlessness which she has observed, especially in big cities like New York, where people, especially the upper middle class, aren't part of communities. "Their families don't live here," she said. "Instead, they hang out with people who are like themselves, people who are their age, their economic level, their profession. Their lives are based in their offices or their health clubs or where they have a country house. It's not intergenerational, and so people's experience of life is very limited and pre-scribed." By contrast, in her synagogue, a genuine community takes shape among diverse people. "Some people like a rabbi who gives great sermons, or a great cantor," she said. "In our synagogue there doesn't happen to be a rabbi, so the style is more egalitarian and informal. But there are Holocaust survivors and an old Egyptian Jew. There are Jews by choice, women who'd be Orthodox except for sexism, and people who were Communists and now have found re-ligion. There's a lot of life history, a lot of different family dramas, a lot of different personal dramas. It's not a community where you do things only if you feel like it. There's an ethic of doing more than that, a religious world view that says that if somebody's sick, you visit them even if you don't like them very much. And if they don't have a home, you make a shelter. The people in your synagogue might not be the most fun people to have in your social life, but you're connected to them in a very real way."

Aside from calling it "religious," however, not much about her notion of ethical behavior toward others differentiates it from secular humanism, and Cowan admits she had acted the same way before she considered herself a religious person, and certainly before she became a Jew. But if her behavior did not spring from her conversion, she still discovered a positive value in the influence of religion on personal ethics. "Nobody today considers visiting the sick to be terribly sexy," she said. "They visit their relatives, but they don't visit the sick unless they come from some organized religious group. In Judaism, there are laws about visiting the sick. It's not just a mitzvah, a good deed. It's a commandment, a sense that a community depends on people taking care of and being responsible for each other."

Likewise, according to Cowan, you can't be a serious Jew without thinking about social justice. "If you're Hasidic, you probably think of it as applying to other Jews," she added. "But the Jewish idea of tzedakah isn't the same as charity. It's giving ten percent of your income, not because you're nice but because social justice requires this commitment." A synagogue or an institutionalized religion, Cowan reasons, helps keep alive the demand for that commitment. People can show a similar commitment without religious ties, some-thing she refers to as the "cut flower theory" of ethics. That theory holds that a person can be ethical without being rooted in religion, but, as she put it, "If I don't have roots in religion, what do I pass on to my children?"

In a sermon which Cowan delivered at her synagogue one year after Paul's death, she analyzed the distinctions between her secular humanist parents and her religious community. "Wonderful as my parents' values are," she said, "they don't exist as part of any community. They don't exist in a full context that embraces the foods I choose to eat, the language in which I pray, the joy of celebrating and the shared grief over losses, the concern for the dignity of every life. I can argue with my parents, point out their hypocrisies, yield to their despair. With God I cannot escape the sense of command."

Rachel Cowan sees religions as "vessels that contain very important ideas. The Communist Party was that for a while, but it was a flawed vessel. Yet even religions can be flawed." Echoing Lex Hixon's words about the importance of the self-critical function within religious traditions, she pointed to the "right-wing view of Judaism" that she said is developing among the Orthodox in Israel. "It's terrible, but nonetheless, the seeds of dissension also exist and others are beginning to challenge that view. When any religion lacks that capacity for self-criticism, the people lose their recourse against individual abuses of power, whether it's a large, organized faith, or a small community united under a charismatic guru." Religion also comprises a vision of "what God expects of humanity," and that vision "is always higher than we're able to achieve. The prophets are still yelling today the same way they did in the Old Testament. In the Communist Party you didn't have prophets, you had Lenin and Marx. So, even though you had a higher vision of what society could be, you couldn't go beyond them. The end was still just people. When it became authoritarian and totalitarian, people could not go back to a source, to higher standards."

As a non-Jew who converted, Cowan is acutely aware of how easy it is to feel excluded from the community, especially in Israel itself, where she would not be allowed to marry a Jew by birth. That situation is changing gradually as many Americans convert to Judaism, and as Judaism becomes integrated into American society to the extent that Jews feel more comfortable with converts. But since Judaism doesn't share the Christian goal of converting people, for American Jews the motivation for conversion nowadays derives from marriage. Judaism has traditionally been passed on from generation to generation in the home, but if one parent isn't Jewish, there is less chance of transmission. Rachel still meets other Jews who don't consider her Jewish. "There are a certain number of people who have that prejudice," she said, "who believe that if you scratch a Gentile you find an anti-Semite, or who for whatever reason are racist, or don't like change, or feel threatened by it. But that has lessened a lot, and I happen to be part of a community where people are extremely accepting."

Beyond genetic identity, then, is there an essence of Judaism? "There's a famous story about Rabbi Hillel," Cowan said, "who, when somebody asked him that question, replied, 'Do not do unto others what you would not have done to yourself, and all the rest is commentary. Go and study.' That really does sum it up. Along with a strong sense of concern for others is concern for what they call tikkun, or repairing the world, which is why Judaism is a very 'this world'-oriented religion and why so many Jews are involved with social justice. It is up to us to do our part to repair the world. Also, in traditional Judaism, study is more central to life than prayer. Prayer is the ritual, the spiritual discipline, but study is the way of understanding God's will." Cowan laments that much of modern Jewry has stopped studying, and she feels that, had the many Jews who have turned to Buddhism, for example, had better teaching or searched more deeply, they would have found in Judaism what they sought in Eastern religion. (That phenomenon is hardly limited to Judaism. The Eastern Orthodox priest Thomas Hopko told of meeting a Quaker-turned-Buddhist teacher who was preparing a tour of Asia with forty-three students. For a week, the teacher and students sat in on Hopko's lectures on Eastern Orthodox Christianity at the Naropa Institute, the Colorado Buddhist learning center, and she later approached him with a message from her students. "I was told to tell you," she said, "that we all agreed that had we heard of a version of Christianity the way we heard it this week, none of us would probably be Buddhists today.")

Asked about the disproportionate number of Jews involved in alternative religions, Cowan speculated that growing up in a tradition that blends ethnicity and a religious life, as Judaism does, might leave one with an expectation of a unified world view. "American Judaism had become so segmented and so dry that the only people doing it in that wholehearted, integrated way are the Orthodox," she said. "And Orthodoxy is impossible for a lot of modern Jews, who can't go back to a sexist, particularist, in some sense racist community. But Reform Judaism, or Conservative, synagogue-based, minimal practice, wherein you don't talk about God and don't pray, is not satisfying to many people. Granted, a lot of people are happy as Reform Jews; but if you're a spiritual seeker, you won't be happy in a highly orchestrated and controlled service with responsive readings in English."

Some of the dryness of modern Jewish practice could be attributed to the fact that, as Cowan put it, "Jews were trying hard to be like Protestants, and when they succeeded, they paid the same price. You could always be Protestant without having to do very much about it. But Protestants in this country go back quite a few generations, whereas many Jews are only third generation here, so they still have all the myths they grew up with about life back in the old country. So much got shattered in that transition, so much was abandoned. Paul's father, for example, totally shunned his Orthodox childhood, yet left Paul with a sense of a gap, something that he needed to mend. It would not have been meaningful for Paul to go to a Reform congregation where the rabbi, in effect, used the *New York Times* as his Torah. He was attracted instead by Rabbi Singer, an Old World Polish Jew and an extraordinarily humble, pious man, who lives his Judaism in every aspect of his life but is not a great intellectual. Paul did not become Orthodox, because he was a totally unorthodox person and could not have been orthodox *anything*. But that Orthodox chord appealed to him, the total commitment of a Rabbi Singer. Paul searched to bring that totality into his religious life at our synagogue, Ansche Chesed, but at the same time he was an American journalist and never wanted to give up that freedom."

After studying for six years—two years on Hebrew alone—at Hebrew Union College-Jewish Institute of Religion, the seminary of the Reform movement, Rachel Cowan was ordained a Reform rabbi. She had planned to be a congregational rabbi, but after Paul's illness and death she didn't feel strong enough to take on a congregation. Now she counsels members of her community who call on her and leads services for learners. The synagogue she belongs to is Conservative, and she considers herself more observant than most Reform Jews, although she likes the fact that Reform Judaism "acknowledges the reality of choice" at the level of observance. "One of the things we're trying to do as a movement," she said, "is encourage people to take on more observances because it makes their Judaism more significant. For a long time, Reform was what you were because you didn't have to do anything." She also liked the feminist awareness in the Reform seminary, where women have been ordained for over ten years. "It transcended simply changing prefixes or pronouns, gender language, and was involved with the question of whether there are female ideas of God, or if the role of a woman as rabbi is different from that of a man."

Besides teaching the learner's minyan and presiding over weddings and funerals, Cowan works as program officer for the Jewish Life Grant at the Nathan Cummings Foundation, a new foundation that makes a quarter of its grants to Jewish projects. She makes recommendations for grants in areas of Jewish concern such as spirituality, social justice, relations between Jews and non-Jews, arts and culture. As a "rabbi for the unaffiliated," her work often has a free-lance feel to it, and includes a lot of telephone counseling. During our first interview, for instance, she took several phone calls from community members. One was from a couple who had just returned from their honeymoon and wanted to share their joyful feelings; another came from a man who had lost his wife and was having difficulty getting through the holidays alone. Because she is known to have dealt with the especially painful death of a loved one, she is often sought out to help others through similar crises.

As for private prayer, Cowan spends "a certain amount of conscious time at home, not exactly praying but somewhere between praying and meditating, something I plan to do more regularly next year. I keep kosher. I don't work, travel, or spend money on Shabbat. On Friday nights I always have Shabbat dinner, and sometimes go to services. I pretty much keep the Jewish calendar." Her current goal is to delve more deeply into the relationship between healing and Jewish spirituality, an area of enormous need that she does not feel is being addressed. Not that there is a specifically Jewish approach to healing that she knows of. "Judaism has always relied on doctors," she said. "Last year I did my thesis on the Psalms of Grief, and a long paper on the laws of visiting the sick. From very early on, way before Christianity, it was decided that although illness may have been the way God taught the need for repentance, people still had the right to try to cure themselves and others. In fact, it was a commandment to save lives, so Jews became skilled doctors very early in history. The Jewish tradition is to pray and rely on your doctor—and get the best one you can."

Cowan's guiding vision is of a place where people suffering from serious ailments like cancer might come for supplemental care. "The center I imagine would never try to take the place of oncologists," she said, "but would be able to do things including group work, massage, acupuncture, meditation, prayer, studying Psalms, learning. When Jews get cancer now and go for any kind of holistic approach, they end up chanting in Sanskrit. But that's the time when you most need to feel connected to your roots. Why couldn't they do something in Hebrew? When Paul was in the hospital, he had a wonderful yoga teacher who is a follower of Swami Muktananda. She would come in and chant *Ommmmmm*, and Paul would always respond, *Shalommmmmmm*."

While he was hospitalized, Paul was besieged by Jewish friends who insisted that Judaism was too materialistic a religion and what he really needed was to meditate or go on a macrobiotic diet. He thought about their advice for a while and then said to Rachel, "Look, I'm Jewish. What makes me feel good is knowing that my friends are taking care of me. I want to eat the food my friends make, like chicken, and kosher food. I don't want to eat seaweed and rice." Bernie Siegel, the former surgeon and best-selling author of *Love, Medicine, and Miracles*, is an example of what she means. "He's Jewish, but none of what he talks about has anything to do with Judaism. There isn't any voice in the Jewish community that understands both alternative and conventional therapies and Judaism."

To know Jewish law involves studying the Talmud and the commentaries on the Talmud, "enormous volumes of business ethics and sexual ethics." Cowan found the latter "very conventional," in that they do not condone homosexuality or extramarital affairs. "But even in the old, traditional teachings, there's also the idea that making love on Shabbat is a special thing to do, a good way to honor Shabbat. And a woman is entitled to sexual satisfaction as much as a man. There's not as much emphasis on the division between body and spirit. Your body is very much part of who you are." For similar reasons, the Judaic tradition places no value on monasticism, suffering, self-denial, or voluntary poverty. Contrariwise, some Jews throughout history have become extremely pious and ascetical, including medieval Jews who beat themselves. "Jews have always been influenced by their surrounding cultures," Cowan said. "In Christian or Islamic societies, their Judaism has taken on those aspects." But in general, Judaism does not hold that to help the world you need to impoverish yourself. One tradition says that if everybody gives 10 percent, then funds will be available. And an ancient Hebraic tradition commands farmers not to glean the corners of their fields at harvest time, leaving them for the needy. Both traditions are emblematic of the importance of community in the Judaic scheme of things.

Very often, Cowan insists, people think of the Talmud as merely a body of dry, legalistic reasonings. That may be partly so, but the core ethical teachings are more lively and involved, as in the Talmud's expression of concern for causing embarrassment to others. "The Talmud says that if you cause somebody embarrassment, to the point that their face goes white with shame, it's as if you've drained the blood from their face and you've killed them," she said. "It also gives an important teaching that you not 'stand on the blood of your neighbor,' a phrase from the Book of Leviticus that has been the subject of debate but which probably means you should not stand idly by when another is in danger of dying. All the laws of Halakah are suspended if it's a question of saving a life. Another teaching says that if you save one life, it's as if you've saved the world; but if you take one life, it's as if you've destroyed the world."

By Jewish law, only three acts are considered heinous enough that one should die rather than commit them: incest, idol worship, and murder. On the whole, Cowan considers it a very healthy system of ethics. "God creates good and evil, and all of us have both an evil inclination and a good inclination within us," she said. "These are manifestations of God, so even the evil inclination has some beneficial aspects. One of the teachings about Passover I really like is that when you eat only matzoh for a week, it's as if you take bread—the staff of life—and remove all the yeast. Yeast is what puffs it up and makes it arrogant. You reduce it to a small self, as you reduce yourself to your essential nature. Then you ask, What am I doing that is falsely puffing me up? On the other hand, there's no sense that you should go around as matzoh your whole life. If you didn't have ambition, you'd never get ahead. These instincts which, when uncontrolled, become greed or cruelty, are, in their moderate state, part of what a person needs to do in the world."

As much as anything else, Rachel Cowan's spiritual search has been for a community in which she can feel at home. Her comments make clear that the relation of the individual to the community—and by extension the world—something of vital importance to most religions, is even more central to Judaism. That isn't to say that Jews do not have an esoteric tradition or do not talk about the relationship between humanity and God. They do. But the emphasis on community, coupled with the absence of concern with self-abnegation, asceticism, or monastic life, creates a religious world view that is uniquely Jewish. As we will see much later, however, it has certain of these elements in common with another religion born in the Middle East—Islam.

CHAPTER 5

Dan and Harriet Carew: Encountering a Marriage

■ ■ ■

The prayer of the heart must penetrate every aspect and every activity
of Christian existence.

—Thomas Merton, *Contemplative Prayer*

■

Many Americans experiencing spiritual transformations are doing
so within the context of the faiths in which they were raised. These
experiences may be somewhat less dramatic than the ordeals of con
version or lifelong search that make up much of this book, but they
are no less real or powerful. Enrique Fernandez, the Cuban-born
American journalist and lapsed Catholic whom I interviewed for a
previous book, laid out fairly clearly the ground rules for many people
who were raised in one of the major religious traditions of America.

"I know—although I'm no longer practicing the religion—that I
will be a Catholic all my life, like most Catholics," Fernandez told
me. "I would feel silly as anything else, including the Eastern religions
such as Buddhism and Hinduism. The only religion that could ever
tempt me would be one of the Nigerian religions that were, and still
are, so prevalent among Cubans and Caribbean peoples, because I
also grew up with them. . . . I would feel silly putting on saffron robes.
Going into a Protestant church would do nothing for me at all. I still
think of myself as a Catholic, in part because it's part of my culture,
the way I was shaped. . . . I never really rejected the Church com-

pletely, and now having outgrown that period of adolescent rebellion, I admit that it is a route toward enlightenment, transcendence, spirituality, God, or whatever you want to call it. Whatever that other thing is that religion is all about, the Catholic Church is a fine, legitimate route, and it's a way that is available to me. I've already gone through its rites of passage. . . . No, I won't learn anything else—this is it. If I'm going to be saved, I'm going to be saved as a Catholic."

For some people, the early experience of religion is so riddled with traumatic events, obscured by overly strict or legalistic teachers and clerics, or rendered so oppressive by an intolerant atmosphere, that they have to remove themselves from all connection with it. In other cases, a believer born into one tradition may find it ineffectual, and evolve belief in a distinctly different faith. Yet most Americans seem generally more comfortable in the traditions in which they grew up than in any other.

Up to a certain point, the narratives of Dan and Harriet Carew are so typical of American Catholics in the mid-twentieth century as to be almost paradigmatic. The Irish-immigrant parentage, parochial schooling, marriage to another Catholic of similar background, church on Sunday, a larger-than-average family, and winning the good life were all part of the script. But midway through their marriage the story changed into one that differentiates theirs from the old, perfunctory, Sunday mass and rosary brand of Catholicism that is being emphatically left behind by younger Catholics in this country. That style may have served their parents well and may have been the source of a certain mystical devotion (although there is also reason to believe it never worked as well as is commonly thought). But it has little chance of firing the devotions of the latest generations of believers.

What the Carews found was a way of intensifying both their marriage and their faith through something known as Marriage Encounter, a weekend-long composite of encounter group and spiritual retreat that led to a major change in their lives. Marriage Encounter may be somewhat passé now among younger Catholics, but it served a useful function for the Carews, driving them to explore alternative styles of faith and community. Simultaneously, they discovered forms of private prayer unlike those they had been taught. Rather than withdrawing into an exploration of Christian esoterica as some have chosen to do, however, they have carried their new realizations into the hurly-burly of everyday life. This last distinction is significant, and deserves a brief explanation.

Quite a lot has been written lately about a resurgence of so-called esoteric Christian practices—the Jesus Prayer, Gnosticism, and so forth—as an attempt on the part of some contemporary Christians to recapture the immediacy and mystical fervor of the early Church. In his intriguing book *Lost Christianity*, Jacob Needleman examines the Western response to the infusion of Oriental religions, and some of the problems they have raised for Christians. Quoting from the manuscript of a priest identified only as Father Sylvan, Needleman distinguishes between the mystical experiences that seem to be in such demand these days (not only by Christians), and the quotidian practice of religion as conscious awareness. "Everything, absolutely everything about the Teaching must be experienced in ourselves and assimilated in our own being before we attempt to guide others," Father Sylvan writes. "Call this mysticism, if you wish, real mysticism. Once, the Church understood this; there must be a perpetual mysticism, perpetual experience. This is the origin of the Church's distrust of so-called 'mystics.' Mysticism in the real sense is the natural state of the human mind. 'Mystics' who have occasional 'experiences' often end by mocking the human creature through treating these experiences as extraordinary. But what is extraordinary is the rarity of this level of experience."

Needleman is searching for what he terms an "intermediate Christianity," somewhere between the mundane version with which modern believers are all too familiar and the high-flown cosmic experience available to only a few. As he puts it in his conclusion, "Mysticism and spirituality by themselves are not enough. Social action and therapeutic caring by themselves are not enough. Nor is it enough merely to reach for both at the same time. The lost element in our lives is the force within myself that can attend to both movements of human nature within my own being and can then guide the arising of this force within my neighbor in a manner suited to his understanding."

Talking with the Carews, and later considering their words and actions at length, I realized that the Christianity they are living, probably without being aware of Needleman's scholarly distinctions, lies somewhere in that "intermediate" neighborhood. They have explored personal spirituality, but in the context of social action and "therapeutic caring," and have sought to guide these forces within their neighbors. And all of that seems to have grown ineluctably out of their experience of Marriage Encounter. At the very least, their approach appears more relevant to today's Catholics than the old, hierarchically dominated version, and more accessible than the purely mystical one. Nothing they have done is extreme in terms of current Christian practice, and they sound less rebellious than many radical Catholics. But their lives nonetheless have radical implications for the direction of spirituality in America.

The Marriage Encounter movement within the Church originated in Spain but was developed in this country chiefly by Father Chuck Gallagher, a Jesuit priest and former chaplain for the Christian Family Movement. It consists of a weekend presentation by a team composed of a priest and a Catholic couple who have already been on a Marriage Encounter, and is also open to non-Catholics. In his landmark book *The Marriage Encounter*, Father Gallagher writes: "What the Marriage Encounter weekend offers is a sensitivity to how I am feeling and a willingness to share this with my spouse. Marriage Encounter reveals the importance of feelings and a freedom to express them." In a typical Encounter weekend, that expression might range from how one partner feels when the other goes away on a long trip to feelings about sex, death, God, and possessions. By the standards of post-Esalen encounter group therapeutics, this sounds like small potatoes. Yet, according to many accounts, the release of emotional openness in a religious setting yields unexpected results for marriage and faith and the couple's response to the world.

Dialogue, the principal technique used in Marriage Encounter, occurs orally and in writing between husband and wife, but differs from standard marital communications in that it suspends judgment and concentrates on feelings. "In dialogue there is no right or wrong," Gallagher writes. "There is no problem to be solved, no decision to be made, and therefore the issue is not the issue. We are not trying to formulate a decision or a plan, only to come to a greater awareness of each other." In its own humble, home-baked way, this sentiment runs parallel to the language of spiritual unfolding in many non-Western traditions. When Gallagher says that "a tremendous release" occurs on Marriage Encounter weekends "when it is emphasized that feelings are neither right nor wrong, they just *are*," he is echoing the advice of spiritual teachers from the East who tell us to look at our thoughts, feelings, and actions without judgment, to watch them without attempting to praise, condemn, or rationalize them. "To live with something like jealousy, envy or anxiety," wrote the modern Indian sage J. Krishnamurti in *Freedom from the Known*, "you must care for it, not condemn it or justify it. When you care for it, you are beginning to love it. . . . It is not that you love being envious or anxious, as so many people do, but rather that you care for watching. Can we live with all that, neither accepting it nor denying it, but just observing it without becoming morbid, depressed or elated?"

When I first met Dan and Harriet Carew, they were living in a walk-up flat in Cambridge, Massachusetts, with their thirteen-year-old daughter Molly, the last of five children. With his close-cropped dark hair and trim features, Dan Carew at fifty-six resembles a more kindly Jack Webb. Harriet was the livelier and more outspoken of the two, and at certain moments, as when she questioned the limited roles for women in the clergy, she became visibly infused with the kind of passionate intensity I'd witnessed among Catholics in the peace movement. The Carews' digs could best be described as cozy and lived in, not at all the kind of place you might expect to find the family of a former senior pilot for United Airlines. There were no antiques or Ethan Allen sectionals, just furniture that looked comfortably unpretentious.

Inspired partly by the example of their oldest children, who had become involved in social welfare causes, Harriet and Dan had brought their standard of living into line with the work they hope to accomplish. Not long ago, they had sold their home in Connecticut and moved to this apartment so that Dan could pursue his desire to teach grammar school in Roxbury, one of Boston's toughest ghettos. Harriet had enrolled in a three-year master of divinity course at the Weston School of Theology in nearby Weston, Massachusetts, although she acknowledged that, in a church that has little official place for women in hierarchical or ministerial roles, she's not quite sure what she'll do with it.

Both Dan and Harriet were raised as Roman Catholics and have stayed in the Church through their adult lives. Although they may have experienced the doubts and questions familiar to other American Catholics, they have never left the Church, even for a short period.

Dan describes himself as "a New York Irish Catholic" whose father came over as an immigrant in 1928 and whose mother was born in New York City of Irish immigrants. Dan's family was not especially religious, he said, but "in an era when everybody was either practicing Catholics or Catholics who had fallen away, we were practicing Catholics." Dan was taught by Dominican nuns in grammar school, Jesuits in high school. He wrapped a degree in aeronautical engineering at Notre Dame around five years of service as a Navy pilot from 1954 to 1959. He counts himself lucky in that he "got in the Navy in time to get the GI Bill to go back to college, but never saw active duty." His résumé reads like a prototype of the education afforded to children of upwardly mobile Catholic immigrants, the sort that was repeated, with variations, in thousands and perhaps hundreds of thousands of families across the country over the past century.

By the time he finished college, Dan was "pretty fed up with the Church, not necessarily with my faith." More intellectually curious than spiritual, he attended mass "as a cultural thing. The way I was brought up, it was the thing to do. My intellectual curiosity, my reading, was probably my way of asking, Doesn't there have to be something more than this to religion?" He read some Zen and Thomas Merton on his own, but otherwise had "what you would probably call a classical Irish Catholic upbringing."

The only thing missing from this "classical" Catholic journey is the angst brought on in many Catholics by the Second Vatican Council of 1962–65, which wrought massive and often disturbing changes in Catholic life. Vatican II affected clergy and laity alike, infusing some with a new zeal while disheartening others to such an extent that many clergy felt their vocations were no longer meaningful and left their orders, and many lay Catholics left the Church altogether. But the Carews escaped the turbulence that roiled around them when they moved to Taiwan after Dan landed positions there with Civil Air Transport and Air America in 1964, three years after getting married. "We kind of missed Vatican II," Dan said. "We kind of missed the whole sixties. When we came home, we said, 'Gee, the world has changed.' "

On the whole, they were attracted to the changes in the Church. "We both thought there was need for change. We didn't know that these were the right changes, and I still don't. I still see the Church as a rather medieval institution. People have said it is a pilgrim church, that it's in process. But the institutional Church is not something I have great attraction to." His admiration for individual Catholics has led him "to want to be part of this *community*, more than part of the institution or the hierarchy or the dogma."

Here Harriet broke in to point out that Dan had jumped "from the sixties to the eighties and left out the seventies, which was really our turning point." Like Dan, Harriet Carew is "a product of Catholic school from kindergarten through college." She was born to second-generation Irish and German immigrants, but unlike Dan, with his perfunctory and indifferent religious upbringing, Harriet relished her Catholic childhood. "I loved the mystery of the Church," she said. "When I read about these awful nuns in these tell-all books, well, that wasn't my experience. I was one of the smart kids who didn't get hit on the head with a ruler."

Born Harriet O'Toole in Bridgeport, Connecticut, she was raised there and in New Haven, and in Brussels, Belgium, where her family lived briefly. She went to college in New York and met Dan through his sister, a college friend of hers. She had "a rather benign experience of church. Church was family. It filled my need for music, mystery, and imagination. It had a lot of cultural overtones and was part of my life. But I wouldn't say I claimed an adult faith until much later— the sense of the faith I know now, which you claim on a very deep, personal level. The deadest part of my faith was that period as a young married. But the turning point was going on a Marriage Encounter in 1973."

Dan's sister had gone on a Marriage Encounter and told Harriet about it. "I thought it sounded wonderful," Harriet said. "I hate to be sexist, but I think women care and fuss over their marriages more than men, and this supposedly got your husband to talk, to open up. So I wanted to go, expecting it to be something for my marriage, not expecting it to be connected to the Church in any way. As it turned out, it was a powerful experience of integrating faith and marriage and your life. It was an exciting renewal of our marriage and a whole new way to look at life." Like a lot of Catholics who grew up in the forties and fifties, Harriet was left with the feeling that marriage was "a second-rate thing," and that "priests and sisters were on a higher level than you were. They had a *real* vocation. Although I knew from the time I was in kindergarten that I was going to get married, I always felt that a lot of people had their eye on me to go into the convent. Now suddenly this thing that was in my gut to choose was being highly valued. That was a tremendous validation of our life as a married couple."

But Marriage Encounter became more to Harriet than a validation of marriage. "People usually come to God individually, but in that particular experience something happens to you as a couple," she said. "You see each other in a new way, and somehow this dynamic of the love relationship is revelatory of God." Just as inner practice can be hollow without a sense of community, the Carews found that their relationship to each other and to God was only the starting point for a broader relationship to the world. "We saw that loving each other was meant to explode out," Harriet said, "and that our love is meant to be a sign of God in the world, and we took that to heart. So we did our weekends, but we also got involved in life in a different way. In that Marriage Encounter movement, people reached out." When she learned that Dan had invited me to stay for supper, for instance, she laughed, because they wouldn't have done that before Marriage Encounter. "That open hospitality to a stranger, among other things, sank into us from that experience and became part of our life."

Marriage Encounter also represents for them a shift of the balance of power in the Church from the hierarchy to the people, the grass roots, more like the way it had been in the first days of Christianity. During their two and a half years of leading weekends, they felt, in Harriet's words, "a sense of ourselves as early Christians. We felt like disciples, going out and spreading the gospel. Suddenly we were attracted to reading Scripture as a living thing. It was a conversion experience."

For Dan, "It got to where the experience of doing this Encounter helped us to know each other much better than we had previously, and to understand, beyond any intellectual way, the relationship between our love for each other and our faith. I first read Martin Buber's *I and Thou* during Marriage Encounter, and after rereading it recently I realized how much *I and Thou* was the premise of Marriage Encounter. What Father Gallagher was trying to do was to have people experience real presence to another person, and that would lead you to the same sort of presence to God. It was such an intense period that it did change us very much."

After several years of participating in and running Marriage Encounters, the Carews "retired" by having a fifth child, a direct result of "the renewal of being in love." They redirected their energy into the parish, where they discovered that most of the other active parishioners had gone, at some point, on a Marriage Encounter. "We lived in a small country parish with two hundred fifty families. So we started a Catholic Youth Organization program and we started exploring different things." That included adopting Vietnamese refugee babies and foster-parenting teenagers. The adoption didn't work out, but the Carews did foster several children.

The experience of the Marriage Encounter had significant subsidiary effects on the Carews' personal spirituality. For one thing, they discovered prayer. They also discovered, in a way that was difficult for them, that they were two very different personalities. "We were doing everything together in Marriage Encounter," Harriet said, "and we found that prayer was just you standing naked before the Almighty. It was painful for me to realize we couldn't do it together, but had to go on the journey alone. No one was telling us how to do this. For me it was tracking down people I thought were holy, meaning that they were full of life and had a commitment and were living it out. Whether it was a priest or a nun or a lay person, I would develop a friendship and go on retreats."

Harriet discovered a Jesuit retreat house outside of Boston, and she and Dan began making retreats there as a way of intensifying their personal practice. But whereas Harriet got up every morning and had a quiet prayer time, Dan rarely did. He had grown up when it was common for Catholic families to "say the rosary together as a sort of devotion: 'The family that prays together stays together.' That was as long a prayer as I'd ever had." Learning to pray as an adult was "a long, slow process. Not that it's a major effort. I've always tried to make time for prayer, and in the last few years I have formalized my practice to the point where I try to take a half hour every day. But I don't have a sense of urgency about praying better."

"We were not frantically searching for how to pray," Harriet said. "It was an organic process of figuring out that we couldn't pray together. We had to allow each other the freedom to do that in our own way." They did investigate the Charismatic Catholic movement, which incorporates emotional elements similar to born-again Christian services such as shouted prayers and talking in tongues, but didn't find it to their liking. They took a course in Christian meditation and learned about the Jesus Prayer, which fourth-century Christian anchorites known as the Desert Fathers had developed and which evolved over hundreds of years. The Fathers would repeat "Lord Jesus Christ, Son of God, have mercy on me, a sinner," as many as a thousand times at a sitting, using beans to keep count. But when Harriet went up to the attic with her sack of a thousand beans and tried to say the Jesus Prayer for forty-five minutes, she didn't find it rewarding.

Over time, the couple evolved individual prayer forms, which for Harriet meant getting up early in the morning before the family and "having a cup of tea with God, sitting in silence and allowing myself to be in God's presence." For his part, Dan became interested in something called centering prayer. Although Catholicism does have a rich contemplative tradition, it has fallen into disuse for the most part. That tradition goes all the way back to the Desert Fathers and continues through writings such as the anonymous fourteenth-century work *The Cloud of Unknowing*, and St. Ignatius Loyola's *Spiritual Exercises*, written in the sixteenth century. Although there is still some debate among scholars as to whether the *Exercises* were meant to be repeated or were intended as a "once in a lifetime" retreat, they continue to be used by both clergy and laity to intensify their connection with God. Recent advocates of contemplative prayer for the laity have ranged from Thomas Merton to Father Basil Pennington of St. Joseph's Abbey in Spencer, Massachusetts, who developed the centering prayer.

Furthermore, a definite connection appears to have existed between Christian contemplative prayer in its earliest stages and Eastern forms of meditation. According to the Baptist theologian Harvey Cox, St. John Climacus, one of the early proponents of the Desert Fathers' methods, "taught his followers to concentrate on each breath they took, using the name of Jesus as a kind of mantra to accompany this breathing." And St. Nicephorus "instructed his disciples to attach a prayer to each breath and to focus their attention on the centers of their own bodies while meditating." Focusing on the breath and the use of repeated sounds or mantras are both basic elements of Eastern meditation. The late Audle Allison, an American meditation teacher and founder of the Lotus Center in Oklahoma, argued on scriptural evidence that Christ practiced meditation in the Gospels. And even in Genesis we read that "Isaac went out to meditate in the field."

Basil Pennington has picked up this tradition. According to Jacob Needleman, Pennington designed his centering prayer "for people outside the monastery who were seeking a more simplified kind of prayer than is generally taught in parishes and Catholic educational institutions." Part of what he sought to address, Needleman writes, was "the need many young people feel to come home to their own tradition after having explored Eastern spiritual disciplines." To that end, the methods of Transcendental Meditation, or TM, created by the Indian teacher Maharishi Mahesh Yogi, "were a principal stimulus and standard of comparison of the centering prayer." (In essence Maharishi's methods involve being quiet, taking a comfortable posture, and repeating a mantra or sound.) In his book *Centering Prayer*, Pennington writes that "In Centering Prayer we go beyond thought and image, beyond the senses and the rational mind, to that center of our being where God is working a wonderful work." He based his prayer as much on the methods of the Desert Fathers as on TM, but points out that by the fourteenth century, when the Jesus Prayer reached its "most highly developed, psychosomatic expression," it reproduced "even to details the dhikr method of the Sufis of the thirteenth century." During the dhikr (or zhikr), a kind of ecstatic dance, the Islamic Sufis were chanting the name of Allah instead of Jesus, but the rest was similar enough.

Father Pennington's centering prayer formed a substantial part of Dan Carew's prayer life. Using a modified yoga position, he learned to sit for twenty minutes at a time "without fidgeting, and to relax and empty and be very conscious of any sensual input, sound, anything. I have my eyes closed, not to try to isolate myself from my surroundings, but to relax into them, to quiet the mind and listen for God from within the heart, not the head. Exactly how to do that I don't know, but there is almost an expectancy to hear the word come this way." Most days he gets up feeling relaxed, and comes away with a sense of something that has been missing from his life.

The Carews found other ways to grow spiritually, by "sniffing things out." Faced with the question of how they could "live life fully," they determined to do "some radical Christian thing," but didn't know what it would be. When United's pilots went on strike, they decided they ought to "go someplace and be teachers." The strike lasted for only two months, but they were left with the idea, so they kept playing with it. Harriet wasn't interested in teaching, "because I'd been teaching children for years—ours. Dan had an idea about going on an Indian reservation. He'd say, 'I could teach and you could . . .' and there would always be a long pause. Finally I said, 'I know what I want to do. I want to be the leader of prayer.'" Harriet decided that she would enroll in the Weston School of Theology.

Their plans were delayed when Harriet's mother was diagnosed with terminal cancer in 1986. But her mother's illness and death clarified for Harriet that she wanted to pursue the ministry. "I had something burning in me to do or say: that the Church was in transition, that I wanted to be a part of that transition, that my experience as a married woman was not reflected anywhere in the Church. I kept thinking, This is my Church and I am not going to shut up. I felt very angry at the way faith was presented on a parish level—the lack of expectation that God was truly there in your life, the lack of dynamism, the dried-out, dogmatic sermon that I heard Sunday after Sunday. When I felt I could tell people what God's like but I wasn't allowed up there, I experienced a lot of frustration for a long time." She finally enrolled in Weston and began her studies. "They talk about that as a preparation for lay ministry," Harriet said. "But I don't think anyone really knows what lay ministry is. I couldn't tell you."

They also "poked around" in other areas of communal spirituality offered by the Church, including *curcillo,* or "little course," a program begun in Spain and offered by Hispanic communities in America in Spanish or English. *Curcillo* is another example of the small group approach in which members listen to talks by their peers. "People want to read and hear about other people," Harriet said. "That's what turns them on, not the theory, not the doctrine. They would prepare a little talk to a group, and you would then discuss the talk. It's very Hispanic. The men went first and then the women went, on separate weekends." And then there was Renew, a movement sponsored by the hierarchy of the Church possibly as a response to Marriage Encounter, which had been organized and run largely by the laity. Originating in the Newark, New Jersey, diocese in 1984, Renew soon spread throughout the country, again suggesting that people meet at home in small groups. "We had had a lot of experience with small groups," Dan said, "so it was odd to go to a group and realize that most of the people had never sat with ten others in a room and shared faith, or talked about experiences in their life, without a priest leading them, telling them, 'This is right, this is wrong.' "

The significant element in all three movements was what Harriet characterized as "people coming in contact with living faith in other people. The idea of Marriage Encounter was that you went on a weekend and afterward you formed a group and had an ongoing place to talk about the experience and how it continued in your life. *Curcillo* and Renew had that same possibility—people coming together, sitting with Scripture, talking about faith in their life. Whenever that happens, something starts to cook. Doing centering prayer or going to monasteries may or may not happen to an individual. People catch the spark from other people, and then do something with that which is very personal. How you continue it comes out of your own personality."

Although Vatican II changed the traditional presentation of the mass by turning the priest around to face the congregation and putting the liturgy into English, that wasn't enough for the Carews. "The group needs to be eight or ten people who look eye to eye, face to face, talk of their normal life and tribulations and joys, and connect that with God and faith," Harriet said. "That's where faith starts to mean something and where those little connections are made. People will take a piece of Scripture and say, 'How does that connect with my life?' Someone will tell you a story that you wouldn't have thought of, and it's down to earth. You keep waiting for the priest to do that in his homily, but he rarely does it."

What is remarkable in these descriptions isn't that the notion of connecting with a small number of other believers in homey surroundings is so unlike the Catholicism most people of my generation grew up with, but how similar it sounds to less conventional disciplines. Eckankar, for instance, uses Satsangs, groups of twelve meeting in a member's home, with a leader who might have a few more years' experience in spiritual practice. Christian Science communities hold

Wednesday evening services in which members express gratitude, talk about spontaneous healings and transformations in their lives. Those modest testimonies resemble what you might hear in the informal teaching session preceding formal prayer in an Islamic mosque, or at a Quaker meeting. I get the feeling from the Carews that if religion has a future in this country, which it certainly seems to, it doesn't lie in massive outdoor stadiums or over the airwaves with millions tuned to one preacher, but in small groups.

Harriet and Dan share an admiration for radical Christians such as Dorothy Day, who founded the Catholic Worker movement in the 1930s as a Christian alternative to communism. But only in the last few years have they been able to move in that direction and take some risks. Spurred by their children's interest in social justice, the Carews began to pursue idealistic activities themselves. It began when their sixteen-year-old daughter Peggy spent a summer in the Dominican Republic, living with a native family and giving inoculations to children in the outskirts of Santo Domingo. "Now she's working in California on a pittance of a salary," Harriet said, "running a St. Vincent De Paul home which is a shelter for homeless women." Their oldest son is no longer a practicing Catholic. "He's probably a practicing Marxist," Dan said with a trace of resignation. "He's a very idealistic young man and is teaching at a black high school in Manhattan." A second daughter is teaching English on an Indian reservation in New Mexico. The Carews wondered how they could challenge their children to do such idealistic things when they were sitting back comfortably. "We believe you should die with your boots on," Harriet said. "We never played golf anyway, and what people were doing when they retired didn't look like fun. Airline couples do a lot of traveling because you get free airfare. It's hardly unpleasant, but it didn't seem very dynamic. We wanted to live life fully, so we decided to do that 'radical Christian thing.' But we still didn't know what it was."

Dan had just reached his "big money years" with the airline. "Last year was the first year in my life I made over a hundred thousand," he said, "and it'll be the last year." Teaching in Roxbury meant earning $12,000 a year and dipping into their savings. "But in fact our needs are taken care of. It's austere in comparison to the way we were living, but we sat down and looked at a budget and said we'd be able to make it and not have the extras." They decided to sell a house and some land they owned in Connecticut, and in six weeks they closed the deal at near the asking price, which was more than they had expected. That allowed them to get rid of one mortgage, buy a smaller house nearby without a mortgage, and prepay the next three years of their son's tuition at Yale. "We imagined ourselves being vagabonds and doing a radical thing, and it's not radical at all," Harriet said. "Sometimes we feel embarrassed telling our story, because it sounds like we're so heroic. We're not heroic. We're doing something that gives us life."

"In a sense," Dan said, "we don't have a great feeling of giving something up. What we're going toward is more attractive than anything we're leaving behind." While Dan was coming to terms with his changeover from $100,000-a-year senior pilot to $12,000-a-year inner-city teacher, Harriet was confronting the implications of working toward a master of divinity degree in a church that does not recognize a pastoral role for women. When she realized that she would never be ordained after completing the same course as the young men at Weston, she was "very depressed. I got an A from my Eucharistic Theology professor, who said, 'You understand this with passion.' I almost felt tears come in my eyes. I thought, Yeah, and I'd make a damn good priest too, because I understand it with passion." That passion was evident when she discussed the irony of a Church plagued by a growing shortage of priests at a time when more and more women want to serve in that capacity. "Hey, I'm a hot number," she said. "My faith burns holes in my socks. But there's no place for me in the structure."

Harriet's frustration with the hierarchical framework of the Catholic Church presents a particular problem because her faith is so deeply embedded in her loyalty to the Church. If we accept the dictum that religion is not primarily about doctrines but about living in religious communities, then we begin to see how difficult it can be for people like the Carews to extricate their inherent faith, even their understanding of Catholic theology, from an ecclesiastical structure that they find unfair or unresponsive. Harriet may wonder how the Church became divided between "hierarchy and laity," but that is the superstructure that holds together a world institution with 900 million members. As to whether the Church could exist without that superstructure, neither she nor Dan has any simple answer. That frustration came to a boil one day when Harriet confronted the president of Weston. "You don't believe this," she said to him, "but if they blew up the Vatican, the Church would still go on."

Dan's view of being a Catholic within the Church is more pragmatic. To him, it's a matter of being "like the supply sergeant in the Army who manages to do exactly what he pleases—just don't catch the boss's eye. I think there's a lot of latitude in the Church to lead an individual life. Teaching in a Catholic school isn't very difficult. No one has ever said, 'Don't teach that.' I'm able to speak my conscience without feeling I'm violating my contract with my superiors or teaching anything un-Catholic. And yet it wouldn't always sound like Catholic dogma to some people. So it's possible to live under a rather oppressive hierarchy without catching their eye. As the Church, we can proceed with our mission while the hierarchy is concerning itself with maintenance."

I came away from my encounter with Dan and Harriet Carew feeling that the tension between their personal faith and sense of community on one hand, and their frustration with the male-dominated clerical hierarchy on the other, is part of their particular spiritual ordeal. The problem may even be peculiar to Catholicism as a whole because of its structural rigidity. I haven't, for instance, found such potent dichotomies among American Protestants, Buddhists, or Jews, whose institutional organizations are generally much less rigid (and all of which, not coincidentally, have made room at some level for women in their clergy). But I can hardly envisage a couple like the Carews, given their history, as anything but Roman Catholics. At one point, Harriet spoke of being evaluated by her supervisor at Weston for a course in Clinical Pastoral Education, part of her training for chaplaincy. He had written that Harriet could be highly critical of the Church, but that she had a great love for it. "That touched me deeply, and I thought, Damn it, it's true," she said. "This is what I was born into. I have a great sense of loyalty and love for the Church, and I'm as angry as anything about it. A young woman here completed her Weston course, then left and joined the Episcopal Church and is now in their ordination track. I'm glad she's doing it, and I understand why, but I could never do that. The Catholic Church is an extended family experience that has formed me. Maybe it even formed my rebelliousness, who knows? But I couldn't leave it."

When I last spoke with Dan and Harriet, they had moved on from Boston to New Mexico, where they have begun to work with Catholic Pueblo Indians as part of a Franciscan mission. Dan is teaching religion, math, and science at the mission school, and Harriet has taken a position as coordinator of pastoral ministries—a nebulous, nonclerical role that at least lets her help direct the spiritual lives of pueblo residents. She still sounds ambivalent about the prospects for a lay ministry, and a little disoriented by the new surroundings. Their living conditions are even more simplified, and they are reaching out to a culture that is admittedly foreign to them, but they both sound excited. The transformative process that had begun on a Marriage Encounter seventeen years before is continuing to be played out in their daily lives.

CHAPTER 6

Jim McCloskey:
The Dark Pit

■   ■   ■

For your hands are defiled with blood, and your fingers with iniquity;
your lips have spoken lies, your tongue mutters wickedness. No one
enters suit justly, no one goes to law honestly; they rely on empty
pleas, they speak lies, they conceive mischief, and bring forth iniquity.
They hatch adders' eggs, they weave the spider's web. . . .
    Justice is turned back, and righteousness stands afar off; for truth
has fallen in the public squares, and uprightness cannot enter.
            —Isaiah 59:3–5,14 (*Revised Standard Version*)

■

Walking into the basement offices of Jim McCloskey's Centurion
Ministries, an organization he founded in 1983 to help free men and
women wrongly convicted of murder, you see little in the way of
religious imagery. On one wall, however, a picture of a grieving Christ
hangs between a photo of two Sioux Indians and another of a white
mob lynching two black men. The latter photo, it turns out, was taken
not in the Deep South but in Indiana. Between the fate of Native
Americans and African Americans in this country, you begin to see
just what Christ is grieving over.

    Jim McCloskey took the name Centurion Ministries from the ac-
count in the Gospel of Luke of the Roman centurion who stood at
the foot of the Cross and, looking up at the crucified Christ, said,
"Surely, this one was innocent." The Gospels, of course, make another
famous reference to a Roman centurion, one whose faith Christ found

greater than that of anyone in Israel. "It takes a lot of faith to do this work," McCloskey later said of his Ministries, "and to raise money to do this work. Raising money is more difficult than freeing innocent people." Still, the main focus of McCloskey's work is not religious faith but bringing a very practical kind of salvation to the innocent.

At first glance, he looks an unlikely character for the role. In his late forties, round-faced and balding, a forcible speaker, Jim Mc-Closkey wouldn't be hard to picture sitting in a sales meeting or executive boardroom. Even casually dressed in an open-collared shirt and neatly pressed bluejeans held up by maroon suspenders, as he was when I first met with him in 1990 after a long telephone interview the previous year, he had an unmistakably businesslike air about him. That's not surprising, considering the mileage McCloskey clocked years ago traveling the globe as a management consultant for American firms. And I could easily imagine him in the black tunic of a Protestant minister, an occupation for which he spent several years preparing after he left the business world.

Fate, however, had other ideas. As part of his ministerial training, McCloskey counseled prison inmates, and, through a series of events he "could not avoid," he helped to win the release from prison of an inmate who was serving a life sentence for a murder he didn't commit. Jim McCloskey never did go on to be ordained, choosing instead to devote all of his time to work for the release of others wrongly imprisoned for murder. In the decade since he began, he has helped free seven men and one woman (four black, three Hispanic, one white), and is at work on dozens more cases. But his Spirit-driven commitment to social justice may be undermining the spiritual life he originally sought when he turned his back on the material rewards of a business career. Now he wonders if he hasn't gone from one rat race to another.

Jim McCloskey is a Protestant by birth, and a Protestant by practice, although his understanding of Christianity has been transmuted from the evangelical fervor of the Presbyterian Church in which he grew up to the social justice activism of the United Church of Christ where he now worships. And the inner transformation that accompanied that evolution is rooted in the corporeal world in a way that adds a new dimension to our understanding of the word "spiritual." The only apparent ambiguity in his experience of faith lies in his continuing struggle to balance the tangible satisfactions of his daily work, which he considers to be inspired by God, with his unhappiness over an inner prayer life for which that work leaves little or no time. It's a curious contradiction, but only one of many that seem to pervade the lives of those who follow their innermost spiritual impulses. And it was a decidedly spiritual impulse that led McCloskey into his current work—work so far out of the ordinary that he may be the only person in the country engaged in it full-time.

McCloskey was raised in a very conservative Presbyterian community in the suburbs of Philadelphia, "not quite fundamentalist, but certainly Evangelical," called the Bethany Collegiate Presbyterian Church. It was an offshoot of the Presbyterian Church of Philadelphia founded by John Wanamaker, the famous nineteenth-century merchant and conservative religious figure. The focus of McCloskey's church was evangelizing, "going out and telling the world about Christ, and saving their souls. Nothing at all about justice and helping others, no sense of a practical application of Christ's teachings in contemporary society." As a child, McCloskey was forced to attend services by his parents, who were active in the church. Along with his younger brother, he went every Sunday from fifth through twelfth grade.

"We'd go to Sunday School," he said, "and then to church—that's three good hours in the morning—and then come back at night for the young people's group, and then night church. Six hours every Sunday. By the time I graduated from high school, I was sick and tired of church." When he came home for Thanksgiving in his freshman year at college, he felt he was finished with worship. "That Sunday, Dad said, 'Okay, let's get ready for church.' I said to him, 'Dad, I'm never going to church again.' And I didn't for fourteen years."

McCloskey allowed that his father, who "kind of understood" his refusal to attend church, "wasn't really an ogre. He wasn't a severe, religious, distant figure at all. He just thought his kids ought to go to church, and he made sure they did. He felt that we should have that kind of background and those values built into us." From age seventeen to thirty-two, McCloskey would stay away from religion of any sort.

In 1960, he went to Bucknell University in Louisburg, Pennsylvania, where he majored in economics and led a "typical fraternity, *Animal House* kind of college existence and social life. My entire four years at the university centered around my fraternity: drinking, girls, having a good time." The sixties had not yet gone into full swing, and so McCloskey missed that generation. "I was never even offered a joint in college. We just drank. We never demonstrated, were not socially conscious or active at all. We just had a party. Bucknell cranked out very successful, conservative, suburban Republican businessmen." To this day, McCloskey's social contacts are mostly old friends from that era. Jim fit the Bucknell mold closely. "The only thing I thought of when I graduated from college," he said, "was to make a niche for myself in the world, earn a good living, compete with my peers, go up the corporate ladder, and become a successful business person. My main concern was to do as well as others had."

Following his graduation from Bucknell in 1964, McCloskey went into the Navy. Unsure of his career goals, he enlisted through Officer Candidate School and became a commissioned officer. He had a long-standing fascination with the Far East, and so, following the first of many interior urgings, he put in for duty in Japan, where he was sent as a young ensign with shore duty. After a year and a half, he wanted to get to where the action was. It was June 1966, and Vietnam was starting to heat up, so McCloskey volunteered for active duty. He was assigned as an adviser to the South Vietnamese Navy, and lived on a South Vietnamese base in the Mekong Delta. "Our job was to patrol the rivers on what they called the 'junk fleet,' forty-foot wooden boats with .30 and .50 caliber machine guns at either end, looking for VC moving contraband," he said. "We also did search-and-destroy and troop-lift missions. We did a variety of things, all very poorly."

After a year in Vietnam, McCloskey was awarded the Bronze Star. All he will say about it is that it was "for performing well under fire on several occasions." When his tour was up, he separated from the Navy and enrolled in business courses at the American Graduate School for International Management in Phoenix, Arizona.

American business was at its zenith then. "We were the real superpower of the world in terms of our business prowess," McCloskey said, "and from that point on it has been downhill." He still was not giving much thought to the way society operated, or to social and racial injustice. "I was consumed by the American Dream," he added, "and so I was asleep for thirty-seven years." Like most other Americans, he never imagined that the criminal justice system might not be functioning as efficiently or as fairly as he thought. "I couldn't have cared less about civil rights or what was going on down South with Martin Luther King, Jr., and neither could my friends," McCloskey said. While he was in graduate school in Phoenix, he heard that King had been assassinated, and figured it was just as well. "I thought he was a troublemaker. It never entered my mind to be moved by the plight of black people, or in any way to participate in their cause. To expend oneself on the part of the downtrodden was just not part of our ethic."

A year later, McCloskey was on his way back to Japan, this time as a management consultant for an affiliate of First National City Bank of New York and Fuji Bank of Japan, a joint venture. He worked primarily with American companies wanting to do business in Japan, performing market research there from 1969 to 1973. During those four years in Japan, McCloskey's internal life gradually fell into turmoil. "To the Japanese, there are two kinds of people," he said, "the Japanese and the *gaijin*—literally, 'outside people,' which means the rest of the world. All non-Japanese are 'outside people.' Even though I was in Japan and enjoying my work, I could never become part of that society, and I felt like flotsam out there, a nonperson. Nor was I happy with the whole corporate structure and the chances for advancement within my employment situation. I was famished for my own culture, and I was unhappy with the way my career was going, so I decided to come back. The Prodigal Son returned."

On his way home, McCloskey made a stopover in New York, where, through a friend, he landed a job on Wall Street, but the troubled feelings that had been festering in Japan didn't go away. "I realized that I needed something within myself that came from beyond myself, that was not just myself. I felt that I wasn't invincible and self-reliant, and I needed something from outside to stir me, to fulfill me, to satisfy me. There was some kind of emptiness, a spiritual emptiness." He started going to Norman Vincent Peale's Marble Collegiate Church. The denomination is Dutch Reformed of America, not Presbyterian, but that didn't matter. McCloskey felt like "a baby Christian, starting all over," and he was nourished by Peale's brand of Christianity. "I couldn't wait for Sunday to roll around," he said. "He inspired me and gave me hope and confidence, self-esteem."

Best known for inspirational self-help books such as his 1952 best-seller *The Power of Positive Thinking*, Peale preached regularly in his church on the corner of Fifth Avenue and West 29th Street, attracting a large congregation. At the time, Peale's message was enormously popular, seeming to embody the perfect marriage of the vaunted Protestant Work Ethic and the American Dream, proclaiming that a positive attitude enabled us to achieve all our goals and desires on a material level. If we imagined success, we would become successful. In some ways, it is similar to New Age teachings of today that stress certain mental techniques to improve our health or finances. Peale suggests, without labeling them as such, creative visualization, positive affirmations (in the form of Biblical quotations), and silent meditation, all of which have become staples of the New Age approach to life. The first lines of Peale's book, in fact, sound as if they might be introducing the latest work on crystals, healing meditation, or subliminal affirmations: "This book is written to suggest techniques and to give examples which demonstrate that you do not need to be defeated by anything, that you can have peace of mind, improved health, and a never-ceasing flow of energy. In short, that your life can be full of joy and satisfaction."

In its practical applications, however, Peale's approach turned out to be considerably more materialistic than it appeared. "His whole thing, as I look back on it," McCloskey said, "is really a success motivation institute. He somehow perverts, or subverts, the Christian gospel. There's no *Cross* in his message, which consists of: 'You can be what you dream you want to be.' Peale uses examples of how a person started from nothing and became a millionaire or a successful executive. The Christian gospel is submerged. He weaves it in using Scripture, but he stresses all the ingredients that enable one to succeed in the world, which to my mind is antithetical to the Christian gospel message."

Today, McCloskey finds Peale's message "very unrealistic." But given where he was at that time, "feeling lost as a result of my disillusionment in Japan, coming into the big, bad city of New York and starting a new career, he was just what I needed. I was in a state of emotional and economic brokenness." Under Peale's influence, he started reading the Scriptures again, especially the New Testament. Slowly, the faith of his childhood was rekindled. "It began to take root within me, in my inner person. But the way I was living externally, you never would have known it. I was sexually promiscuous with women, including 'professional' women. I wasn't applying the message of the Scriptures in business in the way I expected myself to. Although I wasn't an *evil* person, I was an unthinkingly selfish person. I wanted only to get ahead in the business world."

Unhappy with life in New York City after just a year, McCloskey returned home to Philadelphia in the summer of 1974 and took a position with the Hay Group, a prestigious international consulting firm. He bought a house in the suburbs and for a time things went well. He enjoyed a lot of freedom and flexibility in his work, and drew a high salary. "I was living the good life. I had the house, the Lincoln Continental. I was an eighties-style yuppie living in the seventies—a man ahead of my time," McCloskey said with a self-deprecating laugh. But during those five fat years, from 1974 to 1979, when everything was going well in a material sense, a gnawing emptiness revisited him. "I was feeding myself, and the more I fed myself, the emptier I became. My life was like a rainbow: it looked pretty, but there was no substance."

In time McCloskey found the Paoli Presbyterian Church, twenty miles west of Philadelphia, and became a fast friend of the minister, Dick Streeter. His new pastor's preaching was on key with his own understanding of the Gospels, of "how Christ was asking us to live our lives, and it was more scripturally rooted than Peale's. It compelled one to serve others, and the only person I had been serving was myself." Streeter was preaching, in essence, the social gospel, the first time McCloskey had heard anything like that. He was struck by passages such as the one in Matthew 25 in which Christ speaks of choosing the elect at the final judgment, "as a shepherd divides his sheep from the goats," based on their performance of what are sometimes referred to as the corporal works of mercy. "Christ is saying, 'As you did it to one of the least of these my brethren, you did it to me,' " McCloskey explained. "And he uses concrete illustrations, specifically saying that 'the least of these' are those who are hungry, homeless, or imprisoned. 'For I was hungry, and you gave me food, I was thirsty and you gave me drink, I was a stranger and you took me in, I was naked and you clothed me, I was sick and you visited me, I was in prison and you came to me.' I don't remember hearing that in church as a kid."

Pastor Streeter's "social gospel" struck a responsive chord in Jim McCloskey. "It started to touch me," he said, "and drove me back to the Scriptures again, to read the Gospels for myself." The Gospels impressed him as depicting "the real stuff, an authentic life." By comparison, his own life seemed false, superficial, unreal, and he began to question the worth of his work. "So what if I get another sale?" he asked himself. "So what if I bring in another good account? It doesn't mean anything to me because I'm not touching the hearts and souls of people, and I'm not doing anything for anybody." He felt dry and empty, without any real mission. He wanted to live in a spirit of authenticity, and as he read the Scriptures, he "kept coming across passages about 'He who loses his life gains his life,' about washing the other person's feet, going out and serving others. That's the essence of the Christian gospel as I understand it, in addition to the forgiveness of sins and that kind of thing, and I certainly wasn't measuring up at all in the eyes of Christ."

Once again McCloskey became disillusioned with the corporate setting and the corporate attitude. "People didn't care about delivering a qualitative service," he said, "just quantity. Get the client, do the work, and move on to the next client. I saw the exploitation of employees by employers intent on squeezing every last dollar out of the worker for the profit of the corporation. I saw how people lived in quiet desperation, and I was beginning to live that way myself. So I decided that if I was going to be exploited by anybody, I wanted to be exploited by God, not the corporation."

For about a year, McCloskey struggled with the idea of entering the ministry, where he "could touch people where it counts the most, in their hearts and souls," an opportunity he knew the business world would never afford him. He had an image of the minister preaching social justice. "The word 'justice' was ringing in my ears a lot," he said. "And what was I doing for justice for anybody? Not a damn thing. Both in the Gospels and in the Old Testament prophets Isaiah and Amos, the imperative is that if you love your God, you will seek justice for others. I thought that if you can do something great for other people, it must be self-fulfilling as well, and must give you a sense of purpose in life, which I didn't have. I'm not saying that others could not have a sense of purpose in business, but I didn't."

McCloskey increasingly identified with Old Testament characters such as Moses, called by God to lead the Israelites. "Moses was scared to *death*," he said. "He complained to God that he was not articulate, didn't have the capability. And God said, 'Don't worry, I'll take care of that. I'll give you Aaron to be your spokesman.' Jeremiah castigated God as a deceiver, saying, in effect, 'You called me into this work, but you didn't say it was going to be like this.' He called God 'as crooked as a brook.' The fundamentalists wouldn't *dare* criticize God, but that's the beauty: God can take it. We can hurl spears and daggers at him, as long as we're honest. It was Kierkegaard who said, 'Just give me honesty.' I think all God wants is for us to be honest with him and to speak our mind if we feel betrayed by his service. I saw the internal and honest struggle these old figures of faith had, yet they followed God and everything in their lives flowed from that. John the Baptist said what he thought, even though it cost him his life. Peter and the disciples left their secure lives and went out into the unknown. Abraham did the same thing because of his faith in God. Those were inspirational figures to me, and still are. If they did it, then maybe, *maybe*, I might be able to give up the secure, the stable, the known, because I felt famished and unsatisfied and empty anyhow. Going into the unknown, serving God, I would have to believe that God would provide and lead me where he wants me to go. And that's where I eventually arrived."

The idea of devoting his life to a spiritual pursuit involved a great struggle for McCloskey. "I thought I was crazy," he said. "Me? Into the ministry? Holy Jesus! If my friends and family ever discovered that, they'd think I was a fool, and a hypocrite as well." What he called "the crystallizing point" came on a Saturday night in the early fall of 1978, as he was reading the Bible. At the time, he said, "I took counsel with no one other than God, the Scriptures, and Dick Streeter. I'm flipping through the Scriptures and by coincidence—and this is at a particularly poignant moment when I'm struggling with whether to stay in the business world or leave and go into the ministry—I come across Chapter 21 in John. There Christ tells Peter, 'When you were young you walked where you would, but when you get older, you will hold out your hand and another will guide you to where perhaps you don't want to go.' I felt that Christ talking to Peter in that Scripture was talking to me. When I was young I walked where I wanted to go, I did what I wanted to do, all over the world, for me. Now it was time to give that life up, time to hold out my hand and let Christ take me where he felt I should go in serving him."

The next week he told his boss that he was leaving the business world and going into the ministry. "And his first words to me were, 'Gee, Jim, I didn't even know you went to church.' I had been a real closet Christian, and now I was coming out of the closet." His transition from lapsed Presbyterian to renewed believer had been slow and subtle, leading to this one moment of choice that was to limn his future course. Other, more dramatic, events loomed ahead, but they could all be seen as springing from this apparently accidental reading of the Scripture. McCloskey agreed to stay at his job for one more year to complete his work, but it was purely pro forma. "Once I made that decision," he said, "once I surrendered my life to God, I felt liberated and completely at peace with myself and the world. I knew that I was doing what God wanted me to do and what I as a human being wanted to do. To this day I'll drive by a corporate building, see all those cars, and say to myself—for me, not for them inside—There but for the grace of God go I."

Applying to Princeton Theological Seminary early in 1979, McCloskey was accepted for matriculation that September. His managing partner at the Hay Group asked Jim to "put off this seminary business" and go to Tokyo. "He had absolutely no idea where I was coming from," Jim said. "We were on two completely different wavelengths. He thought it was just some foolhardy midlife crisis." McCloskey said no thanks, and at thirty-seven, he rented out his house, sold the car, and went up to Princeton to live in a dormitory. It had been fifteen years since his college days, and as he started a three-year master of divinity program, he dreaded writing papers and giving up his privacy. But he met a few men he liked in the dorm, including one his age who had been a fraternity man in Florida and then an executive with the Hyatt Corporation, and had experienced the same kind of internal struggle that McCloskey had. They became good friends, and that helped ease the transition to seminary life.

At the time he entered the seminary, he was unaware of the realities of racism and social injustice—"how the other half lived. I'd been a white Protestant male, never discriminated against in any way, except in Japan, but I didn't associate the two at that time. In my first year at the seminary I had a heated argument with one of the black students who was telling me that racism was rampant. I didn't believe that. I had never run into racism. How could I have?" Once McCloskey settled in, the seminary unveiled a whole new realm of learning. It challenged him intellectually and spiritually, and it opened his eyes to a world of injustice and suffering to which he hadn't been exposed in the affluent culture of the suburbs and the business world.

By the time McCloskey wrote his senior divinity thesis, he had immersed himself in the life and writings of Martin Luther King, Jr., entitling his thesis "Radical Discipleship." To formulate his personal expression of what it meant to be a Christian in contemporary society, he paralleled the lives of four men from different eras: George Fox, the founder of the Quakers; George Whitfield, a colonial evangelist; the Japanese reformer and evangelist Toyohiko Kagawa, a convert from Buddhism to Presbyterianism who founded the first labor union among the dock workers of Kobe, spent many years living in and ministering to the slums of that city, and was imprisoned for his pacifist beliefs during World War II; and Martin Luther King, Jr., the man whose death he had virtually cheered years before.

As part of his seminary training, McCloskey was required to undergo two years of field education: working in either a church, a nursing home, or a prison. In the fall of 1980, he chose to serve as a volunteer chaplain at Trenton State Prison and, because of his age, was assigned to the maximum-security unit. Those two tiers of cells housed forty inmates considered incompatible with the prison population. Among them was a man by the name of George De los Santos, who proclaimed his innocence very provocatively to anyone who would listen. De los Santos was serving the sixth year of a life sentence for the murder of a Newark, New Jersey, used-car lot proprietor, and he challenged McCloskey, as a Christian, to help him. McCloskey took the bait, got hold of the trial transcripts, and read them carefully in his few spare hours. After studying the documents and asking the prisoner a lot of questions, he came to believe that the man was innocent.

At the time, Jim had no experience in law. "I never have pretended to be a lawyer," he said. "But I'm like Joe Friday: I'm interested in the facts. I can read transcripts. If you study them hard enough, you can see the glaring contradictions and inconsistencies, and they raise questions. All it takes is common sense. You don't have to be Perry Mason."

Once McCloskey accepted De los Santos's innocence, he faced a major dilemma. "This guy was alone," he said. "He had nobody working for him. He was buried. All his appeals had run out. But I had stumbled across him—he's in my way, so what am I to do now?" He decided to take a year off from Divinity School and work on the case. Interviews with private investigators led nowhere, and he was forced to become an amateur investigator himself. Along the way, he formed a defense committee of prominent local citizens who helped raise $25,000 over the next two and a half years to finance his researches. In 1983, with the help of a criminal lawyer, McCloskey succeeded in proving that De los Santos (nicknamed "Chiefie" because he used to head a Puerto Rican gang in the Newark housing projects) had been set up by the Essex County Prosecutor's Office. A federal judge overturned the original conviction and sent Chiefie home, vindicated at last.

Among other things, McCloskey had discovered that the witness who originally identified De los Santos had been in trouble with the office of the prosecutor who was trying the case, and had made a secret deal to help himself by fingering Chiefie. And a fellow inmate, who came to know the details of Chiefie's case on the pretense of helping him, had taken the stand to swear that De los Santos had confessed the murder to him in prison—another lie, and another deal with the DA.

"That was my introduction into the criminal justice world," McCloskey said. "It was a classic case, and it had the same ingredients and themes that I've seen in a lot of other cases. One is that there is often a secret deal between the prosecutors and their star witnesses, who are criminals themselves: In exchange for their false testimony, they receive extremely lenient treatment by the DA. Jailhouse confessions are also very common in murder cases, but I have yet to see a jailhouse confession that was not bogus. Inmates do not go around confessing their crimes, because they know jail is a treacherous place where you can't trust anyone, so you keep your mouth shut."

During the last year and a half he worked on the case, McCloskey

also worked part time in the seminary, completing his degree requirements. But by then he had been drawn into another kind of vocation.
"That experience opened my eyes to the innocent in prison. And as
I was visiting George in the various prisons where he was moved over
those two and a half years, the word was getting out in the New Jersey
jails. Other inmates began presenting themselves to me." When De
los Santos was freed in October 1983, McCloskey had just finished
his senior thesis, but he passed up the chance to lead a congregation
in favor of working with convicted prisoners.

That same year, McCloskey incorporated Centurion Ministries, the
organization he had created to free the wrongly imprisoned, and
started work on his next case. Although he graduated from Princeton
Theological Seminary with a master of divinity degree and joined the
United Church of Christ (formerly the Congregationalists of New England), he was not ordained and is not seeking ordination. "*This* is
my life's work," he said, "pure and simple. I can't imagine doing
anything else. I love what I'm doing, and I feel fortunate to have this
door open to me because it matches my human peculiarities. I genuinely believe that Christ has appointed me to do this particular work
based on who I am and what my gifts are."

But in the area of personal spiritual growth, an ironic shadow has
fallen across this otherwise exemplary tableau. During McCloskey's
seminary days and the first few years of establishing Centurion Ministries, his private devotional life consisted of quiet reflection, prayer,
and Scripture reading. Now, he admits, he is "so caught up in 'the
work of God' that my devotional life has really slipped. This is something I think and worry about, and have to get to. I'm back in the rat
race. Practically every waking moment I'm thinking about this case
or that case. And while I like to think I'm serving God, I have drifted
away from the roots. My prayer life is almost nonexistent. For the last
few years I've spent little time in the Scriptures. When I try to go back
to them, I end up thinking about a case. I need to reroute myself into
the center of Christ. Martin Luther King, Jr., had the same problem.
Before he was assassinated, he was completely unraveled, and was
on the verge of a psychological breakdown. King was such an activist,
and was so completely involved in the vision and energy of the work,
that he couldn't sit still and just reflect. He once went to India to learn

their meditative ways, but when he came back, it didn't do a damn bit of good.

"I'm not comparing myself to him by any means, but I'm finding the same thing happening to me. I'm discovering that you can't totally abandon the inner life for the outer, no matter how 'worthy.' One flows from the other and is rooted in the other. That's where you get your nurturing and strength and confidence. For example, this morning I was feeling antsy, so I went over to the Princeton University Chapel to pray. They call it a chapel, but it looks more like a medieval cathedral. I was only there for a couple of minutes before I started thinking I ought to be doing this, or I ought to be doing that, I'd better get back. I can't sit still for thirty minutes. That's part of my nature, but I'm starting to worry that I'm distancing myself from my center of gravity."

McCloskey's problems in this regard are only likely to worsen. Centurion Ministries has been steadily intensifying its level of activity as donations increased over the last few years, from the time in 1980 when McCloskey was "just an anonymous little figure working away on two or three cases in New Jersey." In November 1986, when he succeeded in reversing the conviction of a third innocent lifer, the Ministries received national attention: radio, television, and press coverage. As a side effect of all that, McCloskey was inundated by over a thousand requests for help, all of which he says have been processed with the help of a small staff. But just as requests for help mushroomed, much of the original funding dried up, and he now has to spend additional time trying to raise money to pay his staff, his own expenses, and two full-time professional investigators.

His life sounds like a classic struggle between the two paths the medievalists refer to as the *via activa* and the *via contemplativa*, between altruistic action and inner growth. Clearly some balance is necessary, especially when altruism leads into the murky fields that Jim McCloskey wades through almost daily. For one thing, the people he deals with are either serving life sentences or are on Death Row, putatively for the crimes of others. "You talk with them on the phone, and with their family members, and it sucks you dry," he said. "You're always dealing with their pain and suffering, and the pain and suffering of others tires you out. It exhausts you. You're always in the

dark pit either of suffering or of the lies that put them there: misbe-
havior by authorities, corruption. This goes to another existential level
with me, namely, that my whole life is my work, and that's bad. In
addition to the decline of my spiritual life, I have no personal life."

A lifelong bachelor, McCloskey would like to marry and raise a
family, but he acknowledges that by the nature of his work, he has
neither the time to pursue a relationship nor the money to marry and
start a family. He does not have a close friend of either sex in whom
he can confide, and that, too, troubles him. And what he calls "the
profound irony" is that, as a result of doing God's work, his relationship with God is not as close as it was. "It's not unraveling, but it has
lost its clarity. I'm struggling with that right now, and with the journey
of faith. That's what it is, a journey that goes up and down. You can
go back to any scriptural figure of faith and see that the same thing
happened in his or her life. That's where I am right now."

In the eighteen months that intervened between the time I first
spoke on the telephone with Jim McCloskey and the time I went to
see him at his Princeton office, I was surprised to find that the state
of his personal and spiritual life continued to weigh heavily on his
mind. Although he had scheduled several retreats, he had not yet been
able to attend one. "It's just the demands of the work," he said. "My
prayer life is in tatters because when I get home from work, I'm tired
and I don't feel like reading Scripture. I'm on the road a lot, reading
transcripts and thinking about all the mothers who come to see me,
asking me to take on their sons' cases. I have to tell them I'm sorry
but I can't do it, and that's debilitating."

McCloskey now works six days and fifty to sixty hours a week,
about 40 percent of that time on the road. When he was in the business
world and dissatisfied with his life, he spent several hours a day reading
the Scriptures, looking for help. "Of course, the Scriptures were new
to me then," he said. "It was like new food, and it was fulfilling,
inspirational food. Sometimes I'll go back to the Scriptures now and
say, 'Oh, I read this story. I know this story.' " His voice sounded
bored as he said the words, and then he laughed that self-deprecating
laugh. "I'm just tired, you know? I don't fear burning out, because I
love the work, and it suits me. But still, every life should have some
balance to it, and mine doesn't."

Despite this absence of balance, McCloskey cannot imagine finding as much satisfaction in any other work, including the ministry. The patient persistence which he learned from his Japanese colleagues while in Tokyo has served him well. "The Japanese take the long-term approach," he said. "They look years down the road for fulfill-ment. The work of freeing one man, for instance, takes constant, steady, detailed work. The Japanese taught me to stick with the job. And I get along with people whatever their socioeconomic status. I'm a good listener, which facilitates my work. I have to convince people who have lied and sent innocent men or women away to prison to come forward, years later, and tell the world they sold out. And a lot of them do."

Whatever ambivalence McCloskey may feel about the imbalance between his inner and outer lives, he has no doubts that his work is spiritually inspired. More than ever, he feels grounded in religious texts, especially the Old Testament. "It's even more interesting than the New Testament in terms of stories that you can apply to contem-porary society and the problems we all have in everyday life," he said. Asked for examples, he referred to a parallel he often draws when invited to talk before church groups.

"America is an extremely hardened, bloodthirsty, vengeful society," he began. "We're still in the Old West, somehow. But I believe that people can change their lives regardless of the grievous deeds they have done, including murder. After all, the three greatest figures of faith in the Old Testament were murderers. Moses was on the lam for forty years because he had killed an Egyptian and buried his body in the sand. That's Murder One. If he were ever tried in America for that, he goes away for life, or death. David was a murderer. He spied a beautiful woman, Bathsheba, and he wanted her. But she was mar-ried, so he set up her husband, Uriah, in the battlefield and had him killed. Paul, as Saul of Tarsus, went looking for Christians to kill them. But God used these three murderers to do great things to advance his work. If God can see something in these people, with all the atrocities they committed, why can't he get other murderers just to lead normal lives?"

Although the prisoners McCloskey worked with were not guilty of murder, they had often had brushes with the law: car theft, drugs, assault and battery, prostitution. Once they got out, though, seven of eight have stayed out. His lone recidivist was the first man he helped free, George De los Santos, whom he described as "a classic junkie. I never thought I'd say this about anybody, but he *belongs* in prison. He's become institutionalized, and knows not only how to survive but how to *thrive* there. In prison, he's a man. When he gets out on the streets, he becomes a little child lost in the big, bad world, illiterate, with no skills, no self-esteem, and no motivation."

As much as McCloskey believes in people's capacity for change, he is the first to admit that jail is an unlikely catalyst. He describes prisons as "ovens that bake hate and anger." Nonviolent offenders come out of the prison experience full of bitterness and often more violent than when they went in. For McCloskey, the criminal justice system is "an insensitive beast that devours people, especially those of color or those who have no money." He compares our system unfavorably with Great Britain's, where, after it was discovered that a number of innocent people had been executed, the death penalty was outlawed. Yet he believes that even if it takes a couple of generations, America will abolish capital punishment and stop "seeking blood from those who have been accused of bloodying others."

When people accuse McCloskey of being naive for believing cons who protest their innocence, he counters that it is more naive to believe that the system always gets the right man. "Where did Americans get this idea that the criminal justice system is practically flawless?" he asked. "From TV, from *Perry Mason*. An innocent person in prison is about as rare as a pigeon in the park. It happens far more often than the public wants to think about." Not that McCloskey hasn't been misled himself at times. He told of one case on which he had spent a year doing research before he came to doubt his client's own veracity and finally tricked him into admitting his lies. But that has been the exception for him.

"Twenty-five hundred years ago," he said, "the prophet Isaiah lamented how people go to court and lie, and weave their spider's webs of deceit. Nothing's changed. It doesn't matter what century or what culture you're in. You're dealing with human beings, and people lie to save themselves. We suburban Americans who have no dealings with the police unless we happen to be the victims of a crime have no idea how they run roughshod over inner-city people. We like to think we're strong and we could not be intimidated into saying something that's not true, when, in fact, we don't know how weak we would be, faced with that kind of situation. As a number of these men who lied for the prosecution at a trial have said to me, 'It's a matter of survival. Either I go away or your guy goes away, and I'm not going away.' "

Fortunately, many witnesses feel remorseful enough about what they have done that, years later, they can be urged to come forward and recant. And here the underlying spiritual theme of McCloskey's work emerges most clearly. He contends that just as the lives of the unjustly imprisoned are turned around at that point, so are the lives of the people who have lied and cut deals with the DA to save their own skins. In this sense, his work is not unlike the kind of work certain spiritual teachers seek to do: to get us to look within, to face the shadowy areas of our souls, our deepest fears, guilt, or self-loathing, and to come clean. "Their lives become redeemed along with those who have been wrongly convicted," he said of the witnesses who retract their false testimony. "It's very cleansing and healing and redemptive for them, and it lifts them up and gives them self-esteem. It rights *their* lives to an extent—and I can give you chapter and verse on that."

McCloskey cited two examples of reclamation. One involved the main witness against his second client, Rene Santana, a man named Roberto Gutierrez who falsely claimed he had seen Santana fleeing the scene of a murder. Gutierrez had been in trouble with the prosecutor's office (something he denied at trial), and in return for giving testimony his slate was wiped clean. Ten and a half years later, McCloskey located him where he was living with his common-law wife, and, at her suggestion, took Roberto to visit Santana at Rahway State Prison to ask for his forgiveness. "I'll bet that's never been done in any other case in the United States," McCloskey said, "for the star witness who lied to send a man away to prison to visit that man in prison before he got out and ask for his forgiveness. How do you think that made Roberto Gutierrez feel? It was a great healing experience for him."

In another case, McCloskey and a coworker located the only witness to the rape and murder of a Texas schoolgirl—a white janitor who had stood by and watched while two other white janitors committed the crime, and who later testified that their supervisor, a black man named Clarence Brandley, had been the culprit. "I let one innocent person go to her death," the witness told McCloskey when he finally convinced him to come forward. "I'm not going to let two die."

In the end, does McCloskey draw more spiritual sustenance from his relationship with God or from his work with the despised and rejected? For him, the two are integrated. "Even though my personal prayer life is not what I want it to be at this time, I've never lost the inner fire," he said. "I know that at least this aspect of my life is highly pleasing to God. I know I'm doing what he wants me to do and has appointed me to do, and that's to free innocent people in prison. God knows who I am, as he has created me and as I have developed through my life experience, and he sent me to do this work. I don't think it's a coincidence that I happened to stumble upon Chiefie De los Santos at Trenton State Prison when I was a student chaplain. God opened that door for me, and inspired me to go into it. And I am forever grateful for this door being open for me, because without it, I would be totally lost. Life would not be worth living. Nothing else would integrate my particular abilities with my personality, even in the ministry. If I had become an ordained church pastor, I would have come unglued because of the constituent work that you have to do in that position: the administration, the petty arguments that have no meaning. Which isn't to criticize that work. It's important work, but I'm just not suited for it."

Before I left his office, McCloskey showed me a photograph of his parents, and then told a story that had been passed on to him as a child. In 1947, when his mother was thirty, she suddenly contracted polio and was paralyzed from the waist down. In those days, the general, if erroneous, belief was that polio was contagious. Neither friends, neighbors, nor minister would enter their house for fear of catching the crippling disease. The McCloskey house was quarantined, and strangers crossed the street to avoid walking by it. The only exception was a woman named Mrs. Boyd, a friend of his parents' who lived nearby and who volunteered to nurse Mrs. McCloskey. She was not a churchgoer or even a believer as far as Jim McCloskey recalled. She didn't know that polio was not contagious and that she didn't risk infecting her own family by caring for his mother. "She really served my mother, and nursed her. In her own way, she gave herself to the forsaken person," he said. "That was a great thing she did, and she was unheralded. Nobody wrote any stories about *her*."

CHAPTER 7

What Is Meditation?

■   ■   ■

What we would like to do is find a way to meditate in everyday life, so that we do not have to open one door only to close another.
—Pir Vilayat Inayat Khan, *Introducing Spirituality into Counseling and Therapy*

Now the easiest way, if you wish to do this . . . is to take this mantram without any training, without any help from the teacher and begin to chant: *Whoooooooooo am I? Whoooooooooooo am I?* . . . This, to me, is the simplest way of meditation, because you don't have to have any super training, you don't have to have any master teacher help you. All you have to do, which is the most difficult of all, is to do it, once or twice a day.
—Audle Allison, *Basic Meditation*

Commune with your own heart upon your bed, and be still.
—Psalms 4:4

■

Even if we accept at face value the Sufi proverb "The Ways unto God are as the number of the souls of men," the multiplicity of paths does not exclude the likelihood that many of them will resemble each other in certain fundamental respects. Take, for instance, what John White labeled "the highest state of consciousness." In the Introduction to his book of the same name, a collection of writings on consciousness by prominent psychologists, philosophers, and spiritual writers, White lists the different names and conceptions applied to this state:

St. Paul called it 'the peace that passeth understanding' and R. M. Bucke named it "cosmic consciousness." In Zen Buddhism, the term for it is *satori* or *kensho*, while in yoga it is *samadhi* or *moksha*, and in Taoism, "the absolute Tao." Thomas Merton used the phrase "transcendental unconscious" to describe it; Abraham Maslow coined the term "peak experience"; Sufis speak of *fana*. Gurdjieff labeled it "objective consciousness," while the Quakers call it "the Inner Light." Jung referred to individuation, and Buber spoke of the I-Thou relationship. But whatever the name for this old and well-known phenomenon—enlightenment, illumination, liberation, mystical experience—all are concerned with a state of awareness radically different from our ordinary understanding, our normal waking consciousness, our everyday mind.

Another thread that runs through most of the major wisdom traditions is the recognition of a need for what is variously called meditation, contemplative prayer, contemplation, or inner silence. The mainstream religions of America—Protestantism, Catholicism, and Judaism—have for a variety of reasons chosen to ignore or de-emphasize meditation in their popular teachings. But the absence of just such a practical technique and discipline may be one reason so many people have sought out either Eastern and New Age religions or deeper, more radical versions of their own Western traditions.

If we can agree that there is an apparent gulf between, let us say, the Zen Buddhist practice of *zazen* (sitting meditation) and the ecstatic Sufi *zhikr* (chanting and dancing), or between Transcendental Meditation and Christian contemplative prayer, we must also recognize that the intentions behind these practices have a good deal in common. The key to most Eastern forms of meditation is a silence or stillness of the mind, in which the meditator creates an internal environment that may allow him or her to contact what the Buddhists call their True Nature, or what others characterize as a Divine Self, an experience of the unity of all being. Specific techniques vary widely from one tradition to another and even within the same tradition. Different sects of Buddhism may gently call the wandering mind back from its stream of thoughts to no thought at all by various methods, including counting, following the outgoing breath, contemplating mandalas, or chanting aloud a mantra such as *Om mane padme hum* or *Namu myoho renge-kyo*. Practitioners of Transcendental Meditation allow the mind to wander where it will while silently chanting a highly personalized sound or mantra. The mantra is even common to some forms of Christian meditation such as the Jesus Prayer.

Eckankar encourages a more active technique it terms "contemplation," the creation of interior scenarios, imagined interactions with the Mahanta, or spiritual guide, in which you can ask questions and receive answers, or simply go on an inner voyage of discovery. "The ECKist does not meditate, but sits in contemplation, doing the spiritual exercises of ECKANKAR. He does not work to bring about the stillness of mind which is said to invite invasion of the spiritual forces," wrote the late Paul Twitchell, who might be called the founder of Eckankar but for his insistence that it has always existed and that he merely gave the religion a name and a shape in its modern incarnation. (In making this distinction between passive meditation and active contemplation, Eckankar follows the Eastern tradition. Worth noting, perhaps as a sign of how out of phase Christianity has become, is that in recent Western Christian traditions, as Basil Pennington pointed out, the terms have been reversed. Christian "meditation" connotes a discursive prayer that reflects on some aspect of life or the Scriptures, whereas "contemplation" signifies "having passed beyond thinking to simple presence.")

Modern-day teachers such as the Englishman Paul Lowe and the American Da Kalki have offered variations on traditional methods that emphasize intention and openness over specific techniques. And Brother Charles—a former disciple of the late Indian teacher Swami Muktananda with a peculiarly American bent—has created a program of deep meditation through prerecorded tapes that combine sophisticated technology with readings and chants taken from ancient Eastern texts. This raises the intriguing issue of the connection between venerable mystical techniques and modern scientific knowledge of what actually happens to the mind during deep meditation. A number of studies concerning this connection have been published, proving conclusively that meditative practices, particularly among meditators with at least five to ten years of experience, significantly alter brainwave frequencies and produce effects that are generally agreed to be beneficial, both to physical health and to mental well-being and creativity.*

At least part of the connection is implicit in the fact that most of the classical techniques involve an attempt to blank out or bypass the rational mind. Whether we are considering the Buddhists' chants and koans, Hindu mantras, the yogic practice of *tratakum* or "steady gaze" (fixing the concentration on a single object such as a candle flame or flower), the repetitive spinning of certain Sufi Dervish Orders, or Western practices derived from any or all of these, the effect is strikingly similar. Focusing on one seemingly arbitrary sensory process withdraws the attention from common thought patterns, activities, and material concerns, something which recent scientific research has shown to reduce stress, improve relaxation, and favorably alter brainwave activity, creativity, learning ability, memory, and other desirable attributes. A similar premise may underlie the common spiritual instruction—often badly mangled and misapplied by doctrinaire religious teachers of all sects—to free oneself from attachment to material things. If not only the anecdotal reports of vast numbers of experienced meditators but also an increasing body of scientific literature are to be believed, the process of being, at least for a short time each day, "in the world but not of the world" can have salubrious effects for the mind, body, and spirit that we are only beginning to understand.†

The range of approaches to meditation is clearly extensive, although the connection between spiritual and material well-being is not necessarily accepted by all proponents of the various systems. Even those who might acknowledge that a goal of some sort is involved would be unlikely to agree on the nature of that goal. Some seekers eschew the notion of meditating with eyes closed for a specific period of time in favor of a more demanding practice of "moment-to-moment" awareness, a way of observing what is actually happening within oneself in relation to the outer world at any given moment and in a continuous succession of such moments. Those who forgo association

---

* See especially Akira Kasamatsu and Tomio Hirai, "An Electroencephalographic Study on the Zen Meditation (Zazen)," and B. K. Anand, G. S. Chhina, and Baldev Singh, "Some Aspects of Electroencephalographic Studies in Yogis," both in Charles T. Tart's classic anthology, *Altered States of Consciousness* (San Francisco: HarperCollins, 1990).
† For a complete discussion of these effects, see Michael Hutchison's meticulously documented book, *Megabrain* (New York: Ballantine, 1987).

with any major tradition often evolve idiosyncratic formats for their meditative work. Arch Crawford, the New York-based stock market timer, for instance, finds in the words of Christ not only a "great psychological truth," but also, "if you tried some of the things he said, an experiential truth." Crawford is referring to Christ's teaching from the Gospel of Matthew, which reads in the King James Version: "But thou, when thou prayest, enter into thy closet, and when thou hast shut thy door, pray to thy Father which is in secret; and thy Father which seeth in secret shall reward thee openly."

In his readings, Crawford came across a description of that as a literal mystical technique, so he went into an actual closet, tried it, and reported "wonderful results." He acknowledged that "it was just to quiet the senses more than anything else. And it probably means, metaphorically at least, to quiet the mind before you seek the truth." But it worked for him in some fashion. Crawford now meditates with the aid of Brother Charles's high-tech tapes, and claims they have helped him to achieve higher levels of self-awareness. The principle behind the tapes is "sound phasing," the use of sound waves set at differing vibratory rates equivalent to brain waves in the beta, alpha, theta, and delta ranges, barely audible underneath the music or chanting. Generally speaking, beta waves correspond to the active waking state; the alpha range is related to a relaxed state with eyes closed; the theta range covers the twilight area between waking and dreaming; and delta waves indicate deep, dreamless sleep, the state most conducive to healing. "The brain has a tendency to entrain itself to the lowest sound frequency when listening to music or any reverberation," Crawford explained. "That low wave is set at alpha in the tapes that are available to the public. In the meditation program, they start up in that range and get deeper and deeper during a half-hour meditation tape, ending in the high delta range. They will knock you out if you're not a highly meditative person." In other words, if your brain waves begin to entrain, or vibrate sympathetically, to a rate associated with sleep, there's a good chance you will go to sleep. It isn't exactly sleep, Crawford said, "but you'll go unconscious if you're not used to those frequencies."

Prolonged participation in a deep meditation tape program teaches the brain to deal more readily with the lower frequencies. After a while, "the first tape doesn't do anything to you anymore, so you send for a deeper tape, and that does it to you all over again. Coming out of that state you have ecstatic experiences. After you settle in for a while, you have a catharsis, because as your brain slows down, you become more and more aware, and the first thing you become aware of is what you're barely repressing. In slowing down your brain pattern, all of your 'stuff' comes to the surface. Some people who work with psychoanalysts can go for weeks or months in a dry period where nothing comes to the surface. Well, if you do these tapes, it will come to the surface all the time."

That may sound implausible, or like another shortcut to enlightenment. But the principle of entraining also applies to having one's consciousness altered by being in the presence of a spiritual master or teacher. Crawford feels that the two approaches probably have about the same effect, although he noted that Brother Charles recently "changed his tune about that. He was saying originally that the technology did it all, and he was just our brother in this process. But now he has gone into his high guru phase, saying that you need a personal touch. I don't agree with him, and I'm not going with his guru trip. But I still like his technology." As Crawford sees it, technology is generally more accessible to the Western mind, which can be distrustful of gurus and the idea of complete surrender. These days, Crawford uses newer technological devices that incorporate sound phasing with flashing lights and Brother Charles's tapes, but the entraining principle remains the same.

Asked whether such tapes could be dangerous for the uninitiated, Crawford acknowledged that possibility. "Meditation is not for the weak," he said, "because when you meditate, you face yourself. All of the stuff that you don't want to look at and have repressed starts coming to the surface, beginning with the worst stuff about yourself. You're required to work with that as you would with any spiritual or psychological process. It's not exactly a free lunch, but it will make it happen faster than any other way I know."

Advocates of more traditional and time-tested techniques would probably disapprove of Brother Charles's tapes while agreeing with Crawford's last observations. Michael Chender, who runs a consulting firm for mining and mineral development staffed entirely by fellow Buddhists, has been practicing Tibetan Buddhist meditation for over twenty years. "One of the signs of meditating properly," he told me by phone from Nova Scotia, "is that your neurosis seems to intensify. This idea may differ from a lot of meditative systems which tell you that your mind will become clearer, that you'll feel better and be more in control. That's regarded in Buddhism as subtle hypnosis. Actually, when you begin to see things more clearly, you see your neuroses much more prominently because you're stepping away from them in some sense. But at the same time you have much more humor, so you're up to dealing with the increased intensity." And the Catholic mystic Thomas Merton wrote that in the practice of meditation, "aridities grow more and more frequent and more and more difficult as time goes on. In a certain sense, aridity can almost be taken as a sign of progress in prayer, provided it is accompanied by serious efforts and self-discipline."

There is an up-side to all of this, however, an understanding shared by most teachers that at a certain point beneficial effects do begin to accrue. "The basic idea of meditation," Chender said, "is that it should make you more available to what is actually going on, and less caught up in your own preconceptions or emotional reactions to things." It may also make the meditator kinder and more compassionate, but that is considered a by-product.

Meditators from different disciplines also share the belief that meditation as a practice evolves over long periods of time. For Richard and Barbara Klein, who live in Annapolis, Maryland, with their two young children, after more than twenty years of Transcendental Meditation it was time to move on to other levels of practice. Richard, who works as a statistician for the federal government, was emphatic that conventional meditation is not part of their spiritual life any more. "The closed-eyes thing has been left behind," he said. "My practice is with eyes open. People keep calling me a meditation teacher, and I do still give meditation courses, always with some ambivalence. But, except in our formal groups, I don't do that anymore." His practice is difficult to describe, but he refers to it as "noticing," a variation of moment-to-moment awareness. "I notice the human tendency for attention to be lost into something, absorbed into some state, thought, feeling, mood, object," he said. "We lose ourselves. And when I notice that, I see that as the self-contraction, the motion of suffering. As much as possible, I release it, and in that moment I'm free. Then it has to come up again and again and again. Most of the stuff is very subtle, not big things. It's just seeing the awareness get lost."

Although he no longer practices Transcendental Meditation, Klein agrees that simple meditation is still appropriate for someone starting out. He doesn't require it in the spiritual awareness group The Community, which he leads in his spare time, but he encourages it. "There's no other way you're going to get the mind to quiet down in the beginning," he said. "There's just too much going on. But at some point that practice evolves naturally—at least that's my experience. Maybe for some people it would go on, but with our life, we don't meditate. What are Barbara and I going to do? Say, 'Children, leave us alone for twenty minutes. We're going to meditate now'?" Those practices were appropriate, he said, when he and his wife were living a single or childless life. "They were all generated in the monastery. They were shortened, but they're still monastic practices."

Richard Klein brings up an important point. Meditative practices that were once the sole province of mystics and renunciates, the priest class, or cloistered orders of men and women, whether in Western or Eastern cultures, are now to be considered appropriate for those who remain active in the workaday world of jobs and families. Just as, in the seventh century, the Prophet Muhammad was inspired to have his followers adopt the practice of praying at different times during the day, as he had observed Syriac Christian clergy doing in the deserts of Arabia, so today spiritual instructors across a wide spectrum are advocating meditative techniques that were once relegated only to monks and ascetics.

By no means is the understanding of meditation limited entirely to silent sitting or contemplation. Taoist teachers such as Mantak Chia and T. K. Shih give instruction in meditation focusing on the Microcosmic Orbit: the circulation of "chi," or bioelectric energy, through crucial body centers called chakras. In some cases, those meditations can involve forms of autoerotic stimulation, using sexual energy to charge the entire system. Chia believes, for instance, that many past masters of meditation experienced sexual arousal during their practice anyway. The late Bhagwan Shree Rajneesh, the controversial Indian master who was deported from America after his experimental ashram in Oregon ran afoul of the law, developed a variation he called Dynamic Meditation. As described by his disciples, Dynamic consists of equal ten-to-fifteen-minute periods of chaotic breathing, jumping up and down and hollering, standing in a frozen posture, lying down in silence, and celebratory dancing, all generally accompanied by loud, rhythmic prerecorded music. The idea behind Dynamic, as explained by Paul Lowe, was to combine Eastern methods of meditative "emptying" with more cathartic Western techniques developed largely at human potential centers like Esalen in California.

As Lowe, a former disciple of Rajneesh who left to teach on his own, told me, the Eastern method of dealing with inner rage or turmoil held that "if you sit long enough, it will go away. The Western method was to keep throwing it out, keep catharting, find out where your hangups are, and do the opposite. Neither of them in themselves is complete. The Eastern method worked for Eastern people a long time ago, but I don't think it's relevant to Western people now." Eastern meditation styles evolved thousands of years ago, during times of extreme physical hardship in parts of the world where material suffering was an inescapable fact of daily life.

The meditative tradition of the Christian West is being revived increasingly by individual clerics and theologians like Harvey Cox, who teaches a popular course on Jesus at Harvard, and who has acknowledged the value of incorporating nontheistic Buddhist meditation into his life as a Baptist. And Basil Pennington's centering prayer combines elements of the Western and Eastern meditative traditions in one technique or system.

Less specialized Christian writers such as the Protestant novelist and screenwriter Dan Wakefield have discovered meditation for themselves. In *Returning: A Spiritual Journey*, Wakefield speaks of a daily practice which began by contemplating blades of grass and then progressed "to trees to passages of Scripture and psalms, and sometimes pieces of music I loved. Sometimes I just kept silent and tried to do the kind of 'listening' described by Jean-Pierre Caussade in *Abandonment to Divine Providence*, trying to achieve a state 'rather like one who, believing himself on the point of hearing music, makes himself alert and attentive. . . . ' The twenty-minute prayerful meditation became a part of my daily routine, like the Exercycle, and I knew after several years that this practice created a kind of interior calm that was cumulative and strengthening for the soul, just as exercise was for the body." Echoing Michael Chender and Arch Crawford, Wakefield adds: "There were times when prayer itself brought up uncomfortable, distressing thoughts and feelings, emotions that shook me up inside, and I remembered our minister telling us once of a Yiddish proverb that said 'God is an earthquake, not an uncle.' "

In a small but eminently useful book entitled *Meditation in Action*, the Buddhist master Chögyam Trungpa Rinpoche identifies two basic types of meditation, one which seeks to discover the nature of existence, and another which "concerns communication with the external or universal concept of God." In the latter case, he writes, "one feels oneself to be inferior and one is trying to contact something higher, greater. Such meditation is based on devotion. This is basically an inward, or introvert practice of meditation, which is well known in the Hindu teachings, where the emphasis is on going into the inward state of samadhi [meditative union with the Absolute], into the depths of the heart." He finds a parallel here with the Eastern Orthodox Christian "prayer of the heart," which is "a means of identifying oneself with an external Being and necessitates purifying oneself. The basic belief is that one is separate from God, but there is still a link, one is still part of God." In the Hindu or Christian format, the meditator is seen as imperfect, imprisoned, and trying to make contact with some exterior Being. Such was precisely Thomas Merton's understanding when he wrote, in *Contemplative Prayer*, "The whole purpose of meditation is to deepen the consciousness of this basic relationship of the Creature to the Creator, and of the sinner to his Redeemer."

The other form of meditation that Trungpa describes takes an opposite approach: "Here there is no belief in higher and lower; the idea of different levels, of being in an underdeveloped state, does not arise. One does not feel inferior, and what one is trying to achieve is not something higher than oneself. . . . This basic form of meditation is concerned with trying to see what *is*." The emphasis is on developing the knowledge of *nowness*, "simply, without any object or ambition, trying to see what is here and now. One has to become aware of the present moment through such means as concentrating on the breathing." This is the approach Buddhism takes, as we shall see in the next chapter in Herbert Moss's experience with the Zen master Dürckheim. Without going into the further ramifications of these two different styles, it's enough to infer a great diapason of meditative ways, the precise nature and value of which is a subject of some disagreement among even the most highly evolved spiritual teachers.

When I asked two Americans who had worked with Paul Lowe and who now lead workshops and seminars of their own, Ariel and Shya Kane, if Lowe taught specific methods such as Dynamic Meditation or some variant, they told me that he had placed increasingly less emphasis on formalized meditation. Ariel recalled wondering why Lowe had once called his group the International Academy of Meditation. "We didn't really talk much about meditation," she said. "Then I realized that everything was a meditation—for instance, if you bring awareness to how you put down your teacup. You're going to hear a few clinks on the tape of this interview because you've put your cup down and you weren't there when you did it. If you have awareness, that's a kind of meditation."

"People have a whole idea about what meditation is," her husband Shya added. "They think it's better to have a quiet mind than to have a noisy mind. This is better and that's better. This is right and that's wrong. But that's an idea you have about what meditation is, so that there's a 'right' way to meditate. We've done a lot of meditation, a lot of different kinds, but we don't meditate now. I don't get up in the morning and sit for twenty minutes or an hour. I get up, and my meditation is to make a cup of tea for my wife. But is it a meditation? I don't know. My meditation might be to sit and teach myself to type on the computer."

"Or to iron," Ariel said. "I do ironing meditation, dishwashing meditation."

"Anything that you're doing can be a meditation if you're present," Shya added. "Meditation is just bringing yourself to the moment."

"Right now," Ariel said, "we're doing an interview meditation."

In his book *The Experiment Is Over*, Paul Lowe speaks of the difficulty of describing meditation, saying, "It isn't anything, and therefore you may have descriptions about something that's not. What most people do are meditation techniques, and they may lead to a place that people call meditation. . . . What most of [the techniques] are doing is helping you to be present, because most of the time most people are not present. They think they're here, but they're not here now." He finds it useful "to go to somebody regularly, to share with them what is going on . . . to get some advice on how to hold the body in a more relaxed posture." On the other hand he warns about the schools that tell you to stop your mind or to suppress it, which may only make you more uncomfortable. "What I found most useful is just to watch. You sit, close your eyes or have them half-open, look ahead, and watch the whole situation. You hear the noises outside, you can feel your mind moving, a disturbance in the body, or the emotions, and you watch. And you watch. . . ." On the whole, Lowe endorses meditation, with the proviso that one's intention not be "to attain anything," because meditation is "a passivity, it's just sitting and allowing. As Jesus and all the masters have said, 'The Kingdom of God is within.' Now. You don't have to develop it, it's there now. You just have to learn to listen."

Yet when I spoke with Lowe in New York, he emphasized mostly this last point. "I recommend that people don't meditate," he said, "because if they meditate, they meditate for something. They meditate for peace, for enlightenment. And meditation isn't for anything. If it's for something, it can't happen, because when it happens, it happens in neutrality. So what I suggest is just to be conscious and present as much as you know how, every moment. And that means, if you're angry, be angry. Don't suppress it, and don't dump it. If you're attracted to somebody, get attracted to somebody. Don't wind it up and make it into something, and don't suppress it. Just be attracted, and see what wants to happen.

"And then one day you'll be moving around and you'll feel like you want to sit, and usually you'll want to close your eyes. It's not meditation. It's just sitting and closing your eyes. It might be for a minute or two minutes, but then it might get longer and longer. And then some day you might be there for five hours and not even know it happened, since you're doing it because it came out of the moment. It wasn't an idea, because if it's an idea, it's somebody else's idea. Even if it's the right idea, it's not your idea. It was fine for Buddha to meditate, because that's the way he did it, but it might not be fine for you. Yours might be dancing or singing or painting or sky diving. But usually silence is needed, because you need to stop and disconnect from other activities to hear what you need to hear, which may mean silence or it may mean a message. But to do it to get a message, or to get to silence, then all you're doing is what you normally do—and doing isn't it. Nondoing is it—which isn't inactivity, as the Westerner thinks, but not doing, or effortless effort, or all the ways that try to describe something that can't be described."

What Lowe seems to be saying is that if you use meditation to escape the pain of the moment, as people have traditionally done in the East, you're in trouble. Then meditation becomes just another anodyne. "I'm saying your way to freedom is exactly the opposite of that," he concluded. "You've got to be totally *in* this moment. And if you're upset, you need to be upset—not to meditate but to be upset—because that is you in that moment, and you're upset because you need to be. And you need to be there so totally that you realize what the upset is about. If you say, 'I'm upset, I'm going to meditate,' it's no different from taking drugs."

From this perspective, the notion of meditation is both more simple and more complex than it might appear. Even more succinctly, Da Kalki says in *The Knee of Listening* that after experimenting with every method he came across, involving many years of intense work both on his own and under a variety of masters, especially Swami Muktananda, the "mature form" of his meditation was no longer to seek so-called higher states of being. Without special techniques, breathing methods, mantras, or mandalas, meditation became for him "simply a direct approach to whatever experiences arose." In that state, he would ask himself, in regard to whatever "tendencies, thoughts or experiences arose: 'Avoiding relationship?' Thus I was constantly returned to a prior state of unqualified awareness." (Through this repeated inquiry, Da recalls the principal teaching tool of the Indian saint Ramana Maharshi, who urged his students to ask of themselves in all endeavors the single question, "Who am I?")

In this way, Da was led to understand the motivations behind all experience. Later in the book he spells it out a bit more concretely. "I do not recommend that you meditate," he writes. "There is only understanding. Therefore, understand. And when understanding has become observation, reflection, insight and radical cognition, then the state of consciousness itself is meditation. . . . When you have understood that seeking is all a function of dilemma, and when you no longer are voluntarily motivated by the physical, mental or spiritual problem, then you are already meditating." Having said that, he then goes on to give detailed instructions in formal meditation.

Swami Muktananda emphasized that his followers should perform all their devotional acts—meditate, repeat the mantra, chant—without expectation. They should not demand or expect to gain psychic powers or mystical experiences; when they are ready, the gifts will come as part of a normal process. In *Play of Consciousness*, he wrote:

> I did not meditate out of fear, but with enthusiasm and faith and love. I did not meditate to please anyone or to get any benefits from anyone or to satisfy a desire, sensual or otherwise. I did not meditate to rid myself of any illness, physical or mental, nor to gain fame through the miraculous and supernatural powers I might acquire. No one forced me to meditate. I did not meditate because religion says that it is good to meditate. I meditated solely for the love of god, because I was irresistibly drawn toward the Goddess Chiti Shakti, and to explore my own true nature.

An especially lucid view of this apparent paradox of meditation that summarizes and expands on many of the points just made comes from the brilliant teacher and philosopher J. Krishnamurti. Krishnamurti, who came to prominence in India in the early part of this century and later traveled to the United States, where he lectured extensively, has often been belittled by other spiritual teachers for his purported inability to pass on his enlightened wisdom to his students. In fact, Paul Lowe has less than complimentary things to say about Krishnamurti's teaching ability. He likens him to the seventeenth-century Zen priest Bankei, generally considered to be one of Japan's three greatest Zen masters, who became enlightened only after sitting for over twenty years on the cold stone floor of an isolated mountain hut. Perhaps as a result of this isolation, when Bankei came out to teach, Lowe says, he "never really connected with people." Krishnamurti, he adds, found enlightenment, "but he found it in such an artificial way, he could never really connect. He didn't connect with people who are sexual, because he hadn't been through that part in himself." And Chögyam Trungpa Rinpoche, who once shared a dais with Krishnamurti, reportedly said that he was "like a realized, enlightened baby," that what Krishnamurti had to say "was absolutely on the dot except for the fact that he couldn't give his students the skillful means to go further."

Regardless of Krishnamurti's ability to pass on the specifics of his wisdom to others, his writings—which, like many books in this field, including Lowe's and Trungpa's, are mostly collections of lectures compiled and edited from tape recordings—are witty, compelling, and often acerbic. (The relationship of the teachings to the man may finally be problematic. The works of Trungpa, who died an unremitting alcoholic, and Rajneesh, who died under a cloud of accusations of sexual and fiscal malfeasance, are both compassionate and extremely useful.) In his 1969 book *Freedom from the Known*, Krishnamurti gave one of the most incisive descriptions of meditation I have read, anticipating many of the criticisms just cited, so perhaps he had the last word, figuratively if not chronologically. After acknowledging all the different schools, systems, and methods of meditation, including those that say, "Watch the movement of your big toe, watch it, watch it, watch it," and others that stress sitting postures, breathing, or practicing awareness, he adds:

> All this is utterly mechanical. Another method gives you a certain word and tells you that if you go on repeating it you will have some extraordinary transcendental experience. This is sheer nonsense. It is a form of self-hypnosis. By repeating Amen or Coca-Cola indefinitely you will obviously have a certain experience because by repetition the mind becomes quiet. . . . By repetition you can induce the mind to be gentle and soft but it is still a petty, shoddy, little mind. . . .
>
> Meditation is not following any system; it is not constant repetition and imitation. Meditation is not concentration. It is one of the favorite gambits of some teachers of meditation to insist on their pupils' learning concentration—that is, fixing the mind on one thought and driving out all other thoughts. This is a most stupid, ugly thing, which any schoolboy can do because he is forced to. It means that all the time you are having a battle between the insistence that you must concentrate on the one hand, and your mind on the other, which wanders away to all sorts of other things, whereas you should be attentive to every movement of the mind wherever it wanders. When your mind wanders off it means you are interested in something else.
>
> Meditation demands an astonishingly alert mind; meditation is the understanding of the totality of life in which every form of fragmentation has ceased. Meditation is not control of thought, for when

thought is controlled it breeds conflict in the mind. . . . Meditation is to be aware of every thought and of every feeling, never to say it is right or wrong but just to watch it and move with it. In that watching you begin to understand the whole movement of thought and feeling. And out of this awareness comes silence. Silence put together by thought is stagnation, is dead, but the silence that comes when thought has understood its own beginning, the nature of itself, understood how all thought is never free but always old—this silence is meditation in which the meditator is entirely absent, for the mind has emptied itself of the past. . . .

Meditation is one of the greatest arts in life—perhaps *the* greatest, and one cannot possibly learn it from anybody, that is the beauty of it. It has no technique and therefore no authority. When you learn about yourself, watch yourself, watch the way you walk, how you eat, what you say, the gossip, the hate, the jealousy,—if you are aware of all that in yourself, without any choice, that is part of meditation. So meditation can take place when you are sitting in a bus or walking in the woods full of light and shadows, or listening to the singing of birds or looking at the face of your wife or child. In the understanding of meditation there is love, and love is not the product of systems, of habits, of following a method.

Having read that, the reader may still choose to follow a method, or elaborate upon or simplify one that already exists, or combine elements of several different forms. For that reason, I have included descriptions of techniques that have worked for a number of people in this book, with the understanding that they may not work for everyone.

CHAPTER 8

Herbert Moss:
The Pebble in the Pool

■ ■ ■

Here is the fulfillment of every religion in the simple practice of Transcendental Meditation. This belongs to the spirit of every religion; it has existed in the early stages of every faith, it is something which has been lost. . . . Fortunately this technique has come to light in the present generation. Let it be adopted by the peoples of all religions, and let them enjoy it while being proud of their faiths. Let the intelligent minds of all religions and the custodians of the various faiths delve into the deeper essence of their scriptures, find Transcendental Meditation in the textbooks of their own faiths, learn the practice, and adopt it in the light of the teachings of their religions.
—Maharishi Mahesh Yogi, *Science of Being and Art of Living*

All the masters tell us that the reality of life—which our noisy waking consciousness prevents us from hearing—speaks to us chiefly in silence.
—Karlfried Graf Dürckheim, *Zen and Us*

■

Those Americans who might have missed the books of D. T. Suzuki and Alan Watts and the vogue that Zen Buddhism enjoyed in the fifties and sixties would have had a harder time avoiding the media impact made by the Hindu holy man known as Maharishi Mahesh Yogi after the Beatles "discovered" him lecturing in a London hotel in August 1967. Although the Beatles disowned Maharishi less than six months later, his influence continued to grow in America, and his particular distillation of Hindu meditation techniques, which he called (and copyrighted as) Transcendental Meditation, became a household word.

In the nearly twenty-five years since Maharishi's emergence as the most influential Eastern religious figure of his day, some of the events surrounding his rise to prominence have faded from memory. Readers may recall that his fall from favor with the Beatles had to do with their perception of his sexual misconduct toward members of their party. Since then, however, the sexual peccadilloes of Eastern gurus who have encountered all-too-willing Western followers have been well documented. Nor, as we now know, are such apparent contradictions between preaching and practice limited to men of the mystic East.

The fact that any one man could exert such a powerful influence on popular figures with as many options as the Beatles was not lost on certain segments of the American population. Centers for the learning and practice of Transcendental Meditation, or TM, began to spring up across the country as word of this new technique spread, and other pop culture icons, from Mia Farrow, Merv Griffin, and Mary Martin to Clint Eastwood, Burt Reynolds, and Mike Love of the Beach Boys, were revealed to be practitioners. At least part of what presumably made Maharishi's system of meditation so appealing to Americans may have been its utter simplicity. All you had to do, in essence, was to sit quietly for twenty minutes each morning and evening, close your eyes and repeat a personal mantra, or sound, which had been supplied by a teacher. This was considerably easier than the rigorous demands of Zen meditation—which requires years of training and long hours of daily practice—and it was not necessarily linked to a specific religious or devotional system with new rituals, liturgies, and scriptures to learn. Boosters of TM, who appeared on TV talk shows wearing suits and short haircuts and talking in businesslike tones—perhaps to counteract the suspicion that TM was yet another manifestation of hippie culture—were careful to emphasize its practical application. There was little reference to the Hindu school of Siddha Yoga out of which Maharishi developed his techniques, and Maharishi himself has consistently downplayed this link. The back cover of his guidebook to Transcendental Meditation, *Science of Being and Art of Living*, which first appeared as a Signet paperback in 1968, refers to TM as "a simple, effortless technique that can be practiced by anyone," and, in language that wouldn't seem out of place on a box of oat bran cereal, makes the following claim:

Scientific research has found that TM

- Eliminates stress and fatigue

- Improves health

- Increases energy and well-being

- Expands mental potential.

As a representative of the TM movement explained to me, the word *Veda*, the name for the oldest texts upon which Hinduism is based, means "knowledge." According to Maharishi, the ancient Vedic science from which he derived his meditation technique actually predates the Hindu religion. He insists that the religion grew out of the science, not the other way around, and so TM is not really religious at all, but scientific. TM instructors claim that the practice of their form of meditation need not interfere with your own religion, whether Muslim or Mormon, but can actually enhance it. One spokesperson insisted that some of the most ardent supporters of TM in Thailand are orders of Buddhist monks.

If you attend the introductory lectures at one of the country's two hundred or so TM centers, however, you may sense, as I did, a curious mingling of this scientific approach with heavy-handed salesmanship. You will be told that you must commit to taking the training during two-hour sessions on four consecutive days, that the fee for an individual is $400, for a family of any size $600, $250 for the retired, $155 for college students, $85 for those age ten through high school, and so on. Those fees are not out of line with what you can expect to pay for workshops, retreats, or instructional weekends in almost any of the new spiritual sects or teachings that are eager for students, and barely approach the kind of money some individuals contribute annually to parish churches and synagogues. Still, the coupling of that price list with reiterated assertions that TM is the only effective form of meditation enhanced my feeling of being pitched a product line.

The man who delivered the lectures I attended in Manhattan characterized as ineffectual other kinds of meditation involving "concentration" or "contemplation." But when I asked him if he was referring to specific systems such as Zen, Taoist, or Christian meditation, he admitted that he had no knowledge of those, nor of any meditation system that employed the methods he had just disparaged. It soon became clear that he was sticking to a lesson plan, and that he wasn't trained to go far beyond it. That may be the inevitable result of franchising any teaching system, of course, rather than a reflection on the teaching itself. But if nothing else, it implied poor training at the higher levels—not unlike the nuns and Sunday School teachers who imparted distorted and narrow-minded versions of Christianity to generations of schoolchildren.

TM bears other similarities to religious organizations that at a certain point become more important to their members than the spiritual values of love, openness, and tolerance they claim to foster. One couple I interviewed, for instance, told of the hostilities they encountered when they left the TM movement after nearly twenty years. They weren't overtly threatened, but were generally shunned and bad-mouthed by those who stayed on. Still, one cannot argue strenuously with the assertions of people who say their lives have been altered for the better through the daily practice of TM. Whatever its shortcomings, Transcendental Meditation is helping to fill the void created by the increasingly flimsy satisfactions of secular humanism.

Although the common perception may be that TM disappeared from the scene along with the Beatles, its membership has continued to grow steadily. Today, TM has centers in fifty countries. Although Maharishi himself has effectively dropped from the public eye over the past decade by staying in India, he maintains a center in Washington, D.C., and an accredited institution in Fairfield, Iowa (Maharishi International University, in which thousands of students congregate to study and meditate), as well as other centers around the world.

One of the 3 million people worldwide and close to a million in the United States who have taken up the practice of TM is Herbert Moss, a former radio and television producer now in his seventies who divides his time among lectures, workshops, and working one to one with clients referred to him by various doctors for training in deep relaxation techniques. He administers a six-session course in which he attempts to help those clients uncover and reverse some of their negative childhood programming. Along the way, he seeks to give them a "spiritual orientation to things beyond the materialistic side of their lives, so that they develop some balance and have some perspective on their relationship to the universe." Moss considers this work a nearly ideal utilization of his life experience, the end of a long and tortuous trail that has led him to where he is now.

Sitting back in a chair in his apartment in one of the last Art Deco buildings on Central Park West, Moss described that journey as a seemingly haphazard series of events and influences that urged him to "turn to the silence and the power within." Dressed comfortably in sport clothes and speaking in a soft, gravelly voice, he explained that Transcendental Meditation "develops your nervous system the way physical exercise develops your body. Then you bring the experience of the body being at rest, and the mind being totally free to move in any direction it wants, back into your daily life. Your mind is a little clearer, your fuses are a little longer, your perceptions of life are a little more sanguine, and that is how growth slowly evolves. It's a process, not a magic wand. Little by little you train your nervous system to respond more appropriately to the stimulus of the environment, to use the mechanisms that nature has given you to defend yourself and to survive." Moss feels that the combination of a highly competitive environment and a materialistic way of life makes it difficult to maintain an internal sense of order. Meditation helps to release the deep-rooted stresses within us and to overcome the "enormous amount of negativity that has been laid down on our nervous systems."

Moss himself emanates an aura of calm and concern, an abiding gentleness and politeness of manner that lends a certain credence to what he has to say about the workings of TM on the psyche. But how do these developments relate to spirituality and, for that matter, to his earliest religious training? For one thing, he said, spirituality grew out of his contact with meditation, his "understanding of our spiritual relationship to the universe and how the universe works." By contrast, his childhood was not in any sense religious. In fact, it was what he described as "a formalistic, middle-class Jewish upbringing," which he left after his bar mitzvah. Moss "never was really close to the temple," but was instead "a disconnected youngster with no liking for organized religions." Like many disillusioned youngsters, he came to feel that religious institutions "were all motivated by survival and power." And like so many of the people who have undergone spiritual transformations in this country, his major religious influences were charismatic individuals who functioned "outside of the structured religions."

Raised in Queens, New York, Herbert Moss had a father who was president of an Orthodox Jewish temple, and "a rather strict martinet," more concerned with future attainments than present pleasures. He wanted his sons to grow up to be great regardless of whether they were happy or liked him. In Moss's words, "He believed in religious public service, but he never had time for fun. He never smiled, never laughed, was never flip." Through exceptionally long hours and hard work, Moss's father parlayed his job as a merchandiser at Macy's into a business of his own, which left him with little time for fun or for anything else.

None of Moss's five older brothers ever seemed to have time for fun, either. "They all grew up with heart conditions or got cancer or had strokes," he said. His father died of a heart attack at a relatively early age, which left Herbert with "an ingrown anxiety about health. He had his first heart attack when I was five years old. I saw them carry him down to an ambulance in the middle of the night, which was terrifying. For the next ten years, he was semi-invalided. After that, I wasn't allowed to go out and play or be exuberant. You know, 'Pop's here, you have to be careful.' I always remember him taking his pulse and taking his Digitalis. Those memories are very difficult to erase. Every one of my brothers grew up the same way: bright but claustrophobic, with all kinds of problems. I had to fight like the devil to overcome some of those early conditions."

After Moss was bar-mitzvahed at thirteen, he stopped going to temple. "I didn't like the feeling of the people there," he said. "Nobody ever explained anything about Judaism to me, so I learned it by rote. It was just like elementary and secondary school: they pour things into you and you don't know what the hell it's all about. It was of absolutely no value."

As the youngest of the six boys, Moss felt lost in the mêlée of growing up, and compensated by developing an early "poetic streak." He attended drama classes in school and enjoyed playing romantic parts such as that of the swashbuckling character L'Aiglon in the Edmond

Rostand play of that name. "Then I'd come home," he recalled, "and my brothers would say, 'Get my shirt! Where are my shoes? Get the laundry out!' And here L'Aiglon was walking around. In so many ways, I felt absolutely separate from everybody as a child. I grew up with my inner life being much more powerful than my outer life." He had already started taking dance classes, and at age seven he became a professional dancer. Expressing himself by dancing or singing got the attention that didn't come any other way.

"I danced in vaudeville time," he said. "My partner was a grown man and we did a shadow act: I did everything he did. I did that for a couple of years until they found out I couldn't read or write." That was when the Geary Society, which kept an eye on children in the entertainment field in those days, got after Moss's mother to put him back in school. But he had had a taste of applause and of people hugging and kissing him when he danced nicely. "That became an important part of my life, and when I did grow up I was always attracted to the entertainment world."

Maybe that explains why he later decided to become a director and producer rather than a lawyer, as his father had wanted. One of his father's brothers was a famous lawyer, and another brother was a famous doctor, so Moss had to choose between the two. Although he chose law when he was seven or eight, he "never really got interested in it," but stuck with it through college as a way of staying in school. At the same time, he was also booking orchestras and talent for parties as a sideline, never thinking that he could earn enough money from that to support himself. After four years at Cornell University in Ithaca, New York, Moss signed on for three more at Cornell Law School. But by the time he received his law degree in 1937, he had lost interest in practicing law and had become fascinated with broadcasting.

"I liked college life," he said, "but it didn't make much of an impression on me intellectually or spiritually. I found formal education extremely empty. They taught subject matter, but they didn't teach me anything about life." While at Cornell Law School, Moss started a radio guild that eventually became well known enough for the networks to come up and check it out. They liked what they saw, and he was soon helping produce network shows out of the campus studios. "Finally I said to them, 'Where do I go when I graduate?'" They told him to go to NBC, where he quickly landed a job as a producer, even though he had never been in a commercial radio studio and didn't know how to function in one. "I was never so scared in my life," Moss said. Nonetheless, he moved to New York City and went from success to success in the radio and television business, going on to produce popular TV shows including "Truth or Consequences," "Songs for Sale," and a series of children's specials with David Susskind. He lived a very different life from the sheltered existence of a college campus in the Ithaca countryside, and within a few years the hectic pace of New York life had made him quite ill. "My whole body rebelled against the lifestyle I had chosen," he said. "I was eating badly, drinking badly, sleeping badly, overworking, and creating an enormous amount of stress on myself. I had a bad case of colitis, bad ulceritis, and severe skin problems."

This crisis led Moss to the first of four major influences which he credits with transforming his life. After he had been to twenty-two different establishment doctors, somebody took him to see a naturopathic physician. Naturopathy is a method of treating illness by using nutrition, exercise, heat, and other natural elements to assist the body's inherent healing powers. The physician he saw was Max Warmbrand, now recognized as a pioneer in the field of naturopathy, who had begun his medical career by curing himself of tuberculosis of the bone at the age of eighteen. "He went on a fast for something like forty days, drinking just water," Moss said. "He recognized that if a body does not take in any more poisons and is allowed to detoxify itself, it will heal itself. The body has an amazing redundancy system for healing, with twenty very nice antibodies to fight one germ. Warmbrand's idea was that we are constantly putting poisons into our bodies, and the immune system has to work harder and harder to get rid of the toxins in the air, soil, food, and water, plus all the emotional toxins we put in. The immune system becomes overwhelmed, and when a tuberculosis germ comes along, there is no one at home to knock it off. He decided to get rid of all the poisons in his body, purify it as much as possible, and see if it would take care of the germs that were beginning to eat his life away. And that's what happened. He cured himself of a tuberculosis that was said to be inoperable and incurable. The doctors had said he was finished."

Warmbrand's impact on Moss was appreciable from the first. "He could just hold your hand and look in your eyes, and you would feel better already," Moss said. "I told him I had trunks full of ointments, unguents, and pills, but I still felt awful. He said, 'Oh, no problem, you'll be fine. You'll give up alcohol and coffee, and throw those cigarettes away.' I told him I could never give up those things, but he said, 'Of *course* you can.' And he was so confident I could do this that I threw the cigarettes away and never smoked again. I gave up my three-martini luncheons, I gave up my coffee and Danish and heartburn for breakfast, and before I knew it, every part of my body that had been in rebellion seemed to become more harmonious. Every symptom disappeared and I regained my energy. Before that, I had been falling asleep by five o'clock in the afternoon."

At first when Moss started eating the food that Warmbrand suggested and laid off the bad stuff, his whole body rebelled. He had headaches and couldn't sleep, his breath smelled, and he was about to give it up. "I said, 'This is not for me, it's for the guy next door. I'm going back to my pills.' He said, 'Hold the phone. You don't understand what's going on. You're getting rid of all the poisons in your system, and they're surfacing as your skin and every organ in your body releases them.' When I understood the process therapeutically, it didn't disturb me, and when the symptoms left in a few weeks I felt marvelous."

Moss thrived on Warmbrand's then revolutionary nutritional regimen of primarily vegetables and grains. "Two salads every day with a baked potato," he said. "Occasionally he would let you have a little fish or chicken, but he believed that vegetables and grains were the essence of life. And he did it again and again with thousands of people—arthritic people, asthmatic people, mostly systemic disorders. He also cured cancer patients this way."

Moss's experience with Warmbrand taught him two basic lessons that began a long string of changes in his life. The first was that nature has the power to restore balance and harmony in the body if given the chance, and the other was that the establishment didn't know everything. "It had never occurred to me that authority wasn't right," he said. "I was brought up to believe that my father was right, the teachers were right, everybody was right, and who was I to challenge them? But this little man from Europe without any degrees, who had cured himself of tuberculosis, was saying, 'Don't take this drug, don't eat that, and throw all your pills away.' He never went to college and he wasn't a doctor." In fact, the New York State Department of Health made Warmbrand cease and desist the practice of medicine for a time because he was not a medical doctor. He finally left New York and moved to Stamford, Connecticut, where he had a successful practice. But Moss was impressed that Warmbrand had nothing to do with the establishment and yet was the only man "who really understood how nature functioned. So when Maharishi came along later and said, 'This is the way the universe functions, and this is the way the body functions,' that felt comfortable to me. I was ready for him."

The second formative experience for Moss was more spiritual than physical. He had been going through a "typical midlife identity crisis" in his forties. A successful producer-director in both radio and television, and owner of his own recording company with sixty employees, Moss was knee-deep in the American Dream. "I had a house in the country, a place in the city, secretaries, lawyers, accountants, charge accounts, all the jazz that went with success—and I was a very miserable guy. I was not comfortable with what I was doing, and when all those stimuli passed and it got quiet again, I would become very depressed and anxious. So, like Siddhartha, I went searching to find out who I was and what I was doing." Over the next few years, Moss subjected himself to Freudian, Reichian, Jungian, and Zen therapy, finding something valuable in each of them. "It was as if somebody put a pearl of truth in my hand," he said, "but it wasn't the whole truth. Through all these therapies, I was being *in*formed but I wasn't being *trans*formed. They were merely intellectual experiences."

Then one day, through "a real coincidence of nature," Moss changed his travel plans at the last minute. Relinquishing a golfing trip to Florida, he accepted an extra ticket from some friends who were going on a skiing trip to Europe. Before he left, a colleague suggested that he visit a German Zen master by the name of Karlfried Graf Dürckheim, who lived in a small town in the Black Forest. So at the end of his trip around Europe, when Moss had some free time, he decided to visit Dürckheim. "I arrived at this tiny Hansel and Gretel village with all these smokestacks coming out of straw-thatched cottages," he said. "His people met me at the station and drove me to his home, where I was ushered into his presence in a marvelous room of oak-rimmed walls hung with tapestries. Dürckheim was about six three, with steel blue eyes, white hair, and ruddy complexion. He looked like an oak tree himself, he was such an imposing individual. He held my hand and tears practically came to my eyes. Then we went to sit down. Normally when you visit a professional man or any person of authority, he sits behind his desk and you sit in a chair pulled up to the side. Dürckheim reversed this and offered me *his* chair behind the desk, while he sat in a little unprotected chair in the middle of the room. It was a wonderful gesture because it put me at ease and filled me with a sense of security."

By the time the meeting was over, Moss had formed a profound attachment for Dürckheim and couldn't stand the idea of leaving the next morning. "In his presence, the energy began to flow, until I finally said after our first hour together, 'Dr. Dürckheim, there's no way I can leave this place. I physically cannot get on a train and go back to Zurich.' He said, 'You don't have to. If you want, you can get your luggage and stay here.' That was the beginning of ten remarkable days. He got me out of my head and into my feelings, and my senses became enlivened. Before that, my entire life had been split: my intellect in charge, my feelings always suppressed. I was never in touch with them, despite all the therapies I had gone through. There, I walked in the woods and meditated. Every time I touched a piece of fruit or bread, it had such a 'liveness' that I couldn't believe it."

As an experience, it was difficult to describe. One night when they were having Chinese soup, Moss was overwhelmed by a feeling of "presence"—a heightened sense of awareness similar to that described by certain mystics. The feel of the porcelain spoon in his hand, the taste of the soup as he swallowed it, was a totally different sensory experience from anything he had ever had. This he attributed to Dürckheim's suggestion to focus his full attention on each moment. "We do everything by rote," Moss said. "Our consciousness is not there. What he was saying was that life is in the moment. There is no past, no future, *only this moment*. And you fill it with your whole being. Somehow that got into me and I began to experiment, walking in the woods, feeling the trees and the earth below me. When you start feeling that, your hair stands on end."

Dürckheim brought in an expert to teach Moss deep breathing, and although the experience didn't seem like much at the time, it wrought substantial changes. "I walked around as though I were twenty feet tall," Moss said, "and my mind became lucid. Everything seemed simpler and clearer, and I had energy for twenty-two hours a day. I said, 'My God, all my life I've been living with about twenty percent of my energy available to me.' I realized that I had a battleground within me: the intellect and the emotions, being grown up and being a kid, wanting and not wanting. But there in Dürckheim's place you just were what you were, and you were one thing. It was more a matter of what he was than what he taught me. He was the quintessence of aliveness and sensitivity and unity."

They talked every day, Moss spilling out his problems with his work, his marriage, his therapy. Dürckheim said, in effect, "Don't worry about them. You'll have your answer by the time you leave." But he never answered Moss's questions directly, never gave advice. "He just talked. And sure enough, by the time I left him, the questions that had been plaguing me about my marriage and my career seemed to answer themselves. And I knew damn well I wasn't going back into therapy. I had had five years of it, and I had never had an experience like I had with him. I knew that if I had any growth potential, it was through the spiritual path."

The kind of entraining effect that Moss experienced is described by the Sufi teacher Pir Vilayat Khan in his book *Introducing Spirituality into Counseling and Therapy*. When people went to see his father, the great Indian musician and sage Hazrat Inayat Khan, Pir Vilayat writes, "they expected to have to bow before this great master and then to have an opportunity to ask questions. But when they found themselves in his presence, he would just welcome them with both hands and invite them to sit next to him on the sofa, and he would speak like an old friend. They would forget all their problems, and then when they left they would often feel as if they had missed the opportunity to ask questions. Later, they would realize that they didn't have to ask the questions . . . because [he] had, by working with a higher attunement, brought them to a level of consciousness at which they were able to see into their problems themselves."

When Moss got home, his wife hardly recognized him as he stepped off the plane. "My face looked totally different," he said, "no longer guarded and withdrawn but open and in touch." He went back to his business thoroughly refreshed; but over the next few months all the anxiety-producing irritations and annoyances slowly began to come back. "As I put it at the time," he said, "the clouds came over and blocked the sunshine."

Besides producing television programs for NBC and running his own recording studio, Moss was putting together packages of audio material for use in public school teaching programs. Audio-visual innovation in teaching—prerecorded cassettes to accompany textbooks—was just beginning, and Moss worked with Reader's Digest, McGraw-Hill, Harcourt Brace, and other major publishers in producing and packaging educational material. He also recorded popular music and advertising jingles in his studio. But while he enjoyed the creative side of recording, he was not attuned to the business requirements of running his own company, and became more and more removed from his work.

In the early seventies, Moss experienced the transition that was to alter his life irreversibly. The underlying cause seemed innocent enough; as with many of the people who report such changes, only in retrospect did the events stand out as crucial. It all began when Moss noticed changes in his son, Rick, who had acquired all the earmarks of a classic, tie-dyed-in-the-wool hippie. In Moss's terms, "He was into the headbands and the beard and the guitar and the drugs. He was a very lost soul." One day Moss realized that the guitar playing and loud music had stopped, that Rick had shaved off his beard and was acting friendlier than he had in some time. When Moss asked him about the change, he found that Rick had begun practicing Transcendental Meditation, which had recently been introduced to America by Maharishi. Out of curiosity, Moss accompanied his son to a lecture and was surprised to discover that TM represented nothing less than the daily implementation of what Dürckheim had been doing in the Black Forest.

"It was the same thing," Moss said, "except that they had a technique for maintaining it in your life on a daily basis, which Dürckheim never really showed me. So I started practicing the technique, and sure enough, I began to get back into that feeling of being connected, of opening myself, of my consciousness growing, of being able to see and listen to other people apart from my own neurotic problems. My anxiety level dropped. Little by little the technique became part of my everyday life. I began going to lectures, going away for weekend retreats, and finally became part of the movement."

The technique fit easily into his life because of its simple regimen of twenty minutes in the morning and twenty minutes in the evening. "Just closing my eyes and following the technique put me back in touch with the experiences I had had in the Black Forest," he said. "The knowledge that there was a path to this kind of fulfillment, this kind of sensory experience in life, and to the avoidance of all the ridiculous conflict that pulls us in many directions, created a sense of inner peace and orderliness in me that I had not gotten from the professional work I had been doing. That experience started me on my spiritual path."

But Moss didn't think of it as spiritual at the time. As he put it, "Maharishi was smart enough to introduce the technique to America in terms of physiology and scientific verification, and to underplay the whole concept of consciousness expansion, which was sort of a dirty word then. There was no way of verifying something called 'expanded consciousness,' and the American public was not about to accept Eastern culture and philosophy with all the mysticism attributed to it." At least not the adult public, so Maharishi gravitated to colleges, where he began setting up campus TM centers. Some students learned his technique, practiced it, and reported significant results. "Don't forget," Moss added, "this was at a time when many students were anti-establishment, and quite a few were into the drug scene and dropping out. Here they found some kind of inner strength and an alternate way of getting the feeling of being high on drugs. The reports of people stopping excessive drug and alcohol use, smoking, eating red meat, and all sorts of negative behavior, were dramatic. Not that there was any discipline for this, because Maharishi never said not to use drugs."

What apparently happened instead was a generic change in meditators, by which "they found that they were not interested in doing something that violated the quality of life they were beginning to experience through TM. They'd say, 'That's just too heavy, that makes me feel down and it's contrary to what I want to feel.' Little by little these things fell by the wayside, and people began to find that they had strength and structure in other values."

Moss was skeptical at first. When Maharishi announced that it was possible to achieve a state of enlightenment by sitting for twenty minutes in the morning and evening, he snickered. "Everyone said,

'This is exactly how the snake-oil salesmen are in the back of the truck.' It was as if he had a bottle of elixir that he was trying to push off on everyone, and it made no sense. We're living with nine thousand vibratory negatives in our life on a daily basis, and this guy says, 'Close your eyes for twenty minutes and you're going to achieve a state of purity, enlightenment, and freedom.' It took me years to understand that Oracle of Delphi statement, but what he really meant was that gradually everything in your life begins to change a little bit because you feel a sense of orderliness, just a touch of it. The next day your fuse gets a little longer, and you find you're not dribbling at the mouth, not getting as involved in negative things. It's like a pebble thrown into a pool that begins to make bigger and bigger ripples, and without your realizing it, your life has changed dramatically. There's more room for loving and openness, more room for understanding your limitations and the limitations of others.''

The effects on Moss's life also began to expand. After doing the work at home for eighteen months, he decided TM was too important for him to have just a superficial knowledge of it. So he sold his business and became a student again. "I had spent nineteen years in schools, but I didn't mind going back twenty years later and learning something on a level that I really cared about." After a year of study in Switzerland and Spain, he was accredited as a teacher of TM.

What he taught people was that Transcendental Meditation is "a mental-physiological technique in which we turn our attention inward and allow the body to settle down to a very deep state of rest. We allow the mind to be free to move in any direction it wants to, not concentrating on anything, not contemplating anything." He differentiates the TM approach from prior classical techniques of meditation which require concentration on a candle flame or the hypnotic drawing called a mandala, or cleansing the mind of all thought and keeping "an open, clear, empty mind. Maharishi says this is a misunderstanding of how the mind naturally functions." Maharishi came to the conclusion that the mind is like a monkey jumping from tree to tree, from thought to thought, and that trying either to clear the mind of all thought or to stay with one thought is almost impossible. So, working under his own master, Shri Guru Dev, for thirteen years, Maharishi evolved a way of allowing the mind to move in any direction it wanted. The only thing he used to guide it was the mantra:

a sound or syllable that has no rational meaning. "The only value of the mantra is that it has a vibratory rate," Moss said. "The vibration of that sound in your nervous system creates a soothing state of being, much the way a cello does, or a flute, as opposed to a brass or trip-hammer. It creates a different internal environment, allowing the mind to settle down to more and more subtle levels."

The actual techniques of TM begin by sitting with eyes closed in a quiet room, either in a chair or cross-legged on the floor. Moss said it is important to keep the back perpendicular to the ground "so that the energy flows between the top of your head and the base of your spine. After making sure that the whole body is in a state of relaxation as deeply as you can achieve it, you introduce a sound that has been chosen specifically for you from a series of mantras taught by the master." He declined to give examples, warning that to give someone a mantra without the entire structure of the teachings is "like putting a weapon in the hands of a child. The mantra also has its greatest power when it's used only internally, and the vibration soothes the nervous system."

As you repeat the mantra silently, you allow your mind to settle down to quieter and more subtle levels. You may have ordinary thoughts concerning the events of the day, anxieties, or fantasies, but the content of the thought is of no concern. "The thought is only a process," Moss said, "an energy field leaving the body. It's like having a steam valve on top of the head. When you open the valve, all the thoughts come out, all that energy is released, and then the body is free to be quiet again. By virtue of the rest that results, our bodies throw off some of the fatigue and deep-rooted stresses that have accumulated in our systems since we were infants." Moss spoke about the negative conditioning that is believed to result from the traumatic events in our early lives, and the negative comments of parents and teachers "that create a feeling of being inadequate and unwanted, and that remain in our nervous system like a block of cement."

By allowing the mind to settle down, he reasons, TM lets the body release these accumulated stresses and blocks and develop some flexibility. "It becomes flexible in much the way your muscles would if you became involved in an athletic or aerobic program. This experience is different from any other because it's not waking physiology, not sleeping physiology, not dreaming physiology. It's so different from all those physiological parameters that it has been called the fourth state of consciousness." When you emerge from this state into action, some of it presumably stays with you. The sense of peace that creates in the meditator again functions like the pebble in the pool. "The more you experience that feeling of peace in activity, the more you say, 'This is the way I'd rather function.' The other way—becoming anxious, frustrated, furious—doesn't seem so natural anymore."

What makes the technique work, according to Moss, is that "the body achieves a state of rest twice as deep as the deepest part of an eight-hour sleep." This was documented by a young Ph.D. named R. Keith Wallace at UCLA, where Moss worked for several years. Later Herbert Benson of Harvard Medical School heard about Wallace's findings and invited him to come to Harvard, where, after two years of scientific study on hundreds of meditators, they replicated what Wallace had done in California. They determined that the state of rest resulting from Transcendental Meditation was as deep as the sixth hour of sleep. "We know that's important," Moss said, "because nature does its best healing in a state of pure rest. If you have a broken wrist or a broken arm, you put it in a cast so it's totally immobilized. In that state, nature knits the bones and heals the injury, whereas if you kept it loose and moving around, it would never heal as well."

After Benson and Wallace's results were published, other scientists moved in. "The physiologists and applied psychologists, the people who study brain waves, retention, and stress in the body, looked at the phenomenon and wrote studies on it," Moss said. "Most of the studies verified that if you did this on a regular basis, you would achieve a state of physiology that was much healthier, and you would feel better about yourself." Among other things, the scientific monitoring showed that TM served to lower oxygen consumption and blood lactate (a substance associated with anxiety), while producing alpha waves in the brain, a sign of deep relaxation. The research gave TM a believability that helped to counter the image of a gray-haired, white-bearded holy man wearing flowing robes and speaking in a high-pitched Punjabi accent. Herbert Benson's book *The Relaxation Response*, which describes these results in lay terms and proposes a secularized version of meditation, became a best-seller and further legitimized the movement. That the technique functions unattached to any system of spiritual beliefs or practice helped it spread more quickly at a time when secular humanism was at its peak in intellectual and professional circles. In Benson's words, Maharishi "eliminated from yoga certain elements that he considered to be non-essential. He left India, bringing with him this revised form of yoga which could be grasped more easily by Westerners."

TM, then, had the advantage of being a simple, durable technique that was easily assimilated by believer and agnostic alike, without the inconvenient inner trials associated with so-called mystical experience, which could lead to a classic "dark night of the soul." "Maharishi used to say that meditation is a sticky experience," Moss said, "like dying cloth in the old days. You put a little cloth in a vat of dye, and then you put it in the sun and most of the color disappears. Then you put it back in the vat and bring it out, and more of it stays. If you do that enough times, the cloth becomes colorfast. No matter what environment you put it in, you don't lose that color. You can be in the most stressful, dynamic environment, and if you're evolved enough so that your nervous system is flexible, you don't lose your center. Psychologists speak of 'centering,' by which they mean that you are inner-directed. I use the image of that big inflated plastic toy called Bozo the Clown which has a lead bottom, so that every time you sock it, it comes back to its own natural position. No matter how we get buffeted by life, we always want to come back to our center of balance."

Like Maharishi, Moss emphasized that "meditation is not an exotic experience. It's not designed to replace taking LSD and achieving a chemically altered state of consciousness." He did acknowledge that it is possible, however, to "transcend the thought field and get to a place where there are no thoughts and no fields of perception at all but just a state of total bliss, or State of Being, as we call it, which is more subtle than the subtlest source of thought. That does take place from time to time, and it's called transcending. You transcend the material field into the field of timelessness, so called because you can experience it only in retrospect. Obviously, if you were experiencing while you were there, you would be having a thought or a feeling, and so you can't do it. But after you've had it for thirty seconds, one second, or whatever, you say, 'There was that time when I felt very quiet. There were no thoughts, nothing going on. I wasn't asleep, but there was that wonderful feeling of. . . .' "

Moss's involvement with the Transcendental Meditation movement ultimately led him to produce radio programs for TM and to become part of its inner circle. While studying in Europe he spent time with Maharishi and in the company of other meditators, something which profoundly deepened the effects of meditation for him. "I was with a thousand people of all ages and nations, and each of them had only one interest in life—personal spiritual development," he said. "It was an environment of pure brotherhood. Nobody was trying to be better, nobody was richer, poorer, smarter or dumber. They were there to learn and to live out their meditations every day. Just walking with that many people, being on the beach or eating with them, was an opening experience. And all the vibrations from a thousand people meditating in one room were not to be believed." In fact, Maharishi believes that the vibrations created in each meditating individual revolve around the world and affect conditions on the planet and ultimately in the universe. According to figures released by Maharishi International University, the precise number of people meditating at once required to produce such effects is seven thousand. Is there any truth to this? Unfortunately, the very word "vibrations" has been vitiated by its popular colloquial use in phrases like "good vibes." But as used by students of the Vedic sciences and other Eastern schools of thought, the notion of differing vibratory rates parallels the quantum mechanical view of modern physics. If we can conceive of our bodies as composed of waves of intelligent energy rather than merely of gross physical matter, then the rate of vibration of those waves can be seen as affecting the way we feel, think, and act. And if meditation has the power to affect our vibratory rate, at least in theory, then by extension it can also affect our daily actions on a personal and, ultimately, a global basis. For this reason, practitioners of TM like to take credit for apparent recent advances in world peace, although scientific evidence for a claim of such magnitude would obviously be difficult to accumulate.

When Moss returned to the States, he was determined to do TM work exclusively. As one of the few older initiates of TM in America— most devotees here were of college age—he was invited to lecture to the growing ranks of doctors, lawyers, psychiatrists, performers, athletes, and other professionals who were interested in TM. Leaving his media career behind, Moss turned his Manhattan apartment into a training center in which he instructed hundreds of people in the science of meditation. From there he went to California to oversee pilot programs and workshops in the resort spas of La Costa and Palo Mesa, combining his practices with the work of nutritionists and physical therapists. On one such trip he met Hans Selye, the founder of what is known as Stress Medicine, and the man who became the fourth major influence in Moss's life.

The author of thirty-two books and over seventeen hundred articles, Selye presided over the Institute of Stress Management in Montreal. His work emphasized the relationship of mental attitude to physiology in the development of stress, and demonstrated that stress is the determining factor in 75 percent of all illnesses. Selye and Moss became close friends, and in 1979, Selye invited Moss to deliver a paper at the Second International Symposium on Stress in Monte Carlo. In Moss's words, "There were five Nobel Prize winners delivering papers, and little old me delivering my little paper on deep relaxation techniques. It was a watershed experience for me."

After Moss returned to New York, many of the doctors who had heard him speak at Monte Carlo referred patients to him, and so began his work of one-to-one therapy, which he carries on today. The doctors couldn't help these clients in their offices, "yet their patients needed this kind of work." Moss begins with five sessions, and then lets clients decide if they want to continue once a week. He no longer teaches the TM technique, which must now be taught at a TM center, but he recommends it. In the meantime he gives them Benson's "relaxation response" technique, which they can take home and practice "until they decide it's powerful enough or they want to learn TM." Added to his lectures and symposia, one-to-one therapy now takes up most of his time. Herbert Moss is doing what he likes most and, as he put it, "What more could you ask for?"

One of the issues that most frequently arises in any discussion of Eastern religions or of practices based on them is the apparent discrepancy between their relatively passive orientation and the need for action to remedy the world's glaring dilemmas, the *via activa* versus the *via contemplativa*. What is one to do in the face of chronic starvation and misfortune on the level of Ethiopia and Bangladesh, or of flagrant political or social injustice? For some, the answer is to turn inward, to perfect themselves and wait for the world to be uplifted by this process. Others, as we saw in the case of Jim McCloskey, choose to pursue justice even at the expense of their personal spiritual life. Moss's answer seems to combine both approaches.

"Our job is to open our hearts as completely as we can to helping others," he said. "Altruism is the highest form of human endeavor. We do our best to alleviate suffering, recognizing that all that exists is part of a cosmic plan far beyond the ability of our limited intelligence to understand. As for actual physical efforts to alleviate pain, it's a matter of what you feel attuned to. But I don't believe that you purify your own system and stop there. When you perfect as much as you can this instrument that you've been developing, it is ultimately for the purpose of sharing it with, and doing for, others."

According to Moss, Maharishi never teaches that you must become a recluse to transform yourself, which can be accomplished in the context of working and having a family, or that you have to reject material things because they are somehow evil. "One of Maharishi's favorite expressions was that you should have 'two hundred percent of life,' by which he meant one hundred percent of the material world and one hundred percent of the inner, spiritual world." As Moss points out, people often misquote Scripture when they say that money is the root of all evil. The verse (I Timothy 6:10) actually reads: "For the love of money is the root of all evil." It's a matter of proportion.

On another level, the impulses toward personal spiritual growth and altruism are interrelated. Moss believes in the "connectedness" of life—a process at work in both the physical and spiritual realms, by which one small action in the right direction has a ripple effect on the rest of one's being. This is what lends such significance to the transformational moment; as small and seemingly inconsequential as that moment may be, its effects grow until they encompass the whole of one's life. "The minute you enter on this path of closing your eyes for twenty minutes and then coming out into activity," Moss said, "you begin changing many other things without realizing it. With every step your breath is different, your interests are different, you desire to read different things, to talk differently, and to meet different people from before."

Told that this sounds like the popular theory of aerobic fitness, whereby accelerating the heart's activity for twenty minutes or so raises the metabolism for the entire day and starts a chain reaction of positive physical change, Moss agreed. "Exercise not only changes your metabolism," he went on, "but it creates psychological changes, too. Your self-esteem changes, your sense of purpose and growth changes, your brain functions more efficiently, all stemming from one twenty-minute exercise. Everything has such a connectedness that you really *can* change the world just by changing one act in your daily life."

Characterized by such optimism, Moss's story shows little of the anguish which is often part of the classic spiritual journey—the "desert times" to which one priest referred, those dark periods when God seems absent even to the firmest believer. In retrospect, Herbert Moss's darkest hours seem to have come *before* he embarked on the spiritual path. "I was very successful in my twenties, thirties, and forties with show after show, and it meant nothing to me," he said. "I thought, It's really *Kinderspiel*, it's nonsense, selling cigarettes and soap with game shows and situation comedy. But that was as far as I had grown. I had no self-esteem at that time. Little by little I evolved and found other values. Once I understood that this is a continuing process, and there are forces at work supporting all of this, I said, 'Great, let them do their job, I'll do mine.' And I saw only light. I didn't see any voids or darkness about it."

Besides his daily practice of meditation, Moss reads books on Hindu philosophy and spirituality, and incorporates that knowledge into his meditative work. "My meditation is really a spiritual experience," he said. "It brings me down to the most profound and deepest part of our personal connection, which is part of all universal life. I feel that the self is indestructible. The body is just the overcoat for it, and we come through each chapter of our growth for the purpose of learning and of purifying our spirit. Until that is completed, we continue to come back in the physical form. Our path is toward enlightenment in this lifetime, as far as we can travel. If we can get rid of negativity, the purity would be here, the state of unity which is called the higher state of consciousness whereby we see only the Oneness of the world. We don't live the illusion of separateness. We see that you and I are the same. We're all the same atoms, individual drops out of one ocean."

Reincarnation and a belief in the ultimate union of humanity with the world and with God are ideas common to Hinduism and to most Eastern religious thought. Is TM a religion or a spiritual system, then, or just an isolated technique? For Moss, it is "not so much a religion as opening oneself up to the spiritual dimension." His sense of God doesn't happen to be of a personal male image, "but God is a tremendous force in my life, and I pray to God. I believe some intelligence is at work, and when you are in what we call the flow of nature, acting in accord with all the laws of nature, then nature is acting for you. When you're violating the laws of nature and there is conflict within you, it's very difficult to achieve a sense of peace or growth." Apart from this "personal religious experience," TM offers the option of belonging to a community of meditators, although "you don't have to go to any church or become part of any formalistic religion unless you choose to." You can even combine TM with Christian or Jewish observances.

Then what is the difference between TM and any secular method of stress reduction, like the "relaxation response"? Moss insisted that TM is "not just a stress reduction technique, it's consciousness-expanding. You see more of the world, and you experience loving and the gratification that comes with it, so it opens you to others. But Maharishi doesn't speak of the death of the ego. He says that eventually ego seems to be an illusion, and as the ego game ends, the self becomes self-less. The *Upanishads* put it this way: 'Having realized his own self as The Self, a man becomes self-less.' This is the highest mystery. Maharishi says that you don't lose the sense of individual ego, you just *add* the sense of Eternal Self. It's that two hundred percent of life. You realize that ego is a small drop of water in a large ocean, and you put it in its proper perspective. You don't artificially renounce it by saying, 'I am nothing. Thou art everything.' "

To illustrate his point, Moss told an old Jewish story about the highest rabbi of the city, who comes to the synagogue on the High Holy Days. "When the ark is opened he kneels down, prostrates himself, and says, 'O Lord, Thou art everything. I am nothing.' The local rabbi sees the big rabbi doing this, so he kneels down beside him and says, 'O Lord, Thou art everything. I am nothing.' The cantor sees both of them, he kneels down and says, 'O Lord, Thou art everything. I am nothing.'

"Then the little janitor—the *shammash*, the smallest officer in the entire establishment—sees what's going on. He kneels down and says, 'O Lord, Thou art everything. I am nothing.'

"So the cantor pokes the rabbi and says, 'Look who thinks he's nothing!' "

CHAPTER 9

Bernard Glassman: But Is It Zen?

. . .

Religion is not to go to God by forsaking the world but to find Him in it. Our faith is to believe in our essential oneness with Him. "God is in us and we in Him" must be made the most fundamental faith of all religions.

—Soyen Shaku

Nan-in, a Japanese master during the Meiji era (1868–1912), received a university professor who came to inquire about Zen.

Nan-in served tea. He poured his visitor's cup full, and then kept on pouring.

The professor watched the overflow until he no longer could restrain himself. "It is overfull! No more will go in!"

"Like this cup," Nan-in said, "you are full of your own opinions and speculations. How can I show you Zen unless you first empty your cup?"

—Paul Reps, *Zen Flesh, Zen Bones*

.

As the classic Zen story concisely implies, our preconceptions about Zen have been so shaped by tidbits gleaned from popular culture, inadequately assimilated readings, and various models of what passes for Zen wisdom, that our vessel of understanding is overloaded. For those who, on the other hand, have had little or no exposure to Zen, even through the usual superficial sources, the severe ellipticalness of the Zen mind can appear so simplistic as to be meaningless or offputting in its presumption of mysterious wisdom. My first response to the now famous Zen koan that appeared as the epigraph to J. D. Salinger's *Nine Stories*—"What is the sound of one hand clapping?"—was, Who cares? It's a trick question, I thought, refusing to be sucked in. Many years later, after a modest study of koans and their uses, I would only half agree with the snotty kid who said that. Koans *are* trick questions of a sort, although you have to let yourself get sucked in for them to work. They are meant to baffle the Zen student out of simple answers, out of rational thought altogether, and into another state of consciousness. Yet they do have answers, even if the right answer is probably the least significant aspect of koan study. As the British author L. C. Beckett puts it in his book *Neti-Neti*,* "It does not really matter what Koan you choose . . . whatever takes the ground from under the feet of the mind."

Besides being paradoxical and mystifying, Zen also presents itself as the essence of living in the moment, free of regrets over the past or fears for the future. A popular Zen parable attributed to the Buddha tells of a man who is chased by a tiger and, in escaping, clings to the root of a vine that hangs over the edge of a precipice. "Trembling, the man looked down to where, far below, another tiger was waiting to eat him," as Paul Reps retells the story. "Only the vine sustained him. Two mice, one white and one black, little by little started to gnaw away the vine. The man saw a luscious strawberry near him. Grasping the vine with one hand, he plucked the strawberry with the other. How sweet it tasted!"

Finally there is the sense of Zen as effortless effort, of achieving without striving or even wanting to achieve. Shunryu Suzuki, a twentieth-century Japanese Zen master who came to America to help spread Zen here, wrote in his excellent introductory book *Zen Mind, Beginner's Mind* of the very simple nature of Zen practice, under t1e heading "Nothing Special." After explaining that, after all, it is human nature to be active, he went on to say: "As long as we are alive, we are always doing something. But as long as you think, 'I am doing this,' or 'I have to do this,' or 'I must attain something special,' you are actually not doing anything. When you give up, when you no

---

* London: John M. Watkins, 1959.

longer want something, or when you do not try to do anything special, then you do something."

To make these kinds of paradoxes comprehensible on any significant level might take a whole book in itself, or several books, and years of study and work. But viewing Zen through the life of one supremely unconventional American master may help to empty our cup of preconceptions and to show that Zen—far from being only a kind of ethereally hip double-talk—can be as grounded in the real world of day-to-day life as any Western religious practice.

A branch of Buddhism generally thought to have been carried from India to China in the sixth century by a man named Bodhidharma, and thence to Japan around the twelfth century, Zen was first brought to America near the end of the nineteenth century by the Japanese abbot Soyen Shaku. It reached a wider audience here through the work of a disciple who became famous as a Zen scholar under the name D. T. Suzuki and whose writings influenced some of the seminal philosophers of his day, from Jung and Huxley to Toynbee, Fromm, and Merton. Following World War II, Zen was further popularized through the work of so-called Beat writers Allen Ginsberg, Jack Kerouac, and Gary Snyder, and through a number of intriguing books that included *Zen in the Art of Archery, Zen and the Art of Motorcycle Maintenance, Zen Flesh, Zen Bones*, and many less-inspired spin-offs. (Titles like *Zen and the Art of the Macintosh* and *A Zen Way of Baseball* by Japanese slugger Sadaharu Oh spring to mind.) The writings of the American Zen teacher Alan Watts—among them, *This Is It* and *The Way of Zen*—broadened the appeal of Zen beyond the initial circle of intellectuals, artists, and musicians.

The Zen mystique was given a further, more superficial ride by the appearance in 1972 of a television series entitled *Kung Fu*, which starred David Carradine as Kwai Chang Caine, a character who had been born in China of Chinese and American parents and raised as an orphan by the monks of Shaolin Temple (where Bodhidharma is said to have settled after coming to China). Besides being gifted with prodigious skills in kung fu, the ancient Chinese martial art from which karate and judo descended, Caine frequently spoke in cryptic, pseudo-Zen utterances. Although the show lasted only four seasons, it nonetheless enjoyed a certain vogue and a kind of cult status in America.

Its elliptical, Oriental inscrutability appealed in passing to the popular mind-set by offering a little painless mysticism, just as the cold, lean aesthetic of Zen—from the tenebrous, quiet starkness of the *zendo*, or meditation hall, to the clean, nonrational language of Zen koans and stories—suited the Beats' cool, crazy stance. However, despite the genuine practice and devotion of followers such as Snyder and Peter Matthiessen, most of the intellectuals who savored the Zen aesthetic eschewed the hard work of rigorous daily observance. In street parlance, they talked the talk but didn't walk the walk.

The difficult truth is that, according to the most authoritative teachers, Zen is a demanding discipline in which beginning students may require a year or more to experience any results, and as much as ten years to evolve a meaningful practice. Although there are many aspects to Zen and many ways in which its practice is manifested, the key is meditation. The word "Zen" is a transliteration of the Chinese *ch'an*, in turn a transliteration of the Sanskrit *dyāna*, meaning "meditation." Zen Buddhism emphasizes meditation as its central practice in the way Nichiren Buddhism stresses the chanting of *Namu myoho renge-kyo*. All branches of Buddhism, including Theravada and Mahayana, use meditation as an integral part of their practice; but some sects focus more on various aspects of the liturgy, prayers, chants, scripture study, and so on. By the same token, Zen can encompass liturgy, work practice, even social action; but zazen (literally, "sitting meditation") is its main focus. You can have Zen without koan study or chanting, but not without zazen.

The larger tradition of Buddhism from which Zen derives had its beginning in the sixth century before Christ, in the historical personage variously referred to as Siddhārtha Gautama, Sakyamuni (or Shakyamuni), Tathagata, or just the Buddha, the Enlightened One. Born in Northern India to a royal family, Gautama at first led a sheltered existence in the court of his father the king. In *The Hero with a Thousand Faces*, Joseph Campbell gives a lively version of the legend of the Buddha's early life in which young prince Gautama, "the Future Buddha," has been shielded by his wealthy father "from all knowledge of age, sickness, death, or monkhood, lest he should be moved to thoughts of life-renunciation; for it had been prophesied at his birth that he was to become either a world emperor or a Buddha. The king, prejudiced in favor of the royal vocation, provided his son with three palaces and forty thousand dancing girls to keep his mind attached to the world. But these only served to advance the inevitable; for while still relatively young, the youth exhausted for himself the fields of fleshly joy and became ripe for the other experience. The moment he was ready, the proper heralds automatically appeared."

These heralds took the form of aging, sick, and dying men Gautama encountered outside the palace, whereupon he was sorely troubled, realizing that "every living thing must decay." How could he enjoy his life of pleasure once he knew it all must end? But upon witnessing the self-possessed and tranquil figure of a passing monk, he determined to become a monk himself. Leaving behind his lovely wife and only child, Gautama fled the pleasures of the palace in search of deliverance from suffering. For six years, the future Buddha studied the philosophy and practiced the asceticism of the prevalent Hindu teachers of his time and place, nearly starving himself to death in the process. He finally realized that enlightenment could be reached only through the vessel of the physical body, however. Shunryu Suzuki explained Buddha's insight into the circular dilemma of asceticism very succinctly in *Zen Mind*. "Buddha found that when he practiced asceticism there was no limit to the attempt to purge ourselves physically," Suzuki wrote, "and that it made religious practice very idealistic. This kind of war with our body can end only when we die. But according to this Indian thought, we will return in another life, and another life, to repeat the struggle over and over again, without ever attaining perfect enlightenment. And even if you think you can make your physical strength weak enough to free your spiritual power, it will work only as long as you continue your ascetic practice. If you resume your everyday life, you will have to strengthen your body, but then you will have to weaken it again to regain your spiritual power. And then you will have to repeat this process over and over again."

And so Gautama abandoned extreme asceticism in favor of what he called the Middle Way between devotion to the pleasures of the senses and complete denial of them. He then went and sat under a nearby bodhi or pipal tree, and refused to move until he had become enlightened and had discovered the secret of release from suffering. When this happened, the Buddha realized that one could be freed from suffering in this life by eradicating its real causes: desire, passionate craving, and attachment. Rather than keep this insight to himself as he was tempted to do, he chose to wander the land for the next forty-five years, begging food and shelter and teaching in the simple vernacular to men and women of all castes. This in itself was a radical departure from the religious conventions of India, which had sought to keep spiritual knowledge esoteric and to allow only members of the highest caste to become priests. Further, the Buddha's Middle Way relied on purely ethical conduct and compassion for others, rather than on the external ceremonies and costumes and Vedic philosophies of Hinduism. In discarding ritual and reliance upon a privileged class of priests, the Buddha foreshadowed Christ's disavowal of the scribes and Pharisees and the retributive orientation of Mosaic law. The establishment of monasteries and orders of monks replete with ceremonies and costumes, liturgies and hierarchical ranks, came later in the development of Buddhism in India and China.

By the time Zen Buddhism found its way into Japanese culture, it began to take on certain martial overtones that seem to have little to do with the Buddha's concepts of love, compassion, and peacefulness. So it isn't surprising that as Zen was translated to America in the twentieth century, it underwent changes that might have appeared odd from a Japanese perspective. A brief but far more detailed history of Zen and its infusion into the American religious bloodstream can be found in the first chapter of Peter Matthiessen's book *Nine-Headed Dragon River*. There the noted naturalist and author also writes about his encounters and studies with Bernard Glassman, the current abbot of Zen Center New York, whom Matthiessen served for a time as head monk. Glassman is the first American Zen master to complete koan study as well as priestly training, and the first American holder of his Soto Japanese Zen lineage—one of only a handful whose credentials for transmitting Zen have been recognized in Japan. His full Zen name is Bernard Tetsugen Glassman Sensei, Tetsugen being a "dharma name" bestowed upon him by his teacher, meaning "to penetrate the mysteries or subtleties." "Sensei" is the Japanese honorific for a teacher who has received "dharma transmission" from a senior teacher; *dharma* is a Sanskrit word with several different meanings for Hindus and Buddhists. It can refer to the essential nature of an individual (dharma name), but it can also mean the entire body of wisdom and teachings that constitutes the tradition of Buddhism (transmission).

Glassman has been recognized as a dharma holder in formal ceremonies at the great Soto temples of Eihei-ji and Soji-ji in Japan, and is considered to be truly enlightened, having experienced, according to Matthiessen, "two classical dai kensho" (breakthroughs or openings). He is, by all accounts, a major influence on the future course of Zen in America. Matthiessen goes on to write that Glassman is also "very ordinary, in the best Zen sense, without idiosyncratic airs or quirks that draw attention to him. He is—and also he is not—plain Bernie Glassman, with a passion for pizza, innovative ideas, and mechanical gadgetry of all descriptions."

Plain Bernie Glassman was certainly on view the day I went to visit him at his place of business, the Greyston Bakery in Yonkers, New York, part of a network of companies congregated under the rubric of the Greyston Family Inn. Short, stocky, almost rotund, Glassman was dressed casually in black trousers and Reeboks and a brown cotton Japanese jacket. His scalp showed the barest margin of new growth (it is traditional, although not mandatory, for Zen monks to keep a shaven pate), enough to reveal that were it fully grown he would be graying at the temples. The absence of scalp hair, though, was compensated for by a pair of bushy black eyebrows that looked as if they had somehow been electrostatically charged. That impression may have been tied in my mind to the knowledge that Glassman is also a mathematician who worked for many years—until he retired to become a monk—as an aerospace engineer for McDonnell-Douglas. He spoke in a soft, distracted tone that sounded more in keeping with the absent-minded scientist than the tough, diamond-hard Soto Zen master and abbot to New York's Zen community. At moments I got the feeling that he was purposely refusing to draw attention to himself, almost to the extent that he seemed barely able to articulate what he was talking about. This, though, would be "trying to do something," or even "trying not to do something" (as opposed to "not trying to do anything"), and as such would not be Zen. Besides, his accomplishments say otherwise.

Glassman's appearance is only one of many ostensible contradictions that swirl around this man like tea leaves in a monsoon. Japanese

Zen has traditionally kept its distance from the realm of commerce, and Glassman has been criticized within his own Zen community for wearing too many hats, for putting business ahead of spiritual matters. In a profile in Helen Tworkov's book *Zen in America*, he is quoted as saying: "If I had to choose between being something called 'spiritual director' and being 'business manager,' I'd choose the business." Maybe it's just his Brooklyn Jewish background, which has more recently urged him into social action, but the bakery is thriving and, according to no less populist an authority than the *Daily News*, is producing the best cheese cake in New York City (the chocolate version of which I was later able to vouch for personally). When I asked him about the Tworkov quote, he insisted that he never said it that way, that what he really meant was that he dislikes the word "spiritual" because he doesn't know what it means. "I'm a Zen priest," he said. "I know what *that* means. I'm a social activist. I teach Zen meditation. I run businesses. I just don't know what's meant by 'spiritual teacher.' "

Quite a few of his former students might agree. Many have left (and occasionally returned) as their abbot has taken Zen Center New York (ZCNY), which he founded in 1980, in unexpected directions. Glassman pointed out that not only is he in a "transition mode" in his teaching, but that "Zen in this country is in a transition mode. I'm not just repeating what was taught in Japan." In fact, the Japanese masters who brought Zen to this country may have had just that in mind. About a century ago, they began to feel that Zen in Japan was becoming, in Tworkov's words, "impoverished, sapped of true spiritual inquiry." As one American student of Zen later pointed out to me, Japanese masters often treat Zen like a family business, passing on the monastery with its lucrative graveyard to their children. Unencumbered by social or financial concerns, he said, American Zen is free to develop along more clearly spiritual lines. But even those prescient Japanese masters who sought fresh soil to implant with the seeds of Zen might not have been able to predict the form some American offshoots have taken. No sooner had members of ZCNY become accustomed to running a bakery business, for instance, than Glassman led his center into a social action project that involves renovating an abandoned building into permanent housing for the homeless and engaging the homeless themselves in construction and maintenance of the apartment house. Members who came to the center after the bakery had already been set up were especially taken aback by the new development. "I went through this phase with the bakery," Glassman recalled, "when people would say of it, 'Yes, but is that Zen?' Then when we were starting our social action work, some people who had arrived after the bakery was established came to me very upset. 'Why are you doing social action?' they asked me. 'That's not Zen. Baking—well, *that's* Zen.' "

He confirmed that when he started social action, he lost "a slew of people" who complained, "That's Christian practice, not Zen practice." Conversely, others who had left, disappointed when he got involved in baking instead of the social action they'd been hoping for, returned. So Glassman is used to people questioning whether what he is doing is "really Zen." But he is steadfast in his belief that Zen practice is one of "actualizing the way of enlightenment, and that it is a manifestation of what you are doing. Many Americans think of the Zen of archery, kempo, or of the sword, kendo, as Zen practice. Can you imagine the Buddha thinking of the way of war as Buddhist practice? That came out of the culture of Japan and became associated with Buddhism. I can't associate with that, and yet people would feel much more at ease if I were teaching martial arts. That would seem normal to them, whereas for me, social action and livelihood are much more normal activities for manifesting the enlightened way. We're more comfortable with things we're used to, and I'm not presenting that kind of comfort."

But isn't the essence of the teacher's job to make people constantly uncomfortable, to get them to wake up? "Yes," he said, "and so to become comfortable in *all* situations—become comfortable in life because life is change. That's what Sakyamuni Buddha said: 'It's all change, and because people want it not to be changing, they suffer.' "

Glassman continually emphasizes that his practice of Zen and his unconventional teaching arise directly out of who he is and what his experience has been, arguing that this is in the best Zen tradition going back to the days when it was taught in the rice fields of China. His life began in the Brighton Beach section of Brooklyn in 1939, in a working-class family Glassman described as a "somewhat typical middle-road Jewish family, going to services on High Holy Days, but not as a weekly practice or as a home practice." The environment wasn't religious, and many of his relatives were active in socialist movements, some in the Communist Party. Because of this socialist streak in both sides of the family, he was led to "a heavy questioning of the existence of God, to the point of actually keeping journals and recording what I read from Dostoevsky and all kinds of books." His religious training was limited to Hebrew school "leading up to bar mitzvah." He graduated and was bar-mitzvahed, but didn't continue his Jewish studies after that.

Glassman's real interest lay in engineering and mathematics, but in his junior year of college at the Polytechnic Institute of Brooklyn, for one of the required philosophy courses, he read *The Religions of Man* by Huston Smith. "I was always interested in studying comparative religion, but that was the first time I ran into Zen Buddhism," he said. "There was a page about Zen in the initial printing of that book, and that felt like home to me." The year was 1958, and Glassman started reading everything he could about Zen. When he graduated from college, he told a close friend that there were three things he would like to do. One was to live on a kibbutz in Israel for a while; another was to live in a Zen monastery in Japan; and the third was to live on the streets, in the Bowery. "In those days the Bowery was a hangout for the bums," he said. "Reflecting back, I see that my interest in community was always strong."

So was his interest in social issues. He felt there was "something to be learned from the streets, a way of looking at life. And that's still a key to my feeling about social action. The people involved in social action who inspire me are those who strongly admit that they are learning from the people they are working with. I'm not inspired by people who have standard answers and are going to 'fix up' the situation." For Glassman, it's a question first of looking at a place that needs improvement, and then working with the people in that environment and learning from them, "to create the changes together."

He forgot all about his wish to live on the streets until about a year after he started working with the homeless in 1987. And if that work wasn't enough of a shock to the Zen community, Glassman has stranger things in mind. He is thinking, he said, of "having a retreat on the streets for people who are doing this work." A Zen retreat is called a *sesshin* (pronounced seh-*sheen*), meaning "a unification of mind," and is actually taken from two words. "The first word is *setsu*, which means 'to join' or 'unify,' and the second word is *shin*, meaning 'mind,'" he explained. "In the sesshin, the point is to become of one mind with the whole group. In our community we're creating a structure of the community which is active in five different spheres: the retreat, livelihood or business, social action, study, and communications. I've been looking for a parallel that would make sense for the idea of a sesshin in each of those series of endeavors. For me, to be of one mind in working with the homeless, to have a retreat living in the streets, seemed a natural thing."

Although he didn't attend Jewish day schools, at some point he did decide that he wanted to get more involved in religious studies, and was drawn to the mystical traditions. "I read in the various traditions, including my own," he said. "My first choice would have been Judaism. But when I did my readings, I was attracted by the Hasidic training, and my liberal, secular upbringing made it very hard for me to accept the male-female dichotomies in that tradition. I felt that in order to study it in a genuine way, I would have to become a Hasid and separate from a lot of things I wanted to do. That was not part of my structure, and in the course of my studies I was struck by the openness of Zen, that they will deliver it to anyone who wants to participate. That is definitely an element of my life, in that whenever I've taken a path I've not excluded any of the others. I stay away from paths that are exclusionary of other paths. Not that I think they're wrong, but they're just not my path."

Nonetheless, Glassman kept reading in Judaica, and became friendly with rabbis who taught that tradition. They were, for the most part, "radical like myself," and today he counts as close friends Schlomo Karlbach and Zalmon Schachter, Orthodox rabbis whose families might have difficulty accepting their connection with a Buddhist. Glassman mentioned but wouldn't name one Orthodox man who "couldn't let it be known" that he conducted workshops with Glassman, "because his kids wouldn't have been allowed to go to the schools they went to if people knew he was associating with Zen." Glassman's nonexclusionary nature finds its expression in ZCNY's interfaith community, which includes a rabbi and a Catholic priest and nun. For him, the practices of zazen and Christianity or Judaism are not mutually exclusive. One of his senior monks, a Jesuit priest named Kennedy, is becoming a sensei. He will be a Zen teacher as well as an active priest.

That is hardly uncommon. Harvey Cox tells in his book *Turning East* of developing a meditation practice in the Tibetan Buddhist tradition while remaining a confirmed Baptist. "I came away," he writes of his experiences at Naropa, the Colorado Buddhist center, "convinced that a sitting-type meditation is perfectly compatible with Christian life. Eventually it might even provide a modern equivalent of something we have lost from our heritage, the idea of a Sabbath or a stated time to cease, to do nothing, to allow what is to be." Cox concludes that meditation will continue to be a vital part of his life, adding immeasurably not only to his ability to function but also to his understanding of Christianity. "Learning to meditate," he adds, "does not entail ingesting the entire corpus of Buddhist ideology, doctrine and world view—or any of it. In fact, I believe there is no reason why it cannot become an integral part of Christian discipleship."

Bernard Glassman's interest in engineering began as "a naive kind of thing," based on a liking for airplanes that led him to go into aeronautical engineering at Brooklyn Technical High School. But his real aptitude was for mathematics. After receiving his B.A. in aeronautical engineering, he took his master's and Ph.D. in math, specializing in applied mathematics. "What's most interesting to me is the philosophy of math," he said, "new fields like fractals and the mathematics of chaos, and questions like What is a line? What is a point? What is a number? What is a fraction? What is zero? What is infinity?" Those fields and questions include mathematical paradigms that are used to try to explain life. "In a sense, the part of math that intrigued me is what religion is about," he said. "They're both working in the same arenas. How do we perceive things? What is the framework that goes into making up our network of conditioning so that we see things the way we do? Even in terms of math, the concept we have of time determines how we perceive time. We're born with Aristotelian logic. In the East there was a whole different logic frame, and logic frames create a way of dealing with what is."

His actual work in the aerospace industry, though, was in the practical realm of developing new techniques for navigation and interplanetary work. There the questions had a harder edge: How do you get from here to Mars with minimal fuel? Most of Glassman's engineering work was done with McDonnell-Douglas, the aerospace giant. Based in Santa Monica and Huntington Beach in Southern California, the firm sponsored Glassman's doctoral work at UCLA. Although he retired three times, once to go to Israel for a year and once to form a Zen monastery, he came back while carrying on his parallel life as a Zen monk, until he quit for good in 1976.

Around the time he returned from Israel in 1963, he started to sit on his own on a daily basis. He was, he said, "creating my own ways of practice, but nothing clicked." Then in 1967 he met his teacher, Taizan Maezumi-roshi, the Japanese master of Zen Center Los Angeles. ("Roshi" is another honorific, the meaning of which varies by use but generally signifies a senior teacher with more experience or authority than a sensei.) Glassman formed a relationship with his teacher that began with coming in every day and grew to taking part in running the center. He was ordained a monk under Maezumi in 1970, and went on to become executive director of ZCLA, where he began his unorthodox ways by buying up real estate, renovating buildings, and running a small publishing company and a clinic for the Mexican-American community in which the center was located.

In 1962, Glassman had married Helen Silverberg, whom he'd met on his trip to Israel. He admits that at first his wife, having been brought up religiously in a Conservative Jewish family in Minneapolis, was very resistant to his work in Zen and his desire to become a monk. In fact, they split up for a time over it. When they got back together, Helen became involved in the practice and is now a Soto priest in her own right. (Zen in America shows the influence of the women's movement: female practitioners are not called nuns here as they are in Japan.) Glassman takes responsibility for some of the difficulties his practice has caused their marriage. "I was a fanatic and probably have always been," he said. "When I got involved with Zen, I was very exclusionary, and that becomes threatening to a relationship. I was putting a lot of time into something which was an unknown, without compromising on it." He acknowledged that, given his current realization of Zen, he "might not have been that fanatical at that period.

But if I wasn't, I might not be where I am now. I would never advise somebody else to be as fanatical, yet I know that if I hadn't been, I wouldn't have gotten done what I did."

Recently, Glassman and his wife separated again after more than twenty-five years of marriage. With their kids grown and out of the house and Helen becoming an independent Zen teacher, Bernie said, "It's like starting new lives. She wants to teach in a different way, not in this community way." Although the separation is amicable, "a separation is a separation. Through those years we had many differences, but she was my student, and she became a teacher under me, so she's my dharmic successor. That was a strong tie, and it was a good life. There were a lot of strains in the kind of life we chose, but the good parts outweighed the bad parts."

Attempting to generalize about how spiritual transformation affects marriage and relationship is probably futile. As with personal development of any sort, when people grow at different rates, they may grow apart. Some with whom I spoke told of how their spiritual growth made them closer, others of how it led to separation or divorce. The Glassmans' spiritual practice probably did as much to keep them together as to tear them apart. They did choose to have their children bar- and bat-mitzvahed, largely at Helen's insistence. Bernard agreed that, since the children were being brought up in a Zen center, it was good for them to experience the Jewish tradition from which their parents came. "I am interested in religion," he said, "so for them to study it in a deeper way felt good to me. They actually had very good Jewish training. They know the Bible and the Talmud and the Gemara, as well as Buddhism."

Balancing a full-time job at McDonnell-Douglas and practice as a Zen monk was more of a problem for his marriage than for his employers—even though he took so much time off work for extended sesshins. "At first that was not the thing to be doing in the aerospace industry," he said, "but in later years it came to be more accepted. In fact, at one point they were looking at me to lead a program on creativity within the corporation, and to give classes on Zen meditation to the Management Club. But even in the early years I was always accepted as an individual, and they were very lenient."

Glassman's work at McDonnell-Douglas included, among other things, the Delta Space Vehicle—weather and communications satellites—and a project to develop interplanetary handbooks, listings of the optimum times to launch flights to Mars and the outer planets. His job required calculating "swing-by trajectories," whereby a craft flies past Venus, for instance, and uses the gravitational attraction of the planet's mass to catapult itself on to Mars. "We created handbooks that showed the right days in the right months for the next hundred years to do these kinds of things, based on the alignment of the planets. You can always do it, but depending on the alignments, sometimes you're going to need less fuel than at other times, and sometimes the path will take longer than others. In the days when I was working on it, they were thinking of manned missions to Mars, and depending on when you went, a round trip could take anywhere from two to five years. It was very important to pick the right windows, and those windows appeared only every two to three years, maybe for one month." The slingshot effect of planetary swing-by is still being utilized on missions to the outer planets. "They use Jupiter, which is so huge that if you didn't do that, it would take forever to get to those outer planets." Glassman still follows space exploration projects with some interest, although he follows new theories in math much more closely.

But what does all this have to do with spirituality? For one thing, Zen teachers create different methods to help their students achieve the openings that lead to enlightenment. "Since the methods are clearly a function of culture, the methods change," he said. "What one perceives doesn't change, and what we're after doesn't change, but the methodology changes depending on the cultures, and the time within a given culture. A thousand years ago we would have come up with different ways, but today I use paradigms that involve math and science because that's part of who I am. What is inherent in our Judeo-Christian background creates methodologies that make it easier for us to do things."

But before we started discussing methodology, I wanted Glassman to explain exactly what the goal of that methodology is. "*Zazen* is translated as 'sitting meditation,' " he began. "One way of thinking of that word is as a technique for Zen meditation. And then there's an absolute sense of the word. The brain functions dualistically—that is, it separates the perceiver from the perceived. Zazen is a way of attaining that state of mind in which one perceives no separation between object and subject, no dichotomy. Logically speaking, that doesn't particularly make sense, because to perceive something implies a perceiver and the thing perceived. But that's just logic, and the reality is that you can directly experience something without that subject-object split. The trick is to *see* that state of mind. That seeing or realizing the state of mind in which there is no dichotomy is called the enlightenment experience.

"Normally, you would think that if you're in that unified state of mind, there'd be no way to know that you're there. So it requires a 'meta-leap' out of the plane in which you can see the Oneness. By definition, to perceive the state of Oneness means that you're *not* in a state of Oneness. But in the true enlightened experience, you do perceive that state. It can be done, and has been done throughout the centuries by all kinds of people. And since, in reality, we're all in that state of Oneness already and only our dualistic mind creates an image that's different, that implies that zazen is the normal state of being."

If only we were aware of our true nature, Glassman is saying, we would not need extraneous techniques to wake us up. Since, however, apart from a few genuine mystics and enlightened beings, we do not generally experience such a unitive awareness—the Cosmic Consciousness of R. M. Bucke, an oceanic experience of being united with the universe or Godhead—other measures are indicated. "There are techniques to enable the individual to perceive that state," Glassman said, "and that's called realization. Then we develop techniques to *actualize* what we perceive. At the moment of perceiving the state of Oneness, there is usually some kind of effect, but we're so conditioned to ways of being that habit takes over. Zen practice continues to try to incorporate that realization into one's actual life."

This is the moment-to-moment awareness of which so many teachers speak, the sense that enlightenment is not a one-time experience but an ongoing process. In the Zen system, that process must be constantly abetted by various methodologies, such as meditation or koan study, or else the most powerful opening will dissipate. It may even become a trap, fooling the student into thinking he or she has really achieved something. For Bernard Glassman, social action is one such methodology. "Social action is so ingrained in the Judeo-Christian system," he said, "that it is more natural for us to do than monastic training or cave living. In China, for example, Zen developed on the farm. Their monasteries became self-sufficient. They emphasized work, and the work was rice farming. In Japan, the arts became very important, so we see Zen being taught in flower arrangement, calligraphy, poetry, Tea Ceremony. One of the things I'm doing here, which some people criticize and others like, is coming up with an American style of Zen. Some people say I'm moving too far away from the Japanese traditions. But I am experimenting with both livelihood business and social action, which are integral parts of our culture."

As an adjunct to the sitting practice, Zen uses the koan to free the mind from its rational predispositions. "Enlightenment always comes after the road of thinking is blocked," as the thirteenth-century Chinese master Mumon put it. Koans are emphasized by the Rinzai school of Zen, and although Glassman is a lineage holder* in Soto, Zen's other principal school, which emphasizes silent practice, he has mastered koan study as well. "In different times and cultures, teachers have created different ways of study," he explained. "Koans are one of those ways, and there are different kinds of koans. A koan could be a problem or question given to a student to work on, the purpose of which would be to try to bring the intellectual process to an end, to present something which could only be grasped experientially, not in a descriptive fashion.

"It could be a phrase or a question like Who am I? What is the taste of coffee? But koans can also arise as part of daily life, which is how they originally did arise. In most cases, a monk was working in the fields, and a student who had a burning issue would ask him about it. They would then work on that issue until they had some realization about it. The question and answer were recorded and became a koan. A student might have read something in a sutra book,

---

* Lineage refers to a continuous line of transmission from the founder of a particular spiritual discipline or school down to the present. In most traditions, a teacher who holds a lineage is understood to be conveying the uncorrupted teaching of the original Master and/or certain other teachers along the way. As a holder of the Soto lineage, Glassman can trace a direct line back from his teacher Maezumi-roshi to Dogen-zenji, the founder of the Soto line, and through Dogen to the Buddha. Of course, lineages are often disputed; the schism between Sunni and Shiite Muslims is based on a dispute over the line of succession from Muhammad. In the West, the Roman Catholic Church bases its claim of authenticity on an unbroken line of transmission from Jesus Christ down through the popes, beginning with Peter—a lineage that is disputed by virtually every other Christian denomination.

and ask his teacher, for instance, 'It says that everyone is the Buddha, and yet we keep practicing for so many years. If everyone is the Buddha, why do we have to practice?' "

That particular question became a major issue for Dogen-zenji, the thirteenth-century Japanese master and founder of the Soto line. "He kept with that question for years, and traveled with it and tried to resolve it," Glassman said. "It wasn't a casual thing. Many issues occurred during the day, and the teacher would use those issues to keep the student in the soup, so to say. A teacher might see that a student was coming to him with a burning desire to resolve something, and he might say or do something that would force the student to ponder, to go into himself. In a sense, work practice is the same thing for me. I use situations where people have to do things they don't like to do, to keep them in the soup. I place people in certain work environments where issues come up which they can't intellectualize themselves out of. They have to experience the solution. Let's say a person has trouble relating with certain kinds of people. I might put him in a situation in which that kind of relation is going to come up over and over, and eventually he either has to give up or experience a way of that relationship's working. What I give a student may be something which came up in somebody else's life but is meaningful for *this* person's life. Once you understand the process, you can create koans yourself. The answers are always in the individual realizing the solution himself or herself. It's never an intellectual answer, and it's never something in which the teacher presents the answer."

Glassman has been known to move students working in the bakery from job to job just as they become comfortable in each new position. It's a training in flexibility, in living with change, but it's not something he does frivolously or at the expense of the work being adequately performed. "For me, work practice also involves being at one with the work," he said. "If we have a bakery, I want it to be the best bakery there is. The workplace is not just a laboratory for transformation, but also to create good products."

Likewise, the purpose of koan study is never just to understand what the question and answer signify. "That," he said, "could be done in five or ten minutes of reading or explanation." Glassman himself achieved his first *kensho*, or enlightenment, while meditating on the classical koan Mu. The story goes that a monk asked Joshu, the great ninth-century Chinese Zen master, "Does a dog have Buddha nature or not?" Joshu's answer was "*Mu!*" which is the Chinese symbol of negation, meaning "Not," or "No thing." Explanations I had read of this and of the "one hand clapping" koan go on and on and make only the most marginal kind of logical sense. Since no rational explanation is possible, I was curious at least to know what Glassman's experience of kensho was like. He was evasive the first time I asked, saying that it had been written about elsewhere. When I insisted I'd rather have it in his own words, he began a fairly abstract discussion of enlightenment that had little to do with his personal experience.

Later I studied the account of his enlightenment in Matthiessen's book, and found it very moving. During a subsequent phone conversation, I again tried to get Glassman to explain it, but he demurred. "It's awkward to describe those things," he said. "And as time goes on, it almost feels like there's nothing to describe." Unlike many Japanese teachers, he plays down the actual enlightenment experience for his students, saying only that "it must come," but deflecting attention from when and how. Yet in the account of his enlightenment in *Nine-Headed Dragon River*, it sounds momentous. After meditating on the koan Mu for three days during a sesshin, Glassman felt that he had passed through it, and his teachers Maezumi-roshi and Koryu-roshi felt he was on the brink of a major breakthrough. "I must have been right at the edge of something very powerful," Matthiessen quotes him as saying. "I was still concentrating when I returned to the zendo, and right away I entered a different space, really beautiful, exquisite, very deep.

"All of a sudden, Maezumi-sensei shook me out of that space by really blasting me with MU! He . . . knew that I was right on the point of explosion. So after I sat down, he stood right behind me, I don't know how long he stood there, but when he saw that I was really settled in, he yelled MU! very loud, right there in the zendo! It broke the logjam; the world just fell apart! . . . Koryu and I spent about half an hour just hugging and crying—I was overwhelmed. At the next meal—I was head server—tears were pouring down my face as I served Koryu-roshi, and afterwards, when I went out of the zendo—well, there was a tree there, and looking at the tree, I didn't feel it was a tree, it went deeper than that. I felt the wind on me, I felt the birds on me, all separation was completely gone."

As if to underscore the point that openings need not occur only in the context of the meditation hall or during koan study, Glassman goes on in Matthiessen's account to relate a second experience, which occurred as he was driving to work in a car pool at McDonnell-Douglas one morning. It was triggered by a book he was reading in the back seat of the car:

> A powerful opening occurred right in the car, much more powerful than the first. One phrase triggered it, and all my questions were resolved. I couldn't stop laughing or crying, both at once, and the people in the car were very upset and concerned, they didn't have any idea what was happening, and I kept telling them there was nothing to worry about! . . . Luckily I was an executive and had my own office, but I just couldn't stop laughing and crying, and finally I had to go home.
>
> That opening brought with it a tremendous feeling about the suffering in the world; it was a much more compassionate opening than the first.

Discussing the koan that had triggered his first opening, Glassman emphasized to me the importance of going beyond any rational understanding of the question. Instead, the student must "get past the realm of discrimination and become Joshu's answer, become Mu itself. We're trying to get the student to get past the discriminative mind and become one with *something*. It could be a rock, or a raindrop, or the sound *Mu*. It doesn't matter. The value of the koan Mu is that it's just a sound, and there's nothing to grasp intellectually. If we ask you to become yourself or to become a dog, there are too many traps. This is very clean, but it requires a lot of concentration to achieve that state. Once you do achieve it, then the point is to try to see that state. Of course, if you're in a state of being at one with something, to see it means that you're coming out of it, so that in itself is a bit of a paradox. But it's a paradox of language and of our way of thinking. Once you get into that state, something will occur. You will make a meta-leap out of that state of Oneness and see what that state is. That is the experience that is called seeing True Nature. That is kensho."

It turns out not to be quite that simple, though, since what matters as much as the experience is the clarity or depth of the seeing. "What you're seeing is always the same, but how clearly you're seeing it varies from incident to incident," Sensei Glassman said. "Even after having a kensho experience, it can take many years to clarify it. Without work, it just fades away into a memory." And so you need to continue the daily practice of zazen. For Glassman, having the initial kensho experience is like "an entrance exam into school." It signals the beginning of real study in a different kind of curriculum.

Some years ago, I heard the story of a Japanese Zen student who passed around a book of answers to koans. Not knowing the particulars, I asked Glassman if this had caused a scandal in Zen circles. Answering elliptically, he said, "It was a scandal and not a scandal. Every time you create a system, there is degeneration of the system. The koan system had become codified, and in some sects you had to pass a certain amount of koans in order to leave the temple. There were pat answers and some students turned to bribes: 'I'll give you some cake if you pass me.' Of course, that's not the point. Since we're looking for the student to experience it, simply knowing the answer doesn't mean anything. If I sense that you haven't experienced this koan, then you haven't passed it. But since that was happening, somebody published a whole series of answers just to try to put an end to it."

The aim of koan study is similar to that of most techniques meant to foster enlightenment: letting go of the self. For Glassman, that means "letting go of the attachments to one's conditioning, one's concepts. We all have certain ideas of how things are, and in and of itself there's nothing wrong with that. The problem is that we become attached to those ideas and think they're reality. If I can let go of that, then from my standpoint I've let go of the self, because the self is that fixed notion of 'This is who I am, and this is how I see things.' I've become part of the whole. Seeing the whole doesn't mean one doesn't realize that each individual is different. If you see the whole of your body, you also see that the hands and the feet work differently, and the heart and the stomach. The whole consists of many pieces, and each piece is operating differently, as it should, but it is all interconnected, all one thing. You can't cut off the heart without affecting the rest of the body."

The way Glassman describes it, moment-to-moment awareness doesn't sound very much like a mystical state. "I don't think it is," he said. "What makes it mysterious may be that it's so obvious we don't see it. The metaphor I like to use for that form of mystery is a fish swimming in water. He doesn't see the water because he's part of it." There are two schools of thought on how to break down habitual patterns of conditioning. "One is to set up an environment," he said. "For instance, I could say that I know the right way to lead a life that's nondualistic or integrated, and set up an environment which will force people to operate that way. That environment will attract people who want to operate that way and repel those who don't. I would form monasteries, communities, structures, rules and regulations, all based on an understanding of what will help people change their patterns. The second approach is to try to bring people to the realization of what life is, so that they themselves start changing their lives in a natural way. Most teaching involves a combination of the two approaches."

In the former pattern, a monastery sets up the rules of the day concerning how monks work, greet each other, wash, eat, sleep, and so forth. The drawback is that those very rules can become habitual. "So you always have people reforming and saying, 'Uh-oh, it's going too far.' That's what happened with koan studies. Even before somebody published that book of answers, famous teachers had burnt all the collections of koans and the commentaries so they wouldn't be recorded. Dogen-zenji created a monastery where he ritualized every moment of the day. Eventually, that became encrustated, and people had to break that apart. It's a constant process." Glassman prefers to mix monastic regulations with individual realization. The mission statement for ZCNY speaks of an integration of "zazen and livelihood and social action and communications and study in order to create an enlightened interfaith community."

The word "interfaith" has a curious resonance in this context. Zen is a school of the religion of Buddhism; zazen is a technique for meditation, and is not religious per se. "A Catholic priest or a rabbi who studies here is studying zazen," Glassman said, "but is not learning Buddhist liturgy. We're not trying to make a mishmash of things. Our zendo had no images and was a place where we could all sit together. I'm a Buddhist priest, and I conduct Buddhist liturgy, just as a Catholic priest conducts Catholic liturgy, or a rabbi Jewish liturgy. The liturgies are different, just as livelihoods are different. We have the livelihood of a bakery. Somebody else could be a carpenter. And yet we can all do zazen."

Still, since most people attracted to Zen Buddhism are fleeing their own religions, things associated with those religions stand in the way. During the center's first year, Glassman dismayed some of the Jewish members of the monastery by having a rabbi lead Rosh Hashannah–Yom Kippur services. "They said they didn't leave Judaism to come to a place where there'd be Jewish services. The Catholics were saying the same thing. The first mass really caught people up short. They didn't have to go to these services, but they didn't even want them in the same building they came to for Buddhist practice."

In any discussion of religious communities, the issue of the relation between the priest class and the laity often appears, as it did with the Roman Catholic couple, Dan and Harriet Carew, in Chapter 5. Glassman does not feel that the monastic life has anything over the lay life. "The person who goes to church or temple and says prayers and leads the lay life is just as valuable as the monk," he said. "As a priest, I'm choosing the street ministry life, so I could hardly believe that the person in the monastery is more of a Zen practitioner than the person in the parish." He agrees that the majority of temple-goers, especially in Japan, have no real practice. They were born into it and they do it by rote. "But that could be just as true in a monastery. You can go away to a monastery for reasons that are not religious. You could be an escapist. You could be doing all the services and still not, as far as I'm concerned, have any religious life. You could be parroting. The key is whether you're putting the teachings into action. Yasutani-roshi [one of Maezumi's teachers] gave as an example that you could take a mannequin in a store window and put it into the form of someone doing sitting meditation, but that doesn't make the doll a Zen practitioner."

The prejudice in favor of monastic existence, however, is as deeply ingrained in the Buddhist tradition as the belief in the superiority of religious vocations is in Catholicism. "The Theravaden tradition in India out of which Buddhism comes was exactly that," Glassman said. "Mahayana was a reform movement that tried to change it, but in the original Theravaden practice you evolved into a monk, and the laity was there to support the monks. If the lay person led a good life, he would eventually be reborn so he could become a monk, but only the monks could be enlightened." In distinguishing zazen from Buddhist liturgy, which involves prayers, chants, rituals, and scripture study, Glassman described sitting as "trying to experience reality, whereas liturgy is the celebration, in your own tradition, of the expression you've found. You're creating a way of celebrating the unity of life, of what you've experienced. There should be time for meditation and periodic retreats, just as there should be periodic celebrations and feasts." He expects at least an hour a day of sitting from his monks, noting that most monasteries in Japan sit for only forty minutes a day.

His method of instructing individuals in zazen is unique to each situation. "Since I've studied many types, it all depends on the individual," he said. "I use different meditation practices depending on the particular individual and what I think would work for the personality. We now have a study program in our community in which new members get to know themselves first. They're here for a fair amount of time before I get involved in a direct practice with them. By then, they have gone through a process of exploring and learning how to befriend themselves, learning about different practices, and dealing with questions such as, What constitutes enlightenment?"

The fundamentals of zazen are simple enough. "The basic idea is to be able to sit quietly and comfortably for around thirty minutes," he said. "We have a number of recommended postures, from sitting in a chair to cross-legged on a cushion. There's nothing inherent in the postures. They're aimed at creating a comfortable, centered body so that you can stay still and quiet, so that the thought process can slow down. In our approach, we are not trying to stop thoughts or to stop any of the methods of perception, whether of the brain or tactile. But we do not want to play with them or be attached to them. If a thought comes, we let it come and then let it go. We don't start playing with that thought. If a sound comes, it comes and goes. This is called 'mirror mind.' It's the same kind of sense as when something passes in front of a mirror and is reflected there. Whatever appears, appears. When it leaves, it's gone. No residue stays in the mirror. That's the process we're looking for in meditation. We're not trying to create silence or some euphoric state, or to keep anything out. Whatever occurs, occurs, and then falls away."

If that's all zazen is, how does it lead to enlightenment? Sensei Glassman explained that, if one follows the process he had just described, "eventually there are gaps between the time when thoughts arise and thoughts don't arise, and that is the space of what I was talking about before: a direct experience with no subject-object split. As those gaps increase, one experiences what that is. Eventually one experiences the state of Oneness." On a more quotidian level, "your functioning also becomes more immediate. The conditioning falls away and you're just reacting to what comes up. Different techniques are aimed at trying to bring about those gaps more quickly, or to increase one's ability to concentrate so that one can penetrate those gaps and focus better. It all gets into the technique."

Although silence is not stressed in conventional Jewish and Christian practice, yet it is there. "In the Bible," Glassman said, "there's that sense of 'out of the stillness comes a large voice.' It's that same gap. The 'still point' that T. S. Eliot writes about is that point. It occurs in every tradition, and that's why we can all sit together. Once we come out of that space of unity, we create different languages, different liturgies, different rituals. If you experience that still point, no matter what language you speak, you will have a sense of recognition, and want to express it to somebody who speaks your language. But even if they don't speak your language, you still know that they've experienced it."

Forced to choose between the solitary and the communal practice of spirituality, Bernard Glassman's orientation is, of course, toward the communal. "In Buddhism we talk about Buddha, Dharma, Sangha as three treasures," he said. "One way of looking at the Buddha treasure is as the enlightenment experience, the Dharma treasure as the teachings of the Enlightened Being, and the Sangha as the community of disciples. Teachers lean toward one or the other, and my leaning would probably be Sangha. Sakyamuni Buddha's strength was that he perceived clearly—that is the Buddha treasure—and he taught, which is the Dharma. But he worked in a large sangha. Some teachers have deep enlightenment experiences and then train people to have that, but they work in very narrow confines. And some people work in large communities, but don't have much depth of perception. I'm trying to work in a large communal parameter because I feel that the enlightenment experience can be broadened only if one works in that community environment. Without communal relationships, you can stay within your confines and still become very accomplished.

But once it opens up, you have to work on difficult relationship stuff. It's like getting married. When you marry, you have to work on relationships, and that starts a broadening of your sphere."

Glassman's sense of community is the driving force behind his latest project of turning a Yonkers building into permanent housing for the homeless. The members of ZCNY looked around the neighborhood of the bakery and saw that they were in a very poor area. As they were weighing where to put their energies, Glassman got a letter of request from the local men's shelter asking for help in preparing meals for the soup kitchen. "We responded to their plea," he said, "but in talking with the people who ran the shelter, we found out the plight of the homeless women and children in our area. That gripped our hearts. It was the closest to us, and I felt we could do something about it."

At the same time, Glassman decided to sell the Zen Center's home, a $600,000 mansion in Riverdale, to raise money for the project. By moving into the neighborhood where the homeless were, the Zen community could also, following his sense of koan study, "become one with the problem. I couldn't live in Riverdale while working on a homeless issue in southwest Yonkers. I put the building up for sale without knowing where we were going to live. If we sold it before we found a place to live, we would be in the streets." The move cost him more members, because the mansion itself, purchased with profits from the bakery, had been an appealing attraction with its aesthetically pleasing zendo. Instead, he put their new meditation center on the top floor of the bakery, "right next door to an all-night bar with prostitutes and a lot of noise—a very different scene."

The renovation project has been carefully thought out, not only in the choice of the building but also in setting up self-sustaining machinery for making sure that the homeless families who inhabit the building will be able to continue living there and supporting themselves without welfare assistance. The overall plan includes a support group for people who move in, a construction company of skilled builders who will train some of the homeless to work on the house and to use those skills for future work, a newsletter, and a fellowship group along the lines of AA to help the inhabitants deal with psychological issues, including drug and alcohol abuse and child care. Prerequisites for entry into the building include the new occupants'

BUT IS IT ZEN? • 165

willingness to get off welfare and to get involved in the fellowship program. They will be required to meet in that support group for about a year before they move in.

Glassman intends for the renovation project to spread out into the wider society and to serve as a model for other programs, succeeding because it avoids the pitfalls of the "welfare model." "There's a business sense to what we're doing," he said. "Our model is to become self-sufficient. Our goal is for people who come into our building to get off welfare within a year." Although none of the homeless has yet become involved in Zen, some of them do work with the Baptist Church. "Transformation of the person is an integral part of our model, whether it's the kensho experience or a transformation that comes about in their own tradition. Without that aspect of religious transformation the project will not work."

That brought him back to the stillness, meditation, that is at the heart of Zen. "Silence plays a big role in that," Glassman said, "and whether it's through zazen or prayer or strict silence doesn't matter. From that silence, the realization of the realm of Oneness appears. Nonsilence creates dichotomies, which is why it's important to have daily sitting practice to keep that state alive and fresh and not just a memory. Any form of liturgy in which you express that is valid. The silence at the center is always the same, but the forms are always different. If you can grasp that center, then you can't have religious intolerance because you see that those forms are just manifestations of it. But if you're hooked up with the forms, then intolerance creeps in because you think one form is better than another.

"Religions go astray in two ways. One is when they become attached to the forms, to the relative world, to the expedient means that those religions have produced. And the other is when they get attached to that still point, to the absolute, and think that's the only thing of value and that everything in the relative world is immaterial. Buddhism teaches that they're both the same thing, and that you have to walk in both spheres at the same time. Normally we get caught in one or the other, and that's the trap. As far as I'm concerned, a life spent in a cave by oneself is just as meaningful as a life spent working in the slums. It depends on who the person is, and how that person is going to manifest his or her life."

CHAPTER 10

Jerome Washington: Minimum Security

. . .

The crucified Christ is a terrible sight and I cannot help associating it with the sadistic impulse of a physically affected brain. Christians would say that crucifixion means crucifying the self or the flesh, since without subduing the self we cannot obtain moral perfection. This is where Buddhism differs from Christianity. Buddhism declares that there is from the very beginning no self to crucify. . . . When we look at the Nirvana picture we have an entirely different impression. What a contrast between the crucifixion-image of Christ and the picture of the Buddha lying on a bed surrounded by his disciples and other beings non-human as well as human! Is it not interesting and inspiring to see all kinds of animals coming together to mourn the death of Buddha?
—D. T. Suzuki, *Mysticism: Christian and Buddhist*

> When I embrace my karma
> as I embraced my deeds,
> waterfalls become quiet ponds.
> —Jerome Washington, *One Crow/One Buddha**

.

Since its inception in the fifth century before Christ, Buddhism has splintered into nearly as many sects as Christianity. Theravada is considered the oldest school, having originated in India but now dominant in Sri Lanka and across Southeast Asia. But in America, alongside

* New York: Dem Dare Books, 1990.

Zen, the most popular forms are the orders known collectively as Tibetan Buddhism. The oldest of these, Nyingmapa, which originated in the eighth century, settled here in the San Francisco area. The latest is the Gelugpa Order, founded in the fifteenth century, to which both the Panchen and Dalai Lamas belong. In between are the Sakya Order, and the Kagyü, possibly the best known here because of the influence of the charismatic and controversial Tibetan, Chögyam Trungpa Rinpoche, who is responsible for its spread in this country. Buddhism has many other sects and subsects, such as Nichiren and Nichiren Shoshu, but apart from Zen, none has captured the American imagination as the Tibetans have.

Jerome Washington is one of close to a million followers of Tibetan Buddhism in America, and like many of them, he was not born into a Buddhist family. He grew up in a fairly conventional African-American Baptist family in New Jersey. But unlike most converts to Buddhism, the greatest transformations in Washington's spiritual life didn't take place in a Buddhist temple or meditation hall, or when he met his first teacher, but in his cells at a series of maximum-security prisons in New York State.

Prior to his incarceration, Washington had been many things: a Vietnam veteran and later an antiwar activist, a member of the civil rights movement who went on voter registration drives in Alabama and Mississippi and took part in the Poor People's March on Washington, a friend of Abbie Hoffman who was dubbed "the first black yippie" by *Realist* editor Paul Krassner, a journalist who wrote extensively for labor and movement publications such as *The Guardian* and the *Panther* (the paper of the Black Panther Party), and for alternative publications including the *Berkeley Barb, East Village Other*, and *The Great Speckled Bird* in Atlanta. He was also a poet and playwright, and by his own account an indifferent student of Buddhism, who liked nothing better than to hang around Manhattan's East Village with fellow writers and frequent jazz clubs.

Washington's status as anti-establishment activist, writer, and bohemian changed radically during the summer of 1972 when he was arrested and charged with two serious crimes. He was working as a copywriter for J. C. Penney catalogues and living on East 25th Street when, late one night, he found himself at an after-hours club, a different scene from his usual jazz haunts. By his own account, Washington "had no business there." But that was where, according to Washington, one thing led to another. "The next thing I know, this guy and I get in a tussle over a gun," he said. "The gun goes off. I leave the guy. He wakes up in the hospital later and says, 'Jerome Washington shot me.' Now if I had gone to the police immediately and said, 'I got in a tussle with a guy, he's unconscious, and I don't know if he's dead or alive,' it would have been a totally different thing. But because I didn't do that, and because I was where I shouldn't have been in the first place, I wound up having to go to prison—not because I was guilty of any crime, but because I was guilty of not taking responsibility for myself."

To make matters worse, the gun that accidentally shot the man he was fighting with had previously been used to commit a murder. Although the gun wasn't his, Washington was convicted of attempted murder and murder. The circumstances surrounding his trial and conviction were hazy at best. As one writer who attended the trial, Kathrin Perutz, later remarked: "Like something in Alice in Wonderland, the trial became curiouser and curiouser. It was the testimony of one man (an admitted felon, loanshark and owner of an after-hours club) against the testimony of another (Washington). The time of the crime could not be pinpointed beyond a 12–14 hour range. Photographs submitted in evidence had been taken a day later. . . ."

Nonetheless, Washington was sentenced to prison for eight and one-third to twenty-five years for the attempted murder and fifteen years to life for the murder. The sentences ran concurrently, and he was paroled after sixteen years and three months. "I did not commit the murder," he said, when we spoke in my apartment in Manhattan. "The attempted murder should have been listed as an accidental shooting. Anyway, the ultimate responsibility is mine, whether or not I'm guilty." Washington's involvement with radical politics made it easier for him to see his unjust conviction as a logical outcome of "how the system works." But it was his Buddhist practice that helped him avoid being devoured by bitterness as he served out his long incarceration in some of New York State's toughest prisons: Greenhaven, Sing Sing, Auburn, and Attica among them.

When I first met Washington in 1989, he had been out of jail for only a few months and was in the process of reacclimating himself to the world. Living in the Bronx, he was teaching a workshop in creative writing to ex-convicts and trying to get his poetry published. He is a slight but compact man, dark-skinned, with a neatly trimmed Afro, dressed in casual but almost conservative clothes. In no discernible way did he present the air of a man who might be expected to wind up in jail, or of one who had just survived sixteen years there. He had certainly kept his sense of humor during all that time behind bars. When I asked him how he had been making the adjustment to life outside of prison, back in New York City, he said, "You mean in *minimum* security'?"

Jerome Washington was born in Trenton, New Jersey, in 1939, the year the World's Fair was in New York. His mother took him to see the Fair, and although he doesn't retain any memories of it, he does have a souvenir penny. "I always tell people I went to the first World's Fair in New York City," he said, "and they say, 'Impossible.' " That may be because, despite everything he's been through, Washington does not look fifty. But he is old enough to remember vividly the de facto segregation he experienced in the local school systems in and around Trenton. He went to an all-black grammar school because there was no other grammar school in the area, and this had a valuable side effect. "In that school I learned more about black history than about mainstream American history," he said. "It surprised me later when I'd run into black students who didn't know about Toussaint L'ouverture or Nat Turner. How could you not know? The answer is that it was not part of 'American History,' and still isn't."

Not until Jerome was in the seventh grade and his family moved to Hamilton Township on the other side of Trenton did he attend an integrated public school. Around the same time, at age thirteen, his aunt made him a present of some four hundred books that had been left in a home she bought. He set out to read them all, from Plato to Shakespeare to Hemingway, including a huge tome called *Bicentennial Studies of Goethe* from the University of Indiana Press, which he struggled to get through with the constant help of a dictionary.

He went to Baptist Sunday School and church, since, as he said, "in black communities, the Baptist church was the hub of the social life of the community. It was a social thing as well as a spiritual thing." But with his precocious readings and his education in black history, Jerome quickly became aware of certain discrepancies in the prevailing attitudes of his church. "In Sunday School, I opened up the book and there was a white Jesus with blond hair and blue eyes," he said. "And the stained-glass windows in the church had a white Jesus with blond hair and blue eyes. I couldn't reconcile that with what I had learned in school about slavery and black history. If Jesus Christ came from the Middle East, then it's unlikely that he would have had blond hair and blue eyes. On the crucifix in church, again Christ was white with blond hair and a blond beard."

This discrepancy wasn't the only thing that bothered Jerome about the Baptist church. "The Sunday School teacher taught a type of afterlife salvation that held that as long as we lived right on earth and suffered and didn't complain, everything was going to be nice in the afterlife. When you die, all of God's children are gonna have shoes, and you're gonna walk all over God's heaven. But I couldn't reconcile that with the fact that when I died, I was going to be on the right hand of this white Jesus hanging on the Cross."

His first confrontation with the forces of organized religion came in that Sunday School. The class had been reading the story of Joshua and the Battle of Jericho, about how Joshua commanded the trumpets to blow and the walls came tumbling down. "At that time I was also getting into jazz," Washington said. "I was turned on to Louis Armstrong, and starting to hear Fats Navarro and some of the bop players. I was sitting in Sunday School when the teacher asked, 'What did you learn today?' That was the standard question, to which you were supposed to give back the party line, the nice little lessons that you should have learned. So I told the teacher, 'I learned that Joshua played a mean horn.' The teacher went absolutely crazy. She couldn't believe that I would say that about Joshua. Shortly after that I began finding reasons to get up too late to go to Sunday School."

Jerome kept going to the regular church services because, he said, "the music was fantastic. I've always loved to hear Baptist preachers preach because of the rhythm. The preaching and the music are in a tradition which jazz and the blues came from." But while going to the Baptist church, he had a feeling for another type of spirituality, for what he called "finding the essence, or making contact with something else." Sometime around ninth grade, he became aware of yoga through a white student in Hamilton High School who showed him some yoga exercises and breathing techniques. "He said that when you do these exercises, you sit in a dark room with a candle and focus on the tip of the flame, and you start to relax and clear your mind. So I tried it." His two brothers shared a room, but he had a room of his own in which he could practice yoga exercises from a book. He had moments of great confusion, but also some moments "when things became very clear and peaceful."

His new practices first came to bear on his life in high school, where he was on the track and football teams. During football practice, as a result of the yoga exercises and breathing, he began to realize "how vicious and violent football really was. I saw that the coach was driving us to beat up other people and to bring blood out of the other team." Jerome quit the football team in his senior year. Over the next few years, through a process of "picking up a little bit here, a little bit there," he learned about Buddhism. One important source of information was the books of Alan Watts, the American interpreter of Zen, where for the first time Washington came across Zen koans. "I'd read a koan a couple of times and immediately perceive the answer to it. Then someone would ask, 'How do you explain that?' I couldn't explain it, but I had a perception of it, a clarity I couldn't translate into words." Meanwhile, he was easing away from his mother and the Baptist community, compelled by his developing desire to be a writer. The community was "based on the principle that you graduate from high school, learn a trade, get married, and have children. You read a book once in a while. A big thing is to go to a movie or to one of those roadhouses and have a barbecued steak dinner with potatoes. Going to Tad's Steak House, that's a big night out."

While the Baptists with whom he grew up were strict moralists, they were not as strict as some of the fundamentalists and Southern Baptists Washington later encountered—followers of Jerry Falwell, for example, who are very different from black Baptists. But he was turned off by the Baptists' passive acceptance of their social position, buttressed by the belief that everything will work out in the sweet by-and-by. "It wasn't until later, during the civil rights movement in the sixties, that Baptist ministers became activists," he said. "And not until the sixties did Baptist churches start taking out those stained-glass windows and putting in windows with black Jesus Christs and black Marys and saints."

In the early sixties, Washington attended Columbia University, then spent three years in the Army as one of the first combat troops to see action in Vietnam. When he returned to New York, he took part in the civil rights and antiwar movements, working with the Southern Christian Leadership Conference (SCLC), the Student Nonviolent Coordinating Committee, and the Congress of Racial Equality. He worked with SCLC during the Poor People's Campaign to March on Washington in 1968, and with the Tompkins Square Community Center at the corner of Tompkins Square Park and East 9th Street, an area of Manhattan's Lower East Side that is now luxury co-ops and condos. That summer, because he had worked in security for the civil rights movement and had a military background, he was sent to select the sites for counterdemonstrations at the Democratic Convention in Chicago.

Around the same time he organized peace rallies for the National Mobilization Against the War in Vietnam, and went on voter registration drives in Mississippi and Alabama. Throughout this period, he also witnessed a proliferation of religious cults. Amid all the social upheaval, "a lot of people were looking for new directions, whether they had been Baptists or Catholics or Jews or whatever. There was a lot of astrology, a lot of Tarot cards. Eastern philosophies became very popular and, to some extent, commercial."

Something else that was becoming popular was drug use. Particularly among college students and certain artists, musicians, and writers, the combination of psychedelic drugs and Eastern philosophy often opened a door to exploring the spiritual realm. Washington's experiences with drugs were modest by sixties standards, limited to smoking grass and experimenting with LSD. "By doing those mind-altering drugs, I felt as though I'd made contact with some force," he said. It was the same kind of force that he had come across in his readings of Eastern religious literature. "I didn't find that in Christianity or Judaism," he said, "but I found it in the stories from the East. I read about mind things like teleportation, being able to transmit yourself over long distances. When I was high on LSD, I often felt I was doing these things, or I saw things that I wasn't normally aware of. You start feeling as if you can see atoms. You look in the refrigerator and you see stringbeans, and you've never seen any stringbeans like that before. This is immediate realization, the enlightenment that you read about in books."

The concatenation of having these kinds of extrasensory experiences on drugs and reading about altered states of consciousness in Eastern religion helped move Washington along on his journey, even after he stopped using drugs. The next step came in the form of an introductory book on Zen by D. T. Suzuki, "written expressly to put Buddhism into a logical or understandable form for the Western mind. It was a history, more academic than mystical, and it explained a lot of things that I didn't get from reading the Buddhist texts. I read it two or three times, and I carried a copy of it for years." That book more than anything else got Washington started in the practice of Buddhism "as a religious belief, as a philosophical belief, as developing a way of life. I now had an understanding of how some of the aspects of Buddhism functioned, how the world functioned and how I related to it. Some people say they were exposed to a teacher, that they happened to hear a certain person speak. One person told me he turned on the television when Alan Watts was on, and the moment of seeing Alan Watts triggered him. Another friend heard somebody give a lecture. But for me it was that book."

After reading Suzuki's book, Washington took courses at the New School, where he was further influenced by a charismatic teacher named John Brzostoski. Teaching a survey course on Buddhism, Brzostoski injected it with his own brand of Zen attitudes. Washington recalled one time in the class that was "a major turning point. He threw me a book of matches, and at his direction, I took one of the matches out of the book, struck it, then put it out. He said, 'Did you waste a match?' And I said, 'No. The match was intended to be struck and create a fire. That's not a wasted match. Whatever you *use* it for is something else.' John just stood there and laughed, and the way he laughed opened my head and unified everything in one moment. I don't know if I could call it spiritual, or a sudden realization, but after that I became interested in understanding how Buddhist concepts were put into everyday practice."

Besides his civil rights and antiwar activism and his work as a journalist and editor throughout the sixties and early seventies, Washington spent his time writing poetry, reading it with Allen Ginsberg, Ted Joans, and others, and hanging out with jazz musicians. But the fun came to an end on that fateful August night in 1972, outside the after-hours club. After being arrested, he was sent to the old Manhattan House of Detention, known as the Tombs, and he spent more than a year there awaiting trial, an experience he refers to as "very traumatizing." But one of the first things he discovered was that, "in prison, religion is very big. Everybody in the place is looking for something to save them. There are Bibles all over. Once again I could not identify with the Christian religion, so I found books on Buddhism to read, and never talked with the other guys about it, because you can become ostracized by being different." Upon being sentenced, he was sent to Auburn Prison, where he started the practice of meditation in his cell. "For close to twelve years, my practice was a monk's practice, getting up in the morning, doing meditation. Since I was in prison, I had no one as a teacher, no instructor."

In the prison system of that day, inmates had access to a Catholic priest, a Protestant minister, or a rabbi. There were occasional Quaker services and a number of Muslims, but as a Buddhist, Washington was out of luck. From Auburn, he wrote to the American Buddhist Churches in San Francisco. They sent him a large silk hanging print of Sakyamuni Buddha which he promptly hung on the wall of his cell above his bed. He met other inmates at Auburn who were interested in doing yoga, and together they formed a small Buddhist group and tried to find out how to perform Buddhist services. "We wrote again to the Buddhist Churches of America and they sent us information and material, incense and holders and burners," he said. "We got the authorities to give us a schoolroom on Friday evenings where we could chant and sit in meditation. That went on for some months until one by one the guys were transferred to other prisons or released. Finally I was the only one up there. All those years I just did the meditation practices that I learned from books." Then his former wife, Ellen Maslow, who had become a student of Chögyam Trungpa Rinpoche, sent him information about Trungpa and his books *Cutting Through Spiritual Materialism* and *Meditation in Action*, which provided Washington with another kind of breakthrough.

He was surprised to discover that some of the things he had come by on his own, through trial and error, were in those books. "All I had to go by at first was a photograph of a guy sitting in meditation," he said. "I didn't know that you sat on a little cushion. I tried sitting on the floor, but there wasn't enough room in the cell, so I had to sit on the bed. Then I learned to fold up a pillow to put under me. Reading

Trungpa's book, I realized these things are part of traditional practice, so now I had names for them."

Traditional Buddhist meditation also requires the instruction of a master, but Auburn was too far from the nearest Buddhist center to make that feasible. Instead, Ellen put Washington in touch with an old friend from the sixties, Ann Doubilet, a former activist who had been authorized by Trungpa Rinpoche to teach meditation. Doubilet was given permission directly from Trungpa to instruct Jerome by mail, and she did. Meanwhile, Washington was transferred to Attica, where he ran a writing workshop to which he invited Gwendolyn Brooks, whom he counts as his "literary mother," Ishmael Reed, Dennis Mahoney, and Allen Ginsberg, among others. Remembering Ginsberg from his East Village days, he invited him as much for the fact that Ginsberg was a Buddhist as for his literary ability.

After the end of the writing workshop period, they talked about Buddhism. "We sat together in one part of the classroom, just Allen and Peter Orlovsky and I, and Allen instructed me in meditation and sitting and practice," Washington said. "He gave such clear, quick, concise instructions that it took me only six months to understand where he was coming from. One thing Allen said, for example, was, 'Let the meat hang from your bones.' From that I got further into the practice, and I practiced every day in Attica. I'd get up in the morning and sit for a half hour, then forty minutes, and then one hour. At night I would sit for an hour again. Sometimes at noon I didn't go to the mess hall because I didn't want to eat what they were eating, and I would have a chance to sit for another twenty minutes. I noticed that things were happening a lot differently in my life. There were changes in the way I saw things, the way I heard things, the way I related to people, and the way people related to me."

One example of the way he was changing internally while in the belly of the beast had to do with a Buddhist practice of listening and projecting. At Attica at night, he could hear "far-off sounds," a truck on the highway, for instance. But beyond the trucks, in the morning, he could hear crows. "Crows became a very big thing for me," he said, "and I started learning to listen to the way the crow calls in the morning and to understand what the calls meant. There's a call the crow makes when he's out feeding or checking out his territory." By listening to the different calls of the crows in the morning stillness, Washington learned to focus his attention as part of his everyday practice. "Not just sitting in meditation, but focusing and paying attention and really hearing what is being said. Looking at a color and really seeing the color. Smelling something and really smelling it. I would take a week and just practice looking at a color and really seeing it."

At about this time, Washington was given a copy of Shunryu Suzuki's *Zen Mind, Beginner's Mind*. Reading the book, he was again amazed to find a teacher talking about things he had already experienced on his own. For instance, Suzuki wrote, "The most important thing is to express your true nature in the simplest, most adequate way, and to appreciate it in the smallest experience." That appeared to be a confirmation of Jerome's experience of listening to the crows from his prison cell. "In Suzuki-roshi's book," he said, "he talked about satori in the Zen practice and in all Buddhist practices, where there's a little flash of light, as if a light bulb goes on and then goes out. But when it comes on you have an immediate, clear perception of everything. I'd had that a number of times when sitting, but until I read his book I didn't have a name for it or an understanding of what it was." He had already been doing many of the things Suzuki catalogued in his book, focusing his attention on the outgoing breath, for instance, or "constantly going back to the basic practice of right thought, right word, right action. 'Right word' would be the right breath. 'Right action' would be checking my posture and doing it over and over and over, focusing attention on that."

At Attica, Washington stayed out of trouble and worked in the prison hospital as the dental-lab technician, training to make false teeth. There he served under Dr. Swami Krishna, a Hindu who taught him more meditation techniques, such as visualizing a pendulum swinging. "Just as I would visualize a pendulum reaching its outermost arc, I would feel it touch my forehead before swinging back," he recalled. "Dr. Krishna also said, 'If you are a holy man, fire does not burn.' It took me a long time to understand what he was saying— that if you are a holy man, you don't harbor hatred or animosity toward people." Washington was also learning to do his practice "not just for its own sake but to apply it to my life."

One shape that application took was in relation to the prison guards.

He "began to realize in dealing with guards that they were as much victims of the system as anybody else. I learned to apply the peacefulness of meditation to everyday life in a violent prison. I learned that when a guard says something to you, you always address the guard politely. Not subserviently, not shuffling, but never getting loud or violent with him, either. And if he gets loud, you react by getting softer. It's like the practice of karate. As a matter of fact, I used to call this mental or oral karate, using the adversary's energy to defeat him." In many instances during his prison term, Washington's confrontations with guards "could have become nasty had they been handled another way. But I would continue to get softer in my approach and absorb their energy. I pointed out to them that they shouldn't be angry at me, but at themselves. That's what I mean by putting into everyday practice what I learned in meditation."

Although the guards usually left Washington alone, on several occasions he took the prison system to court to keep them from interfering with his practice. In 1985, a friend sent three Buddhist artifacts to Washington which were intercepted by the Deputy Superintendent of Security. Two of the artifacts were "lost," and the third, a mask of the Buddha's face made out of papier-mâché, was deemed a security violation: "Since it was a mask, they said it could be used to escape with. But they damaged it so badly, it was beyond use anyway." As a result of that incident, he filed a First Amendment lawsuit against the Department of Corrections and the Superintendent at Greenhaven, alleging religious discrimination. "He wouldn't let me have an image of the Buddha, but he would allow me to have a statue of Jesus Christ." Today, partly through the efforts of Jerome Washington, there is an active Zen sangha in Greenhaven Prison.

Most of the inmates at the state prisons were tolerant of Washington's Buddhism, on the principle that "whatever helps a guy get through the day" is all right. The predominant religion in prison these days may well be Islam, because of its popularity among the black population, and Jerome became closely associated with many Muslims "because there was a certain moral foundation these guys had developed that was much closer to Buddhist morality than to Christianity. They practice their religion every day the way Buddhists do, unlike most Christians who go to church on Sunday and act differently the rest of the week. It even affects the clothes they wear and the kind of food they eat." If he had any problems because of religion, it was more likely a misunderstanding on the part of a guard. For instance, all prisons ban the practice of martial arts. "You're not even supposed to have books on martial arts, because the guards are scared to death of them," he said. "They buy into the myth that one karate guy can take on fifty people. So there were times when a guard would come by my cell while I was meditating in a half-lotus position and would hassle me because, out of ignorance, the guard thought I was doing martial arts."

Washington doubts that he would have gotten through the sixteen years in such good shape without his daily practice of Buddhism. The first hurdle to get over was the perceived injustice of being sent away for crimes he didn't commit. "People say, 'Wow, you spent all that time in prison. Why aren't you bitter? Why don't you hate the guards?' But I know that I was there because I did not assume responsibility for myself. I wasn't escaping the fact that I was in prison. I was very much in touch with where I was. There were a lot of opportunities for me to go insane in prison. I had opportunities to check into the mental joint and stay whacked out on Thorazine and other drugs, or to stay drunk all the time. There's jailhouse wine all over, made with the sanction of the guards, and drugs are all over. Guards are routinely busted for introducing drugs into the prison system. The opportunities are there, but when you give in to them, you're not in touch with where the hell you are. And prison's a dangerous place not to be aware."

What he learned from his Buddhist practice was the need to be in touch with each experience. "It's not a matter of practicing and then going off in a corner and doing something else," he said. "I practice Buddhist belief and then put it *into* practice. As a Buddhist, I dealt with prison first of all by taking absolute responsibility for putting myself in the position to be sent away. This wasn't something that snapped on overnight. It came by a slow process, like a snake shedding its skin."

As Washington's spiritual practice ripened in prison, his literary and journalistic skills bore fruit. At Auburn Prison, he founded and served as editor of the *Auburn Collective*, the first New York State prison newspaper to be nationally recognized. During his four-year term as editor, the *Collective* won fifteen awards for journalistic excellence in feature and news writing and editing. While leading writers' workshops in Auburn and Attica, Washington increased his own output. His plays have since been broadcast on radio, and his short stories, articles, book reviews, and poems have been published in the *Transatlantic Review* and elsewhere. But in 1978, authorities at Auburn, labeling his writings "venom," transferred Washington to Attica and confiscated his typewriter and manuscripts. The following year he sued the State Department of Corrections for First Amendment violations. In winning that suit in 1985, he won for fellow inmates and all future prisoners the freedom to write uncensored material for publication outside of jail.

In the title story from his book *A Bright Spot in the Yard*, a collection of remarkably spare short stories, notes, and sketches written while in prison, he tells the tale of a con named Jomo who finds release from the oppressiveness of prison life by standing in a spot from which "the prison disappears." The other inmates give Jomo a wide berth, with the exception of the narrator, who befriends him and in return learns his secret. Standing on Jomo's "spot" and looking up at the sky, the narrator discovers that Jomo was right. "There was only the open sky, dotted with fluffy, slow moving clouds riding eastbound zephyrs. . . . I relaxed and the weight of the prison was gone. I was a caterpillar suddenly transformed into a butterfly." The narrator's "escape" from the confines of the prison walls begins, as he is transported to foreign shores and experiences in his mind the sights and smells of the Far East and Africa.

The scene recalls Jack London's novel *The Star Rover*, in which an imprisoned narrator escapes his brutal confinement at the hands of a sadistic warden through a series of extended out-of-body visits to past lives. London's story was based on the reportedly true experiences of the turn-of-the-century California outlaw Ed Morrell, and Washington's story is clearly drawn from his own years in prison. In his case, the metaphorical parallels with the author's sitting practice of meditation are hard to ignore. As we know, Eastern spiritual practices such as Buddhism were based on finding ways to escape from suffering. For Washington, writing from prison, the image of the "bright spot" in the prison yard does double duty, representing at once the freedom Buddhism granted him to transcend the dimension of the material body and the relief it offered from prison life.

Now that he is living on the other side of those walls, Washington finds his Buddhist practice no less real or serviceable. "Of course, I'm relearning a lot of things that I knew years ago," he said, "getting back in touch with certain experiences. Maybe I'm overdoing it, but I feel that it's no good to practice any religion if you have to hide behind it, if you always have to stand up and say, 'I'm a good Christian,' or, 'I'm a good Buddhist.' That's of no importance if you are not doing the right things. Sometimes you do what is correct and someone else says it wasn't. But as long as you understand it was correct, that's all you can be accountable for. Sometimes people use their religion to accuse others of infidelity or blasphemy. That is not the way. Religions have to be lived. And I don't even think of Buddhism as religion. I think of it as a system of life. I don't pray to Buddha in the sense that people pray to Jesus Christ."

Since leaving the maximum security of Attica for the world of "minimum security," Washington has found the practice of his spiritual path easier, despite abundant distractions. "I was fortunate to practice in prison," he said, "because now the practice is a cakewalk. I mean, it's baby food out here in the world. It's just a matter of trying to stay on point. Having dealt with the hard stuff in prison, it's much easier to do what I have to do and to set my agenda so I'm not doing harm to anyone else. Taking a vow to do no harm is a very important part of Buddhism."

When it comes to recognizing the validity of other paths, Washington has "very little tolerance for intolerance. I don't care what your belief is, whether it's organized or disorganized, or whether it's just you standing on the street corner by yourself. That's cool with me as long as you're not doing harm to another person. If what you believe in becomes harmful or dangerous to someone else, that bothers me. I don't have any problem with somebody who does TM, but converting by the sword bothers me."

Washington's sense of religious tolerance is fairly inclusive. "Jesus Christ was a prophet," he said. "Muhammad was a prophet. Abraham was a prophet. They were great thinkers in the same sense that Gautama Buddha was. Those were four of the great prophets. Removing the mysticism, you can say that they all taught the same thing. When you read one, you read the others. And I'm quite sure that if any of them was around today, he would say, 'Hey, what are you people talking about? This ain't got nothing to do with anything I said.' As a matter of fact, none of the teachings of the great prophets were organized into religion until after they died. And they were always organized by the disciples, the people who came along later.

"On the other hand, if the message is good, you don't throw the message out because you don't like the messenger. Trungpa was merely a messenger. Gautama Buddha was merely a messenger. When Buddha died, Buddha was dead. He was cold meat. When Trungpa died, Trungpa was dead. He was cold meat. He was a great teacher, but there's a teaching in Buddhism that says 'Kill the teacher,' meaning that you become the teacher and no longer need the teacher. When people get hooked up in gurus and worshipping another being, then they're setting themselves up for extinction."

Since Washington witnessed and participated in several kinds of violence, and since he professes a belief system that holds as one of its chief tenets the avoidance of violence to all sentient beings, I asked him for his feelings on this subject and, by implication, the interrelation of spiritual practice and worldly activity. "We are in a golden age, and at the same time we're in a terrible age," he said. "There's major violence. And even though you can say there's not a major war, if you could talk to the people who are getting killed, they'd tell you it's a major war. People are talking about East and West. I say the whole thing is North and South. The Southern Hemisphere is where all of the emerging nations are looking for their independence, and that's where the wealth of the world is. All those nations have raw materials, the resources that have been plundered and exploited by the nations in the Northern Hemisphere. We've always played the East-West game, but the whole political shift is North-South."

Washington feels strongly that "the 'spiritual' people in the United States who are talking about doing something need to come out and put their spirituality into practice. All these people prophesying about the world to come—that's the same thing that turned me off with Christianity. 'The great pie in the sky in the hereafter.' Show me something now. If you raise your consciousness, put it into practice. If you stay sitting on the side of the mountain, you're not helping anybody else live. It's absolutely important to go out and apply it. In everything, I go back to Gautama Buddha. Gautama was the first teaching Buddha, but he was not the first enlightened person. We don't know who the first enlightened person is. I think the Buddha said, 'I stand on the shoulders of twelve previous Buddhas.' But he went out and taught. If he had just said, 'Man, I'm cool,' and sat back on a rock, we'd never know. Jesus Christ was a prophet. He went out and taught. Muhammad was a prophet, went out and taught. Abraham was a prophet, went out and taught. That's the whole message. They went out and taught, and by doing so, they helped change the world. And they all taught about going forth and spreading the word. So if you come to the realization yourself and find peace and comfort, that's all cool. But if you don't go and deliver that somewhere and put it in some kind of practice that's going to influence somebody else to be cool, then you ain't doing nothing. And that's my whole belief."

CHAPTER 11

Is the New Age Really New?

. . .

There's a new energy coming which is making things very different. In the past, we had to work through things. We had to complete things because there was karma. Now that's not necessary. We're coming to the end of this phase and all that is needed is a waking up. That's just awakening to who we are. The old methods of working through things are no longer appropriate because there's no time for them.
—Paul Lowe, *The Experiment Is Over*

Because America is so fertile, seeking spirituality, it is possible for America to inspire charlatans. Charlatans would not choose to be charlatans unless they were inspired to do so. Otherwise, they would be bank robbers or bandits, inasmuch as they want to make money and become famous. Because America is looking so hard for spirituality, religion becomes an easy way to make money and achieve fame. So we see charlatans in the role of student, *chela*, as well as in the role of guru.
—Chögyam Trungpa Rinpoche, *Cutting Through Spiritual Materialism*

The business of America is business, and that includes the religion business. The greatest irony of the neo-Oriental religious movements is that in their effort to present an alternative to the Western way of life most have succeeded only in adding one more line of spiritual products to the American religious marketplace.
—Harvey Cox, *Turning East*

.

Depending on your predilections, the catch phrase "New Age" can signify a field of fascinating literature and practice that bodes well for the planet, combining personal spiritual growth with physical and psychological well-being to create a new sense of harmony between man and environment, or it can describe a grab bag of laughable, deceptive, potentially dangerous claims made by a bunch of American neo-con men and women who are out to make a quick buck on false hopes. The truth, as usual, is a lot grayer than all that.

Behind the term "New Age" is a significant body of religious practice, much of it spun off from classical Oriental wisdom traditions such as Buddhism, Hinduism, and Taoism, along with a much broader collection of practices that would be hard to classify as religious at all: alternative approaches to healing, creative amalgamations of body-work, psychology, and spiritual techniques, and psychic phenomena such as trance channeling. Part of the difficulty in dealing with the New Age is its enormous diversity. As Jay Stevens wrote in the *Utne Reader*, the New Age presents us with such curious aspects as "the surrealistic collision of the technofuture with the archaic. Discussions of how we will soon be downloading our consciousness into non-destructible robotic objects dance cheek to cheek with disquisitions on how to be a modern shaman or how to perform neolithic mother goddess rituals in your backyard."

Academia has gotten its robes enmeshed in the gears of the New Age machine as well. Take the Tao of Voice, a workshop series taught by a New York University professor. This course promises to "transform your singing/speaking voice for professional advancement and personal joy" by utilizing "the best of Western technique and modern psychophysical approaches unified with ancient Chinese philosophy and breathing practices." Whether you consider it spiritual depends on your definition of spirituality; whether it sounds like a good idea or a rip-off depends on your feelings about New Age practitioners as alternative entrepreneurs.

And if you don't think the New Age is a business, take a look at the ads in *Free Spirit* or *New Age Journal* or *Newlife* or *Fireheart* or any one of the publications that have sprung up in the last decade to service this fast-growing industry. Beyond spiritual practices, New Age advertisements offer psychotherapy, holistic healing, foods, and cleaning products, homeopathic medicines, crystals, music, arts and crafts, oils, perfumes, weight loss and addiction-control services, massage, and countless kinds of bodywork. You can take a holistic vacation, hire a holistic house-cleaning service, and hang out at the New Age Cabaret, "a night club for the personal and social transformation so many people have made a priority." And as if all the subliminal suggestion tapes for self-improvement already on the market weren't enough, you can now Dial-An-Affirmation. (In the name of research, I did, although the ad for this New Age service—which was headlined "What You Need Is A *Good* Talking To"—did not specify the cost per minute. What I heard was a five-minute prerecorded lecture by someone who identified himself only as Jay. "Hey," it began, "I'm really glad you called. You don't know it yet, but soon you will feel how important this call will be for you." Jay explained how valuable it is to take care of ourselves, and how affirmations—sayings that reinforce positive attitudes, e.g., "I am feeling healthier with each passing day"—could help me to get what I want out of life. Finally Jay said, "Enough of me flapping my gums. It's your turn. Hey, don't be shy." I was instructed to press seven-seven on my touchtone phone. When I did, a synthesized-sounding voice came on to say, "You've made an invalid entry. Please press seven-seven to hear the menu." Once more I did, whereupon Jay came back on the line in his calm, nonjudgmental voice. "Let's go through it again," he drawled. "Like I said, just about every week there will be more options for you to play with on this menu." Tired of listening to Jay, I hit seven-seven again. The synthesized voice returned to tell me I had made another invalid entry. "I'm sorry," the voice concluded before I could go any further, "You've made *too many errors*. Please call again soon." With that, it hung up on me. Contemplating the dial tone in my ear, I reflected on my affirmation for the day.)

To make matters more confusing, the New Age goes on to include areas so speculative that the old dictum, which I first heard voiced by a television mentalist named Joseph Dunninger in the mid-1950s, applies with a vengeance: "For those who believe, no explanation is necessary; for those who do not believe, no explanation is possible." Once we start to talk about crystal channeling and magnet therapy ("Few people are aware of the healing energy in magnets," read one ad which would be hard to dispute), then we have crossed the line between the verifiable and the conjectural. A number of people have told me they have experienced almost miraculous cures through obscure, unverifiable therapies, but in my own experience these therapies have produced no more or less dramatic results than allopathic medicine or more established alternatives such as Bioenergetic Analysis or chiropractic. Nonetheless, medical approaches that treat the whole organism rather than symptoms, such as the Indian science of Ayurvedic medicine popularized in this country by Dr. Deepak Chopra, are not only growing in popularity but are also having a salubrious effect on medical doctors trained in conventional Western methodology. If nothing else, those doctors are learning that patients may now expect much more from them in terms of preventive and holistic care, and are being forced for purely economic reasons to provide it.

But there is a big difference between Ayurvedic medicine, which derives from a tradition thousands of years old, and magnet therapy; the only similarity is that both can be labeled "New Age." And if we accept principles espoused by many Eastern schools of wisdom, from Taoism to Kundalini Yoga, that enlightenment is inextricably connected with psychic energy that moves through various energy channels and centers in the body, then the line between the spiritual and the physical can be further blurred to support any number of New Age claims. If body and spirit are one, and spirit is energy, why not heal with magnets?

Precisely how New Age healers are connected to the spiritual practices also labeled "New Age" is unclear, although one thing they have in common is a sense of being "alternative"—either to traditional religion or atheism, or to the medical and psychiatric professions as they are commonly constituted. Unlike traditional religions, New Age beliefs place less emphasis on large communities, elaborate disciplines, and complex moral codes (partly because they haven't been around long enough to accrue them), and more on what Norman Vincent Peale popularized as "positive thinking." For this reason, New Age philosophies are sometimes criticized for avoiding the darker, disavowed feelings and urges which Carl Jung called the "shadow" side of the human psyche, and they may lack the profundity of traditions that have evolved over centuries. Still, for those who have been wounded by the arbitrary strictures of orthodox religion, the New Age does offer a nonjudgmental, do-it-yourself approach to spiritual development, free of old moral and ritualistic baggage.

But just how new is the New Age? Around the turn of the century, William James, in his landmark study of the psychology of belief entitled *The Varieties of Religious Experience*, identified a movement that can be seen as a forerunner of Peale's positive thought power and the New Age in general. James called this the "mind-cure movement," although it referred to itself as, among other things, the "New Thought." As promoted by writers such as Horatio Dresser and Henry Wood in books with titles like *Voices of Freedom, Ideal Suggestion Through Mental Photography,* and *Happiness as Found in Forethought minus Fearthought,* the school included the sect of Christian Science, which sees all illness as an illusion of the mind, and for which evil itself is considered a lie. According to James, mind-cure had several doctrinal sources, including the Gospels, Emersonianism, and Hinduism. "But the most characteristic feature of the mind-cure movement is an inspiration much more direct," he wrote. "The leaders in this faith have had an intuitive belief in the all-saving power of healthy-minded attitudes as such, in the conquering efficacy of courage, hope, and trust, and a correlative contempt for doubt, fear, worry, and all nervously precautionary states of mind."

After enumerating some of the actual cures and cases of moral regeneration laid at the feet of this movement, James remarked that the "mind-cure principles are beginning so to pervade the air that one catches their spirit at second hand. One hears of the 'Gospel of Relaxation,' of the 'Don't Worry Movement,' of people who repeat to themselves, 'Youth, health, vigor!' when dressing in the morning, as their motto for the day. Complaints of the weather are getting to be forbidden in many households; and more and more people are recognizing it to be bad form to speak of disagreeable sensations, or to make much of the ordinary inconveniences and ailments of life." One also hears adumbrations of such latter-day phrases as Herbert Benson's "relaxation response" and the self-proclaimed avatar Meher Baba's "Don't worry; be happy," not to mention the overall triteness and blandness of much of the literature of the New Age movement of today. As James said of the mind-cure movement, with a pungency that still applies, its verbiage "is so moonstruck with optimism and so vaguely expressed that an academically trained intellect finds it almost impossible to read it at all."

From a purely etymological perspective, according to Jay Kinney of *Gnosis* magazine, the term "New Age" was apparently first used in 1914. That same year the Freemasons, a popular esoteric society said to have derived from the Sufi master builders of the Middle Ages, called their publication *New Age*. And Samuel Bercholz, editor-in-chief of Shambhala Publications, a Buddhist-oriented house, points to a pre–World War I weekly newspaper published in London by A. R. Orage* entitled *The New Age*. Orage's paper combined articles on spiritual, political, and psychological subjects by the likes of Shaw, Eliot, and Wells. But origins are less important than what has become of the term, a catch-all for practitioners who are united mainly by their claim that new ways of conceptualizing and healing age-old problems are suddenly available to a vast number of people. If we accept a broad range of quality and authoritativeness, and the vagueness of expression which James derided, then we will have a recognizable, if suitably clumsy, working model of the New Age.

Perhaps predictably, the most skeptical critics of New Age thought are those who most value traditional religion. Lex Hixon, for instance, is a traditionalist, even if his practice of four distinct belief systems makes him a markedly unconventional one. "The New Age concept is the microwave concept that you can cook something instantly," he said when asked about it. "It remains to be seen whether that's good for you in the realm of food, but in the realm of spirituality, you can't concoct a tradition overnight, and you can't reach high realizations except through a whole lifetime of practice. The New Age impulse has so many varieties and shades that it's hard to know what is the thread running through them all. I would say that thread is acceleration, the notion that you don't need to be connected with an ancient tradition with complexities that take a long time to learn. The New Age is saying that in a matter of months or so, you can reach the same spiritual levels that the mature saints and Gnostics reached in traditional contexts after a lifetime of practice. There's a kind of arrogance to that, a modern-world idea that says that since we've been so successful in technology, why couldn't we develop a psychological or spiritual technology more accelerated and maybe more efficient than the earlier ones?"

Conversely, Hixon believes that the longing for a New Age has been around long before Norman Vincent Peale or mind-cure. "Actually,

---

* Among other things, Orage made the first English translation of Gurdjieff's *Meetings with Remarkable Men*.

St. Paul called it the New Aeon," he said. "St. Paul's entire discussion of Christ and his teachings was in the light that a New Age had dawned, that circumcision and certain other factors of Jewish law had been superseded, and something else had been introduced by God. The other disciples were upset by that because they felt that Gentiles should first be circumcised, then baptized. Eventually Peter allowed Paul to carry out his vision, which was a kind of universal Judaism in which you no longer had to have a physical circumcision. In fact, Paul talks about a 'circumcision of the heart.' You could say that was New Age thinking also, but the difference is that it has proved to be justifiable and authentic."

The test of time is precisely antithetical, however, to many New Age proponents who talk in apocalyptic terms not unlike those of fundamentalist Christians, and who believe we are living in the "last days" or the "end time." Paul Lowe, as the epigraph at the start of this chapter indicates, might be considered an advocate of the microwave concept based on his premise that we no longer have time for conventional methods. But when I questioned Lowe about this, he made a finer distinction. In the ancient East, he explained, the process of awakening was long and arduous. Seekers went to a master who determined whether they were ready to learn meditation. "Then the masters gave them a hard time," he said, "having them meditate eighteen hours a day in some cases. This kind of total surrender is almost inconceivable to a Westerner, whose mind tells him it's nonsense. But in the East, you went beyond your own mind. This process took years and years, and even then, only one in hundreds of thousands of meditators actually woke up. Now it's as though the New Age has a casual thing that you can do in half an hour a day."

Among the people with whom Lowe worked, the ones he felt had awakenings "were not New Age people, but ordinary housewives or businessmen. The main thing needed is the intent." So for Paul Lowe, the New Age expectation that half an hour a day of meditation, or listening to peaceful, trance-inducing music, will result in a genuine transformation is misguided. Awakening is not the result of a few painless procedures but of an intense desire to wake up, and time for that may be running out. Lowe's feeling that we don't have much time has been absorbed by his former students, the Kanes (who commented on meditation in Chapter 7). "There's no more time," Shya insisted when we spoke. "You don't have the luxury of time anymore. The planet is on its way out."

"It doesn't take a psychic to notice that," Ariel said.

"Land is getting eaten up faster," Shya said. "There's not much time left for people to wake up. They have to find somebody who's awake and discover how to wake up fast."

Arch Crawford sounds as if he would agree. "I don't know how much Brother Charles was joking about this," he said, referring to his guru of the high-tech meditation tapes, "but he said that in the past it took thirty to fifty years of intense work in a cave, doing a mantra, hearing the reverberation and looking at a mandala on the wall, to coalesce with a Higher Power. He said that his tapes will get you to the same place in twelve years. Of course, nobody's been on the tapes for twelve years, because they haven't been developed that long, so we're watching closely. But people who've been in the program three to five years are having very significant breakthroughs that are like the experiences talked about in the Eastern traditions. Brother Charles said, 'What the heck, this is America. We've got McDonald's. Why can't we have high-tech meditation?' "

Fast food for hard times? We certainly have a right to be skeptical about extreme or unverifiable claims. But what Chögyam Trungpa Rinpoche was warning Americans about in his seminal work *Cutting Through Spiritual Materialism* was not merely the onslaught of opportunistic gurus, cults, and New Age entrepreneurs. He was also calling attention to the tendency of spiritual seekers to collect teachings, paths, and practices to the point where they begin to put faith in their hoard of spiritual knowledge rather than to learn from it and move on. "Our vast collections of knowledge and experience are just part of ego's display," he wrote, "part of the grandiose quality of ego. We display them to the world and, in so doing, reassure ourselves that we exist, safe and secure, as 'spiritual' people. But we have simply created a shop, an antique shop."

The Eastern Orthodox theologian Father Thomas Hopko was not sanguine about the New Age in general or accelerated spiritual practice in particular when we spoke at St. Vladimir's Seminary in Crestwood, New York, where he teaches. "Sometimes I see signs on churches: 'Enter, rest, relax,' and so on," he said. "I think you can sue them for libel, because once you get in there you're going to get smashed, killed, burnt, and redone if you do it right. And you'll say thank you for it in the end. I worry that people will be searching, and what will be given to them? Will it be Shirley MacLaine and crystals? As Chesterton said, When you don't believe in the truth, you don't believe in nothing—you believe in anything. Or as St. Paul would say, 'Any wind of doctrine that comes down can blow you around.' Is there a strong enough root of experienced people onto which the seeking person can graft a community that's authentic, where they can find communion with God, the Ultimate Reality, or whatever you want to call it? I'm not thrilled by the New Age exactly for that reason. I wonder how deep and how serious it is."

On the other hand, Hopko refuses to rule out the possibility that good can come through any avenue. "Without doubt, a type of post-materialistic searching is going on," he said. "People are satiated with things that cannot satisfy, and the emergence of all these pop religions, even the dark Satanic ones, is still positive in that it shows a hunger and a thirst, some kind of longing. I believe in the living God, and if you are a pure-in-heart seeker, God will find the way to satisfy that hunger and thirst. He will raise up people who will be his agent for that. What do the Jews call them? The *lamedvovniks*, the [thirty-six] righteous upon whom the world depends, who keep God's wrath off the rest of us. So if a person is hungering and thirsting and hears that he's got to meditate for twenty minutes a day, and he does it because he wants reality—not because he's looking for the Uncreated Light, or to levitate three feet off the ground—then I believe the living God will lead him or her. There's a Hindu saying, although you can find similar sayings in our tradition: 'When the disciple is ready, the master will appear.' If you're genuinely hungering and thirsting, you're already blessed, and God will work out the details."

One idea on which New Age advocates and traditionalists may be able to agree is that spiritual devotion need not imply a life of extraordinary physical hardship or withdrawal from the mainstream of society. John-Roger, the leader of the Movement of Spiritual Inner Awareness (MSIA), a Los Angeles-based New Age church which combines meditation, positive thinking, and Christ-centered prayer with more esoteric practices such as "aura balancing," takes a stance that is representative of most New Age practitioners. He writes in an introductory pamphlet:

Students of MSIA learn to recognize the illusions of this world and lift beyond the negative forces of jealousy, anger, depression, disappointment, hurt feelings, and upset emotions; they may learn the spiritual exercises that MSIA teaches, learn to use them throughout the day, learn to move in consciousness to those areas of Spirit and Light that lie beyond the physical. They may do all these things and never change their names, their residences, their jobs, or anything outwardly. They may still have families, watch football on TV, go bowling, eat hamburgers, and work on their cars. These are outer things; they have very little to do with spiritual growth. Some people, as their consciousness lifts, may feel it necessary or more comfortable to alter their physical surroundings. This might happen, but it is not necessary. The work of MSIA primarily goes on inwardly. Any outer changes are the choice of the individual involved.

Compare John-Roger's attitude to that of the Gnostic Christians, a disparate group of believers who flourished during the first six centuries after Christ. Their Christianity was infused with elements of Eastern mysticism and esotericism that the established Church ultimately condemned as heretical (and succeeded in eradicating from orthodox Christianity, along with most of the alternative Gospels and other writings of the Gnostics). Vis-à-vis both the non-Christian world and the orthodox Church of their day, those Gnostics may have been in a somewhat similar position to that of New Age believers today—confronted on one side by atheistic humanists who find their beliefs risible, and on the other by traditional believers who find them threatening. The way the Gnostics responded to their dilemma is instructive in its scope. "Some radical Gnostics," writes Marvin W. Meyer in *The Secret Teachings of Jesus*, "apparently retreated from the world to the solitary life of the monk or the ascetic, and refused to participate in the everyday business of human society. Other equally radical Gnostics seem to have flaunted their disdain for conventional human values by disregarding the amenities of polite society and practicing a libertine way of life. Most Gnostics, however, probably led normal lives in society, while engaging in an inner, spiritual quest for God."

That last course, which the Buddhists call the Middle Way—a path somewhere between renunciation of the material world and unquestioning absorption in it—is the one that many of the spiritual seekers in this country have chosen. They may have moved, changed their diet or their life's work, or become active in spiritual communities that are out of the mainstream, but they haven't left the world. Their willingness to remain in it, in fact, may be an indication of their understanding of the process of spiritual transformation.

Whether the New Age is qualitatively different from previous historical movements or eras that have augured massive changes in human consciousness is a fascinating question, but one that is impossible to answer at this time. In the Canadian psychiatrist Richard M. Bucke's classic *Cosmic Consciousness* (1901),* written around the same time as James's *Varieties*, he argued the case for an evolutionary change in mankind from self-consciousness to cosmic or spiritual consciousness—a change that would parallel the prior shift from animal to self-consciousness that had ratified our very identity as human beings. Bucke presented evidence, based on certain extraordinary individuals, that such a change was beginning to occur at an accelerating pace, but even he talked in terms of "many thousands of generations" before this new consciousness would become a universal fact, present from birth in each human heart.

Stepping back further, we might look to the first millennium before Christ, the era Karl Jaspers referred to as the "axial period" of human history. As described in *The Golden String* by Dom Bede Griffiths, the Catholic monastic who has spent his later years in a multisectarian ashram in India, this period saw the simultaneous emergence of many of the world's great wisdom traditions, as if, Griffiths says, "the real meaning of life seems to have dawned upon the human mind. In India and China, in Persia and in Greece, a movement of thought began, by which mankind finally pierced through the barrier of the senses and discovered the mystery of the world which lies beyond." This era gave birth in India to the Buddha, the *Upanishads*, and the tradition of the Vedanta, in China to the Tao, and in Greece to the Logos. "To each people the mystery was revealed in a different way. To the Indian it came rather as a sense of the utter unreality of the phenomenal world in comparison with the reality of that which lay beyond. To the Chinese it appeared as a principle of harmony, a cosmic order uniting man and nature in an organic society. The Greek saw it as a law of Reason by which 'all things are steered through all things,'

* New York: Citadel Press, 1984.

which gave rise to Plato's conception of the 'world of ideas' and to Plotinus's vision of the One, transcending all thought and all being." Based on that assessment, we could say that the New Age of Consciousness began in the first millennium before Christ, and that the New Age of today is merely a term of convenience to characterize widely divergent elements, the modern implications of a chain of events set in motion over two thousand years ago and held together tenuously under one ponderous logo.

Whether Bucke's estimate was too conservative, or whether those who have proclaimed the arrival of a critical mass of new consciousness are premature in their pronouncements, is difficult to judge from where we stand in the eye of the maelstrom. All around is evidence of massive turbulence, but also of increasing awareness of the overwhelming need to change. One could argue that the number of enlightened souls has increased exponentially in this century, but so has world population. But should it matter in the long run, as Aldous Huxley once said of chemically expanded consciousness, what kind of key is used to open the door, when the real issue is what we see once the door is opened? Today the door of spiritual awareness is at least ajar, the light is seeping through, and we are going to have to learn to live with what is on the other side.

CHAPTER 12

Paul Lowe:
It's Not Supposed to Work

■ ■ ■

Nobody needs to learn anything. In fact, what you know is in the way
of your knowing. The answers to all your questions are within you.
Stop holding onto your life the way it is, and it changes on its own.
— Paul Lowe (from his last talk, July 1990)

Finally U.G. asked, "This thing called enlightenment, can you give it
to me?"
  Looking the serious young man in the eyes, [Ramana Maharshi]
replied, "Yes, I can give it, *but can you take it?*"
— Terry Newland (from the Introduction to
Mind Is a Myth by U.G. Krishnamurti)

■

Early in 1989, while in the beginning stages of gathering information
for this book, I received a strong recommendation to hear Paul Lowe
speak. I had never heard of Lowe, but the person who advised me,
Howard Finkelson, insisted that he was "on the cutting edge" of
spiritual teaching in America. I subsequently did hear Lowe speak,
read his book *The Experiment Is Over*, watched many of his half-hour
programs that ran on a public access cable channel in Manhattan, and
spent several hours interviewing him. This gave me a chance to observe a contemporary teacher who has experienced firsthand two very
different but related developments in awareness in the West: the hu-

man potential movement that gained popularity in Esalen in the sixties, and discipleship with an acknowledged Indian master.

Lowe doesn't follow any easily categorizable school of spiritual beliefs, opting instead for a kind of "bootstrap" approach, to use the physicist Geoffrey Chew's term. The bootstrap theory of particle physics developed by Chew has been described concisely by Fritjof Capra, who combines his knowledge of high-energy and quantum physics with a grasp of Eastern mysticism in his books *The Tao of Physics* and *The Turning Point*. As explained in Capra's *Uncommon Wisdom*, the bootstrap approach dispenses with the conventional notion that all matter can be reduced to certain fundamental building blocks: the atom, electron, quark, and so on. Furthermore, Chew's approach rejects all fundamental constants, laws, or equations. "The material universe is seen as a dynamic web of interrelated events," Capra writes, and the properties of any part of this web "follow from the properties of the other parts." Hence, the structure of the universe is determined by "the overall consistency" of the interrelationships between the parts.

In a similar way, Lowe has pulled together various elements of Eastern and Western teachings into a "dynamic web" that resists reduction to specific belief systems. Although he shows the influence of both the humanistic psychology work of Esalen, where he spent some time, and the Tantric philosophy of the late Bhagwan Shree Rajneesh, with whom he spent many years in India and America, his teaching is very much his own.

Lowe is tall and lanky, with a full beard and a coif of gray-white hair meticulously arranged in a kind of nimbus around his face. That ethereal aura may be less than accidental, for although Lowe fixed me with an intense gaze when we first met, throughout our talk he seemed to be strangely absent, as he does during his appearances in person and on television. (I later thought of Richard Klein's description of his first meeting with Maharishi Mahesh Yogi, during which he felt "there was no-body there." Klein's explanation was that Maharishi had effectively expunged his own ego and was simply mirroring Klein back to himself.) Lowe was dressed casually and, except for a pair of black bedroom slippers, entirely in light shades of blue. Again this was probably no accident, since Lowe says that he consciously chooses everything he does, from the food he eats to the clothes he wears. I had read in Annie Besant and C. W. Leadbeater's book *Thought-Forms* that blue is the color of religious devotion and spirituality. We met in an elegantly furnished East Side townhouse lent to Lowe by one of his followers, a light and spacious place with windows looking out on a backyard of early-blooming forsythia and magnolia. Although until recently Lowe has lived an itinerant life, his followers apparently take very good care of him.

Paul Lowe was born to working-class parents in Warwickshire, England, in 1933, the first of three children. When he was very young, he joined the local Church of England choir, where he sang for seven years. "My life revolved around singing in the choir," he said. "I had an exceptional voice—very high, very clear, very loud—and people used to come from miles around just to hear me sing. I think I used to go into what we now call meditation, into nothingness, when I was singing. My life revolved around that, and everything else felt secondary." It was not the religious lyrics of the hymns that put Lowe into that early meditative trance, though. It was "just the sound," he said. "In fact, I didn't buy anything that was being sold in the church because nobody lived what they were talking about. And I didn't believe Jesus ever was born. I thought he was just a wonderful story, and I loved him and the story, but I didn't think that anybody like that ever really existed. I couldn't imagine there being such a contrast between what was being told about him and what was being lived round about. I equated him with truth and the world with lies." Lowe later changed his thinking about Jesus. "I think he existed," he said. "But I didn't change my thinking about the world."

Nevertheless, Lowe attended all the church services in which he could sing, including weddings and baptisms. "As I sang, the 'I' was God," he said. His statement reminded me of the concept of the Audible Life Stream or Sound Current as it was propounded by Charan Singh Ji and other Sikh masters and propagated in this country in the beliefs of Eckankar. I asked Lowe if he thought he was tapping into this "life stream" when he sang. All he would confirm was that "Certain sounds touch certain places or vibrate them." His wonderful singing experience ended abruptly at the age of fourteen, when his voice broke. "It was over," he said. "Except that it came back later. I can still sing soprano."

Like many of the people I interviewed, as a child Lowe felt that his family's religion held nothing for him. "The way I saw people live," he said, "I didn't really want to live, although I didn't know there was an alternative. But I didn't like the way people treated each other, and the way they told lies, the destructiveness that went on all the time. I didn't enjoy that at all, but I thought that's all there was. For a long time I thought there was something wrong with me."

One day, Lowe came upon a copy of George Bernard Shaw's five-play cycle *Back to Methuselah*, with its long, witty Preface excoriating the foibles of institutionalized religion and education, among a host of other things. "When I read the Preface," Lowe said, "I suddenly realized that there was somebody in the world who thought the way I did. And then everything instantly changed, because if somebody had written a book and had it published, then he was really 'somebody' to the somebody who I was then. I started to read and look around, and to see that there was possibly more than I had been told, that it wasn't just getting married and having children and avoiding illness and getting as much money and security as possible. I could see that that wasn't working for anybody I knew. It meant there was something else, so I started looking for the something else. I still didn't equate what I was looking for to the nothingness of the singing. I didn't know what that was. I didn't even think about that. But I knew there was something else."

Looking for the something else, Lowe got married, held down various jobs, and started to travel outside of his parochial Warwickshire world. None of these activities fulfilled his inner desire. "I felt that being married wasn't it," he said. "And where I was looking wasn't it. So I found my wife a boyfriend. I moved him in, and I moved out. I went to London and I was there for a while, and I didn't find it there. I didn't find anybody who knew as much as I did. I mean, they didn't know what I was talking about. And so I gave up, really. I said, 'It isn't working. I'm not happy with what I'm doing, so I'll get a job where I can contribute to the planet in some way, and just earn my food and keep.'"

In quintessential seeker fashion, Lowe began hitchhiking around the world. In East Africa, he worked in the field for the Red Cross and managed the Kenya Charity Fundraising Organization, but that wasn't it, either. He didn't meet anybody he felt could teach him anything worth knowing. "I met people who *knew* more than me, but they *weren't* any more than me. They were all lost," he said. In 1968 he heard about Esalen and immediately headed for America. The Esalen Institute, founded by two men named Michael Murphy and Richard Price on a piece of Murphy family property overlooking the Pacific Ocean at Big Sur, had become one of the most influential centers of the human potential movement in the sixties. Innovative psychologists, including Carl Rogers, Rollo May, Fritz Perls, and Abraham Maslow, led workshops which focused on an experiential approach to psychology and personal growth. There Lowe spent nine months, "doing everything there was, every weekend, studying with everybody." His studies included encounter and Gestalt groups, and psychodramas with John Pierrakos, Betty Fuller, and Will Schutz (who encouraged physical confrontation), among others. "That kept me busy for a while, because that was an expansion in finding out about myself and discovering levels that I didn't know were there, feelings I didn't know existed. I could see what my patterns were about, and my attitudes, and all the things I was stuck in. That started to unravel things."

Much has been written about Esalen and the human potential movement, but I asked Paul to characterize his own memory of being there. "Above all," he replied, "it was experiential. And of course it branched out from Esalen, which was a center of it but not the originator. It was about experiencing, not talking about it, not theory, not philosophy. But if you had a theory, then you tried it out. If you had a theory about anger, you found a way of getting angry. If you had a theory about sex, then you got yourself into sex—not in the groups at that time, but you experienced things. You experienced your sadness, your frustration. You dealt with it in an ongoing, alive way. All sorts of structures and methods and techniques were developed to help people experience parts of themselves that they probably didn't know about, or knew about only in theory. The leaders accomplished that through words, through psychological means, through movement, through massage, through sounds for meditation, any way they could get people to experience themselves."

Through a wide variety of encounter groups and bodywork techniques, Esalen encouraged and enabled people to discover and then come to terms with aspects of themselves that had been previously unexamined. Although Lowe stayed only briefly at Esalen proper, he continued to work on the outside with many of the influential members of that circle, including Alexander Lowen (a student of Wilhelm Reich and founder of Bioenergetic Analysis), bodywork pioneers Ida Rolf and Moshe Feldenkrais, and Charles Berner, who developed a radical form of encounter known as the Enlightenment Intensive. Lowe returned to London in 1969 and with his second wife, Patricia Solway, opened a growth center called Quaesitor ("seeker") that was patterned along the lines of Esalen. Quaesitor was successful, but after three years Lowe began to feel limited by the kind of work he was doing there. "I could see where all the innovators of the growth movement were stuck," he said, "and I stopped working in that direction. That's when I went to India."

Before we discussed India, I wanted to know how he determined that the leaders of the human potential movement, whose work is still highly regarded, were "stuck," and in what sense. "Because I know that," he replied. "And now I know that everybody knows that—that everything there is to know, you already know." Lowe's answer sounded evasive to say the least, but in the course of my interviews I'd become accustomed to responses that seemed not to answer my questions. As both William James and Aldous Huxley, two of the earliest Western analysts of Eastern religions, have pointed out, the mystical experience in general has about it a quality of ineffability which makes description difficult and explanation often confounding. With that in mind, I asked Lowe if he meant that he knew *intuitively* that the human potential movement had reached a dead end.

"You can call it intuitive," he said, "but that's putting a restriction on it. 'Thou art That.' You are everything there is in existence, and you've forgotten that." ("Thou art That" is a phrase from the ancient Hindu holy book known as the *Bhagavad Gita* which implies that the individual self is identical with Brahman, the Godhead or Absolute Principle of all existence. This notion was summarized by the ninth-century sage Shankara, who wrote: "Caste, creed, family and lineage do not exist in Brahman. Brahman has neither name nor form, transcends merit and demerit, is beyond time, space and the objects of sense-experience. Such is Brahman, and 'Thou art That.' ")

"So when I say I knew more than these people," Lowe continued, "I mean that I was in touch with more of myself than they were in touch with themselves. It's like when you've reached a certain standard, you can see the people who haven't reached that standard. Even though there are more standards up above you and you can't see up, you *can* see down. I could see where people were not, so to speak."

But something Lowe had seen at Esalen interested him enough to make him want to seek it at its source. Several of the group leaders with whom he worked had integrated aspects of Eastern religious practice, including yoga and meditation, into their work, and he wanted to look more deeply into those methods. One practice which particularly intrigued him was being taught in Bombay, on the west coast of India, by a man named Bhagwan Shree Rajneesh. At the age of thirty-eight, Lowe set out to meet him. "I went to India because I'd heard about a method of meditation called the Dynamic," Lowe said. The Dynamic Meditation taught by Rajneesh consisted in its earliest form of equal periods of chaotic breathing, catharsis, and silence. "From what I'd seen and worked and practiced with previously," Lowe said, "people in the West didn't know how to sit and empty out. They knew how to sit and be quiet on top of their fullness, but they didn't go empty. So people came to my workshops who had been meditating, and they had a certain peace about them. But at some point they were touched, and then they were even more raging in anger than anybody else because they hadn't dealt with it." The combination of Eastern passivity and Western catharsis in Dynamic Meditation was unique, the result of Rajneesh's exposure to Western techniques through the many Esalen "graduates" and therapists who spent time with him in India.

When Lowe heard about Dynamic Meditation, with its active elements, he thought it might be more suitable for Westerners. "And it was. Dynamic consisted of ten minutes of chaotic breathing, then ten minutes of catharting, and then ten minutes of silence. Later the time proportions were changed." "Chaotic breathing" was a term I was unclear about, so I asked Paul to explain what he meant. "If you breathe regularly," he said, "it ties up with a pattern of the brain. When you're calm, you have a breathing pattern, and when you get upset or when you're having sex, you have a breathing pattern. Chaotic breathing is *not* a pattern. You keep breaking the pattern by breathing fast and slow, and more and less, so the mind can't keep its pattern. Even though you think you're going to go mad, you hold that breathing chaos, and then at a certain point you cathart, and just throw stuff out—screaming, shouting, jumping up and down. Then after that you feel more silent than before."

What Lowe found when he first encountered Rajneesh was "a very powerful being who was in touch with more than anyone I'd met before. I felt that he was capable of teaching, so I became a disciple and stayed." He remained in Bombay for two or three years, and when Rajneesh moved to Poona, about eighty miles southeast, Lowe went with him. Eventually he became the Bhagwan's "right-hand person. I led the meditations and I performed the initiations. I slowly took over many of those things from him." When Rajneesh traveled to America and established a large community in Oregon, Lowe went along, staying with him for a total of thirteen years.

Stories of the rise and fall of Rajneeshpuram near the town of Antelope, Oregon, complete with accusations of rampant sex and violence, machine-gun-toting bodyguards and a private fleet of ninety-three Rolls-Royces, occupied the news media briefly in 1985. After all, how could any tale of cult sex, guns, and Eastern religion run afoul of the law not be expected to make great copy? Rajneesh was even interviewed from jail on "Nightline" on the eve of his deportation to India for violating U.S. immigration laws. Those events have been well documented in a number of books, and Lowe would not go on the record concerning what he observed there, or make judgments against Rajneesh, saying only, "And then for me the whole thing didn't work anymore. It didn't work for me, and it didn't look as though it was working for anybody else.

"Ever since I can remember as a child, I've had this feeling that I was supposed to be involved in something big," he continued. "Later I came to realize that it was something to do with the planet. And then I realized that it was something to do with the change in the consciousness of the planet, and that I was to be one of the key people in this change. But I didn't know how. I still don't know how, exactly. So when I came to Rajneesh, I thought he was going to do it. I chipped in with him because I didn't care who did it, as long as it happened, and then I wouldn't have to take all the responsibility. While I was there, I listened to everything he had to say. I heard all the English lectures and I watched every movement of his hand. There were still lots of things that went on that I didn't know about, but I didn't find that out until later. I was watching his awareness. He was very aware and present. Since the change happened, I've learned that if you're really present, you don't exist." (Lowe later described this "change" as "an opening beyond the restrictions of the mind," perhaps a veiled description of enlightenment.)

"When you're really present, you're not aware of yourself," Lowe said. "Rajneesh was not that sort of aware, but very aware. So I watched how to build communes, what to do, what not to do. I was totally in it, and I had experiences that nobody else has had. In Poona, there were no-limit groups. In other words, you could die in those groups, and people got close to death. People broke bones. It was an experience of living life with no limits. Nobody died, and nobody got any permanent injuries, but there was incredible intensity, incredible reality and liveness."

As Lowe told his story he showed neither excitement, braggadocio, nor reticence. It was merely a recitation of steps along a way, but it caught me off guard. I was prepared to hear about arduous ascetical practices or long periods spent in meditation at the feet of a master; instead I was hearing stories of initiates beating each other within an inch of their lives in encounter groups. In the psychotherapist James S. Gordon's book about Rajneesh's exploits in India and America, *The Golden Guru*, he confirms that Lowe, under his sannyas, or initiate's, name of Swami Ananda Teertha, was in fact one of Rajneesh's closest associates, and ran some of his most extraordinary—and most physically violent—encounter groups in Poona and Rajneeshpuram. And in *Drunk on the Divine*, an account of the Poona ashram written by a female devotee named Ma Satya Bharti, Teertha is portrayed as an intuitive and relentless leader of the ashram's toughest group, the one to which Rajneesh invariably sent psychiatrists, therapists, and other encounter group leaders from the United States and Europe. "They were the hardest nuts to crack; they knew too much," Satya Bharti writes. "But Teertha cracked them." Her book describes in vivid detail Lowe's alternation of violent free-for-alls and group lovemaking, aimed at tearing down the barriers of artificially socialized behavior. In Satya Bharti's accounts, everything works out in the rosy fashion that only a devotee might see; but her story does corroborate Lowe's descriptions of the kind of work he did.

"The process was one of sitting there and sensing what people were avoiding in themselves," Lowe said of those groups. "Most people deny their anger. If there's sex there, they deny their sexuality. They deny all the things that are embarrassing to them or are not approved by other people, and which therefore they don't approve in themselves. In fact, that's what judgment is: What you don't like in somebody else is the part of you that you don't accept in yourself." Lowe's aim was to provoke the denied aspect of his subjects' characters, "so that the people would undeniably see that and experience it for themselves. Then it was up to them what they wanted to do with it. But what we all need is to see this part in ourselves, accept it and, of course, love it. And as soon as we do, it balances and disappears. The group was bringing this part out for people to see. Of course, people who say they want to work on themselves don't want to work on themselves. What they are saying is, 'I want to see the part of me that I can accept, not the part I don't want to accept.' They want to hear what they want to hear, not what they *need* to hear. Because when you *do* hear it, then you have to make some adjustments. So most people who go for change don't go for change at all."

Leading such groups seven days a week for several years gave Lowe an unparalleled chance to learn. "I learned a lot about people and about myself," he said. "I learned about violence and hate and love, and way, way beyond. Because after things have been that intense, when you reach a silence, it's very silent. I did conscious-awareness work with people off the street. There was a scheme in Oregon by which people were collected and given a home for a time." Lowe was referring to the Oregon commune's Share-A-Home program, which, according to Gordon, brought 3,700 street people from 41 cities around the country to Rajneeshpuram, purportedly for "humanitarian" reasons, although it was widely believed they were bused in to help influence a local election. "Up to three hundred people would come for groups with me, and I had a lot of assistants," Lowe said. "I got them to the place where they would talk—because most of them don't talk—about their lives and their experience, and then allow themselves to have the feelings that go with that."

Toward the end of his thirteen years with Rajneesh, Lowe began to have inner experiences as well—the "change" he spoke of earlier. "And then," he said, "it was totally, absolutely, and completely over, so I moved out. By this time I had reached a place of choicelessness, which is one of the things that happens when balance is reached in the system. It's choiceless," he said, referring to the body-mind complex which he calls simply "it." "It doesn't particularly want to go anywhere, do anything. It has no preferences. But it responds to whatever is available. I was invited to start an institute in Italy, in a beautiful villa there on Lake Maggiore, and we called it the International Academy of Meditation."

The IAC lasted about three years and ended with a six-month intensive group of sixty or so people. When I asked Lowe how he selected the people to work with in this situation, he replied, "Let's say they were suitable for a certain level of experimentation. They were the core members who had not only worked with me before, but worked with me on other planets and in other places before. Several levels of things were possible. One was helping these people wake up to who they are, what they came to this planet for. They came to work as a team. They came to disappear to themselves so totally that only the 'is-ness' was there. And when a number of people are in the same place at that level, a very powerful energy is created. But none of them wanted to let go. They didn't want to let go of the personality. They wanted to have spiritual advancement, but they didn't want the total let-go to happen."

Did he say "other planets"? Lowe, who believes in something akin to reincarnation, also believes that the people he has worked with on Earth made a pact to come here fro n other planes in the universe. Still, the more interesting issue for me was the "total let-go"—people who "disappear to themselves"—a phrase I had already heard from spiritual practitioners. Richard Klein had told me about his inner work of learning to disappear, to remove his ego in any given situation. This is, of course, a frightening proposition for most Westerners. We have always been taught to value individuality and personality— whether in the conservative sense of "rugged individualism" or in the liberal notion of artistic and academic freedom. The Eastern ideal of disappearance, or loss of ego, appears to be antithetical to everything we value. Klein, who studied firsthand with Maharishi and secondhand, through books and tapes, with Da Kalki, explains this apparent contradiction as well as anyone.

"Being born into this existence," he said, "we're not disposed toward happiness. We're disposed toward fear and worry about death and disappearance. And so our work is the continual realization that we're not this limited, fearful self that's going to disappear and die. We have to realize that we are the context of it, the consciousness of it, and that consciousness is unaffected by all experience." The realization Klein refers to is that the separate ego—what we commonly identify as the "self"—is dispensable, and is not necessarily identified with the larger Self of which we are all part. Eastern ideas of reincarnation do not usually imply that the "soul" which is reincarnated is the identifiable ego or personality, but rather something akin to what the Buddhists (who do not believe in the individual soul) would call character. As Klein sees it, the teaching that says that "this self we've built up, this important person, has to be completely sacrificed," will never be acceptable in the West.

"I come up against wanting to hold on to some experience or some hope that life will be better or different," Klein said. "But I constantly have to give that up and come back into what the Buddhists would call Nothing. To deny that Nothing part is to be very Western. It's Nothing, but it is also Everything. It's also pure happiness. And I can't see why that teaching would ever be popular. We used to teach in TM lectures that TM would help you to use more mental potential, have better health and better relationships, and therefore we would have more harmony, and world peace. *That* teaching will always be popular, and has always been taught." Mentioning Norman Vincent Peale's "variation on that," he added that "the spiritual teaching of sacrifice—that he who loves his life loses it and he who hates his life has eternal life—has never been popular. And it never will be popular, because if great numbers of people got that, we'd literally disappear. There literally is nobody there—no 'body' in the sense of an individual that's separate from everything else."

I asked Paul Lowe if Klein's sense of "nobody there" was what he meant by letting go of the personality, but he said it wasn't. "If there's nobody home," he said, "everybody's home. So you couldn't say there's nobody home now. There's no personality. I don't have an experience of my self. But there is a sense—none of these words are true, but these are the only words we've got—that everything is here. You're not separate anymore from the whole. I know that I'm not separate from you, that I'm not separate from the chair I'm sitting on or the air I'm breathing. That happened as a knowing that there is only One. We've heard that over and over: There is only One."

Nevertheless, among Lowe's sixty handpicked troops, none opted for "the total let-go. Nobody gave total permission as they would to a Zen master, first of all because I wasn't interested in being a master, and because it's not suitable for Western people. But I was a presence, and people weren't ready to let go to that presence of themselves. So their resistances were there, which is fine. That's the way it was. Many things happened out of that for many people, all sorts of things at all sorts of levels, very high levels of vibration and what's called meditation. And then, to me, it was over. I had contributed what I'd set out to contribute, so I let it go. After that I made myself available to anybody who wanted to hear anything about my experiences or whatever. I started to go around the world making myself available. I've made videos, gone to conferences and talks and seminars. But it's not a teaching anymore. There are no techniques. I just talk."

At various times during our discussion, Lowe made reference to ascended masters, the White Brotherhood, and other terms for spirit entities. I asked him if he could explain these references in a way that might make sense to the lay person. "There are other levels of reality," he said, "so what you see here isn't what's here. You're seeing what you're trained to see. If you let go of your training, you'll see other levels. But the other levels are not reality, either. They're just a higher level of vibration. And if you let go of everything, then there isn't anything. There's no universe, there isn't anything. The mind can't understand that, because the mind can only understand things that are or things that are not. But what you think is, isn't. It's not like that."

Since Lowe believes that the logical mind is not much use in understanding most of what he has to say, like others in his line of work he uses stories and metaphors to clarify his points. One intriguing metaphor that he had recently developed, and which I heard him use later the same night before a few hundred people in a downtown Manhattan art gallery, involved the image of a flight simulator. "You know what a flight simulator is," he said. "You go in and put your seat belt on, close the door, and it's as though you're in an airplane cockpit. You have a screen in front of you and you see the runway and all sorts of conditions. There are computer games like that, too, but the flight simulator is a complete experience because you feel as if you're really in the cockpit. It tilts or crashes and does all those sorts of things. You don't actually get hurt, even if the plane crashes, but it gives the same sounds and feelings.

"Now imagine that you're existing in a dimension that is indescribable, so we won't even bother to try. But somebody says to you, 'Listen, we've devised this game. If you go through that door and close it, it'll lock automatically, and you'll be in that room for no time at all. It will take no time because there's no such thing as time. But while you're in there, you'll have an experience of time.' Because you've never had an experience of time, you say, 'What does that mean?' They say, 'Well, if you go in there, you'll know what time is. And it'll seem like a long time.' You say, 'What's a long time?' And they say, 'It doesn't matter, because we can't explain it to you until you go in that room.'

"When you're in that room, nothing will happen to you. But you'll think *everything* is happening to you. You'll have to get into a certain suit to go in there—call it a spacesuit if you like. And when you're in there you'll get identified with that suit, so anything that's happening with the suit you'll think is happening with you. It's a whole level of experience. You say, 'What's experience?' And again they say, 'We can't tell you what experience is until you go in that room.' So you go in that room and you come out in no time. But while you're in there, you're in there for three score years and ten. And everything happens to you. You have illness, and you die. Or somebody close to you dies and you get damaged. You have trauma. All these things happen to you, but of course they don't happen to you because it's a simulator. So, welcome to planet Earth. That's what Earth is, it's a simulator for experience. It's not supposed to work. It's a school, a learning place. You're here for experience of duality. If there's no duality, there's no time, there's no space, there's no you, there's no other."

My first question was, "Where and when do we get to use that experience of duality?"

"You never get to use it," Lowe said. "The classic example is that if you're a fish in water, you don't appreciate water. But if you get thrown out, you're very glad to go back in. So you could say the purpose is just to realize that wherever you are, you are. You come out of this experience to realize where you are."

"It must be nice to be back, then," I said, "to the non-Earth experience."

"It's nice to be back until you find that there are other levels that you can expand to. And then you might come back to planet Earth, or you might go to a more advanced dimension."

"What you're saying is that we can choose to go to another place during the reincarnation process?"

"The key word there is 'choose,'" he said. "It's not done to you. You choose to do it. And they're not really places. You could say there are other levels of consciousness. We'll call them places, or planets, or whatever you want to call them. It's just a way of trying to describe something."

The notion that things on this planet are not supposed to work forms part of the core of Paul Lowe's teachings, and is tied up with his sense of this being a planet of polarity. A strikingly similar assessment of the human condition is made in a book called "*I Come as a Brother.*" Like the famous Seth books of Jane Roberts, the book is the product of a so-called "channeled entity" (here named Bartholomew), a spirit who speaks through the medium of a human being in a trance state. However unlikely that may sound, the ideas communicated by this and other such books are often surprising. Bartholomew speaks, for instance, about the necessity of recognizing our dark aspects rather than focusing only on the light—a concept that was also dear to the embodied personality of Carl Jung, but which is not terribly popular in New Age circles. "If those of you who think you are spiritual really believe that you have the capacity to be only 'positive,'" Bartholomew says, "I would ask you to look at the nature of the world into which you have been incarnated. It is a planet of polarity. All worlds are not so polarized. It is the basic essence of this planet. You will not be able to move in it freely until you recognize that. It is part of who you are—and it is wonderful." In more conventional psychological terms, the Jungian analyst Roger Woolger speaks of the same need in his beguiling book *Other Lives, Other Selves.* "Dr. Jekyll *is* Mr. Hyde," he writes. "Iago *is* Othello *and* Desdemona. We are each of us one, but multiple at the same time. Only when we can welcome this multiplicity of being within us, especially the distasteful parts, can we become truly whole, truly human." He quotes Jung saying that "we do not become enlightened by imagining figures of light but by making the darkness conscious."

Lowe's reference to other planets, however, was confusing. Did he mean other levels of consciousness, or actual, physical planets within this universe? "If you want them to be, they are," he said. "Here's an ancient Indian story. It's about the kalptaru tree, a wish-fulfilling tree that grows only in heaven. But a seed fell out and fell on planet Earth. One day a man was walking along way out in the wilderness, and he was hot and tired. He sat under a tree, and it was the kalptaru tree. When he woke up, he said, 'I'm hungry. I wish I had something to eat.' And there was food. He started eating. And he said, 'I wish I had something to drink.' And there was wine. When the wine appeared, he suddenly realized he'd come out of his sleep. He said, 'Oh, this must be an enchanted place.' And he became enchanted. And he said, 'If it's enchanted, there must be demons here.' And there were demons. And he said, 'Well, demons kill people.' So he was killed.

"On planet Earth, it doesn't work quite that quickly, but it works exactly the same way. If you think there are other planets, there are other planets. You create your reality, not only with your actions, but with your thoughts. Your previous thoughts have an effect on now, so things get crossed." By way of example, Lowe told the story of a woman who had approached him a few days before to ask his help. "What can I do about this?" she asked him. "Not long ago, some months back, my life was terrible. It was so bad I wanted to die, and every time I went to sleep I said, 'I want to die. Let me die.'" She did this for months. Then in a very short time she found a beautiful lover, she got a great job, and everything was wonderful. But then she discovered that she had a terminal illness. "So," Lowe concluded, "she got what she wished, but of course it had come out of sequence for her. And everything has this consequence. There's no 'previous.' It's now. What you call the past is happening now. What you call previous lives, they're all happening now."

When it comes to practical areas such as sex, health, and work, Lowe makes specific recommendations for behavior, although their implications are likely to be hard to accept for most people in the West. For instance, he does not favor either monogamous or promiscuous sex, but what he calls being "appropriate." What is appropriate at any given moment in one's life is likely to change considerably, and so it is necessary to remain "choiceless." That is to say, what we do ought to be based on internal rather than external considerations. "If you are angry," Lowe has often said, "then feel the anger. Don't suppress it, don't deny it, and don't judge it." This sounds like an echo not only of Esalen but also of Tantric admonitions voiced by Rajneesh. "Tantra says: Indulge, but be aware," wrote the Bhagwan in *Tantra, Spirituality & Sex*. "You are angry; Tantra will not say don't be angry. Tantra says be angry, wholeheartedly, but be aware!"

Lowe has carried this notion of aware indulgence into all realms of human action. "You reach a balance, and then it depends on what level of vibration you settle at or lie around in for a while," he said. "But it's a balance. And it doesn't have to *have* anything anymore, so there's no desire, and it becomes choiceless. And so if you see a very attractive person of the opposite sex, classically attractive, then you might enjoy looking, as you would at a Lamborghini or a beautiful crystal. You enjoy it because it's a beautiful example of what it is. But you don't have to do anything about it. If you can see an attractive person and you don't have to be with her, then you're free. But as soon as you say, 'I'd like to, and I won't,' you've made trouble. Now if you say, 'I will,' then what you do is stay very aware, very alive, and come to her, and talk to her. Because sometimes your mind might be over it before your body, or your body before your mind. If you start suppressing any of them, you're going to make trouble. But if you go there with total awareness, and total choicelessness about whether you're with this person or not, then when you don't need to be with them, you won't be. And nothing will contract. But it has to be done without condition. If you say, for example, 'But if I do, then it's going to upset my partner,' you're putting in a condition and you're going to suppress something. And it might be you suppress something when it's not appropriate for you to be with that person in the first place. You might have only needed to talk to them. Or look in their eyes, or take them out to dinner. Or you may have gone to bed and not made love. You might choose to remain with your partner anyway, but you won't know until you make yourself available. The whole game is to be totally available at every moment, not only to the opposite sex but to the same sex. To the tree, to the chair you're sitting on, to everything. And if you're not totally available for whatever is appropriate, you suppress something, you close the circuit. If you close the circuit, it'll kill you. That's what your cancer is. That's what all the diseases are. They're just energy that was not allowed to be itself.

"Another way of saying this is that you're here without condition, whatever consequences that has. You don't have a desire or a choice to be this way or that way. Then you'll be in your own harmony, and incidentally, everybody else will be at their maximum potential in relationship to you also. Maybe you're sitting one day and you get a very clear message to leave your wife and family. But you're not going to do it, because you're not choiceless. You're into, Well, what about them? What about their survival? They'll sue me, and I care for them, and then they'll starve. You don't listen to your maximum potential, which is probably their maximum potential as well because they probably need you to go, even though they don't recognize it. If you get to that place, you get your maximum potential, but then do you have the courage to follow it?"

But how do we know when an impulse is genuine or just a response to biological stimuli? And what about other kinds of adventure we feel impulsively drawn to, like race-car driving or sky diving? "When in doubt, do it," Lowe said. "Do it with awareness. Don't take unnecessary risks, and don't be silly, because your body is very precious. Five billion people have crammed themselves on this planet at this time because it's a very precious time to be here. Change of consciousness is coming. So, don't risk your body. But if you're in doubt, do it, because it doesn't matter what you do. There's no right, no wrong. You're here to experience. I once read an article in a magazine that said a tortoise can advance only when it sticks its neck out."

Lowe's advice is not to die with the thought that there is something you still need to experience here, or you'll be bound to come back. I argued that basing relationships on random sexual attraction isn't necessarily the best way of relating, and that it is possible to have a perfect sexual relationship that doesn't work on any other level. "Nothing will work," he said, reiterating his theme. "Perfect sex doesn't work. All the money in the world doesn't work, all the possessions, all the fame. And if you don't buy that, meet the richest, most famous people who have the best. Look in their eyes and see for yourself. Nothing outside works. It's not supposed to work. If you have perfect sex—and there is such a thing as perfect sex, when you are totally in tune, you turn each other on, you become the One, and you both disappear together at the same moment—still it's not enough. Nothing is ever enough. It's not supposed to be. So you keep looking for what you came here to look for, which is a realization of yourself."

Most of what we do is done for approval, anyway, according to Lowe, the approval of spouses, parents, society. And so our approach to relationships is usually based on the wrong premise. "You can be relating for the whole of your life with one person, monogamously, if it's appropriate for you. But it's a relating, and it's choiceless in each moment. It says, If we part, we part; if we stay, we stay. And then it doesn't matter about time. You can let go and say, 'I'll be what's appropriate, and if it's appropriate to be with somebody else, I'll be with them. If it's appropriate for my partner to be with someone else, they'll be with someone else.' If you're appropriate, then you're always with the most appropriate person. That could be the same person moment after moment, but it needs to be choiceless. Most things have to do with survival, and if you let that go, then you're appropriate. Some people live in hell to be close to the money."

Lowe talked about "completing your sexuality," by which he means, as nearly as I could determine, getting to the point at which your actions are no longer determined by fear, guilt, or insecurity. "And when you have completed it," he said, "you do have more energy, and your sexuality also changes. You have a different sort of orgasm. Everything changes when you move to that level." But he also made it clear that completing your sexuality does not necessarily mean going through every conceivable experience for the sake of doing it. "You could sit there and complete it," he said. "It could just be a total and complete Yes, and then the energy's gone through that level. You're aware of all the things you need to be aware of, and then it's over. Or you can go and fuck your brains out for the rest of your life and it won't work, because you haven't opened. You're not aware, you're not experimenting each time. It's literally a masturbation, it's a pattern, a closed circuit. You don't learn anything. Whatever you do, you've got to be present there. And then you'll learn all sorts of things about sex you didn't know existed. You'll learn physical things that go on in the body, mental and emotional things, and things on other levels, too. But you've got to be there for it. The Eastern cultures say suppress it. If you go to India, you'll find they are the most obsessed people about sex. All they ever think about is sex—either doing it or not doing it. They're obsessed with it, and it doesn't work."

The problem with sex, according to Lowe, is that "it's a process that makes you unaware. It's supposed to make you unaware, because it's for reproduction, and naturally you wouldn't want to reproduce. You wouldn't want the hassle and the expense. So there's a circuit built in that makes you want it. It's called the mother instinct in a woman. There isn't such a thing as a father instinct, but it's something that wants to fuck, that just wants to have that pleasure. It's there to make you unconscious, so you'll do it and have children. People say, 'But I love children.' But that's only because they've got that circuit. If their lives were complete and whole, most people wouldn't have children."

Once again, Lowe's debt to the Tantric teachings of Rajneesh is evident. While on the island of Crete after being expelled from America, Rajneesh urged his followers to "go through the sexual experience to such an extent that you are completely satisfied with it. Only then will you be able to become meditative like Buddha."

"It all boils down to this," Lowe said, when I questioned him at a later date as to precisely what he meant by completing one's sexuality. "It's just to be in this moment as totally as you know how, without looking for anything else or thinking of anything else. Another word for that is 'honesty.' You are totally honest in asking, What is the reality of this moment? Which includes the fact that I'm married or they're married, and there's AIDS, and this and that. If I include all that and am totally honest, what is my truth in this moment? And then you live it as totally as you know how." His guideline for knowing whether you are truly *in* the moment is to ask whether you are expanding or contracting. "Contracting" means closing yourself to possibilities, to relationship with others; "expanding" means opening to include every perception, every possibility of what might happen in a given moment. "And if you are expanding," Lowe said, "you are more likely to be appropriate. You are more likely to pick up messages."

But could your truth be that you are conflicted in that moment? "When you say 'confliction,' " Lowe replied, "that means the mind is interfering with the openness of that moment, because there is no confliction in the moment. There is an 'is-ness,' but then the mind says, 'What if?' And as soon as you're in the mind, you bring in time and space, the past and the future, and that's the only place confliction exists. As soon as you think of consequences, you have confliction." But what of the simple biological impulses, the physical attraction of the moment that any human being may feel for any other human? Was Lowe implying that we ought to act on each impulse because we honestly perceive it as being our reality at the moment we feel it?

To Lowe, acting on such impulses is not consciousness. "That's just a wound-up spring that has to do with your biology. Consciousness includes everything that's happening in that moment, including the fact that you have certain chemicals and certain instincts, like survival. If you just go blindly, you're acting on the lower, animal level. And when I say 'lower,' there's no condemnation. It's just a lower level of vibration. But if you are fully conscious, that includes many other things, and in that moment you can include all those things, and then something totally different comes out. Parts of your mind get attracted, parts of your body, of your emotions. But if you expand and say yes to this moment, then all these things just slot into their own place, and you will act appropriately." Something in the animal nature of man is normally stronger than his higher consciousness, "unless you are really present and really in that moment. And then it may say, 'And I want to be with that person.' It doesn't matter if the person says yes. It's nothing to do with being with them. It's nothing to do with sex. It is that at this moment, this being wants to approach that person to say this thing. We're talking about honesty with consciousness, not instinct, not re-action. I don't look at it in terms of enlightenment or anything else. I look at it in terms of, What is your maximum potential in this moment? Are you interested in that, or are you interested in your lower levels, in your survival, how people see you—all the normal things that produce normal, ordinary people? If you're open for that extraordinary higher part, that potential, then your life is not going to be safe. If you're safe, you're dead. You have to live each moment totally, whatever it costs. But of course, hardly anybody is interested in that."

On the surface, not much seems to separate Lowe's teaching of constant self-awareness from the conventional gospel of self-gratifi-

cation as epitomized by the *Playboy* philosophy of uncommitted indulgence. At second glance, it appears that Lowe is not against
commitment but against basing that commitment on fear of loss,
against placing security above an honest, moment-to-moment ap-
praisal of whether a relationship is still vital. "The people who just
go on fucking do so because they are contracted and unconscious and
stuck in that lower level, and nothing ever evolves," he said. "Once
you open up and become very conscious, you also become very sensitive, and nothing is ever the same again. Then that *Playboy* thing
just dies, and something new is born in its place, something that has
to do with love and caring and a dance of vibrations with the other.
Sometimes it evolves into celibacy or into monogamy—not out of
anything that's been taught, not out of morals, but from your own
essence in that moment. How many people live their truth unconditionally in each moment? And how many people are stuck with
somebody else's idea of how to live, a Buddhism or a Christianism
or a something else-ism? Who dares to be themselves? Christ dared,
Muhammad dared, and Buddha dared, but their disciples weren't
themselves. Only Christ was himself, only Buddha was himself."

Lowe's words remind me of another spiritual teacher I interviewed
named Daniel Castro. Castro, who lives in Santa Fe and teaches to a
small group of followers worldwide, is not an advocate of any specific
spiritual path, or "format," as he calls them. He believes that the
established schools have in most cases lost contact with the spiritual
energy of their founders, a notion he elaborates by drawing a fundamental distinction between Buddhism and the Buddha. "From my
perspective," Castro said, "Buddhism is a movement away from Buddhahood. Buddha didn't have a path. Buddha apparently was alone,
with no-where, no guidelines, no rituals. He came to the ending of
rituals before he was Buddha. He tried everything, and in trying everything he came to an aloneness. In that aloneness he had to explore
his nature, without props, without costumes, without disguises, without knowledge. That exploration into nothingness, into selfhood, was
the basis of his Buddhahood. Now we have Buddhism, which gives
you the guidelines, the format, and which explains what will happen.
It is a re-creation of form. The mind that desires Buddhahood, but
then acquiesces to form, is seeking the comfort or security of the form,
and is moving away from the whole intention of Buddha's work. One

is finding security by having a road map, by having a path to this pathless place."

While studying in an ashram in Rishikesh in Northern India, Castro had a breakthrough in which he saw that although the originators of the forms—Christ, Buddha, Gurdjieff—"had some energy," their followers by and large "are trying to use those forms to resolve some neurotic pressure. The original forms had some integrity, but the neurotic mind, which is me-oriented, attempted to use these things as a kind of medicine, and to exploit and perpetuate them." According to Castro, the very process of organization and institutionalization, in early Christianity and elsewhere, corrupted the initial concern of these religions for the general population. Even now, the meditative formats that are available in packaged form "reflect more the condition of the human mind than an attempt to communicate. The people who developed yoga were realized already. They weren't trying to find realization through Hatha Yoga. The people who developed meditative formats had already come to enlightenment, which they deepened by introducing means of communication through certain physical practices. They were monks before they developed Tai Chi. They developed Tai Chi as a means of insuring that they could continue being monks and deepening that state. But in America we have separated the Tai Chi from the monkhood, so we get a chance to wear different costumes and be somebody superior in rank to the other person. This need to satisfy the ego structure came later. The person who developed the form had left his ego behind."

Nonetheless, Castro believes that we can restore these expressions to their original intention. But he emphasizes that this must be done on an individual, moment-by-moment basis. "What I'm saying, *I'm* saying, with no body of tradition to relate it to," he said. "If I suggest that you are stuck in a particular place and that maybe some walks in the morning or sitting quietly would be good, then we're developing the technique ourselves and addressing a particular fact, but we're not saying that meditation is God or the Bible is God's word. We're not trying to cloak ourselves in tradition. These religions have become a habit. Meditation places have become places where one seeks refuge, going to the mountains to escape from the city. The mind that escapes does not have enough internal courage to explore the life as it is, where it is, and that is what is necessary. We're attempting to escape behind meditation, to make meditative formats take away our stress. We go out in the marketplace and create stress, and then we want to use these forms as a retreat. The intense human being wants to *be* with God, doesn't want God as a helper, is not seeking God to relieve his psychological stress. He communes with nature and doesn't seek nature to be a sedative for him."

Paul Lowe takes Castro's notion even further. For him, it's not enough to be sensitive to trees and animals. "You're going to find out it's the same with plastic," Lowe said. "Everything has a consciousness. *Everything.*" His words sounded far-fetched until I later came across a saying attributed to Jesus in the Gnostic Gospel of Thomas: "Lift the stone and you will find me. Cleave the wood and I am there." ("To discover the Kingdom of God exclusively within oneself is easier than to discover it, not only there, but also in the outer world of minds and things and living creatures," wrote Aldous Huxley in *The Perennial Philosophy.* "It is easier because the heights reveal themselves to those who are ready to exclude from their purview all that lies without. And though this exclusion may be a painful and mortificatory process, the fact remains that it is less arduous than the process of inclusion, by which we come to know the fullness as well as the heights of spiritual life.")

As Lowe sees it, we just don't care about anything. "Not because we're bad, not because we're wrong. It's just we're ignorant here on planet Earth. Somebody was going on about their dog, one with three-inch-high legs and a flattened nose, and I said, 'You put that being in constant torture. It can't breath properly and can't jump anymore. It can't do all the things it wants to do. It can't feed itself, so it has to wag its tail every time it sees you. You've put that thing in torture because you want a toy.' They were fairly upset. But when I said you've done the same with children, it produced a lot worse upset. Children are not children. They talk baby talk because you talk baby talk. They act like children because you treat them like children. They're full-grown beings inside—they're just in miniature bodies. But we want children to be children so that we can feel superior. And a lot of the children, especially those being born now, are vastly superior. They're very advanced beings, but we want to keep them down. Christ came along and said, 'Don't do that,' and Buddha and

Gurdjieff and Krishnamurti came along and said, 'Don't do that.' But you don't want to hear because you have to give up your inner pattern. You're addicted to what you're doing, and if you give up an addiction, you have to go through withdrawal."

I proposed that one of the reasons we resist spiritual development is that we are afraid we'll have to renounce worldly goods. "If you renounce anything," Lowe responded, "you're doing the opposite of what you were doing before, but it's the same energy. But if you become more present, and find time to disconnect from what we've been told is right and wrong, you start to hear yourself. If you hear yourself, you'll start to hear what's appropriate: what to eat, what not to eat, where to go, where not to go, what music to listen to, what colors to wear, what air to breathe, what water to drink. You will hear and you will know through your own sensitivity. You won't have to read a book. It may mean letting go, but it's not pushing it away. You won't take a step to stop yourself from eating sugar. You just stopped eating sugar by the very realization that you are addicted to sugar, and sugar is poisoning you. But then your system will go through withdrawal, and your system will tell you it's natural to eat sugar, because your system is now unnatural. When you first smoked a cigarette or drank alcohol, your system screamed NO! But you did it because other people did it. And then your system contorted itself to be able to handle it. So when you stop doing that, it's going to put itself right, but in the meantime, it will go through withdrawal."

Apart from one reference to his childhood at the very beginning of our talk, Lowe hadn't mentioned God, so I asked what his conception of God was. "It's a cute idea, God is," he said. "People have created it for some sort of security, that there's something bigger than me, greater than me. So I'm a child, and therefore there's a father. It's a comforting thought, except you have to pay the price, because fathers want their way and you have to do as you're told. But it's just another way of not being responsible. And there's no way of answering whether there is a God or isn't a God, because each person has a different idea of what it is: the 'is' and 'is-ness' and 'Thou art That.' Jesus said, 'The Kingdom of God is within.' But he also said [in the Gnostic Gospels], 'When you see the within is without and the without is within, then you're in the kingdom.' In other words, as we say over and over again, 'This is it.' And so somebody else says, 'That means I am God.' Well, the 'I' is not God. When all the boundaries have gone, then *It is*. God is just a neurotic idea."

As for enlightenment or realization, Lowe said that it is always available, but often a matter of how much someone wants it. "Anyone can take any step they want any time. It's whether they will or not. But they can. Most people do it either because they have a near-death experience, or because they get a terminal illness, somebody close to them dies, they lose their money, or they get bored and say, 'What else is there?' Or they have a religious experience in the form of a dream or a vision. But everybody has the chance. How many Bibles are there? Even though the Bible has been hacked to pieces and distorted, the truth is still in that Bible. The Koran, the *Tao-te Ching*—everybody knows somewhere to look. But if they want to make their little world work, they won't listen. There's that old story of a man who falls off a cliff. He catches onto a branch, and he's hanging over certain death. He says, 'If there's a God, tell me what to do.' A big voice comes out and says, 'Let go!' And the man says, 'Can I have a second opinion?'

"All the techniques people do and all the groups that people go to, they do because they don't want to wake up, not because they want to wake up. If you want to wake up totally, completely, unconditionally, you're awake." I told Lowe that this reminded me of Krishnamurti, who eschewed any talk of a belief system or followers or specific methods, and challenged his listeners to wake up in the moment of hearing him. "I don't think there is a system and a method," Lowe said, "and I don't think it's appropriate if there is. Krishnamurti worked very hard, and so did Gurdjieff, and nobody got realized around them, it seems.

"There's the story of Bodhidharma," Lowe said, referring to the man credited with carrying Zen Buddhism from India to China. "He sat in front of a wall for nine years and he said, 'I'm not turning around until somebody comes who really wants it.' Eventually a guy cut his arm off and threw it in front of Bodhidharma, and said, 'If you don't turn around, I shall cut my head off.' And Bodhidharma said, 'You're the guy I've been looking for.' People all think they want it, but they don't want what it takes. Bodhidharma talked for forty years after that, a very beautiful man. But it didn't happen. Gurdjieff did exactly the opposite. He beat people and fucked them and gave them all sorts of grief, and it still didn't happen. Jesus didn't seem to have any of his disciples wake up, either. So I don't think there is a way."*

Some time after I spoke with Paul Lowe, I tried to contact him again to update our interview. That was when I discovered that in July 1990 he had retired from speaking publicly after delivering his last talk in London. It isn't unusual for spiritual teachers to lapse into silence for a time. Meher Baba imposed physical silence on himself, and Da Kalki retreated to Fiji and announced that he would no longer take on new disciples. But before bowing out, Lowe reiterated the apocalyptic sense of the impending dissolution of the planet that he shares with Jehovah's Witnesses and the Christian fundamentalists. Whether they are all onto something or merely coming to the same conclusion from diametrically opposed directions remains to be seen. In a curious way, though, their predictions can be taken as metaphors with the same implication: a major change in consciousness is necessary in order for existence to continue, but that new existence may not bear much resemblance to the one we take for granted in our daily lives.

"I haven't wanted what most people want," Lowe said in his final talk. "At one time I wanted to find a true guru, and I never found one. I wanted to find someone who really knows, and I never found anyone. When I read the books and I tuned in to the energy of the ascended masters, it didn't feel to me that any of them had it either. Anything that has ever been said on this planet is not it. So what does it matter? In one way it doesn't, except that there is a change happening on this planet. All over the world the weather is in absolute chaos. There is tremendous political and economic instability. Earth-

---

* Philip Kapleau records the following account of the Bodhidharma story in *The Three Pillars of Zen* (New York: Anchor Books, 1989): "Hui-K'e, a scholar of some repute, complains to Bodhidharma, who is silently doing zazen, that he has no peace of mind and asks how he can acquire it. Bodhidharma turns him away, saying that the attainment of inward peace involves long and hard discipline and is not for the conceited or fainthearted. Hui-K'e, who has been standing outside in the snow for hours, implores Bodhidharma to help him. Again he is rebuffed. In desperation he cuts off his left hand and offers it to Bodhidharma. Now convinced of his sincerity and determination, Bodhidharma accepts him as a disciple. Whether these episodes are historically true or not is less important than the fact that they symbolically reveal the importance which Zen masters attach to the hunger for Self-realization. . . ."

quakes are increasing in their frequency and strength. The hole in the ozone gets bigger. Anyone with any intelligence can see that things cannot go on as they are. The planet just doesn't work the way it is. Everything in every way is on the edge of change.''

When I reached Lowe by phone in Maui, where he has retired from public teaching, he sounded calm and relaxed. Although he was no longer speaking publicly, he did say that among friends he had once again been singing with something very close to his childhood soprano voice. ''A sound comes through that is not just a single note,'' he told me. ''Sometimes it carries five or seven tones with it, and it seems to affect people's bodies and vibrations. Changes happen when they hear this. It seems to shake everything up. 'In the beginning was the Word'—and it probably wasn't a word, it was probably a sound. Vibrations are very powerful.''

He acknowledged that he stopped teaching not only because people don't want to hear what they need to hear, but also because the process can be counterproductive. ''If people are growing,'' he said, ''they get to a certain point where they feel comfortable and then they stop. And it's worse than if they didn't start at all. When you're in pain, you often look for a way out, and that looking is helping the whole planet. But when you get complacent, as the New Age has on some level, then the process stops. Then, in a way, that burden has been transferred through the teacher, because when someone reaches a new level of awakening, they go out and use it in marriage or in making money or in politics. They use that energy to spiral down the energy on the planet. So, as you can see, I don't know what's going on and I don't know anything anymore.''

Among the things Lowe doesn't know is what his truth is. ''I have a feeling,'' he said, ''that whatever we call Truth is beyond anything that's ever been spoken, that's ever been written, that's ever been on the planet before. There is something else, and I don't know what that thing is. I could say that I've stopped talking and stopped doing anything to see if it wants to come through, but in fact, that isn't my truth either. All that's happened is that I've stopped talking. It's as though something else wants to come through, but it won't come through in words. And when I say I'm not talking because people aren't getting it, there's no judgment in that. It's just not appropriate for this system to continue the way it was.''

His words reminded me of the book by L. C. Beckett I'd read almost twenty years before, called *Neti-Neti*, a Sanskrit term roughly translatable as "Not this, not that," and I mentioned it. Lowe said, "I used to have a group called Neti-Neti. That's my favorite." The basic theme of the book, as best I could remember it, involved a principle Beckett called "the Nothing Between," a sort of cosmic emptiness out of which new matter and ideas are created. "It's not a very popular concept," I said to Paul.

"No," he said, "because you have to let go of everything, and you have no idea whether anything else is coming. Through my life, that's what has happened. But this time I really have no idea at all whether anything else is coming. I go to psychics, and I've had readings saying that this is a preparation period, there's a whole new level coming, and so on. That may be true, but it's not my reality. I'm just living moment to moment, eating when I'm hungry, sleeping when I'm tired, making love with my beloved when I feel like it and she feels like it, and anything that wants to happen, or doesn't want to happen. I'm having a great time."

CHAPTER 13

Kathryn Quick:
At Home with the Serpent Power

■   ■   ■

Worldly people constantly repeat this refrain: "Babaji, I try to meditate,
but as soon as I sit down, worldly things come before me—the office,
the factory, the children. What should I do about it? I just can't
meditate."

I answer, "But you certainly are getting meditation. To have your
office or factory appear within you is meditation. To see visions of your
children is meditation."

—Swami Muktananda, *Play of Consciousness*

■

Of all the Eastern teachers to make their magnetism felt in America,
the late Swami Muktananda was one of the most warmly regarded,
and among the most influential. Perhaps not as widely known here
as Maharishi Mahesh Yogi or Chögyam Trungpa Rinpoche, he nevertheless had an impact on many American teachers, including Brother
Charles and Da Kalki. What Da got from Muktananda, with whom
he studied in India, was not merely initiation into the mysteries of
Kundalini Yoga, but also the practice of extreme devotion to a guru.
"A man becomes like the object on which he meditates," Muktananda
wrote in his spiritual autobiography, *Play of Consciousness*. "He becomes
permeated by whatever object he holds in his heart with love." This
process of reflection works two ways: the disciple ultimately becomes
what he or she beholds, and the guru shows his followers who they
are by reflecting their very being back to them. In a book devoted to

exploring guru-disciple rapport, *The Perfect Relationship*, Muktananda wrote, "There is a great mirror in the Guru's eyes, in which everything is reflected. The eyes are very active and reveal one's personality. The body can hinder one's self-expression because it is inert and gross, but the eyes are very subtle and offer no obstacle. . . . Whether the Guru tells you so or not, your entire personality is revealed before his eyes. You are seen in every detail as in a clean mirror."

But Muktananda's advice to achieve the spiritual level of the guru by continuously concentrating and meditating on him and showering him with love and devotion can present problems for Westerners, who put a premium on independence and individuality. And, as we now know, there have been enough instances of abuse of power by Eastern gurus in this country to give one pause. Yet for disciples who have been able to avoid such pitfalls and overcome their socialized resistance to out-and-out devotion and imitation, this process has yielded remarkable results. Particularly in a practice as arduous and potentially dangerous as Kundalini Yoga, the guidance of a spiritual adept or teacher is almost essential. One of the most powerful forms of yoga, Kundalini is also one of the fastest ways of reaching self-realization. Muktananda defines Kundalini, which he characterizes as a goddess, as "the primordial Shakti or cosmic energy that lies coiled" in the base of the spine. "When awakened, Kundalini begins to move upward within the *sushumna*, the subtle central channel, piercing the *chakras* and initiating various yogic processes which bring about total purification and rejuvenation of the entire being." When the Kundalini energy reaches the crown chakra at the top of the head, "the individual self merges in the universal Self and attains the state of Self-realization."

In his book *The Kundalini Experience*, Dr. Lee Sannella, a San Francisco-based psychiatrist and co-founder of the Kundalini Clinic, treats Kundalini awakening as a physical event as much as a spiritual transformation. Sannella explains that whereas most spiritual traditions stress the subjective side of the transformative process, the Kundalini experience is an exception. Traditionally, Kundalini—the Sanskrit word means "she who is coiled"—has been referred to as (in the title of Sir John Woodroffe's classic book) "the serpent power" whose uncoiling parallels the unfolding of spiritual awareness in an individual. "According to this Indian tradition," Sannella writes,

the Kundalini is a type of energy—a "power" or "force" (*shakti*)—
that is held to rest in a dormant, or potential, state in the human
body. . . . When this energy is galvanized, "awakened," it rushes
upward along the central axis of the human body, or along the spinal
column, to the crown of the head. Occasionally it is thought to go
even beyond the head. Upon arriving there, the Kundalini is said to
give rise to the mystical state of consciousness, which is indescribably
blissful and in which all awareness of duality ceases.

Sannella underlines the largely physiological nature of Kundalini,
and says it is not necessarily to be confused with "authentic spirituality." Like Gopi Krishna, the great Indian scholar of Kundalini, Sannella contends that "the Kundalini is a fundamental evolutionary
mechanism underlying all psychic and spiritual phenomena," a step
along the way, but only a step. Borrowing from the teachings of Da
Kalki, Sannella continues: "Authentic spirituality, by contrast, is
founded in the moment-to-moment transcendence of the ego, the
body-mind, and all possible experiential states. It has nothing to do
with the search for God or higher evolutionary possibilities. It requires
living on the basis of the intuitive recognition that there is no real
separation from Life, or God, or the Transcendental Reality." But the
bulk of his accounts of clients who reported typical symptoms of
Kundalini awakening make it clear that in the long run, and despite
some uncomfortable early side effects, the experience does leave most
people considerably better off mentally and emotionally than before.

That Kundalini is not limited to practitioners of Hindu meditation
or Siddha Yoga is clear from Sannella's citation of classic Christian
mystical variations of the experience, including St. Thérèse of Lisieux,
and the !Kung people of the Kalahari Desert in Botswana, Africa, who
undergo a Kundalini-type experience they call *n/um*. St. Thérèse's
descriptions do sound something like Kundalini explosions, although
the Catholic Church would undoubtedly dispute such an implication.
(In fact, in December 1989, the Congregation for the Doctrine of the
Faith at the Vatican released a twenty-three-page document caution-
ing Roman Catholics that Eastern meditation practices such as yoga,
Zen, and Transcendental Meditation can "degenerate into a cult of
the body and can lead surreptitiously to considering all bodily sensations as spiritual experiences." It is curious but not atypical that the

Vatican should be so wary of experiences that have been recorded in detail by some of its greatest saints.)*

We ought not underestimate the power of Kundalini at any rate. Dr. Sannella's work often requires him to intervene in the cases of men and women who have undergone Kundalini experiences that have been misdiagnosed, frequently by professional psychologists or psychiatrists, as psychotic episodes. In a series of clinically documented cases, Sannella records instances of clients who "began to worry about going insane," "developed laryngeal spasms, which were accompanied by the fear of choking to death," "suffered from recurring migraine headaches, mental disorganization, and impulsive disruptive behavior," or feared that they "would be labeled and treated as insane"—all of them having undergone various degrees of Kundalini awakening.

However one chooses to view the experience of Kundalini, accounts of those who have undergone it leave little doubt of the transformative impact it has had on their lives. Kathryn Quick, who now lives with her husband and three children in the rural seclusion of Divine Corners, New York, can attest to the changes wrought within her by the serpent power. Divine Corners is nothing like the exclusive North Shore Long Island enclave of Sands Point where Quick raised her family. Neither is Pine Bush, the upstate town where she operates a religious book and gift shop, and where she lived for several years after leaving Sands Point. "It's conservative but friendly, with a live-and-let-live attitude," she said, when we met in the meditation center

---

* The document, signed by Cardinal Joseph Ratzinger and approved by the Pope, apparently misunderstands the nature of most Eastern practice, yet is prescient about the distinction between physiological sensations and authentic spirituality. It first refers to "impersonal techniques or . . . concentrating on oneself, which can create a kind of rut, imprisoning the person praying in a kind of spiritual privatism," a description of meditation diametrically opposed to the teachings of most Eastern masters. But in a segment that seems to echo the concerns of Da Kalki, it then warns: "Some physical exercises automatically produce a feeling of quiet and relaxation, pleasing sensations, perhaps even phenomena of light and of warmth, which resemble spiritual well-being. To take such feelings for the authentic consolations of the Holy Spirit would be a totally erroneous way of conceiving the spiritual life. Giving them a symbolic significance typical of the mystical experience, when the moral condition of the person concerned does not correspond to such an experience, would represent a kind of mental schizophrenia, which could also lead to psychic disturbance and, at times, to moral deviations."

she runs above the gift shop. "They may not join you, and they may not share in what you're doing, but they won't harass you." Her store sits unobtrusively on the main street of Pine Bush, amid the delis and coffee shops typical of small-town America, as if emblematic of the mundane surface of much of the spiritual change going on in this country.

About eight months before, a trance channeler named Robert Johnson had told Quick that someone would be coming to interview her about her life story. Channelers supposedly act as conduits for information and advice from spirit "guides" who speak through them while they are in a self-induced trance. Although she usually gives credence to such sessions, Quick found this information so incredible that she erased the tape recording of the session and immediately put it out of her mind. Now she was sitting in front of another tape recorder, relating the curious skein of events that had brought her to this pass. Aside from being dressed entirely in white, she didn't look unlike the Long Island housewife and mother she was. Her accent, hairstyle, and features resemble softened versions of the ones I encountered growing up there over thirty years ago.

Looking back on her childhood, Kathryn Quick does not find it improbable that she has made such a considerable transition. "I always felt that I was observing, that things did not make sense and were not as they appeared," she said. "I naturally gravitated to the people who were poor and didn't have what I perceived as enough to eat. I brought them home and made sure they ate. My mother would say, 'Why are you always bringing home the poor kids?' In her eyes, I should have been seeking out those who had money. Then maybe some would rub off on us, because we didn't have any. It didn't make sense to her, but a lot of what I did and felt never made sense to her, or to my family in general."

This took place in the blue-collar neighborhoods of Hunts Point in the Bronx, where Quick was born, and Yonkers, just north of New York City, where she went to school. In the Bronx, Quick's family lived with her grandparents, members of a Conservative Jewish community that she credits with having had a "great influence" on her. But when her family moved to Yonkers, her parents joined a Reform temple there, and Kathryn began to lose interest in the faith. "It had no juice, no life, no emotion," she said of the new community, "and

I got nothing out of it." Conservative Jewish practice is "more meaningful, more ritualistic, more traditional" than Reform. "The home is more observant. They light candles on Friday night, they go to the temple, they observe the fact that they should walk and not drive on the Sabbath. Judaism is integrated into their family life, not separate." In her Reform temple, observance was relegated to religious holidays. "Reform is an intellectual exercise," she said. "The sermons are timely with current events, politics, and all that, but they don't touch your heart. For me to relate to God and spirit, I have to feel it in my heart. The mystical tradition, the incense, the chanting, all open the heart so the spirit can come in."

One thing didn't change in her new neighborhood, however. "If people are prejudiced, they don't care if you're Reform, Conservative, or Orthodox," she said. "They hate you. I always got the taunts. Growing up in a Christian area, it was 'Jew' this and 'Jew' that. I didn't like that, and I always defended myself and my people." On the other hand, Kathryn was distressed by what she perceived as the hypocrisy in the Reform temple, where members seemed more interested in dressing up and gossiping before the services than in "focusing themselves." She was turned off further by the constant emphasis on the Holocaust. "I wanted to go to a service and hear about joy, and about life and God," she added. "But it seemed that all we were talking about was death, destruction, and despair, the pain and suffering of being a Jew. That's a fact, but I don't want to keep hearing about it when I go to worship my God." And so she gradually drifted away from active practice.

Although Kathryn wasn't drawn back to Judaism, she did feel that she was searching for something. While still in her teens she decided to try the religion of her friends (and, with no little irony, her taunters), Christianity. She was reluctant to attend Christian services, though, for fear that it might offend her parents. Still, Quick said, "I loved the whole story of Christ, which was very romantic. I wanted the experience of Christ without the experience of the Church. The more I read the New Testament, the more I knew that Christ really had something, that what he said was true."

When, much to the distress of both families, Quick married a Presbyterian at the age of eighteen, she at last felt free to attend Christian services. "But I didn't get it in the Protestant religion either," she said, referring to the kind of transcendent spiritual feeling she had been looking for since childhood. "They're very dry. I wanted the experience of Christ, but each time I went, I felt I was among enemies, that if they knew who I was they would never accept me. And I could never swallow everything the priest was saying, like 'Only those of us who accept Christ can go to heaven.' I knew that my mother was a good woman and my father was a good man. Why couldn't they go to heaven?" Quick and her husband tried many different churches. "But every time they started with 'only our way,' something went click, and I walked out and never went back."

After the birth of her third child, Quick was feeling "very, very unhappy. I didn't know why, but I just thought, This can't be all there is. It didn't make sense, and I started to ask myself, Why am I here? Who am I? Now I know that when you start awakening, the first question you ask yourself is, Who am I? Some spiritual teachers tell their students to keep asking that question."

The Indian sage Ramana Maharshi did just that. "Ramana's method for awakening into primal awareness, or awareness at its Source, is called *vichara*, which simply means inquiry," writes Lex Hixon in *Coming Home*. "It consists of continually asking, and eventually living, the existential question: *Who is it that is having this particular thought or perception I am now having?* or, more simply, *Who am I?* The purpose of the questioning is not to isolate an individual *I* but to trace the rootedness of the separate *I* in the universal *I am*, which itself ultimately dissolves into primal awareness." Or, as Ramana himself put it, "The Self, though obvious, is hidden. It is hidden because of the mistake made in identifying It with the body." Ramana held that the true Self resides in the right side of the chest, opposite the physical heart, and that by the constant process of vichara one can learn to distinguish this Self from the bodily consciousness. In a biography of Ramana Maharshi, his disciple T. S. Anantha Murthy tells how Ramana reduced his teaching to the following: "I am not this body. If so, who am I? I am He." "The seeker of spiritual wisdom should realize," Murthy writes, "that he is not the physical body but is a wave in the Ocean of *Satchidananda*, or God, and that he has been and is abiding as part of that Ocean. This is the crux of the teaching. . . ."

Without knowing any of this, Quick had begun using radical inquiry as a form of contemplation. "And the more I questioned the existence and the purpose of my life," she said, "the more in despair I became. There was no answer. I couldn't figure it out." As her inner doubts dovetailed with external dissatisfactions, Quick asked her husband, Edward, for a divorce and then set about trying to find herself. She went through a long period of psychoanalysis, and took the est training with Werner Erhard, a group experience that had more to do with psychological grounding than with spirituality. The first time she got a sense of something closer to what she was looking for was when she read about psychic phenomena, "ESP, Edgar Cayce, things like that," but she still lacked any direct experience. Analysis and group therapy helped clear up a number of childhood conflicts but left the larger questions unresolved. She would take her kids to school, then sit home "and read and read and read. I started to pray every day to Christ, because I didn't know who else to pray to." One afternoon she was sitting on a staircase by a window with the sunlight shining on her. "I said, 'Dear God, if I ever get out of this mess and get my life back together, I will devote my entire life to you.' But I never thought that I would actually be doing that."

The trauma of the divorce had only added to her growing doubts about the direction her life was taking. In an attempt to fill the void, Quick began going to healing groups, intensifying her study of Edgar Cayce and of the Seth material, a large body of work by the trance channeler Jane Roberts. She studied Silva Mind Control, a secular system of meditation and visualization, and delved into books about Eastern religion and mystical thought in general, including all the writings of Baba Ram Dass. Soon Quick was practicing a form of meditation she had picked up from books, which consisted of sitting in a chair and visualizing a white light.

After more years of study and meditation, Quick reconciled with her husband, and they moved in together without getting remarried. Edward's manufacturing business in Elmhurst, Queens, began to prosper, and he moved the family from Bayside to Sands Point. Known as the home of Perry Como (and later of the tennis star Bjorn Borg), Sands Point is a well-to-do community on that stretch of the North Shore of Long Island that Quick refers to as "the Gold Coast." Living in a house that they later sold for three quarters of a million dollars, Quick once again felt out of step with her surroundings. "Everyone around me was going to the health club three times a week," she said, "exercising to aerobics, wanting to be gorgeous, and spending fortunes on clothing and jewelry. I went through that, and it was meaningless. That kind of activity fills time but it doesn't get you anywhere. So I started turning to God in my own way. I started to read the Bible every day at the kitchen table, and prayed every day. And I started to experience a 'Christ consciousness' awakening in me, a direct communication with God."

Suddenly, Quick became ill with internal hemorrhaging, and went to see a doctor who recommended an immediate hysterectomy to remove a large fibroid tumor in her uterus. She asked for two weeks to prepare herself, and spent the time in intense prayer and meditation. When the two weeks were up, she entered the hospital and had the surgery. "The next day," she said, "the doctor walked into my hospital room and said to me, 'Who are you and what did you do to prepare yourself?'

"I said, 'I'm nobody. Why?'

"He said, 'There was a miracle on the operating table, and we want to know who you are.'

"I said, 'I was unconscious. You tell me what happened.' " The doctor reported that when they cut her open for the hysterectomy, there was virtually no blood loss. "He said he had seen more blood loss from a tooth extraction," Quick said. "This was at Long Island Jewish Hospital, no rinky-dink place, with the chief gynecologist assisting. The doctor also said that during the operation, as he determined in his mind each vein and artery to clamp off in succession, that vein or artery seemed to pop out and 'present itself.' He was astounded at what was happening between his mind and whatever energy was working in my body. He didn't have to say any of this to me because I had been unconscious the whole time and would never have asked about it. But when he told me, it was clear to me what had happened. Just before I went under from the anesthesia, I felt a presence descend on me and the whole room. In my mind, I said to the doctors, 'Let this presence work through you.' At first the doctor told me that he was planning to write an article for one of the medical journals about his experience, but later he changed his mind, saying he had no time. I said I understood, and I did. He probably didn't want to look like a fool."

A phone call to the surgeon in question, Dr. Allan Warshowsky of Port Washington, confirmed most of Quick's recollections, but also revealed a man unlikely to be bothered by the opinions of his peers. He said he is considered "quite a maverick, almost a heretic," because he suggests patients use visualization to help prepare for surgical procedures. And he spoke highly of unorthodox healers such as Carl Simonton of Texas, who has done pioneering work on the role of emotional stress in the onset and development of cancer, and Bernie Siegel, the controversial former surgeon who recommends healing meditations. "Five years ago I tried to get a cancer chemotherapist to acknowledge that the emotions have some effect on the immune system, and he tried to laugh me out of the conference," Warshowsky said. "Today they're talking about how immunity is affected by stress. So it's coming slowly, but it's coming."

If Kathryn Quick had any doubts about the value of meditation and visualization, that experience wiped them away. While she continued her spiritual readings and meditation, she maintained an appearance acceptable to her family and North Shore neighbors. She dressed well and drove a nice car, and never stopped thinking of herself as a traditional housewife and mother. "On the outside," she said, "I was no different from anybody else. I picked up my children at school every day at three fifteen. They did their homework and I made supper." But when the kids sat down to watch television after dinner, she slipped into her meditation room in the basement for an hour or more to chant and pray. Her husband was working long hours, six days a week, at his business in Queens, leaving her lonely in her marriage. But this proved advantageous as it directed her into deeper spiritual pursuit. "I couldn't lose myself in my relationship with my husband," she said. "I could only turn to God. I was lonely, but it was perfect for my growth at the time."

One of her major breakthroughs during this period came on the eve of Yom Kippur, the Jewish Day of Atonement. It was a Sunday and the house was quiet. Even though Quick had not practiced Judaism for years, she felt odd not being in temple on the holiest day of the year. At least she would say some solitary prayers in her basement room. She sat in a familiar yoga posture known as the *chin mudra*, with her hands on the arms of her chair, thumb and index finger forming a circle, and started to pray. " 'Dear God,' I prayed,

'I've been seeking you for so many years. When are you ever going to reveal yourself to me? When are you ever going to remove this pain from my heart?' The pain of separation from God was so great that my heart felt broken. Searching the world for your beloved is a horrible pain, although I didn't understand it at the time. I read about it in the lives of saints who lived hundreds of years ago, raving and looking for God, not understood by anyone."

All of a sudden as she prayed, she felt an explosion of energy at the base of her spine. Having read about Kundalini, she knew enough to identify the experience, yet still found it "awesome and frightening. But having prayed for God to give me something, I wasn't going to run away. When this explosion occurred, it started to rise up through my whole body. It was as if a fire hydrant had opened and the water was gushing at full force. I didn't know if I was going to die, or if I was going to have a heart attack. I just knew that something was happening *in my body*, not in my imagination."

Kathryn's body started to sway back and forth, and when the sensation of energy reached her heart, she felt as if her heart might explode. When it got to her throat, she spontaneously began repeating mantras she had never heard before. Then the energy reached her "third eye," a spot between the eyes just back of the forehead, and her head began to rock back and forth, "like a serpent's." She prayed for God to protect her because she didn't know what was going to happen. "Then the energy went to the top of my head and shot out, poured out," she said. "I felt as if I had become a vessel, and whoever I thought I was inside was now merged with everything on the outside. It was total bliss, just joy. I don't know how long it lasted."

The description she gave frankly sounded so unbelievable that I later searched the literature of Kundalini for something to compare it to. Perhaps the foremost Indian authority on Kundalini is Gopi Krishna, who earned his expertise less by theoretical study than by dint of careful and detailed observation of the Kundalini experience in his own body over twenty-five years. In *Kundalini: The Evolutionary Energy in Man*, Krishna describes his first awakening while meditating at sunrise. "Suddenly, with a roar like that of a waterfall," he writes, "I felt a stream of liquid light entering my brain through the spinal cord. Entirely unprepared for such a development, I was completely taken by surprise. . . . The illumination grew brighter and brighter, the roaring louder, I experienced a rocking sensation and then felt myself slipping out of my body, entirely enveloped in a halo of light." Admitting that any accurate description of the experience is impossible, he reports that his consciousness seemed to grow wider as awareness of his body diminished. Finally, he writes, "I was no longer myself, or to be more accurate, no longer as I knew myself to be, a small point of awareness confined in a body, but instead was a vast circle of consciousness in which the body was but a point, bathed in light and in a state of exaltation and happiness impossible to describe."

Kathryn hadn't read Gopi Krishna at the time of her experience, but she did recall a book by Baba Ram Dass that touched on Kundalini awakening. When she came back to herself, as she put it, she got up and went into the bedroom to find the book. In it, Ram Dass wrote that once the Kundalini experience occurs, you must work with a master, and included a section about different religious teachers and where to locate them. One of the teachers listed was Swami Muktananda, who gave workshops in Kundalini at his ashrams in Manhattan and South Fallsburg, New York. She determined to seek him out, but first, she had to deal with the earthly needs of her family.

"It was significant to me that this happened on the eve of the holiest day of the Jewish calendar," Quick added. "It didn't happen on Christmas Eve. I am still a Jew, I realized then, and there's no denying that heritage, but I could not limit myself to being only a Jew. I was also still a wife and mother living in the suburbs and having to be appropriate. When my husband woke up from his nap that evening, his greatest desire at that moment was to go to the movies in our Volkswagen camper!" In a way, having to maintain a balance between the spiritual reality of her ecstatic experience and the physical reality of the household helped to ground her. "So in this blissful state," she said, "we went to the movies and saw the Muppets. I thought it was the greatest movie I'd ever seen."

The humor of the event wasn't lost on Quick, who still felt as if she were in "an altered state of consciousness." Even as they were getting ready to leave for the movie theater, Kathryn was overcome by feelings of compassionate merging with the universe similar to those expressed by Eastern mystics, but with a decidedly Western, suburban, flavor. "All I could feel was love," she said. "I felt love for the kitchen countertops, and I felt love for the Volkswagen camper. I was swimming in ecstasy. When we got to the parking lot of the theater, I was so careful because I didn't want our car door to knock into the door of another car, because it was me. That door was me, the car was me, everything was me."

For all its explosive power, Kathryn Quick's Kundalini initiation couldn't completely transform the environment in which it had occurred. That night after the movie, she tried to explain to her husband what she was feeling, but with no point of reference he had little chance of understanding her. The next day she was back at work, helping him conduct interviews for new factory workers. "I had just had this once in a lifetime experience, but there I was sitting in a dirty, stinking office," she said, smiling at the irony. "It was back to reality, and integrating it. I felt so much love for the people I was interviewing that I wished I could have given everybody a job."

That evening, Quick had her husband drive her to Muktananda's Manhattan ashram. She knew she would need a personal teacher for further development, but that with a family to raise she couldn't just take off for India "like the Beatles did, and hang out." If God wanted her to have a living master, he would have to send one to New York. As she walked into the ashram, she wondered if Muktananda could be the one. He wasn't present that night, but when she sat down and joined in the chanting of *Om namah shivaya*, she had a mild recurrence of her Yom Kippur eve experience. "The same energy started flowing in me again," she said, "and I recognized the mantra as one that had started to come from my own throat the previous night. This was at least one sign that I had found my guru."

Speaking to the hostess afterwards, Quick learned that at the same time that she had been spontaneously chanting the mantra the night before, Muktananda had been giving a program in Carnegie Hall. The hostess suggested that Quick meet Baba (an affectionate term meaning "Father," by which Muktananda was known to his devotees) in person at an upcoming weekend intensive. Kathryn missed the bus from the ashram to South Fallsburg, where the intensive was to be held, but she decided to rise at three o'clock the next morning and drive herself there. Arriving without incident, she was soon standing on the line for *darshan* with Baba. Darshan, or being in the physical presence of a revered master, is considered a great gift by the followers of Eastern traditions, based on the belief that one benefits simply from being in the energy field of an adept. When the meeting occurred, she asked Muktananda for a spiritual name, and he handed her a card from a stack he had beside him. Quick returned to her seat and read the name Gureeja, and, on the back of the card, its meaning: "Energy of the Kundalini."

During the intensive, she felt at home. The men were on one side of the room, women on the other, as they had been in the Conservative synagogue of her childhood. "It brought me back almost to my roots, in a different form," she said, "very conservative, chanting in a foreign tongue, everyone wearing prayer shawls." In what sounds less like a description of a Jewish service than a born-again Christian ritual, she sat on the floor as Muktananda approached and placed his foot against the base of her spine. "Then he placed his hand on my head," she said, "and the energy exploded. It went higher and higher until finally I screamed, '*Baba! Baba!!*' It was as though all the pain and anguish of searching, from childhood on, came out in a scream of 'Baba!' An assistant came over and said, 'Don't be afraid. Baba wants us to have you lie down.' They bent me forward with my head on the floor and my arms outstretched, and Baba put his foot on my hand. When he did that, it felt like all the pain of seeking was taken right up, and in its place I felt that I was filled with peace. With my free hand I stroked his foot and I said, 'Baba.' And he said, 'Baba.' I could see that it was a chain, me with my new teacher, him acknowledging his teacher. I felt my prayers were answered that night, as if God had guided me to my guru, who was going to take me from where I was to where I had to go. And I've never left him."

Quick decided to legalize her reunion with Edward, and they were remarried at a group service led by Muktananda. She carried on with her life as wife and mother, and continued to chant, spending her summers at the upstate ashram and training to lead a center in her neighborhood. She began to hold Thursday night meditations in her home, attracting the disapproval of the Sands Point police department, who allowed her to continue as long as visitors parked only in her long circular driveway and not on the street. Through ads and articles placed in local papers, she drew a small group of people to chant and meditate with her. "I saw my role as that of a mother hen," she said, "encouraging and supporting people who were seeking until they could become established on their own."

That nobody came on Thursday nights from her own wealthy community, but only those from less privileged circumstances, struck her as ironic. She concluded that, with a few exceptions, people need to suffer somewhat before they are willing to seek solace elsewhere. But when I asked if the material suffering of India provides a more fertile ground for Muktananda's teachings, she replied that no matter what country you come from, life is suffering. "People who have to commute two hours each way to and from work are suffering. And we have our own poverty here, spiritual poverty. It takes different forms. AIDS, cancer, all diseases are suffering. It's only a matter of time before New York City becomes like Calcutta." The reason for the connection between suffering and seeking is that "people who suffer become more sensitive. At some point, when the pain of life is so great, they have to turn up and say, 'God, help me.' If you just say that, really meaning it, then help is there. But we have to do it our way for so long that some of us spend much of our lives, usually until middle age, before we are knocked to our knees. When I ask myself why so many people have to suffer, I sometimes feel it's grace in a sense. They're being given an opportunity to surrender."

In the past twenty or thirty years in the West, it has become far less difficult to gain access to spiritual masters from the East, making it possible for people to develop their spiritual inclinations without leaving home and family behind. "Years ago," Quick said, "you had to travel to India or Tibet under great hardship. You had to leave the world, in essence, and renounce everything. You had to give all your wealth to the guru, then you had to serve him for years, maybe picking up cow dung. Here, the time frame has changed because the need is so great. Now this information is being made available to the masses, although in some cases people don't want the information. But if they do want it, all they have to do is come home, give dinner to their children the way I did, come to the center, have Satsang, chant, receive the teachings, learn to meditate, and go home an hour and a half later. Things have changed in that respect, even though the practices themselves have not."

Quick's belief in the process of awakening the Kundalini is so strong that it raises the question of how she feels about other systems of achieving awareness. "I've read that one can attain enlightenment without having the Kundalini awakened," she said, "but I don't see how that's possible. They may call it another name, but you have to meditate and take the time to purify your life, to lead a disciplined, moral life. You have to create the space for Kundalini to happen. You have to earn it in a sense." But how does that attitude differ from the early Christian apologist Tertullian, who said, "Outside the Church there is no salvation"?

"What I'm saying is that everyone has the Kundalini," Quick responded. "Not just the white race or the yellow race. Every human being is divine—it's not an exclusive club. If anyone takes the time to turn within a few minutes every day, he or she will experience God, whether they want to call it Christ, Buddha, or any other name. They can pray to whatever God in whatever form they want. I'm not judging their way of praying, because minds and temperaments and cultures are very different and they need different forms of expression. They can pray to a rock as far as I'm concerned. But at some point, they've got to sit down and worship that rock. They've got to worship God in whatever form. If they follow their breath, if they repeat this mantra or that mantra, it's all valid. And if they do so with faith, sincerity, and devotion, eventually they will get that experience within themselves. It doesn't have to come through an institution or a formal ritual."

In fact, as Quick pointed out, Christian mystics like St. Thérèse never used the word "Kundalini." "Yet she talks about the many mansions and the many rooms within and many levels, and once you've had the Kundalini awakening, you can read between the lines. She herself may not have known about Kundalini, but her experiences are similar." Quick also referred to Michael Talbot, a modern-day Christian mystic and composer, who "talks about the mystical union with the beloved. As somebody who has had Kundalini experiences, I totally relate to what he's talking about." Through long discussions with her friend Chad Roche, a Higher Initiate in Eckankar, she discovered that they shared an interest in the Light and Sound, an esoteric spiritual experience of auditory and visual phenomena that the two belief systems have in common. In the year since we first spoke, she studied to become an interfaith minister at an interdisciplinary institution in Greenwich Village, New York, called the New Seminary, presided over by the Kabbalah scholar Rabbi Joseph Gelberman. "Each person has a unique experience," she said, "and each is different. We talk about the sushumna, but someone else may use other words."

Swami Muktananda defined sushumna as "the central and most important of all 72,000 *nadis* located in the center of the spinal column extending from the base of the spine to the top of the head. The six chakras are situated in the sushumna and it is through the sushumna channel that the Kundalini rises." According to Quick, the sushumna carries within it the unique impressions of each soul for life, thereby defining an individual's specific needs. "Each person's journey is unique," she said, "but at some point, that energy has to be awakened. We may call it different names. In China they call it *chi*, but if you read the spiritual autobiographies of the great beings, you can see that they've gone through some sort of purification process. That's what the awakening of Kundalini is."

What Quick is talking about, in much the same vein as Lee Sannella, is a physiological phenomenon with spiritual implications, and one not limited to those who actively seek it through devotion to a particular master. But she does believe that some kind of devotion is an aid to development, and that her role is helping other people find that devotion. She is fond of a Muktananda metaphor which views the spiritual seeker as a person digging a series of holes in his backyard, searching for water. After a while, the backyard takes on the texture of a fine Swiss cheese, full of holes each only a few feet deep. At some point, you have to stand fast and keep digging in the same spot until you have dug a well. "You may have to go down two thousand feet, but you will get that water," she said. "And it's the same thing with a spiritual path. Eventually you have to stick with one path."

While Kathryn and Edward were still living in Sands Point, she began having a series of dreams which advised her that she would soon be starting a center of her own—dreams that she resisted, not wanting the responsibility. In the dreams she addressed groups of people and had overnight guests in her home. "Night after night, I had the same kind of dream," she said. "It was driving me crazy, as if I would get no rest until I obeyed. Then one night, just before dawn, I had a dream that I was being lifted. I was sleeping, but I was traveling, almost like in an elevator, going up, up, up, up, up. I stopped and a door opened, and my teacher, Muktananda, was standing there. I threw myself down at his feet. I'm not one of these people who have nightly dreams of their teachers. I hadn't dreamed of him in ages, and he had passed on years before. But in the dream he took me on his lap and told me what I was to do, and then asked me if I understood. The whole time he was rubbing my back, and I was crying. 'You will do this and this, and then this will happen,' he said. 'Do you understand?' I said, 'Yes, Baba.' He went on for the longest time, making very specific requests, telling me that he would be doing it through me. I was to remember that he was in charge.''

When Kathryn awoke, she could not remember the specifics, Baba having told her that if she knew consciously what was to happen, she wouldn't be able to focus on the present, and it wouldn't work. "My job," she said, "is to keep the lines of communication clear through doing my practices and surrendering to my destiny, whatever that may be. That isn't to say that everything will be smooth. When I awoke, I sat bolt upright in bed and said, 'My God, I've just been with Baba,' and the tears came. I couldn't talk about the experience for months without crying.''

Shortly after the dreams had begun, the Quicks were forced to move from Queens for business reasons, and her husband established a new factory in the southern Catskills. Now Kathryn told Edward they would have to move again. They bought the storefront in Pine Bush that doubles as the bookstore and meditation center where she holds regular gatherings, and a home where she sponsored appearances by one of Swami Muktananda's co-successors, named Bhagawan Nityananda after Baba's own guru. (Muktananda's other co-successor, Nityananda's sister Gurumayi Chidvilasananda, broke with Nityananda in 1985 and now continues Muktananda's ashram in South Fallsburg.)

Quick contends that the string of Eastern masters—Hindu, Tibetan, Taoist, and others who have recently made their appearance in America—have come here "to seed this country, not to transplant themselves. It's almost the theory of man's beginnings on this planet. On that subject Swami Muktananda was in agreement with the Christian fundamentalists. He didn't feel that we evolved from apes in some simplistic way. His theory was that, according to researches from the East, this planet was seeded by beings called Siddhas from a more highly evolved planet, and that we are descendants of these perfected ones. When the Eastern masters came to the West during the sixties and seventies, they were seeding, and it was our destiny to be their audience. 'Those who have ears to hear, let them hear,' as the Bible says. I drank in what Muktananda had to say, and, as a housewife and mother, I adapted it to the West. Now I can relate to the people sitting around me and tell them how they can also do these practices and be a better mother, a better husband, a better salesman. When your mind is clear and calm, you'll be better at whatever you do."

For Quick, the initial experience of Kundalini was clearly ecstatic and consciousness-altering. "But then you come down," she said, "and you have to function like anybody else. The difference is that for some reason I got the answer to the question, Who am I? I know who I am." Who she is consists of a "divine consciousness manifesting as the particular form of Gureeja Quick. Behind all the exterior movement there is an interior peace, the 'peace that passeth all understanding.' I used to think that if I became enlightened, I would be so ecstatic that I'd be out of my mind, but that's not true. If you're a carpenter, you'll remain a carpenter. If you're a schoolteacher, you're still a schoolteacher. God exists *as* you. You are perfect as you are. You don't have to become anyone else."

The children can still be a challenge, and daily problems don't automatically straighten themselves out. In some ways, though, she credits her spiritual development with helping her children make it through some difficult times. Because she sees herself as divine, she sees the same divinity in her children, regardless of their behavior. "If I'm taking care of little gods and goddesses," she said, "then it can never quite become the drudgery it would be if I just saw them as annoying little brats driving me crazy. If you can keep it clear in your mind that these children are here for your growth, and that you can serve God through your children, then everything you do with them takes on a spiritual quality." Although her kids went through their share of typical teenage difficulties, she feels they were able to get over them quickly because she had imbued them with high self-esteem. And after more than ten years of watching Kathryn's spiritual activities without taking an interest, her husband began sitting in her meditation groups and had a Kundalini experience. He now meditates and chants and continues running his manufacturing business.

From Quick's perspective, a greater impediment to spiritual awareness than the extraordinary wealth and material comfort enjoyed by

Americans relative to most of the world is pro forma faith. It's not so much the attitude of organized religion as of congregants who follow only the perfunctory rules of their creeds without seeking the deeper essences inherent in them. "I don't have all the answers," she said, "so I can only speak from my own experience. But just going to church on Sunday and paying your membership dues, just going to temple on Friday night, standing up when the congregation stands and sitting down when the congregation sits, is not going to get you anywhere. The search has to begin within the individual, and then it doesn't matter what church you belong to."

One day Quick was visited by the minister of a local Sands Point church whose congregation was "concerned" about what she was doing in her home. When she asked the pastor if he had ever meditated, he told her that he meditated daily on the Word, on Scripture. "That's contemplation," she told him. "But do you ever go beyond the mind? Do you ever still your mind and go into the silence?" He said he didn't, so she suggested he try it first and then return to talk about what goes on in her home. She feels that too many of the people who preach in churches and synagogues are themselves not informed by spiritual experiences. "They can quote all the Scriptures and argue me into the ground, but they don't feel the connectedness with God inside their own being, so they can't give it to their followers. You can only give what you have."

That doesn't mean that if people learn to meditate, they necessarily end up leaving the church of their childhood. Quick's experience is that "once they can quiet their minds and meditate, they can go back to their church and experience the God there. It has to come from within, but nobody has taught them how. I got a letter from a Catholic girl thanking me for giving her the knowledge so that she can experience God for herself, within the context of her own church."

Given Kathryn Quick's background in conservative religiosity, I wasn't surprised that, when asked about the tenor of American society, she said that she saw "a definite deterioration in morality." What, then, was the appropriate place of sexuality in the emerging consciousness of which she spoke? Muktananda did teach celibacy, and moderation in married life, and she found that valid. Even beginners at the ashram were urged to consider refraining from sex for a week after leaving, because if they retained their seminal fluids, the teaching he had given them would have a chance to take root. His advice was tied to the notion popular in Eastern thought that sexual energy in general and the sexual fluids in particular are a source of vitality that can be channeled into spirituality. "I've gone through periods during my marriage when I practiced celibacy for a while," Quick said. "There's no right or wrong with sex. There's nothing sinful about it, and it's not harmful. But the sexual fluid gets transformed into the Kundalini energy. If you can conserve the sexual fluid, the sexual energy, both male and female, and continue your practice of chanting and meditation, you can transmute that sexual energy into spiritual energy. What I have found in my own practice is that when I did remain celibate for long periods of time, I would be able to meditate in a deeper way. The internal fire was hotter, and I would experience Kundalini rising in a much more powerful way. Once the Kundalini energy reached the sexual center and moved into the navel area, there would be an orgasm, but it would be an internal orgasm. The bliss would be there, the same release and exhilaration, but then the energy would rise into my heart and I would feel a tremendous amount of heat and love in my heart, universal love."

The idea is not to suppress sexuality, because suppression leads to neurosis. If, according to Muktananda, one can raise the energy of the lower emotions from the lower three chakras—located in the base of the spine, genitals, and navel—to the fourth chakra, the heart, then it becomes divine love and passion for God. "So we use the sexual energy for our spiritual growth," Quick said. "At times in my own *sādhana*, or practice of spiritual discipline, I felt that I was at a critical point and I had to maintain celibacy. And, perhaps because of God's grace, my husband understood. It's not forever, though."

Muktananda believed above all in being appropriate where sex was concerned. Although he encouraged followers to be celibate for brief periods, he also chided spouses who said that they wished to *remain* celibate after entering into a marriage agreement. Sex is part of that agreement, and he didn't feel they could break the agreement and still expect the benefits of being married. Quick feels that seekers have a hard time being appropriate, and go from one extreme to another. "If you are in a married state, then celibacy is not appropriate. But if you start going with this man and that man, or woman, how are you going to have peace of mind? Your mind will be divided. If you want to live a worldly life and not think about God, and you don't want to attain anything spiritual, that's fine. There's nothing wrong with being in love with ten people. If you want to attain God, though, you have to quiet the mind and the passions, and focus within. So then you might as well find one person you can enjoy life with, who will support you in your attainment, and go through life with that one person."

Quick's Kundalini experiences came more frequently early in her practice when she lived a more "reclusive" life at home, "doing intensive spiritual practices for hours a day, not working in the world." In the past few years, though, she has concentrated her energy on building up the meditation center, traveling and working with people, and she hasn't been spending as much time going within. "Now the Kundalini happens just once in a while," she said, "but I know how to get back inside any time. Once you do it often enough, you can do it more easily when you want to."

To the Eastern mind, God is One; suffering stems from the dualistic nature of the material world. Good and evil, life and death, female and male, joy and despair, darkness and light are among the principles of opposition in which Eastern sages locate the roots of suffering and unhappiness. Once there is an "other," once we are separate from one another or from God, they say, it is impossible to experience the bliss that only union with the Absolute can bring—the experience variously referred to as kensho, samadhi, satori, or simply Oneness. But if the world is by definition dualistic, if this is, in fact, "the planet of polarity," what recourse do we have?

"It's true that this world is a world of duality," Quick said. "Those who are asleep, unconscious, think that this is real, that duality is the way it's supposed to be. But every once in a while somebody will wake up and say, 'No, this is an illusion. I want to know the One Truth. Who am I?' Through the process of meditation, through awakening the Kundalini, you can perceive the Oneness in duality. There is just one Consciousness, appearing as many. When you can begin to see that, then you can live in the world, acknowledging the duality. I can see that you're a man and I'm a woman, and I act appropriately. I can also see that there's no difference between you and me. We're one consciousness, one energy, one being. But we still must act appropriately. I don't walk on certain streets at certain hours, because although I may see everybody as God, they don't always see *me* as God. But when you experience that awakening, it's almost like being in love. There's a rush when the heart opens, and the trees are so beautiful. They were always beautiful, but now you see them for what they are. If you can maintain that awareness, then every day is an experience of being in love: How beautiful everything is, how beautiful everyone is."

CHAPTER 14

Vicki Mullen: Moving Energy

■   ■   ■

God cannot be grasped by the mind. If he could be grasped, he would not be God.

—Evagrius of Pontus

The way that can be described is not the way.

—Lao-tzu

God heals, and the doctor takes the fee.

—Benjamin Franklin

■

The time I met Vicki Mullen she had come to my home in upstate New York as one half of a team of itinerant healers. Her traveling companion was a man by the name of Bob Tobey, whose appearance and credentials were, at first glance, far more formidable than Mullen's. Whereas Mullen is a diminutive and unassuming brunette, almost introverted, Tobey presents the ruddy complexion, golden mane and beard of a Nordic warrior-sea captain out of some Jack London novel; his résumé boasts a doctorate in applied mathematics and experimental psychology from Harvard and positions as research scientist with the Atomic Energy Commission, the Air Force, and IBM. But Vicki Mullen, with twenty years of experience in various kinds of physical therapy, was the one who seemed to me to have the power to move energy fields with her hands and to exert a healing influence with very little effort.

Mullen and Tobey had come highly recommended by Roger Woolger, the Jungian analyst who for many years has worked with therapeutic clients by regressing them to experiences of what he calls past lives. Past-life regression is a controversial area of alternative therapy, partly because it is so resistant to proof and so open to misunderstanding and misuse by therapists, and partly because it sounds utterly preposterous to anyone who doesn't accept the possibility of reincarnation in the first place. But unlike many of the past-life regressions I had read or heard about in which the subject invariably relives some grandiose existence as an Egyptian princess, a Renaissance painter, or perhaps Moses or Elijah, Woolger's sessions lead his clients to relive existences so traumatic and unglamorous that nobody would want to know about them unless he absolutely had to.

Furthermore, Woolger doesn't insist that the "memories" he elicits correspond to actual past lives, but feels that they represent states of consciousness that have a significant bearing on the client's current dilemma. In *Other Lives, Other Selves*, he explains that it is not necessary to take these experiences literally if the client chooses not to, or does not believe in reincarnation. "As I always tell my clients," Woolger writes, " '*It doesn't matter whether you believe in reincarnation or not. The unconscious mind will almost always produce a past life story when invited in the right way.*' Indeed, I am sometimes inclined to think that even if the conscious mind is highly skeptical about the reality of past lives as historical memories, the unconscious is a true believer and is simply waiting to be asked."

The overall intelligence and evenhandedness of Woolger's argument, bolstered by several discussions I had with him on the subject, gave him a certain credibility in my eyes, and so I was predisposed to trust the odd-looking couple whom I had invited into my living room on his recommendation. In my first session with Vicki and Bob, I lay down on a standard massage table with my eyes closed while they took turns manipulating parts of my anatomy. It seemed so much like a variation of other kinds of bodywork I'd experienced, such as therapeutic massage and Rolfing (an intrusive realignment of muscular structure), that I wasn't ready for the intense emotional responses that began to rage through me. Two minutes into the session, when Vicki stroked my left temple, I burst into tears. It wasn't just a good cry, but a stream of uncontrollable convulsions that racked my body and felt as if they would never stop. Three days after the session I still had flecks of red under my eyes.

The session went on for almost two hours, as my body was gently assisted in going through a series of contortions. There were times when I was astonished at the feelings Bob and Vicki were evoking, and times when I questioned the reasonableness of going through with it all. But I didn't question the immediate aftereffects of this and a subsequent treatment, which left me feeling extraordinarily exhilarated, if somewhat exhausted.

Undoubtedly, these people knew how to get the energy flowing in my body. As we sat down to dinner afterwards and Bob began to talk about their itinerant life, I thought of Paul Lowe, another traveling teacher. When I brought up his name, Bob seemed surprised, and I asked if he knew Lowe. "I knew him under his sannyas name of Teertha," he said. That was how I learned that Tobey had also been a student of Bhagwan Shree Rajneesh during the time that Lowe had been leading those controversial encounter groups. The more we talked, the more strongly I felt I should interview Bob and Vicki formally. Their one precondition was that I first learn more about the principles behind what they do by attending one of their open seminars. Since none was planned nearby before they were to leave the Northeast, I agreed to host a gathering in Woodstock, and to invite other alternative healers from the area: Rolfers, chiropractors, Trager practitioners, a podiatric surgeon, and a homeopath, among others. It turned out to be an elucidative evening on several different levels, and a few of the issues that were raised then are worth mentioning.

The link between spirituality and healing is increasingly hard to ignore as the successful results of alternative healers with a basis in metaphysical practice continue to be reported in the New Age press. Nonetheless, many people remain very skeptical about such healers, perhaps with some justification. If fully accredited doctors such as Bernie Siegel or Allan Warshowsky, who advocate adding alternative techniques to the healing repertoire, are still treated with mistrust by many of their colleagues, then how much less credibility must be enjoyed by pioneers in these fields who lack any established medical credentials. Unfortunately, few ways exist of evaluating alternative practitioners other than firsthand trial and error. Licensing agencies are rare, and in many cases no established professional groups oversee or recommend such practitioners. One can practice rebirthing, massage, and many alternative forms of healing with only a brief training period, perhaps under someone whose training was equally sketchy. On the other hand, because many of these techniques are so new, it is still possible to study with the originators, providing a direct link to the source no longer available in more established therapies. (For that reason, lineage can be one helpful guide: a Benjamin massage therapist who studied with Ben Benjamin, a Bioenergetic analyst who worked with Alexander Lowen, or a rebirther trained by Leonard Orr or Sondra Ray at least has a better likelihood of having properly absorbed the essence of those techniques.) Still, I wonder whether alternative healers would be thriving if the medical establishment were adequately meeting its patients' needs. Less than fifty years ago, chiropractors were labeled "quacks" by the American Medical Association and were subject to arrest in some states. Yet I have rarely been in a chiropractor's office that wasn't overrun with patients who were presumably not getting adequate treatment elsewhere.

The people who gathered in our home that evening represented a small cross section of the field, tending to the more established end of the alternative spectrum, although to someone not familiar with the language of alternative healing, what they had to say may sound strange indeed. They included Howard Finkelson, a Rolfer. (A typical Rolfing program involves a series of ten one-hour sessions of soft-tissue manipulation and re-education. After five sessions I gave up, deciding the pain wasn't worth the results, which were not clear. Many people, however, announce remarkably helpful effects.) George Quasha integrates several forms of bodywork, including Trager work and the Chinese disciplines of Tai Chi Chuan and Chi Kung. (Named for Dr. Milton Trager, Trager work, or Psychophysical Integration and Mentastics, emphasizes free movement and natural release, and is a far less invasive form of bodywork than Rolfing.) A poet and video artist, Quasha also runs an independent publishing company called Station Hill Press, specializing in books on the body-mind continuum, as well as a literary line. Roger Woolger's spiritual training combines Christian and Theravaden Buddhist traditions. Robert Stewart is a practitioner of homeopathic medicine. A few friends were invited to take part in the colloquy or just observe.

On a cold and snowy night the discussion began with Bob Tobey explaining how he had entered the healing profession in the first place. "I was an itinerant home repairman and carpenter in Saratoga Springs three years ago," he said, "and before that I had a professional career for thirty years as a research scientist. Then the universe started putting me in situations where I began to realize that I was a healer. Somehow I was moving energy, and people who saw energy would tell me so, even though I had no idea what I was doing. So part of it is just trusting that what comes into me to do is the right thing. Vicki is another story."

"I come from a traditional medical background," Vicki said. As a physical therapist who dealt mostly with very young children for twenty years, she had gotten results that baffled her colleagues. "I didn't call myself a healer then," she said. "It wasn't until I had several experiences and started healing myself, a year ago, that I finally made the declaration that I was a healer. But I was also a childhood educator, and it was very easy to be in a group and to tune in to people and find out from them what their energy—as I would now call it—was, and where to meet them. That's what I continue to do when we work."

"I don't feel energy most of the time, and I don't see it," Bob said. "I just somehow know what to do."

The idea of "moving energy" may sound peculiar to anyone not familiar with Eastern or New Age concepts of psychic and spiritual energy. In an earlier chapter I discussed briefly the notion of differing vibratory levels and the potential effects of meditation on those levels. One could likewise distinguish among different kinds of energy and levels or rates of energy movement. That issue came up in the meeting when Bob Stewart, the homeopathic practitioner, asked Tobey what he meant by energy. "For a scientist," Stewart said, "there is a definition of energy, but you're using it in a different way."

"What's the scientific definition?" Tobey asked.

"There are three modes of energy," Stewart replied, "nuclear, electrical, and gravitational. But what do *you* mean?"

"We see the difference in the way people move and present themselves," Tobey said. "Even as we're talking to you, you can pick up different charges or energy on the question or on the answer. There are subtle differences that I call 'energy charge.' I'm not interested in precise definitions because so much goes on that I'm not sure how to frame it in that way. I'd say that we can explain seventy to eighty percent of the work we do in terms of anatomy—a lot of which the medical world is not trained in—and the other twenty percent continues to be a mystery. We feel energy, we sense it, when we're working with other people. Do you understand what I'm saying?"

"It's a word that has crept in and been taken over by the New Age healers," Stewart said, "and it's never been defined. What I'm saying is that they borrowed this term from science—"

"Maybe science borrowed it," Tobey shot back. "I don't know the etymology."

George Quasha knew the etymology of energy. "It comes from the Greek," he said. "What it means in the Greek is a matter of a lot of discussion, because the best etymologies of *energein* in Greek seem to imply that it means everything we want it to mean now in the broadest possible sense. The narrowing of the word into specific external, verifiable forms of energy is a very recent event in the history of that word. Another complication arises because the word is used to translate certain foreign terms which have an environment of their own, such as [the Chinese word] *chi*, and which have an extremely rich range of definition within those languages. There will be many forms of *chi* for which we have no word, so we attempt to make compound words: 'primary chi,' 'environmental chi,' and so forth."

Tobey felt that a couple of stories might illustrate what he meant by energy better than a definition. He described the case of a fireman he and Vicki had treated in Boise, Idaho, who was forty years old but looked fifty-five. The fireman was bent over and walked with a cane because of a spinal fusion suffered two years before. When they got him on the portable massage table, Bob and Vicki performed some gentle myofascial and cranial work. "What we were doing was tuning in to his body, supporting it in moving the way it wanted to move," Tobey said. "We don't move it ourselves. You've all turned off the flow of water in a garden hose by kinking it. When you live through an accident, like being in a car that rolls over, your body goes through different trajectories, and the energy gets locked or kinked in those trajectories. For the release to occur, you have to go back into that same trajectory. The body knows this, which is why we use the phrase 'body wisdom.' In the weekend groups we lead, we've actually had four or five people holding somebody in the air and gradually moving him or her through a weird trajectory."

The fireman went through a number of gyrations as they worked on him, and then he came down off the table onto the floor. "After an hour's work he was on the floor huddled up in a fetal position and his whole body was shaking, releasing blocked energy," Bob said. "There was a lot of pain and fear of pain that we took him to the edge of so that he could let his body do that." When the fireman stood up fifteen minutes later, he appeared several inches taller. Two days afterwards, he was reportedly able to walk without his cane, enjoyed complete restoration of range of motion, and was pain-free. Three weeks later, the fireman reported to his massage therapist that although he still had complete range of motion, the pain had returned "about fifty percent." Whereupon the massage therapist asked the fireman whether the pain would be back if he didn't have a lawsuit pending that was going to pay him close to $700,000, based on the fact that he was in pain. The fireman got the point. As Tobey put it, "He had an investment in keeping his pain. That's why we say we can't heal people, we can only be with them during their healing processes."

He made the point that he and Mullen are "first and foremost energy movers," because "disease arises when energy is blocked," adding that "fear has been used for millennia to force people to sit on their energy." If we accept the notion of energy as a kind of bioelectric force moving through the body—one startling manifestation of which is the Kundalini experience—then it may be possible to discuss other phenomena which are commonly treated with great skepticism, such as human auras. The human aura has been depicted in art for centuries as the nimbus of light surrounding the head of Jesus Christ, Mary, and certain disciples and saints, as well as in Buddhist iconography. Clairvoyants such as Annie Besant and C. W. Leadbeater have claimed to see the auras of ordinary individuals in this century. But recently more concrete proof has been advanced. "First of all," Tobey said, "the human aura has been instrumented in research labs at UCLA Medical School. This work was done between 1974 and 1979 with a healer named Rosalyn Bruyere, who sees auras quite clearly and distinctly. At the end of that five-year period, researchers were able to predict what their instruments would show based on what she said she saw. So there's a direct correlation. It is physically measurable."

Vicki had a more practical way of explaining the idea of energy fields. "Are you sometimes aware that you're uncomfortable because someone is standing too close to you?" she asked. "You keep backing away and you feel you're drawing yourself in. That's two energy fields moving. You have an energy field about you. When you feel drawn to put your hand on somebody, you're connecting with that part of the energy field that you feel in your hand."

Tobey discussed a machine used in Europe for diagnostics called the Voll Machine, or Dermatron, "that involves tuning in to the subtleties of energy vibration." Developed by a German physician, Reinhardt Voll, this machine allows the user to measure the electrical parameters of any acupuncture point in the body. According to Tobey, it uses the body somewhat like the battery in an electrical circuit, and the readings can help homeopathic practitioners to prescribe certain remedies. It is also currently illegal for use by medical practitioners in this country.* Clearly, the measurement and treatment of energy forces in the human body is in its infancy here, and so Tobey and Mullen's work is as pioneering as it is difficult to evaluate scientifically. Even for experienced practitioners, the work is often extremely subtle. "Some people are very sensitive to energy movement in their bodies," Tobey said, "and others are not sensitive at all. Cranial work, for example, involves working on the bones of the skull. You have individual bones there, separated by live tissue, and the conventional wisdom is that those bones grow together and become one solid skull at some point. That's not necessarily true at all. In fact, there is a craniosacral rhythm, a breathing of the skull and the spine that is about twice as slow as your breath, and is also different from the pulse rate. When you open that up, a lot can happen. You can do craniosacral work with pressure no stronger than the weight of a nickel. It's direction of energy, and you're inviting the tissue to let go."

Mullen later told the story of a sixty-five-year-old retired Methodist minister with whom they worked at an introductory lecture-demonstration. He had just moved to Sidona, Arizona, and had developed

---

* For more information on Reinhardt Voll and the Dermatron, see Richard Gerber, *Vibrational Medicine: New Choices for Healing Ourselves* (Santa Fe, N.M.: Bear & Co., 1988).

a sore shoulder while building his new home there. About five minutes into the session, as the man lay on the work table and Bob and Vicki were "channeling energy" through him, he started sobbing and continued to cry for nearly an hour. At the end he said, "Thank you for giving me back my tears. I haven't cried in sixty-four years." His wife, a very demure-looking woman, also had tears in her eyes when she approached them after observing the session. "He didn't even cry when we buried our child," she said.

Alongside energy and craniosacral work, Tobey and Mullen speak about the fascia in the body, from which the term "myofascial release" derives. "Myo" stands for muscle, and the fascia is the body's connective tissue. "The fascia is the thin, silvery layer that you see in beef or chicken when you cut it up, between the fat and the muscle," Mullen explained. According to Tobey, "At a microscopic level, fascia is constructed of collagen fibers tied into each other like a huge macrame net. That very thin transparent tissue wraps every two or three muscle cells, so that a large muscle has fascia all through it. The tendons and ligaments are fascia in which the collagen fibers are organized like the wires in a suspension bridge cable. The bone is fascia in which mineral salts have crystallized to make it solid."

"In high school anatomy class, they just referred to fascia as connective tissue," Mullen said. "That's why we say that eighty percent of our healing work can be explained anatomically. It's just that the majority of the medical profession hasn't been trained that way. They've learned their anatomy on cadavers." One day, Bob and Vicki were being towed to Boise by a mechanic and his friend, and got to talking about healing and about the fascia. "I wasn't sure they were taking in any of it," Mullen said. "Then one of the men said, 'Oh, yeah. I know exactly what you're talking about. When you skin a deer, within ten minutes after the deer dies, that stuff gets hard and you practically can't manage it.' So anyone who works on cadavers doesn't experience fascia the way it is. But now a lot of osteopaths are being trained in myofascial work. It takes *intent* for the fascia to release. You can't force it to release because it's a hundred times stronger than steel—two thousand pounds per square inch anywhere in the body. We have to work with energy and invite it to let go and release the traumas that are involved."

In the growing fetus, the fascia apparently forms first and then forms pockets into which the organs grow. Ida Rolf, the creator of Rolfing, said that the organ of bodily structure is not the bones but the fascia, according to Howard Finkelson. "She also believed that the fascia is malleable, as opposed to muscle and skin, which are contractive, resilient," Finkelson said. He meant that the fascia can be molded and then hold its new shape, a basic principle behind Rolfing.

The implications of energy movement become more significant when we speak of the results of damming up that movement early in life. Bob Tobey conjured the image of a small child in a supermarket, running up and down the aisles, laughing and generally exhibiting more energy than its parents—behavior for which the child might be reprimanded, punished, or otherwise intimidated. "In one way or another when we were small," he said, "we all decided, albeit unconsciously, to shut down our breathing so that we would receive food, shelter, clothing, and love from those giants who couldn't handle our energy. And so part of the work we do is to coach you in your breathing, to watch for where the breath is not the way a newborn infant breathes. When you shut down your breath, you set up adhesions in the fascia, and by working with the breath, we're inviting the fascia to let go in a holistic way. Hence we don't have to diagnose which muscles are taut."

Simply put, we all withdraw our breath from that part of the body which is in pain. "The anatomy is constructed in such a way that it gets the message to hold automatically, but it never gets the message to let go automatically," Tobey said. "So if you haven't let yourself feel or express certain emotions, they're bound down in the fascia, and breathing can help us get there. One thing about the breath is beautiful: no one else can breathe for you. We can work with you and coach you, but only you can bring the breath of life into your own body."

Up to this point, the words "spiritual," "God," or "religion" had not been mentioned, perhaps because all the participants implicitly agree that energy *is* spiritual, that the scientific wisdom of the Vedas, the Microcosmic Orbit of the Taoists, and most yogic and meditative practices imply the indivisibility of spirit and energy. However, the connection was eventually made explicit by Bob Tobey. "The most prevalent spiritual disease of our time is not wanting to be here," he said, "not wanting to be in a physical body. In terms of trauma in the

body, whether in this life—physical abuse, sexual abuse, whatever—
or from past lives, we find that a lot of healers who are very much
into 'spiritual' things have a difficult time being fully in the body. The
healing is often about releasing the pain and torment that is bound
down in the body, so that the energy and the body can function
together."

George Quasha seemed to confirm what Tobey was talking about.
"I do bodywork, and what's been coming to me clearly in the last
several years is that whenever I touch somebody, the first thing I feel
is the degree to which they're not there," he said. "It's almost as
though what one has to do is to attract them back. Somehow by being
there for them, you're making contact with the potential for someone
to be there too."

Tobey talked about the case of a woman whose body exhibited a
strangely contorted anatomy that appeared to conform to past-life
experiences of a deformed, crippled body that had come up in therapy.
"Do you want to hear a way-out hypothesis?" he asked. "What if we
did live past lives, and what if we come into this life with an energy
field that is somehow maimed or deformed, and that energy field is
the template that guides the fascia in the way it grows in the fetus?
That would explain everything, wouldn't it? It's as though, if you've
had significant injury to a certain part of your body in a past life, that
part of your body is prone to injury in this life."

"You could say she was inhabiting a body image that was lopsided,"
Roger Woolger said. "I would postulate that at birth, even at conception, there is the seed form of the body image, and that seed form
contains a lot of *sanskaras*, or past-life wounds. If one has been crippled, that area will repeat at a certain time."

"Roger calls it a body image," Quasha said, "and you call it a
template. We could call it any number of things, but we need something that says that energy patterns have integrity. And when they're
given integrity by some form of intention, whether it's a wound or
something that you actually evolve, it tends to persist until it's
changed, or until something larger supplants it. Salamanders can reproduce parts of their bodies. We can reproduce our mangled members
from past lives. One thing we know about ourselves is that we replicate. We make more of the same with what we are, at whatever
level we're living."

"We have clients," Vicki said, "who remember being animals, so we don't always replicate as human beings."

"I once had a guy who was a boulder," Roger said, to a chorus of laughter. The atmosphere lightened, and Roger asked Bob about body image. "Have you had men experiencing or imagining being in women's bodies, or vice versa?"

"Of course," Bob said. "We've had men being in women's bodies, experiencing female orgasm, giving birth. We've had women in male bodies, feeling that they had an erect penis. Those are the extremes, but whenever that happens, we encourage the person to enjoy it. It may be the only time in their life they'll know what the other sex feels like."

That is only a small sample of the evening's exchange of ideas, and it indicates just part of the scope of thinking among alternative healers. Mullen and Tobey acknowledged afterwards that much of their terminology and theory was influenced by Deane Juhan's book, *Job's Body: A Handbook for Bodywork*, but their refinements and hands-on work are, naturally, their own. Although I interviewed them both, I chose Vicki's story because, of the two, her background was the more mundane, and her narrative showed such a marked divergence from Kathryn Quick's. Both women appear to have had classic Kundalini experiences, and yet they could hardly have been more dissimilar in terms of upbringing and orientation.

Until recently, Vicki Mullen was totally unaware of how healing and spirituality coincided in her, having shown little or no overt interest in the latter. To call her life earthy is probably an understatement. She was born Vicki Dobbins in 1947 in Emporia, Kansas, where her father worked as an oil field gauger. "That was how I became addicted to the smell of crude oil," she said, when we spoke the morning after the group discussion. "I *love* the smell of crude oil." Raised a Methodist, she lived in a house across the street from the church after the family moved to Bogue, Kansas, "a place out in the Western plains, flat land where the only tree is a cottonwood that grows right along a river." Mullen's memory of the Methodist church is less of a religious institution than of a social gathering place. She sang in the choir, acted in church plays, and hung out with friends from church. The only other nearby church was a Catholic one fifteen miles away. "That made life very simple," she said. "All my friends went to the same church."

Around the age of eight, she realized that "God wasn't a big, elderly man sitting someplace in the sky. One day I went to my mother and said, 'I think that God is just a kind of big energy. He's not something you can put your finger on.' I remember using that word 'energy' even then. And she just said, 'Oh.' I didn't necessarily believe that God was Methodist, either. That came to be a telling thing when a couple who had been our Sunday School teachers for several years changed religions to Seventh Day Adventist, and everybody was just horrified. They were all concerned about the kids this couple had taught, but I said, 'Why?' They changed how they were living a little, but they still showed love, which is what the Christian religion teaches is its basis."

Mullen's family found little reason to question their own faith until her father committed suicide when she was eleven years old, at which point her mother stopped going to church. Vicki went along with that for a while, but soon she felt drawn to the church youth group and went back on her own. Her father had been, in her words, "mentally ill" for several years before she was born. "What really started eating on him was that he had had a relationship with a woman who died of syphilis. He actually held her in his arms as she died. And he convinced himself that he had syphilis, or was going to develop it."

Vicki's anguish at the death of her father was compounded by the fact that for some time before his death, she "would lie in bed at night asking God to let him die so we would have peace. I've had to work through a lot of guilt over that, the child thinking that she had killed Daddy." A few months after her father died, she remembered, "A spirit came to me, holding its hand out in front of me and saying, 'Your father is at peace.' It manifested itself as a presence, an energy."

But Mullen traces her career as a healer to a more concrete set of circumstances. "I started being my family's caregiver when I was about four," she said. "When my younger sister got sick, both my parents started getting sick. What we're finding out now about healers is that they have seemingly been the adult forever. In that vein, I took over the adult feelings about religion and the world." Soon after her father's suicide, her sister died of leukemia, and Mullen and her mother went to live with her grandparents in Tulsa, Oklahoma. They later got a home of their own in the area. "Just the two of us lived together," she said. "I didn't have a mother, I had a friend." About a year after they had moved into their own house, her mother started trying to commit suicide. She tried three times unsuccessfully, and Vicki was the one who found her the first time. In high school, she tried to assume the appearances of a normal life, joining the school marching band and studying nursing. Her hopes of pursuing a career in physical therapy did not fit in with a place and time in which women were not encouraged to do anything more professional in the health field than nursing.

Completing her studies at the University of Oklahoma, Mullen became president of the nursing class, and promptly failed Physiology in her second semester. "This was after I'd already been capped, so I had to take it over in summer school." There she met her future husband, Jim, whom she married at age twenty while in her junior year. Jim went on to become a banker, "very secure, someone who would always be there. That was his statement when we got engaged: 'I'll always be there.' And he was, for nineteen years. We had three kids, and he was always there."

During her marriage, though, Mullen was not happy just to sit home with the kids. "I tried that, and that drove me crazy," she said. "I was supposed to love being a mother, but there was another side to me, and I integrated all of it. I was Supermom, a professional and community person who volunteered at church and at school on days when I wasn't working." Following her early dream, Mullen earned a bachelor's degree in physical therapy and began to work at a children's convalescent home. She also worked with paraplegics and quadriplegics, youngsters with cystic fibrosis, muscular dystrophy, burns, and tumors. To her impressive list of physical therapy credentials, she added a decade of work as a childbirth educator.

Throughout, certain gifts began to manifest themselves, abilities that went beyond what she had learned in college or in the field. "I went into physical therapy using my hands," she said, "and discovered that I could work with kids and get them to 'do things,' to move in ways they hadn't moved. People would say to me, 'Oh, you've taken thus-and-such course in using this method.' And I'd say, 'No, I don't know. It just seemed right.' It wasn't until I had certain experiences, and started healing myself, that I began thinking of myself as a healer. I didn't realize then that I was channeling energy and tuning in to a very deep level of the kids' bodies. One of the first times I was given a context or justification for what I did was when I took a professional course in myofascial release. That gave me some of the intellectual background for what I had been feeling in my hands when I touched bodies all my life. It put it into a context that I could relate to professionally, and that was a safe, good feeling."

As Mullen became increasingly aware of her unusual abilities, she began to be more restless in her marriage. She divorced her husband of nineteen years and moved with her kids to a suburb of Dallas. A few months later, she was off to Chicago to take a week-long advanced healing course led by a woman named Barbara Alin, a nurse and Trager practitioner whom she described as "an intuitive healer with many psychic abilities." The first day of the course was characterized by intensive hands-on workshops in myofascial release, and Mullen soon found that people were seeking her out. When she worked on them, they often went into catharsis. Memories of forgotten traumas emerged during the healing, something that continued all week.

But after the first day, she went back to her room and took a bath, which she rarely did, usually preferring showers. "As I was lying there, all at once I felt what I thought were bubbles going up my back," she recalled. "I thought, Hmm, this is strange—I'll change positions and the bubbles will go away. But they didn't. It felt like little charges going up from the base of my spine. I got out and lay down on the bed spread-eagle, a position I never take. All at once, I realized I couldn't move. I was plastered to the bed. I tried to bring my hands up, to bring my fingers together, and I couldn't do it. In language that's used now, what was going up my spine was the Kundalini energy entering me."

The next evening she didn't sleep much, although she had always been a very sound sleeper. "I was aware all night of not really being asleep," she said, "and now I know I was in an altered state the entire night. All at once I needed to sit in the middle of my room. I took a tailor sitting, a cross-legged, Indian-style position that I don't sit in normally, and started having spontaneous visions of being in a red cave up in a mountain. The cave was halfway between a village of people and . . . the phrase that came to me was 'where the eagles live.' I was between the eagles and the village. I could see articles of pottery and things on the walls. I had never studied any Indian lore, and yet I was very comfortable with what they meant. I knew that was me, and the term that came to me was that I was a shaman. I had never heard the word before, although now it's passed around very easily. I knew that I served the people below but that I didn't live with them.''

That night she was besieged by similar thoughts, and when she saw Barbara Alin in the morning, she asked her what "shaman" meant. "She got a kick out of my story," Mullen said, "but I had no idea what was going on. The next night I went to sleep but woke up at about two a.m. and needed to get outside. Since I was staying at a resort hotel in the middle of Chicago, that wasn't easy, so I put my bedding next to the window and looked out. There was a full moon with clouds around it, and for some absolutely unknown reason I looked up at the moon and started blowing at it. As I blew, the clouds separated so the moon showed clearly, and when I stopped blowing, the clouds came back. I thought maybe it was a coincidence, so I did it four more times, and each time the clouds separated and rolled back again. The whole week was like that.''

Unlike Kathryn Quick, Mullen had done no reading in Eastern philosophy or mysticism, had never meditated, and had no knowledge of Kundalini. "I'm very aware that things are happening to me since then," she said. "I feel like I've been on an accelerated course, and I don't feel it's my special gift necessarily. In fact, when people ask me what I do, I can feel very shaky inside about saying I'm a healer. But after that week, when I went back to Presbyterian Hospital in Dallas where I was working then, I started being open to whatever might happen with my hands. At the time I was a clinical specialist in general medicine and neurology, and one of my areas was taking care of people with diabetic feet. They get gangrene, and their circulation is so poor that they start sloughing off their bodies. I did what's called debridement, or taking off the dead tissue so that the viable tissue can heal.''

Patients whom Mullen treated reported rapid healing progress. "I found myself channeling energy on one patient's feet as I dressed him after he'd been in the whirlpool. Seven days later there was almost complete healing, and the doctors were saying, 'Hmm.' But one event that really showed me I was a healer happened after I learned to center myself." By "centering," she means taking a few moments to focus within, be aware of where she is, and concentrate on what she is doing. "Part of the myofascial training is to center yourself and be with the patient as you start work. One day I centered myself, pulled back the curtain, and walked into the treatment room where a woman was lying on a stretcher. The aides had told me that even wheeling her over the bumps in the floor hurt her back so badly that she was almost in tears. I said hello and talked for about a minute, and hadn't even really gone near her when she looked at me and said, 'I know where my pain comes from.'

"I said, 'Yes?'

"She said, 'I had to stand in my kitchen and watch my husband kill our son.' I was thinking, Wait a minute. I'm a physical therapist, and I don't get into these areas. But as I was standing there, she said, 'I've been in psychotherapy for eight years and I haven't told my counselor this.' So it struck me that I must be making a connection with people. That was the first time I realized that just being very present with a person could be healing. I didn't have to *do* anything."

Mullen speaks of energy blocks in the body not unlike those described by Reichian therapists. In Reichian terms, once these blocks are worked through, energy, or life force, flows more freely and easily throughout the body. The process is also similar in some ways to the Kundalini awakening, in which the Kundalini energy is said to flow up the spine, breaking through or purifying the energy centers along the way. As Lee Sannella explains, "In its ascent, the Kundalini encounters these blocks, it works away at them until they are dissolved. . . . Once a blockage is removed, the Kundalini flows freely through that point and continues its upward journey until it meets with the next area of stress." Sannella later states that "the flow of the Kundalini energy through restricted areas of the body-mind causes turbulence, which may be experienced as painful sensations." (Compare that to Mullen and Tobey's theory that "disease arises when energy is blocked.")

The weeklong workshop in Chicago began a healing process in Mullen, during which she was able to retrieve what had previously been only vague memories of childhood sexual abuse and rape by the son of a family friend. At a subsequent workshop in Buckingham,

Pennsylvania, Mullen first met her current companion and healing partner, Bob Tobey. "During that weekend," she said, "the ground rules were that if anyone felt drawn to heal the person who happened to be lying on the table, to put their hands anywhere, they should do so. A lot of the time I put my hand someplace, and a hand would already be there, and when I looked up, it would be Bob. Or vice versa. We connected energetically that way off and on all weekend."

Not long after that encounter, and after working on a number of clients together with Bob, Vicki sold her house and began a period of itinerant healing with him. They had been together for almost a year when I met them, but Vicki sounded enthusiastic about the idea of not having a fixed home, at least for a while. She had chosen to give up a secure life with a good income because "it seemed right. There was no problem at all to selling things or giving them away, because I'd become aware several years earlier that I'd just as soon live a much simpler life. But of course, as a banker's wife, you don't go simpler, you go showing how secure you are in the community." She left her eighteen-year-old son in college, and a sixteen-year-old son and thirteen-year-old daughter living with her ex-husband.

Talking with Vicki Mullen, two major questions arose. The first was how she felt about the relationship of her healing and Kundalini experiences to the absence of any spiritual practice. The other concerned leaving teenage children to pursue a career. She responded that she didn't have an investment in putting her healing work into a spiritual context. "I don't have a routine other than being very aware of what my energy is, and being very centered in myself," she said. "In a way that sounds like the 'Me Generation,' saying that the rest of the world can go hang, but it's not that. It's just that when I'm fully present, and know my inner self and am calm, the rest of the world gets more. That's what I felt with my kids. I said, 'I've got to do this, and then there'll be more of me present for you.' I probably connect more with them now than I ever did. I connect more with other people now, too. I'm not in my own shell. As we heal ourselves, we heal others."

In answering those questions, Mullen implied that a specific belief system is not necessarily a prerequisite for living a spiritual life. Just as Gopi Krishna and Lee Sannella view the Kundalini experience as an evolutionary process with spiritual overtones (albeit one that often arises out of a lifetime of spiritual practice), Vicki Mullen sees a similar connection between her healing abilities and her Kundalini awakening, without having to follow any established format. Her spirituality may take the form of certain characteristics not normally associated with traditional religion. For instance, one of the traits Mullen credits most for her success as a healer is her ability to listen and suspend judgment, which she traces back to her role as caregiver in a troubled family. "I've always been a person who sits back and listens, and finds out where someone else is coming from," she said. "I probably learned that from a very early age. I'm an adult child of an alcoholic. My mother didn't start drinking until I was in college, but she always had that personality. I've had to work through my own feelings, so I don't judge either the alcoholic or the adult child who's lived around one. I'm also very much an introvert. When my sister died of leukemia, my grandmother whispered to me, 'Don't cry. Don't be selfish, because your parents need you.' I think that's a very common directive that people get in different ways: 'Don't express who you are, because it might upset somebody else.' And yet, when you do express who you are, it gives permission to other people to express themselves."

In a word, the direction of Mullen's spiritual development could be described as acceptance. Although her verbalizations sound vague and almost pantheistic at times, the sort of generic theologizing common to the New Age, the core of her belief is a quintessential openness. "Particularly after I first learned that I was a healer," she said, "I began to feel that we are all one, that—and this bothers some people—we are all God, that there's a God part in each of us. It's not a matter of there being an overruling Master. As far as I'm concerned, all of creation and everything in it is God. Even as early as six or seven I remember going outside at night and looking up in the Kansas sky and knowing that it was all a part of some plan, that other things were going on. Everything happens for a reason, and I'm very comfortable with that." After she moved to Tulsa with her husband and two kids, for example, they decided that it was time for him to get a vasectomy. "It was a hard decision and I decided to give it to God, if he would answer. The rational part of me said that if it wasn't supposed to be, we'd have a car wreck on the way to the urologist, or something like that. But everything went fine, and my medical mind said that it really took. Two weeks after he had it, I discovered I was pregnant with our third child, and I realized that the pregnancy had happened the night before the procedure. Although that was not a fun time, a little later I figured out that things are the way they're supposed to be."

Mullen's acknowledgment of the darker aspects of life was in contrast to the attitude of many New Age advocates. "Unfortunately, some of the people involved in the New Age and a lot of the new cult-type religions are on a spiritual level where everything has to be positive affirmations and trying to stay on the light side," she said. "Some of them say, 'Oh, you can't have negative feelings,' and go so far as to say, 'You shouldn't have negative *thoughts*.' But there is also a shadow side to everything, if you want to call it that. Both sides are always there, and you have a choice as to which you want to go into. If you want to go into a low funk for a while, you can, because that's a part of you. You make choices, but you don't beat yourself up for making the choice, and you don't have to stay in it, either."

Some time after interviewing Bob and Vicki, I took part in one of their weekend healing workshops and, after overcoming my usual resistance to opening up in such groups, underwent several favorable experiences working with other people in ways that I had previously found rather trying. One incident especially left me with a new sense of what healing is about. A woman in the group had been very anxious over a scheduled operation to remove a fibroid tumor from her uterus. During a part of the workshop in which we were separated into groups of three to do healing work on each other, I was teamed up with her and another man. Using techniques we had been taught—a combination of deep breathing and massage—I did my best to ease her fears concerning the impending surgery, and to help her come to terms with the abdominal growth, which was apparent through the expensive green track suit she was wearing. In helping her, I also had to confront my own aversion to the physical distortion in her body.

During the group assessment later that evening, the woman made a point of thanking me publicly. I tried to appear humble and nonchalant while secretly enjoying the ego-building feelings of pride and accomplishment. In the midst of this swell of self-satisfaction, it dawned on me that hers was the same ailment for which my mother had undergone surgery less than a month before. At that time, I had failed to do any more than make the requisite post-operative phone call to her hospital room and send the usual bouquet of flowers. The healing workshop had provided me with a chance to see my fear of involvement with my mother's suffering without judging myself for it. Through helping a stranger, I had at least tried to come to grips with my discomfort over my mother's ailment and my inability to cope with it consciously and honestly. That may not sound overtly spiritual, and yet I have increasingly come to see spirituality as involving just such subtle levels of realization.

Bob and Vicki have settled, for the time being, in a small Massachusetts town and established a local practice. They are philosophical about the future, although with a faintly apocalyptic edge. Vicki had given me one reason they spent so much time traveling. "We're being drawn to places we may have to go back to when something major happens in the world," she said. "We may have to know where there are safe places, and to realize where we're needed. We do the group work to teach people to be with one another, to teach them how to find their own strength to survive, and to be with others who aren't going to survive, and how to help them die. That sounds ominous, but it can happen on an everyday basis, too."

She was philosophic about the apocalyptic predictions being made by many of today's spiritual teachers. Conceding that apocalyptic events may happen and that we can't necessarily prevent them, she added, "We can still live this moment and be fully present for each other and for ourselves. Get all the joy out of this moment, and don't worry about the future or the past or putting the two together. I don't think that's a fatalistic view, since we do have this moment. There's a lot of joy, even in the pain, because that's a part of it, too. If we don't continue to experience, we don't live."

CHAPTER 15

Elizabeth Lesser:
Of Cults and Gurus

. . .

The Sufi life can be lived at any time, in any place. It does not require withdrawal from the world, or organized movements, or dogma. It is coterminous with the existence of humanity. It cannot, therefore, accurately be termed an Eastern system. It has profoundly influenced both the East and the very bases of the Western civilization in which many of us live—the mixture of Christian, Jewish, Moslem and Near Eastern or Mediterranean heritage commonly called "Western."

Mankind, according to the Sufis, is infinitely perfectible. The perfection comes about through attunement with the whole of existence. Physical and spiritual life meet, but only when there is a complete balance between them. Systems which teach withdrawal from the world are regarded as unbalanced.

—Idries Shah, *The Sufis*

We don't need wine to get drunk,
or instruments and singing to feel ecstatic.
No poets, no leaders, no songs,
yet we jump around totally wild.
—Jalaluddin Rumi, *Unseen Rain* (translated by John Moyne
and Coleman Barks)

.

One of ironies in the religious perceptions of America over the past decade is that the Islamic faith has been identified with machine-gun-toting mullahs and fanatical crowds of Muslims jeering "the Great Satan," whereas Sufism, a belief system that springs directly from and incorporates virtually all the spiritual practices of Islam, enjoys a growing reputation as a beneficent mystical sect, popularized by teachers who wear Western garb, smoke cigars, drink coffee, and talk about living in "the real world." Does this dichotomy represent an intrinsic difference in two apparently related traditions, or is it only a problem of perception?

"The word 'Sufism' is working magic in our culture now," Lex Hixon said on this topic, "exercising some of the same inflaming power on the spiritual imagination that Zen did in the sixties, when Alan Watts came along and the Zen stories became popular. Very swiftly the name of Jelaluddin Rumi, the great Persian poet, for instance, has entered the culture, particularly through Coleman Barks's new translations. Soon the same number of people will know about Sufism as know about Zen, and probably more so." But whereas Zen offers no belief in God and actually bears a superficial resemblance to a certain spare existentialism, Sufism "is connected with the ecstasy of love, with seeing and encountering God in everyone. In that regard, Sufism and Islam touch our deep cultural and spiritual imagination much more readily in some ways than Buddhism does."

Hixon also recalled that, after Americans' initial infatuation with Zen in the Beat era, "we found out gradually that Zen was a part of the religion of Buddhism and was not just those sparkling stories. It had to do with disciplines and the relation to a living teacher and all the things that make a religious tradition so rich. Likewise, Sufism should be considered part of a way of referring to Islam as a whole. The nonrelation of Sufism to Islam is something which one or two Sufis have developed in the modern world. Certain Sufis in different Islamic cultures at different times may have distanced themselves a little from Islam. But the very clear, overarching truth is that Sufism is an expression of Islam, albeit one which is very appreciative of, and which participates in, other great religious traditions."

Yet one characteristic of Sufism as practiced in America is that many of its followers have little or no knowledge of the Islamic religion, do not read the Koran either in Arabic or English, and do not practice the five-times-daily prayers (said at daybreak, noon, mid-afternoon, after sunset, and in the early night) and other rituals of the orthodox Muslim. The only Arabic they know may be a smattering of prayer, or some of the ninety-nine names of Allah. This is the kind of superficial practice that was common among American followers of Zen some years ago: a little reading, a little meditation, a knowledge of koans and Zen stories, but no total involvement.

Elizabeth Lesser is one of those people who could be classified as Americanized Sufis. She does not practice Islam in any traditional sense, and has even modified her practice of Sufism. But she counts her experience with a Sufi master and the events that followed as a distinct turning point in her life. She was also involved for many years with a Sufi community of the sort that are sometimes labeled cults in this country. But her experience of the commune provides a different perspective on the cult experience from that portrayed in the media. Lesser's devotion to and interaction with a spiritual teacher also reveals some of the advantages and drawbacks of working directly with a guru. Attachment to a personal teacher or spiritual guide is one of the most difficult aspects of Eastern practice for Westerners to accept. The very idea of total surrender to a source of authority flies in the face particularly of American concepts of independence. Maybe that's why the Pope, for example, has had such difficulty keeping American Catholics in line. The majority of Catholics here listen to his preachments, talk with their parish priests, then consult their conscience and in the final analysis follow its dictates. And yet, most of the people with whom I brought up the subject of gurus agreed that they didn't make real progress on any spiritual path until they found and established some relationship with a personal teacher. In Elizabeth Lesser's case, her years of study with the Sufi master Pir Vilayat Inayat Khan were the watershed experience in her life. The very work she does today helping to operate an alternative learning center grew directly from her involvement with Pir Vilayat and Sufism.

Like many alternative learning centers that have sprung up across the country in recent years, the Omega Institute for Holistic Studies in Rhinebeck, New York—built on the site of an old Yiddish cultural center once owned by the great storyteller and scholar Sholem Aleichem—takes an eclectic approach to its summertime presentations of workshops and retreats. "Spiritual Practice" is only one of the categories offered, along with studies in healing, bodywork, fitness, yoga, addiction, and the arts. Guest teachers can range from a Tibetan lama, Catholic priest, or Kabbalah scholar to performers such as Meredith Monk, Sally Kirkland, Spalding Gray, and Olatunji.

If Omega sounds more like a New Age supermarket than a spiritual retreat, it doesn't pretend to be anything other than a summer learning center with a holistic orientation. The word "holistic" is used in different ways, but derives from the philosophical doctrine of holism, which contends that the determining factors in nature are whole organisms, and not their constituent parts. (Although drawn from different languages, both "holistic" and "holy" have roots meaning "whole.") Holistic health, for instance, is less interested in treating specific symptoms with medicines or surgery than in understanding the functions of a healthy body and how the body can heal itself through nutrition, exercise, and stress management. The same holds true for holistic approaches to everything from food and fitness to spiritual practice, and that is the theoretical approach Omega and many other alternative centers take. They should be distinguished from spiritual retreats, such as Kripalu in the Berkshires, Yogaville in Virginia, or Naropa in Colorado, that concentrate on a specific spiritual tradition.

As a member both of Omega's board of directors and of its program department, Lesser is responsible for sifting through hundreds of course proposals and researching new developments to find the teachers and courses that are most likely to interest Omega's varied clientele. She relishes the opportunities this offers to examine new disciplines, discover a gifted teacher, or even to realize that someone the center had taken a chance on has turned out to be an uninspired or uninspiring teacher. When we spoke at her home not far from the Omega campus, where she lives with her two young sons, she acknowledged the occasional mistake, and Omega's vulnerability to faddishness as it tries to suit the demands of its public. At least, she said, it keeps her aswim in the variegated currents of physical, psychological, and spiritual learning.

A similar kind of eclecticism permeates Elizabeth Lesser's personal background. Although her parents are Jewish by birth, her maternal grandfather converted to Christian Science in the early 1920s and became active in the church. As a result, Lesser's mother was raised "a very devout Christian Scientist," whereas her father was raised in the Jewish faith. According to Lesser, though, "he was very happy to give it up after he left his home. His religion was nature and the outdoors." Elizabeth didn't often go to church with her mother, but felt she was "raised spiritually Christian Scientist in that, although I wasn't traditionally brought up a Christian Scientist, that philosophy pervaded the house."

One aspect of the philosophy, she said, is that "the mind governs, that life in the world of form is an illusion, and so physical illness is an illusion. There is an undertone of guilt to that which implies that if you're sick, you've done something bad. You're paying too much attention to your body, and if you weren't, you wouldn't be sick. There's a tremendous amount of judgment on any sort of self-indulgence, which is all negative." But she also found "a mystical edge" to Christian Science, especially as her grandfather practiced it, placing it in relation to mainstream Christianity, "what Sufism is to Islam. There wasn't so much talk about Jesus and the Bible as about mental practice and discipline. Unfortunately, that did not translate for me, at least as a kid, into faith healing, but rather into beating myself up psychologically when I couldn't heal my physical and mental illnesses."

Although her family celebrated Hanukkah and Christmas and stayed home for all the Jewish holidays, Lesser felt a strong desire to attend a church of some kind, and often went to Catholic mass with her best friend. At Barnard and Columbia colleges in New York, Lesser "got into radical politics because that's about all that was going on." She strayed from her "pacifist upbringing" to become embroiled in violent anti-establishment politics with Students for a Democratic Society (SDS), the radical left-wing group that flourished in the sixties. Around that time a policeman had reportedly been shot by SDS students near the Columbia campus, and Lesser's first reaction was one of solidarity. "I said to my boyfriend, spouting the rhetoric, 'Isn't it great the pig was offed?' And as I heard the words fall out of my mouth, I knew this was not right."

Her boyfriend, Stephan Rechtshaffen, whom she had met at the end of her first year of college and who was soon to become her husband, didn't share her political fervor. She was eighteen and he was "into Zen Buddhism. When I met him and started sitting Zen at the New York Zen Center, it was such a relief to get back in tune with who I really was. That was my first exposure to Eastern mysticism, and I was immediately taken by it." But Zen was "a little too mental" for Lesser, and her "real conversion" didn't occur until the summer of 1971, when some friends of Stephan's came into town and announced that they were planning to spend that summer at something called Sufi camp.

"I had absolutely no idea what that meant," she said. "But I wanted to get out of the city for the summer and he had to stay because he was in medical school and had summer school work. So I hitchhiked across the country with them to Mendocino." She described the scene that greeted her in that Northern California coastal town as "a tribe of one hundred fifty people camping out in the Mendocino woods. A man from India, Pir Vilayat Inayat Khan, was coming to lead this thing called the Sufi camp. To me it was like coming home. It was a combination of California and bonding with a community for the first time in my life. I've since watched thousands of people go through that every summer at Omega. There's nothing like the first time you find yourself in a situation where people are forming together around a transformative experience."

Lesser was introduced to Pir Vilayat, the son of Hazrat Inayat Khan, who had brought the Sufi teachings from India to America in the twenties and thirties, the first major figure in that tradition to come to the West. Hazrat Khan later married the niece of Mary Baker Eddy, the founder of Christian Science, and Pir Vilayat was the offspring of that union. Even now, Lesser can't be sure why she resonated so emphatically with Pir Vilayat and his teachings. "I was nineteen, so it's hard for me to know exactly what the connection was," she said, "but it was very deep, because it abided for years." The camp lasted two weeks, but she stayed in California all summer with the same group, taking care of Pir Vilayat's children, "getting close to his inner circle."

Lesser emphasized that there are "many branches of Sufism, and many Islamic Sufis would say that the forms that have made it to the United States have absolutely no relationship to what they do. At that time, a form of Sufism called Sufi Dancing, a kind of spiritual folk dancing, developed here. Some of it involves whirling and is related to the so-called Whirling Dervishes of Turkey, but some of it is completely Americanized, using Islamic phrases and singing and doing circle dances. Pir Vilayat's Sufism is especially Americanized because he is half American himself."

Although Lesser knows a number of Islamic phrases from the practice of repeating the ninety-nine names of Allah, "or God's ninety-nine qualities, as a way of strengthening your personality," she doesn't know the words of any of the Islamic prayers or much about Islam itself. "As I understand the philosophy of Sufism, without actually being a Muslim, it's almost the opposite of the Christian Science doctrine. It says life is holy, and the body is holy. Nothing that we have been given as human beings is separate from God; therefore, everything is spiritual. That's why Sufis don't have monasteries where you have to renounce wealth and sexuality and relationships. Another tenet of Sufism is that all religions come from the same mystical source." In keeping with this mystical orientation, Lesser feels a reverence for the thirteenth-century Persian poet Jalaluddin Rumi, whom she described as "the patron saint of Sufism. He speaks to what Sufism is about—intoxication. The sober drunk is the image that comes through in all his poetry. You are ecstatic in the sensual world, but you're sober. You're awake in the dream. You might say that's no different from the mystical stream in any religion, and a Sufi would agree with you."

After that summer of initiation in Mendocino, Elizabeth returned to New York and began practicing with some of Pir Vilayat's students. She and Stephan married and moved to California, where he performed his internship. They lived in a Sufi household in Marin County, north of San Francisco, and Elizabeth went back to college. She also cut herself off from her family for the next few years. Looking back, she saw this time as "somewhat of a cultish experience" in that she considered the Sufi group her new family. But to hear her tell it, it was a cult experience without the disastrous side effects recounted in books such as John Hubner and Lindsey Gruson's *Monkey on a Stick*, or the films *Split Image* and *Ticket to Heaven*. There was no coercion, no slave labor, none of the power abuses described in such harrowing detail by former members of some of the Jesus cults, nor, for that matter, the rampant sex and violence that characterize stories by members of Rajneesh's Oregon commune. "You could use the word 'cult,' " Lesser said, "but I hesitate to do so because in this particular group, we had ultimate free choice."

Initiation meant receiving spiritual practices, and a course of study. It also meant aligning herself with a group of people and a teacher, which she equated with "receiving Baptism into a Christian fundamentalist group or joining the Lubovitcher Hasidics in Brooklyn. I joined a group of people who were all practicing the same path, who had the same language, even the same way of dressing." And yet she learned a lot. "A tremendous amount of Persian makes sense to me now, not because I studied the language but because I studied the Persian poets and the Sufi lineage. I went to India and visited their tombs. It resonated in me. I was not so impressionable and so in need of group identification, even at that age, that I should write it off as a cult experience."

The group may not have been a cult, but they did want to start a commune. Those annual Sufi summer camps gave Pir Vilayat the idea of creating a permanent camp somewhere. At his urging, Lesser and her companions bought an old Shaker village in the Berkshires, and around 1975 founded a Sufi community called The Abode of the Message, which still exists. "When we started it," she said, "my husband and I were the leaders of the community for Pir Vilayat. In its heyday, about one hundred fifty adults and fifty kids were living there. I completely immersed myself in teaching other people about Sufism. It was not only living in community, but living in spiritual community." She bore and raised two sons there en route to becoming a midwife herself. "I caught over one hundred babies," she said, "and I got into the spiritual dimension of birth." At that time, the commune also had some unusual rules, including one that forbade drug use. "I went from a period in my life when I had been doing a lot of psychedelics and grass to ten years in which I didn't do any drugs. When Pir Vilayat made that rule, about two years after I joined, it caused a break in the ranks."

Some of the members who left had originally been students of an American Sufi named Samuel Lewis. Heir to the Lee jeans fortune, Lewis had been disowned by his family, traveled the world, and studied Zen. He met Hazrat Khan and became one of Pir Vilayat's teachers, ultimately bringing Sufism back to his native San Francisco, where he was known as Sufi Sam (or S.A.M., for Sufi Ahmed Murad, his Sufi name). Sam started the practice of Sufi Dancing, or Dances of Universal Peace, as they were originally known, and Pir Vilayat learned the practice from him. When Lewis died in 1971, many of his students, whom Lesser describes as "a wilder crew," embraced Pir Vilayat—at least until he made that no-drug rule.

"Politics and drugs and spirituality were all dovetailing back then," Lesser said. "The drugs opened us up to a different way of seeing. You can't take psychedelics, especially at that age, without having it change your values." Those changes took different forms, however. Some people "got into harder drugs, and some people quit when it became apparent to them that their careers were very important, and they started going in the yuppie direction. Some went the other way, into the spiritual scene." For Lesser, the choice was easy, since Sufism was so clearly what she needed, "a discovery of something that worked" for her. She could have stayed with Zen or gone to one of the Hindu teachers, like Swami Satchidananda. "But Sufism spoke to me, probably because of its emotional context and its enjoyment of art and music and poetry. And its acceptance of life, its adoration of beauty and the physical form."

Pir Vilayat also brought to American Sufism instruction in all the major world religions. Hazrat Khan's practice of what he called the Universal Worship became their Sunday service. A candle was lit for each of the six great world religions: Hinduism, Buddhism, Zoroastrianism, Judaism, Christianity, Islam, and a seventh candle representing "all those, whether known or unknown to the world, who have held the light of Truth amidst the darkness of human ignorance." They read thematically linked passages from different scriptures and combined Sufi and some Muslim prayers, "but always tying in the unity of religious ideals." They learned more than just religion from Pir Vilayat. Educated at Oxford and the Sorbonne, a cellist who had studied music with the famed French teacher Nadia Boulanger, he taught his chelas about classical music as well as the Koran, the Bible, and the *Bhagavad Gita*.

The Shaker village in which the Abode was founded was "unbelievably dilapidated, with no heating system, nothing," said Lesser. "Part of the ethos in those days—I don't think it was just us, but the whole 'back to the land' movement—was that we had to do everything ourselves. We couldn't think of bringing in plumbers, even if it might have made more sense financially. We put in a brand-new heating system and plumbing, and planted crops. By the end of the first few years we had cows and farm equipment and backhoes and bulldozers. We were building our own houses. We made a lot of mistakes, but we learned a lot." In that environment, Lesser re-established close contact with her parents. During her early days in California, she hadn't entirely lost touch with them, calling "every now and then." But Pir Vilayat and his wife had taken over that role in her life for a time. "I found new parents," she said, "and definitely a new family." Her three sisters, meanwhile, all settled in Vermont, close to where her parents live, and she has no way of accounting for the difference in their lives.

For the most part her parents accepted her new life, unlike some other parents who tried to remove their children from the Abode and have them "deprogrammed." Lesser's parents visited often and liked what they saw. "They thought what I was doing was great because they are Vermonters and homesteaders. And as a Christian Scientist, my mother had had a somewhat unconventional family. For example, one of her uncles was into the Kabbalah and numerology, and had changed all of their names when she was a teenager because they were numerologically incorrect. So what we were doing didn't seem so weird."

In retrospect, Lesser herself views her life during those days as extreme. "Living so alienated from American culture, it was as if we became like Amish people. For all of our sophisticated backgrounds and having gone through the sexual revolution and drugs, we were very Puritan. Our neighbors in New Lebanon, New York, which is the sticks, were probably terrified about what was going on up there, and yet we were living much more puritanical lives than they were. We had a lot of babies and very monogamous marriages. There was not much screwing around, nor a lot of discussion about sexuality. It wasn't as if there were rules within the Sufi Order as to how you conducted yourself. We were just focused so intently on spiritual development that we completely negated relationship and psychology and sexuality. We overdeveloped one side of ourselves and paid for it later."

Some time after she left the Abode, Lesser realized that she had gone through her twenties emphasizing only spiritual experience, so for the first five years of her thirties she "went through adolescence. During that time I got divorced, and really had a wild time of it. I had to, because it was as if I had been in a monastery. Besides, we had been living in the Shaker buildings, and, whether we knew it or not, the lineage of the Shakers was coming through. They had been so devoted to work and spirit and simplicity, as we were, that there had been no time for anything else." The Abode's governance system levied a heavy tax on members, so most of the money they earned went back into the community, including the income from a number of cottage industries, like the Volkswagen repair shop and bakery, the sale of wood stoves and home insulation. In addition, they cooked, cleaned, and farmed for themselves. "It was like Communist China in that we returned college graduates to the fields," she said. "We had our own school for the kids, and a home-birthing team in which I was involved. I started out delivering Abode babies, and then, because my husband was a doctor, I began birthing babies all over the Berkshires in New York and Massachusetts. Finally, it got to be crazy. I had no life except delivering babies, because you couldn't know when they were going to come. But it was wonderful. I still do it every now and then for friends."

The straight life Lesser's community led extended even to music. Pir Vilayat "was very prudish," and didn't value expression unless it was "aesthetically correct." Pop music was out and Mozart was in. Lesser feels she "missed out on a decade of rock-'n'-roll. We were busy getting a classical education. But I didn't mysteriously find Pir Vilayat. It wasn't as if all of a sudden he changed me from a heathen punk rocker. I was raised in a family that listened to classical music, so the training appealed to me and reinforced things I loved."

Adjusting to the non-Abode world proved to be almost as much of a challenge as establishing the commune had been, especially "the transition from living your life under a set of imposed values and practices to re-entering a world where you're setting your own limits and deciding what you want to do." She had no idea, for instance, how to buy shower curtain hooks, or how to cook for just a family of four after all those years cooking for over a hundred people. "And what do you do with your free time? I hadn't watched TV for ten years. What do you want? What do you even like to do?"

Probably the most difficult change Lesser had to confront was in her marriage. Not having had to examine her marriage during the Abode years, because she had "so much stimulation and interaction with other people," when she finally had the time to take a long, hard look, she concluded that it wasn't working. After obtaining a divorce, she had to face more troubling questions, such as how to raise the children by herself. "It was overwhelming," she said. Lesser has remained friendly both with her former husband, who works with her on the board of directors of Omega, and with Pir Vilayat, although she now sees Pir Vilayat differently. "I have a lot of gratitude for what he gave me," she said, "but he's an often annoying, egocentric, out-of-touch person, who expects people to relate to him in a certain way and who makes demands that no other person I know does, like expecting to be picked up at the airport. But that's his attitude about himself, that he's special and needs to be taken care of. I've gotten mad at him several times, and he's gotten mad at me, and it still scares me if he's angry, because he's like my parent. But he's also my teacher, so I forgive him everything, because what is drummed into you in Sufism is devotion to the teacher. When you devote yourself to the teacher, you put all judgments aside."

Lesser feels that Sufism's connection with Islam "has disqualified it as viable" in many American minds because of the stereotypical equation of Arabs with terrorism. But besides that, Sufism is "shrouded in mystery, and it's not intellectually rigorous. Zen appeals to the American mind because it's very mental. It's clean and understandable and it fits into our linear, masculine world. Sufism is much more messy. It's all over the place, and it doesn't necessarily give you a doctrine to follow. It's hard to get a handle on." The reason is not that it's purposely convoluted or obscure for the sake of limiting its appeal to a select group, but that it has developed "a system of checks and balances to keep people from fixating on a teacher or an idea. It's constantly putting the responsibility back on the student. Therefore, unless you understand it in a very sophisticated, responsible way, it doesn't work.

"A Sufi will say, 'We're all Sufis, because we all are mystical light. We all are the One, manifesting itself as the Many.' On the other hand, a Sufi may say, 'You're not initiated. You don't have your own *wazifah*, your mantra. You don't know the prayers. You don't face Mecca five times a day, and so you're not a Sufi. Get out of here. But you *are* a Sufi.' I never know exactly what they mean. So, when they say that Sufis built all the cathedrals in the world, or that the Pentagon was really designed by Sufis, the interpretation might be that we're all Sufis, or that Sufis actually built the Pentagon. I don't know."

Lesser's confusion seemed odd at first. Most of the people I'd interviewed talked with great assurance about their paths and the traditions they follow. Later I realized that she might still be feeling the aftereffects of her long involvement with Pir Vilayat and the Abode. I recalled the warnings I had read about the dangers of starting on the spiritual path, and the confusion that you could expect to encounter if you didn't finish. But I also remembered teachings that say it's an endless process. Elizabeth Lesser may have reached a temporary backwater, a turning point or a real cul-de-sac. But for all her doubts, she is able to express what she has to say about Sufism with an appealing lyricism. When I pressed her about the seeming contradiction in Sufi teachings she had been bemoaning, she said that "it comes from a deep understanding that life is mystery. This is a projection of the obvious truth that we don't know what is going on here. It's web upon web of an intricate joke played by a creative and mysterious God who takes great pleasure in being a trickster."

As if to clarify matters, she read a passage from *The Sufi Message of Hazrat Inayat Khan*:*

"One of the words to which the term Sufi is related is the Greek *sophia*, meaning wisdom, which is a knowledge acquired from within and without. Therefore Sufism is not only an intuitive knowledge, nor is it only a knowledge acquired from the outer of the world. Sufism in itself is not a religion, nor even a cult with a distinct or definite doctrine. No better explanation of Sufism can be given than by saying that any person who has a knowledge of both outer and inner life is a Sufi. Therefore, there has never in any period of the world's history been a founder of Sufism, yet Sufism has existed at all times. As far as we can find out, there have been esoteric schools since the time of Abraham, and many of them may be called Sufi schools. The Sufi schools of Arabia observed Arabic culture and were largely metaphysical. The Sufi schools of Persia developed the more literary aspect. The Sufi schools of India developed the meditative faculty. But the Truth and the Ideal have remained the same as the central theme of Sufism.

* London: Barrie & Rockliffe, 1962. Distributed in the U.S. by Omega Publications, New Lebanon, N.Y.

Hearing that, I could begin to understand some of Lesser's confusion as to what Sufism is. In actual practice, under Pir Vilayat she and her fellow chelas learned Buddhist meditation techniques and Hindu chanting. "We did a lot of ecumenical practices," she said. "But we also did Sufi practices such as the repetition of the ninety-nine names or qualities of God—for instance *Jamil*, or beauty. If a teacher sees that a student needs to develop the side of him which is beautiful, he may suggest repeating that word. Or, say, *Allahu akbar*, the Islamic phrase that means 'God is great.' Muslim warriors going into battle sing *Allahu akbar*. A teacher might decide that a student needs to develop her strength, so he would give her that phrase to repeat as a way of inviting that quality. All these qualities exist in you, and you can cultivate them in your personality through the repetition of wazifah, the Sufi equivalent of a Hindu mantra or the Catholic rosary. If you say twenty Hail Marys, it's the same idea." Since scholars have shown that the rosary is of Saracen origin, the connection is not coincidental.

Other Sufi practices include breathing techniques such as Hindu pranayama, the regulation and restraint of breath, and "a mystical school of meditation. *Fana* means subjugating yourself to the form of something else, and the practice of *fana fi sheikh* means that you're nothing and only your teacher, the sheikh, is real. So you practice focusing on only the sheikh. You also study the teachings of your lineage, and repeat the names of the teachers in your lineage all the way back to Abraham. Some people memorized one thousand teachers' names, and would sit and repeat them as their practice. It's hard to annihilate your own ego, so you do it by going into other forms, or formlessness, however you can do it best."

These practices were taught and reinforced by Pir Vilayat in a series of twelve-day retreats in which followers sat alone in a hut while doing their practices and fasting and "really getting out there." But the one practice that is probably most crucial to Sufism is the *zhikr*, Arabic for "remembrance." Zhikr comes in many forms, but usually includes the repetition of the divine names and the phrase, *la ilaha illa'llah*, the first half of the Arabic prayer central to Islam which, translated literally, means, "There is no God but Allah, and Muhammad is his messenger." But as Pir Vilayat translated it, Lesser said, "it

really means, 'There's no reality except God, and you are his messenger.' '' The so-called Whirling Dervishes of the Mevlevi Order "repeat the zhikr over and over, sometimes all night long, and go into
ecstasy. The whirling derived as an expression of being completely
ecstatic, in the same way as the Shakers just lost it in dance. We had
zhikrs during which we stayed up all night and drank black tea. Some
Sufis smoke cigarettes and drink a lot of coffee and tea, so we never
will know if it's the zhikr or the coffee that gets them whirling! But
the zhikr is a powerful practice that still lives on my breath. No matter
how far I get from considering myself an active Sufi, it's deep in me,
maybe in the same way as somebody who grew up singing hymns in
church.''

Sufism is often portrayed as somewhat more worldly than orthodox
Islam, although one would hardly guess this from the ascetical conditions Lesser lived in at the Abode. But according to Lesser, when
Pir Vilayat came to the Abode he was horrified by what he saw. "In
fact, he built himself a house on the hill which was palatial compared
to all of ours, and he would have been very happy if we had done
likewise. Much of what we were living out was a mishmash of idealism
that was closer to Helen and Scott Nearing—two inspirational figures
in the back to the land movement—than to Sufism. Sufism teaches
that the body is holy and beautiful, that it's part of the earth, which
is part of God. Therefore the concept of sin originating in sexuality
and pleasure is not Sufi. However, Sufism doesn't say to be indulgent
or lecherous, only that if you renounce something before you're ready
to you become neurotic. If you respect all life as holy and your own
body as holy, and you feed it healthfully, you will be guided toward
living a balanced life in which the material world is holy. Home and
a family is holy, and it's wonderful to cook a sumptuous meal, because
it's symbolic of the bounty of God. And if you're really in truth, you
will be guided not to be excessive.''

She contrasted the classic spiritual life of renunciation with the lives
of most Sufis, who ''see life in terms of appropriate stages. You have
a family and you can renounce it, and you can come back to it. But
you have a relationship and children, and work, each of which has
tremendous opportunity for growth. You're not a hedonist. Hedonism
and the ecstatic appreciation of the sweetness of life are not synon-
ymous. The strange paradox of this plane of existence seems to be

that we've been given everything—everything but enough wisdom to know how to use it. The teaching is about how to accept the gifts in a balanced way, so we can abstain when it's appropriate and go for broke when it's appropriate. It's what the Buddhists call the Middle Way."

Pir Vilayat based his initial idea for the Omega center on the ancient wisdom schools of Alexandria in Egypt, "where learning never stopped and people continued their educations forever." The center started small, with a mimeographed catalogue, a few teachers, and a handful of classes, but the idea "hit a nerve. It was a matter of being in the right place at the right time." She credits much of the school's success to her ex-husband, whom she described as "a natural business whiz." When the Lessers left the Abode in Omega's third season, there was some controversy over who owned the rights to the school. This "enraged a lot of Abode people, and there was a real split between us and Pir Vilayat," she said. However, Vilayat now serves as chairman of the board of directors of Omega, which has completed its fourteenth season.

Trained as a doctor, Stephan introduced classes in the relatively new field of holistic health to the Institute along with teachers who shared his orientation, including future luminaries such as Bernie Siegel, who "was just a guy at Yale then," and Elizabeth Kübler-Ross, the mother of the modern hospice movement. Omega has since become a big business, handling about eight thousand students each summer with a staff of one hundred fifty people to cook and clean. Many of Omega's attendees are doctors who come to take advantage of courses in transformational psychology, holistic health, stress reduction, "and all sorts of healing principles. Some doctors come to learn how acupuncture, say, can fit into a Western practice. Although very few people who work there are Sufis, Omega keeps up the Sufi tradition in some ways. For instance, it does not present only one particular way of being." The center's name is taken from Teilhard de Chardin, the Jesuit priest and visionary anthropologist for whom Point Omega represents the convergence of all ideas. "Pir Vilayat originally named our center Omega because it's what happens when all thought and learning converge at one place. It's more like a village than an institution of learning."

She also described Omega as "a meeting ground for cutting-edge learning and a lot of things you could not find in universities. The concept of Point Omega is that the ancient is respected but does not exclude the present and the future. We'll have someone like Joseph Shabalala, the South African singer from the Ladysmith Black Mombazo group, teaching Zulu to a class that might include a singer from the Metropolitan Opera. A doctor might come to study Filipino healing. Even if he never uses the actual techniques, he may be broadening his ability to serve people. That cross-fertilization in time and locale is exciting to me."

A closer look at the syllabus, however, reveals some courses with a certain superficial glamour, like the Tao of Boxing with guest instructor Floyd Patterson. Lesser herself is skeptical about some of the close to 175 different classes scheduled at Omega. "Sometimes," she admitted, "we'll invite someone to come and he turns out to be a total asshole. It'll be the joke of the summer, and we know we blew it." She was not sanguine about a course in crystal channeling, for instance, and some of the other things "that people are very interested in. But we include them because we don't know if they're right or not." As an example of changing fads, she mentioned "the whole addiction thing," noting that recent addiction courses are doing poorly. "Everybody was addicted to everything for the past three years—their relationship, their car, their guru. We had lots of addiction courses this year, but people aren't signing up for them."

Like Kathryn Quick, Herbert Moss, and a number of people with whom I spoke, Lesser holds her guru in great esteem; unlike some other followers, though, she takes a balanced view of the role of the spiritual teacher. She refers to Ram Dass, a close friend, as "an extraordinary teacher who has sat with hundreds of people dying," but who is constantly "testing himself. I hope people like him are happy doing what they do, but I don't want to live like that. And I don't think that's the only way to reach enlightenment, whatever enlightenment is. Ram Dass helps a lot of people on their path, but his life is not what I'd want as a model of a spiritual life."

Not surprisingly, considering her long and sometimes turbulent association with Pir Vilayat, Lesser sees the teacher-student relationship as a double-edged sword. "Sufism teaches that the kingdom of God is within you," she said, "and that it has nothing to do with the teacher, but that doesn't always work. A teacher is telling you this, so it's hard not to project powers and understandings onto him. When you later grow up and individuate from him, you say, 'What was I thinking? What did I do that for?' " Asked if teaching chelas to think for themselves isn't part of the job of any guru, Lesser agreed. "But they don't do that very well," she said. "That's why someone like J. Krishnamurti, who tried so hard to teach nonreliance on the teacher, figured out that the only way to do it was not to have students at all. Teachers say, for instance, 'Don't do what I do, do what I say.' That's the part of this experience that makes you crazy. All the teachings say the same thing: 'God is within you. You are your master.' But the teachers don't act like that, or they wouldn't be writing books and giving seminars. People open themselves to them, saying, 'I'm lost in my life. What should I do?' And the teachers say, 'Do this. But don't do anything I say.' "

Lesser doesn't doubt that teachers like Pir Vilayat are "coming from a sincere and realized place," but does question what responsibility they have. "If they took total responsibility, they wouldn't say anything. The Buddhists say, 'If you meet the Buddha on the road, kill him.' Hazrat Khan had a saying: 'I give my life to my students like a fragile glass and they shatter it.' I think he meant what the Buddhists mean, and that's what students have to do, because it's part of the individuating. But the way Pir Vilayat used to quote that implied that he felt sorry for himself: 'See what you guys are doing to me?' " Nonetheless, she never has doubted his integrity, and doesn't feel he has ever misled, abused, or bilked his students, as more than one guru has been accused of doing in recent years. She wonders, for instance, why certain widely recognized teachers could "live in such contradiction to the teachings. I've met practically all of the teachers whose books and workshops are available, and they are no more or less healthy and genuine than any cross section of society. In fact, they may be more fucked up."

One of the spiritual teachers who was most influential in Lesser's life and whom she most respected, aside from Pir Vilayat, was Chögyam Trungpa Rinpoche. Lesser spoke highly of Trungpa while recognizing that before his death in 1986 at the age of forty-seven, he appeared to do some questionable things. It was reported in various newspapers and widely bruited about the Buddhist community, for instance, that Trungpa's handpicked successor, an American whose dharma name was Ösel Tendzin, had become infected with the AIDS virus. Furthermore, Tendzin had failed to take protective measures or to inform his sexual partners of his condition. Word spread that he had transmitted the disease to at least one male member of the Buddhist community there, who had in turn infected a female lover. Tendzin subsequently went into "retreat," but the stories persisted. One particularly distressing story that Lesser had heard from someone close to both men was that Trungpa had known of his successor's plight and had given him, she said, "certain esoteric Tibetan practices that would protect other people from the transmission of his disease. That level of insane irresponsibility went on a lot at Trungpa's retreats in Boulder."

She is also familiar with the tales, rather widely circulated among the spiritual communities in America, of Trungpa's predilection for wine and women. As brilliant as his books and teachings were, she said, "he was a drunk, a womanizer. I went to his retreats in the early seventies and he would have a pitcher of Colt .45 in front of him during an all-day sitting at the Dharmadhatu in Greenwich Village. He later graduated to sake, but when I sat with him in Vermont, it was Colt .45. By the end of the all-day sitting, he was stone drunk. We'd all be sitting there, and his dharma talks would continue to be incredibly inspiring—until he passed out."

Lesser's account was corroborated by an article appearing in the May–June 1990 issue of the magazine *Common Boundary*. The author, Katy Butler, a longtime member of San Francisco Zen Center and student of its American abbot Richard Baker-roshi (who himself resigned under pressure, according to Butler, "after affairs with women students, including his best friend's wife, were acknowledged"), reports a harrowing story of excess and denial at the Naropa Institute. Even as Trungpa lay dying, only a few close associates reportedly knew the cause. "Few could bear to acknowledge that their beloved and brilliant teacher was dying of terminal alcoholism," Butler writes, "even when he lay incontinent in his bedroom, belly distended and skin discolored, hallucinating and suffering from varicose veins, gastritis and esophageal varices, a swelling of veins in the esophagus caused almost exclusively by cirrhosis of the liver." Members of the community, she speculates, acted like many families of alcoholics, both enabling the alcoholic and denying the reality of the disease.

"The Regent himself suppressed discussion of the crisis," she adds, "creating an atmosphere reminiscent of an alcoholic family's defensive secrecy."

For her part, Lesser said that she had "gone through phases of not accounting for and of rationalizing" the paradoxical behavior of gurus such as Trungpa and Rajneesh. She believes that they are "highly sensitive people, especially the Easterners who are unused to what they find in the West, and they freak out culturally when they come here. I'm not excusing them, but they have lived highly ritualized and disciplined lives in India or Tibet, where they couldn't get out of line. Then they come here and have all these devotees and no rules."

But what about the inner discipline that presumably comes with all that study and practice? Lesser shook her head. "The point of the spiritual path isn't to be disciplined," she said, "it's to be in touch with the ecstatic core of being. They're in touch with it, and maybe they feel they've already disciplined themselves enough. Discipline isn't where it's at for them anymore, and so the outcome of spiritual practice wouldn't necessarily look like a very straight life. It might look like anything. And within that structure there's tremendous room for taking advantage of other people and of the truth. Maybe they're just testing the limits of *maya*."

Maya is the Hindu concept of the world of illusion, described by Swami Muktananda as "the force that shows the unreal as real, and presents what is temporary and short-lived as eternal and everlasting." As Butler points out in her article, Trungpa also taught that all sides of existence, including "neurosis, passion, desire, alcohol, the dark and the light, were to be embraced and transmuted." Lesser recalled a series of profiles of Gandhi by Ved Mehta that ran in *The New Yorker* in 1976.* They stated that Gandhi sometimes tested his realization of *Satyagraha* (the policy of passive resistance which he inaugurated in 1919), and all of his beliefs, "by having two young women sleep on either side of him in the night, just to see if he could really abstain." It wasn't clear from the stories, she added, whether Gandhi proved his point or not. She again invoked Hazrat Inayat Khan's dictum that the act of renouncing something before you've enjoyed it will make

---

* These were later expanded into a book entitled *Mahatma Gandhi and his Apostles* (New York: Viking, 1977).

you very neurotic. These gurus renounced so much, she said, "and then came around our generation of people for whom renunciation had no value at all, so maybe they went into real conflict. It doesn't bother me anymore that there is such a contradiction between the teachings and the teacher. It seems like the name of the game."*

In his book *Introducing Spirituality into Counseling and Therapy*, Pir Vilayat tells the story of a group of Buddhist monks from Ceylon who were visiting Paris and were observed spending most of their time in nightclubs there. "We can only conclude from this," he writes, "that it would have been better if they had lived a married life—or even a wild life—and then become monks, rather than the other way around. It is possible to overstress oneself in following the spiritual path if one is not up to it; some people even develop an aversion to the spiritual way, or find themselves torn because they feel the spiritual path is keeping them from the fulfillment they need in their personal satisfaction."

Katy Butler's article imparts a slightly different slant to this argument, pointing out that while Trungpa was trained as a monk from birth, headed a "huge institutional monastery" by the age of nineteen, and was awarded personal devotion and tremendous power, his freedom was also "rigidly circumscribed" by obligations not only to his monastery but also to the surrounding community. These obligations were part of a tacit but clearly understood reciprocal framework. "Almost everyone's behavior—serf, lama or landowner—was closely but subtly controlled by a strong and often unspoken desire to save face. But these social controls did not exist in the society to which Trungpa Rinpoche came in the freewheeling 1970s."

In a roundtable discussion entitled "Why Spiritual Groups Go Awry," in the same issue of *Common Boundary*, Ram Dass takes yet another view of the problem: "[The Indian sage Sri] Aurobindo said, 'The spiritual journey is one of continually falling on your face, getting up, brushing yourself off, looking sheepishly at God, and taking another step.' I really sense that the errors *are* the journey. I have been taken a number of times. But I have learned how willing I was to deny what I didn't want to know, even though I knew it, because I

---

* A detailed account of Trungpa's rigorous training as a Tibetan lama is given in his autobiography, *Born in Tibet*.

was greedy for something. These experiences taught me to trust my intuition more deeply."

One can be forgiven for feeling both perplexed and somewhat cynical about all these different, sometimes conflicting, explanations of the same phenomenon. And yet we regularly receive many more conflicting opinions on how to view a particular medical problem, or a political, economic, or ecological dilemma. In those cases we are dealing with fairly linear, logical situations, whereas, as we have seen, the spiritual realm is not always so clear or so open to rational answers. Perhaps the most one can do is to try to come to an understanding of the problem that is personally meaningful, while realizing that no one solution can apply to everybody.

In search of some further clarification, I spoke with George Quasha, practitioner of the Dzogchen lineage of Tibetan Buddhism, who has had extensive experience with spiritual teachers. Quasha made the point that there is no denying the *siddhis*, or psychic powers, that certain teachers develop, but that possessing such powers does not make one either spiritually or ethically sound. If one's awareness is focused on "the liberation of all beings," then that focus should turn those powers to something good. "But without that ingredient," Quasha said, "it can go any way. The more one is involved with the higher energies, the more power one has, the more dangerous it becomes. Rajneesh is an object lesson in how someone who had the right ideas—a lot of his books say the same thing I'm saying—did not carry them out himself. He couldn't possibly have injured so many people and allowed so much negative karma to arise around him if he had fully established and grounded an orientation toward the liberation of others. It was all in his head, and that's very dangerous when you're manipulating other people's energies."

According to Quasha, Rajneesh used sophisticated hypnotic techniques that "anchored people in his own image even as he told them that they were being liberated. While they were making love, they were thinking of him. While they were going through heavy encounter sessions during which their defenses and the shell of their identity were breaking apart, he was substituting his own identity." The accounts of Rajneeshpuram do bear out the fact that large photographs of Rajneesh were everywhere in the commune, and that students were instructed to gaze and meditate on them. When it came to using these techniques, which Rajneesh did not discuss in his books, his followers apparently didn't have the personal power or insight to see through them. Yet many legitimate teachers also stress devotion to and concentration upon one's guru as the surest way to achieve enlightenment. The key lies in first determining the level of realization of a particular teacher before submitting to him or her—something that is easier said than done.

For another thing, Quasha feels that teachers like Rajneesh can become "addictive," and that even after disciples have broken from them and seen their flaws and potential destructiveness, the followers may continue to exhibit addictive behavior, if not to those particular teachings then to any number of other things. "How do you break the addiction of everything that you are oriented toward?" Quasha asked. "Gurdjieff put it very succinctly when he said that you have to reverse everything you see as reality. You have to see through every last thing." Rajneesh's students ought to have seen through his self-aggrandizing statements to the effect that he was fully realized, that he was another Christ or another Buddha. Genuine teachers would not make such statements, Quasha said. "Those words never come out of their mouths, nothing remotely like them. There's no self-reference about the stages they've gone through. You have to *find out* how realized they are. They know better than to fall into the trap of saying, 'It's me.' Once you say that, it's finished."

Having known Trungpa personally, Quasha allowed that although he was a very high-level teacher, "when these people incarnate, they incarnate as human beings." The nature of the game, as he put it, is free choice, and, in exercising that choice, Trungpa went awry. Much as Quasha admired Trungpa's work in establishing Tibetan Buddhism in America, he kept his distance from the Naropa community because he "had an instinct that it was going to go wrong in some way. That it took an unfortunate turn is one of those things that require study, thought, meditation, and awareness. There is no quick and easy answer, although, on balance, much more good than bad came from him."

Ösel Tendzin died of an AIDS-related illness in August 1990, and Quasha believes that his and Trungpa's Karma Kagyü lineage of Buddhism will heal itself, largely through the work of other teachers who were not involved in that period of "obscuration" and who have now begun to interact with Trungpa's followers. This is one more version of the ongoing self-critical function of major traditions, another example of how the older, more deeply rooted religions can purify themselves and continue to be effective. By contrast, Quasha feels that Rajneesh's teachings, without a grounding in any discipline or lineage, are liable to die with him. Nonetheless, several former disciples have told me that, whatever their feelings about what happened at Rajneeshpuram and how it was interpreted by the media, they learned things of incomparable value from Rajneesh. They were not talking about esoteric practices but knowledge and experiences that they believe have stood them in good stead in their everyday lives. One psychotherapist I met in Kingston, New York, who had spent several years at Rajneeshpuram running an organic farm there, acknowledged that some abuses of power did occur, and that Rajneesh was probably aware of them. But, he said, if the place were still in existence, he would go back there tomorrow.

For all Elizabeth Lesser's misgivings about gurus like Trungpa and Rajneesh, she has no doubt that great teachers are essential for both spiritual and material development. She acknowledges that the process of determining what to believe and who to trust in the realm of spiritual instruction can seem intimidating even to the experienced student. All the guidelines that have been mentioned here—whether the teacher is connected to a tradition with strong roots, is genuinely realized, is not self-deluded, and so forth—must still be tempered by the individual's instincts about whether that teacher is appropriate for him or her at any given moment in his or her spiritual development. In that light, Lesser's decision to drift away from Pir Vilayat, to attenuate her practice of Sufism, to rely for a time more on her own inner direction than on any particular teacher or system, can finally be seen as a valid part of her spiritual transformation. As long as she is willing to say, "I don't know," then even her apparent confusion becomes part of her truth at the moment.

CHAPTER 16

Lex Hixon:
The Truth About Islam

. . .

All human beings are invited to the truth. We have a longing for the truth, a sensibility about the truth. In Arabic this is called *Haqq*. Haqq is one of the ninety-nine beautiful names of Allah, so sometimes we chant "Haqq," or "Truth," in our Dervish circle. Jesus said, "Know the truth, and the truth will set you free." But it's not an abstract truth like the Truth of Plato, or Hegel's philosophy. Jesus also said, "I am the Way, the Truth, and the Life." It's existentially manifest in the human being. Gandhi subtitled his autobiography, "The Story of My Experiments with Truth." And the great mystic saint Mansur al-Hallaj cried out *An-al-Haqq*—"I am the Truth." This is absolutely equivalent to saying, "I am God." Of course, he was martyred for that by his Muslim compatriots who thought that he might be saying blasphemy.

—Lex Hixon

.

Probably no religion is more feared by Americans, and more misunderstood, than Islam. Part of this perception can be attributed to ignorance, a confusion of the political stances of a minority of Muslim fundamentalists in the Middle East with the religious beliefs of nearly a billion Muslims worldwide, including anywhere between about 2 and 6 million in this country, depending on which source you quote. Further obfuscating the religious issue for Americans is the misidentification of Islam with the Nation of Islam, the black separatist movement now headed by Minister Louis Farrakhan, which is no longer considered by other Muslims, including most Black Muslims in this country, to be part of the Islamic mainstream.

The issue of fundamentalist Muslim attitudes to women also looms large in the West, although the problems it presents are much the same as those Christian and Jewish fundamentalism present for Westerners unwilling to abide by the subservient position assigned to women in those traditions. Even the Catholic Church, not generally likened to fundamentalist denominations, has been accused by its faithful of foisting unacceptable roles on women because it excludes them from clerical and decision-making positions. Moreover, many Muslim communities in this country, like many Buddhist communities, grant a measure of equality to women beyond that of most Middle Eastern and Asian countries.

Yet Muslim laws do not go unquestioned over there, either. Writing in defense of his book *The Satanic Verses* in *Newsweek* magazine, Salman Rushdie makes the point that "disputes about rules"—such as death by stoning for prostitution, or the Islamic law of evidence which requires the testimony of two women to contravene that of one man—"take place daily throughout the Muslim world. Muslim divines may insist that women dress 'modestly,' according to the Hijab code, covering more of their bodies than men because they possess what one Muslim absurdly described on television as 'more adorable parts'; but the Muslim world is full of women who reject such strictures. Islam may teach that women should be confined to the home and to childbearing, but Muslim women everywhere insist on leaving the home to work."

Rushdie's image of a pluralistic Muslim world is borne out by non-Muslim scholars of Islam such as H. A. R. Gibb, who writes in his book *Mohammedanism* that the Muslim community "presents in regard to religious beliefs and practices a wide range of differences, not concealed by common acceptance of certain rituals and doctrinal expressions or by the common activities of clerics and lawyers. The popular forms of Islam differ from one another in almost every Muslim country, and often stand in strong contrast to the rigid system of the orthodox Ulama." (The Ulama is composed of the "learned" or "doctors" of Islamic knowledge, according to Gibb, corresponding to the "scribes" of Judaism.)

Nor is Islam different from other major religions which are composed of liberal and conservative factions, with a great gray area of belief ranged between. As much as the Vatican, for instance, may proclaim the sanctity of natural law in its absolute prohibition of artificial contraception, the Pope has never declared that the 70 to 90 percent of American Catholics who practice birth control are not, in fact, true Catholics, nor is he likely to. Rachel Cowan may be appalled at the sexual politics of Orthodox Judaism, or the real politics of the right-wing Orthodox in Israel, but she does not feel any less a Jew for being part of a religious community that embraces such wide dimensions of practice and belief.

Still, fear and misunderstanding of Islam permeates America, largely in the minds of those who have had little or no contact with Muslim, or Moslem, communities ("Moslem" being a Western adaptation of the word *Muslim*). The evidence seems to support the fact that where American Muslims interact with the larger Christian or secular community around them, they are accepted rather easily, in part, I suspect, because of the Muslims' emphasis on stringent moral codes, respect for family, and generally clean living. In certain inner-city neighborhoods in the New York area, for instance, the mosque has become a very real bastion against the drug dealer. Why then this antipathy to a moralistic religion so close at heart to the conservative fringes of our own Jewish-Christian tradition?

Before we can address that question, we need to know a little more about the Muslim faith. The word *Islām* itself means "surrender" or "submission," specifically to the will of God, or Allah. The image of surrender was reportedly drawn by Islam's founder, the Prophet Muhammad, from Abraham's submission to God's will when asked to sacrifice his son, Isaac. Islam is viewed by Muslims as a final redaction or transformation of the Jewish and Christian traditions of monotheism. Muhammad is considered "the Seal of the Prophets"—the last and greatest—chosen by God to rectify the wanderings of the Jews and Christians who had gone astray and had to be brought back to the original faith of Abraham. And so the Islamic holy book, the Koran, said to be inspired by Allah through the intercession of the angel Gabriel and dictated by Muhammad to a scribe, recognizes a number of figures from the Old and New Testaments. (The other major source of Islam, the Hadith, is the confirmed oral tradition of the Prophet

Muhammad, which encompasses ten to twenty thousand sayings or experiences from his life.) Of the twenty-eight prophets mentioned in the Koran, eighteen are from the Old and three from the New Testament, including John the Baptist and Jesus Christ (the other seven being for the most part obscure Arabian figures). The Koran does not recognize the divinity of Christ, however, holding instead that "God is One, the Eternal God. He begot none, nor was He begotten." Nonetheless, it seems to combine elements of the Mosaic and Christian God, rendering Allah not only omnipotent and omniscient but also infinitely merciful and compassionate, "the Forgiving One." The Prophet Muhammad gave one teaching that a man was walking through the desert and he saw a thorny branch that hung down across the path. The man moved the branch so other travelers would not be cut by the thorns, and for that act alone he was given Paradise—a ruling closer in spirit to the New Testament than the Old.

Islam is not in any real sense, then, an Eastern religion as we understand the term. However, at least in the Middle East, North Africa, parts of Southern and Western Asia, and Indonesia, where Islam flourishes, its spiritual and secular aspects are not always distinguished as they are in Western religions. In this regard Islam may resemble the closed communities of the Hasidim, Mennonites, or Amish, although this is less true of Muslim communities in the United States than in countries such as Pakistan where the very government is Muslim and the entire population falls under the sway of Muslim law. Such an arrangement might seem intolerable to Americans who have struggled to keep Church and State separated. Yet politicians routinely refer to the United States as a Christian nation, notwithstanding the vast numbers of Muslims, Buddhists, Jews, and unchurched who live within its boundaries. And over the last decade or so, elements of the fundamentalist Christian movement have renewed attempts to impose their religious beliefs on the population through law, seeking to render illegal both abortion and artificial contraception, to impose Christian prayers on public school classrooms, and to write fundamentalist creation scenarios into school textbooks.

Other parallels between Islam and Western religious belief systems are more striking. Muslims believe, for instance, in a hierarchy of angels, led by Gabriel, created by God before man, and serving to guard over and intercede for humanity. The Islamic vision of heaven and hell (preceded by a "Last Day," the resurrection of the body, and a "Day of Judgment") should appear familiar to anyone conversant with *The Divine Comedy*. One Islamic tradition divides Paradise, which is said to exist above the seventh heaven, into ninety-nine levels as opposed to Dante's nine, and the Koran speaks of the "seven gates" of hell. (Paradise, however, features a distinctly Arabian decor, replete with couches for reclining, silver goblets full of ginger-flavored drinks, green silk robes with gold brocade, "cool shades and fountains," and heavily laden fruit trees.) The Muslim practices of praying five times a day and of prostrating themselves in prayer may well have been inspired by the monks of the early Syriac Christian Church and the Desert Fathers who lived in caves around Mecca, where Muhammad encountered them. Some scholars even suggest that the word *Kōran* (or *Qur'ān*) is not an Arabic but a Syriac word, which the Desert Fathers used to mean "recitation," as when they recited the Psalms at length while making continuous prostrations. However, Muhammad took these practices a step further by popularizing the daily prayers, and sought to eliminate the priest class, and celibacy, altogether. He also transmitted Allah's command to give alms to the poor and to fast from dawn to sundown during the month of Ramadan (a lunar month that shifts from year to year by about eleven days).

According to Lex Hixon, Islam is also waiting for Jesus to return, "a fact little known to Christians." The Islamic scenario of the last days is that Jesus will return and rule the earth for a thousand years. "Next to the tomb of the Prophet Muhammad in Medina," he said, "there is an empty tomb which will be given to Jesus when he dies." The wooden prayer niche or mithrab which is part of any orthodox mosque has written above it an *ayat*, or verse from the Holy Koran. In many mosques, the verse concerns the Virgin Mary, and the niche itself, which must face Mecca, represents the east-facing room in which the Annunciation took place. Even the Islamic law forbidding the use of pictures or statues goes back to the Mosaic precept against the worship of "graven images." It may also be an extension of the "imageless meditation" of the Desert Fathers, which derived from a desire to encounter the Divine Light more directly and intimately, without any intervening forms. And like some Christians and all Jews, Muslims practice circumcision.

In certain ways, Islam can be seen as a religion that answered the specific needs of the small Arab community in which it arose, a populist creed that offered, as an alternative to the polytheism of Arabia, a direct relationship with God unmediated by a priestly hierarchy. (The born-again movement in America offers its members a similarly immediate personal relationship with Jesus.) In the years following Islam's birth in the seventh century, however, its theological system became increasingly convoluted, until a countermovement, at once more ascetical, mystical, and populist, rose within its ranks. Sufism, as this movement of Islam came to be known, began as a turn away from the rigid dogmatism of orthodox Muslim scholars, and formed a number of Orders, brotherhoods of dervishes (literally, "mendicants") organized around teachers or sheikhs. Across the centuries, Sufism has taken on a life of its own, and is said to have influenced Christian and Buddhist philosophy, and public figures as diverse as Goethe, Charles de Gaulle, Dag Hammerskjöld, and St. Francis of Assisi, and to have provided the spiritual underpinning of the great cathedral builders of the Middle Ages. Sufism has split into many different Orders and has been brought to the United States in what purists consider a watered-down form. Perhaps because Sufis have occasionally run afoul of orthodox Muslims in the Middle East and Christians in the West, they are sometimes secretive. Of the 900 million Muslims in the world today, no one can say how many are Sufis.

Lex Hixon is a Sufi who is very candid about his beliefs. Throughout our first meeting at his home in Riverdale, however, he was reluctant to say much about the biographical facts of his life. Hixon believes that no one set of incidents has more effect on a person's life than any other. To his way of thinking, "It was all there in the beginning, and various obstructions were simply cleared away in a kind of maturing process." For Hixon, the vagaries of life—whether you have been through divorce or a happy marriage, whether you were abused as a child or are a member of a minority—are largely irrelevant. "It would be too superficial," he insisted, "to feel that those things had any fundamental control over spiritual evolution."

About all the personal history to which Hixon would initially admit was that he was "a very passionate child and very uncontrollable," that he "could never conform to the proper way of doing things." Asked for his earliest memory of any seed of spiritual intent, he was more forthcoming. "I first began to aspire," he said, "when I saw a star or some sort of lucky thing, and I would make a wish that I just wanted to be good. By that I didn't mean superficially conforming and making everyone happy, as in, 'Oh, he's a good boy.' I had no concept of praying for this, but I profoundly wanted to manifest that goodness which must have been in me."

As to formal religious upbringing, Hixon was raised in a "nonreligious environment, without any sort of regular religious practices or beliefs," although both parents were nominally Episcopalian. He does remember being baptized at age six, and during the ceremony turning to his aunt and saying, "in a loud whisper that everyone could hear, 'Auntie, what is this man talking about?' It was my first religious questioning." He grew up in "that strange, pluralistic, open environment of Southern California, particularly Los Angeles, where German Tudor houses are right next to Spanish stucco homes. I have always had the kind of semi-crazy, wild openness of the culture there." At thirteen, he came East to the Hotchkiss School, a disciplined preparatory academy, and stayed in the East to attend Yale. "But it was always as if some sort of cultural openness and even craziness was underneath, and a veneer of an Eastern boarding school and Ivy League college was placed over that."

Here he stopped his story. "I'm sharing this with you," he said, "but I don't really like to indulge in these kinds of reflections very much. Maybe that'll be enough." He laughed. For my purposes, such a thumbnail biography could never be enough. I wanted to know where he came from, what had shaped him, what guideposts he'd passed along the way that I and, by extension, my readers could look for. I didn't much care for his theory that nothing is learned from personal history; after all, I was basing my book on a contrary assumption.

But before I could ask my next question, Lex had started speaking again. "Since you asked me," he said, "and since I'm a practicing mystic, maybe I can put it this way. I'm never going to answer questions in ordinary ways. So if you ask where I come from, I'll tell you this story. When my mother and father were married, in their early twenties, they traveled a lot and were just having fun together. They didn't want to start a family right away. But after a couple of years, my mother decided that she really wanted to have children now. And so she said to my father, 'Let's have a special ceremony, because the idea of making love when you're having a child is different. It should be joyful and beautiful for us, but there's something else going on.' My father was not particularly sensitive to this way of thinking, but he agreed to have the ceremonial event. The time they chose to try to start a family was midnight on Christmas Eve. And the next year, on Christmas Day, I was born. So that's where I come from."

The story sounded a little preposterous, and for a moment I thought he was implying that he was the result of a twelve-month gestation. But it did lead Hixon into explaining his reservations about the significance of upbringing in spiritual development. Someone who is well along the path of spiritual evolution, he said, might get a false sense of superiority by thinking he or she must have had worthier spiritual opportunities than someone else, whereas other people might think they had inferior opportunities. "But spirituality is totally democratic in that sense, and that's not true of other things," Hixon said. "Not everyone has the opportunity to learn to play piano or anything like that, which has to do with inequities which exist in every culture. But the beautiful thing about the Divine intelligence and spiritual unfolding is that it is absolutely just, and that the soul is never wronged by God. Different opportunities are given, along with different trials. There could even be the trial of ease or complacency, of having a great deal materially or intellectually or artistically and not having to struggle for it. Everything is a trial and a test from God, administered with infinite mercy. That's what I'd like to emphasize, rather than the specific events that may have triggered my spiritual evolution."

I asked Hixon when it first became clear that some kind of spiritual evolution was taking place, and when he was first drawn to a particular religious tradition. He said that when he was nineteen he went to South Dakota, where he encountered Vine Deloria, Sr., "the first evolved, saintly person I'd met who was conscious of the spiritual path and conscious that the longing for holiness is connected with spiritual practice. I say that because we may meet saintly people all the time who are unconscious of it themselves. The summer I spent with him was the first touch I received from a very blessed and mature soul."

Deloria was an Episcopal priest whose grandfather had been a Native American medicine man of the Lakota Sioux, and whose spiritual practices derived from both Christianity and his Native American background, "long periods of waiting in silence, mystical experiences." Deloria's grandfather had converted to Christianity after hearing a particular hymn sung in the Lakota language at the reservation chapel. "Especially in Protestant Christianity, the hymns are a rich source of the most beautiful spiritual teachings," Hixon noted. "People sing them and the teachings go into them in a unique way. You can't fully evaluate Protestant Christianity from the discursive things you might hear from the pulpit."

On Deloria's recommendation Hixon went back to New Haven, where he was a junior at Yale, and received confirmation in the Episcopal Church. "I took communion once from the bishop," he said, "and then didn't take communion again for many years, without thinking why. I'd gone through a formal procedure, but my inner integrity didn't feel linked up with it." Hixon was not attracted to Christianity again until he and his wife discovered the Russian Orthodox Church in 1984. They were touched by the writings of a nineteenth-century Russian mystic saint named Seraphim of Sarov. They then met Father Alexander Schmemann, "a living saint of the Russian Orthodox Church. Through these two saints, we were brought into the sacramental life of Russian Orthodox Christianity."

But, Hixon protested, this is just one of the many complex lines of spiritual evolution running through his life. "My feeling is that these were not different initiatives," he added, referring to his subsequent initiations into Buddhism, Vedanta, and Islam. "They came directly from what was innate in me because as a little child I had longed to express goodness. They also came from what is innate in the universe, which is what Islam calls the Light of Guidance, the same light which has descended, in the Islamic tradition, through 124,000 prophets beginning with Adam—who in Islam is honored as a prophet—all the way to the Prophet Muhammad in the seventh century of the Common Era in the deserts of Arabia."

That brought us to the subject I had originally sought out Hixon to discuss: Islam, and its relation to Sufism. Hixon is quick to reject what he considers a superficial characterization of Sufism as "a mystical branch or subset of Islam." Instead, Sufism should be considered "part of a way of referring to Islam as a whole." Refusing to separate the two, any more than he would separate the exoteric and esoteric practices of Christianity, Hixon insists that "Islam as a whole is a Gnostic tradition, in the sense that it wishes to know the nature of reality. Knowing that unity directly and not just discursively has certain alchemical effects on one's whole being. This is true not only for a limited number of mystics, but for every sincere practitioner. Hence, my relationship is not just with Sufism or Islamic mysticism, but with Islam itself."

To begin with, he underlines the importance of receiving the tradition from "living representatives" of the faith. For his initiation into Islam, Hixon had two: Bawa Muhaiyaddeen of Sri Lanka, whom he described as "a mysterious Islamic yogi from the jungle, whose lineage transmission is secret and not historical," and Muzaffer-al-Jerrahi, "a highly educated scholar from Istanbul, the nineteenth sheikh of a very prominent mystic Order. The combination of these two very different Sufi masters intensified my spiritual evolution in Islamic terms."

As if amplifying Elizabeth Lesser's remarks on gurus, Hixon insists that his relationship with his teachers is more than just intellectual, that it incorporates "real feeling" and is different from studying with a great academic teacher. He used the analogy of marriage. "In marriage," he said, "sexual union and the children that come forth from that add a dimension which is incomparable to the dimensions of other friendships. And although marriage doesn't necessarily devalue other friendships, it's something much more involving and profound. That kind of union of souls occurs between a spiritual guide and a disciple."

Hixon cited Kierkegaard's contrasting of Socrates and Jesus as two forms of transmission. "A college professor does not want to be a guru, and is not prepared to be, so he takes a Socratic approach," he said. "The Socratic approach is to be a midwife and stand by as someone's ideas are born, but Christ's approach would be to impregnate the person with the truth. Christianity doesn't have much sexual imagery, but Sufism has a lot. The sheikh is said to use the sexual organ of his tongue to implant the semen—the words that he speaks—in the organ, or ear, of the disciple. The womb is the heart, which becomes impregnated and then gives birth to various spiritual states which come forth in the realm of the soul. It's the Sufi way of expressing the kind of difference that Kierkegaard saw between Socrates and Jesus. But if we look at the life of Socrates, we see that he too was, if you want to say, a Sufi. In his own manner, he was impregnating his disciples, and all of the history of philosophy, with a kind of spiritual presence."

The Chisti Order of Sufism into which Hixon has taken initiation was the first Sufi Order to come to America, brought here from India by Hazrat Inayat Khan in 1910; the Jerrahi is a totally Islamic Order brought over from Istanbul in 1978 by Sheikh Muzaffer. Hazrat Inayat Khan's lineage runs from the early disciples of Muhammad all the way to the American Sufi, Samuel Lewis (Sufi Sam), who received the transmission of Hazrat Inayat Khan while Khan's son Pir Vilayat was still a small boy. Lewis was also initiated by some of the early Japanese Zen masters who had come to San Francisco. Hixon regards Lewis rather than Pir Vilayat as his link to the Chisti lineage, and feels "particularly linked to Sufi Sam" because Sam also held lineages in more than one tradition simultaneously.

Hixon feels that Pir Vilayat's distancing of Sufism from orthodox Islam probably has to do with "trying to protect his students from various kinds of Islamic fundamentalism." But what of the Sufi masters throughout history who had reportedly been persecuted by orthodox Islamic leaders, including the ill-fated Mansur al-Hallaj? Hixon began by correcting an assumption. "If you say Sufis were persecuted by Islamic leaders, you're already presupposing a difference," he interjected. "The point is that certain Muslims were not appreciated by other Muslims. If you asked St. Francis, 'Are you a Catholic, or a mystic, or a troubadour?' he would say, 'Of course, I'm a Catholic.' St. Francis manifested a great deal of obedience to the Church, and yet he was obviously a mystic troubadour." (Idries Shah, in his popular book *The Sufis*, makes the case that St. Francis received initiation into Sufism. "Most people know that St. Francis of Assisi was a light-hearted troubadour of Italy who experienced a religious conversion and became a saint with an uncanny influence over animals and birds," he writes. "It is on record that the troubadours were a relic of Saracenic musicians and poets. It is often agreed that the rise and development of the monkish Orders in the middle ages was greatly influenced by the penetration of Muslim dervish organizations in the West." And in *Turning East*, Harvey Cox lumps St. Francis with other "avatars," divine beings incarnated on earth. Ideas of the Hindu conception of the avatar vary widely, he writes. "But one current theory teaches that in each age there is an avatar on the earth somewhere—that Confucius, Moses, Jesus, the Buddha, St. Francis, Mohamet, Lao Tzu and many others were such embodiments of the divine.")

I told Hixon that his response didn't really answer the question, though, because as far as I knew, St. Francis hadn't been persecuted for his unorthodox beliefs. He replied that the Church had brought a lot of pressure on its saints (St. Ignatius Loyola, the founder of the Jesuit Order, was reportedly investigated by the Inquisition, as were John of the Cross and Teresa of Avila), and particularly on those unorthodox believers who never became saints. "We should see that kind of phenomenon happening in every tradition," he said. "There are heretics in different religious traditions, and legitimately so. You *can* make a mistake spiritually. You can be on a dangerous and divisive ego trip and think that that's your sainthood or your new understanding of the tradition. The body politic of the living tradition has to protect itself against that distorted viewpoint. There are various ways of doing that, including burning people at the stake. I can't give my approval to that, but it is a very serious matter that negativity and even evil is at loose in the universe, and we have to protect ourselves. One of the difficult aspects of a religious tradition is that it has to keep its truth as full of integrity as possible—not by killing people, but at least by refuting them. All traditions exist in a blurred state because history is not a clear medium. It's a very milky, cloudy water. That's why religious tradition should never be judged by purely historical standards."

Certainly the confusing array of perceptions about Islam in the current American mind-set is as cloudy as can be. Several million Muslims are now practicing in this country, a significant number. However, many of them are in ethnically isolated communities, and although by most accounts they are accepted by their non-Islamic neighbors and successfully interact with business and society, we still don't know very much about them. In fact, Americans probably know less about Islam, even after the war in the Persian Gulf, than about Zen Buddhism, which has far fewer practitioners here. White America's perception of Islam is also tainted by memories of the Nation of Islam, the Black Muslim separatist group which rose to prominence in the sixties under the leadership of Elijah Muhammad, and has occasionally darted back into the spotlight through the actions of his successor, Louis Farrakhan. Based on the Iranian hostage situation of 1979, and to a lesser extent the Ayatollah Khomeini's death threat against Salman Rushdie, the image of Islam as composed of hordes of fundamentalist extremists ululating through the dusty streets of Arabia is the one that seems fixed in our minds.

The Persian Gulf crisis and war of 1990–91 only served to confuse the issue, as America opposed an Iraqi despot who in many ways resembled the kind of Western military dictators often backed by the U.S. government, and who paid the merest lip service to Islam. In doing this, America joined forces with Saudi Arabia, perhaps the most staunchly fundamentalist Muslim regime in the region, a nation where women may not drive automobiles and alcohol is anathema. And then there were the brave mujahedin in the mountains of Afghanistan who for years baited the Russian bear with hand-held Stinger missiles sent to them largely with congressional approval. They are Muslims, too. And in Azerbaijan and Bangladesh and Sri Lanka, the followers of Muhammad present other images that are not so readily identifiable with American preconceptions of Islam. It may be useful to view the discrepancies between the teachings of Islam's founder and the actions of its followers in the same way one can view the gulf between the words of Christ and the often unrelated behavior of the world's Christians. Much is made, for example, of the Koran's incitement to *jihād*, or holy war, against infidels. The Koran also teaches, "Fight for the sake of God those that fight against you, but do not attack them first. God does not love the aggressors." (2:190.) And according to the Hadith, Muhammad once proclaimed after returning from battle, "Now we turn from the lesser jihad to the greater jihad," the greater jihad being the battle against the limited self, the separative ego that is the enemy of all spiritual teachers.

With all that in mind, I asked Hixon to try to make sense of this country's skewed viewpoint, while dealing with reasonable criticisms of the things that make Americans uncomfortable with Islam, namely, its religious intolerance and its treatment of women. He began by drawing a parallel to the variegated sects of Christianity practicing in America, noting that Evangelical Protestants might be likely to say that Roman Catholics "are inspired by the Devil. So we don't have to pick on Islam as something that is misunderstood. We can find in our own culture that Christianity and Judaism are wracked with misunderstanding, not just among people who are on the outside but also among practitioners.''

Hixon likes to draw an analogy between political factions and the liberal and conservative wings of most religions, whatever the culture or historical period. Just as a bird needs two wings to fly, the analogy goes, so religion has to be ''the collaboration of sincerely dedicated people.'' Inside a religious tradition, a genuinely honorable disagreement often exists among great practitioners, scholars, and even saints. ''Eventually the Holy Spirit tries to bring the truth to the milky, impenetrable medium of history. The Eastern Orthodox Church does not accept the idea of the Catholic Pope being infallible and in charge of everything, because they believe that the Holy Spirit works best in a decentralized way through all the bishops. But they don't think that laymen or local priests should be making decisions on spiritual matters, as Protestants do. They think that's too decentralized. Every tradition has to find its balance.''

Differences do exist among the various Muslim sects: the Sunni and Shiite, to name the largest, and the Wahhabi, an ultrafundamentalist group of Sunnis that rose up in the late nineteenth century. The Wahhabis, located primarily in Saudi Arabia, oppose all practices not sanctioned by the Koran. ''When a somewhat fundamentalist Islamic culture in Afghanistan defeated the Communist invasion of Russia, we were very happy,'' Hixon said. ''When the Ayatollah was going against another Islamic regime in Iraq, which turned out to be much more strange and vicious than he was, we were unhappy with him. All this is the play of historical perspectives.''

Turning the tables, Hixon asked how our dropping a bomb on Hiroshima or Nagasaki could square with the Sermon on the Mount. For a Christian culture, that seemed a highly un-Christian way to choose to end that war. ''Harry Truman was hardly an Ayatollah,'' he said. ''He was a gentle, genuine man who somehow got involved in ordering this. And the second bomb we dropped was much worse than the first, in a sense. You drop one bomb and then you send out negotiators, so there's no need to drop a second one. Does that mean that Harry Truman was some sort of horrible beast, or that we'd gone mad under the pressure of being attacked by the Japanese? What does that mean about Christianity? It's the same with the Ayatollah. Those questions are not relevant. What did the Ayatollah mean about Islam? Islam is something much vaster than he was, just as Christianity is much vaster than Harry Truman and the United States of America were at that particular time of conflict—vaster, for that matter, than Jimmy Swaggart is today. The political sphere is always going to be murky, and spiritual or religious development will itself be infected by the surface of human nature and politics."

Concerning the concept of the holy war, Hixon points out that Muhammad was a reluctant warrior who, after he received his revelation at age forty, spent the first thirteen years in Mecca being "more nonviolent than Gandhi or King, because he not only didn't lift a weapon but didn't start a resistance movement either. The last ten years of his life he had Divine permission to retire to Medina, and that's where he engaged in nineteen battles, but reluctantly, hating the use of the sword." Because Muhammad "sanctified warfare through these nineteen battles, that didn't imply that warfare would always have to be carried on." (Of course, "holy warfare" is hardly limited to Muslims. During the early days of the air strikes on Baghdad, I saw televised images of American airmen writing on the bombs that were being attached to the wings of their planes. One inscription read: "If you're getting tired of Allah, why not try Jesus?")

However Islam is viewed, criticism ought to come not from the local culture or from another tradition, but from within the tradition. "I don't believe that Islam is in a position to criticize Christianity," Hixon said, "or that Christianity is in a position to criticize Islam. Christianity and Islam should criticize themselves in the light of their own standards. When the Islamic nations met recently, something like fifty out of sixty condemned the Ayatollah's death threat against Salman Rushdie. They can't agree that closely on oil prices. The United Nations can't agree on whether Communist China has committed an aggression in Tibet. But the Islamic world is very much in harmony saying that the Ayatollah's death threat was not Islamic. So that should close the issue."

He makes the further point that somewhere between 30 and 40 million Americans—other observers put the figure even higher— would probably describe themselves as fundamentalist Christians, leaving us with a huge fundamentalist population of our own. Islamic countries have much the same fundamentalist problem, he said, adding that "the ratio of fundamentalism to the fuller dimensions of the tradition is roughly the same in every culture. You could probably make a law of physics to that extent. But among the Christian fundamentalists, there are different strands and degrees of intensity. I doubt if all the Christian fundamentalists could be characterized as awful people or people who aren't sincerely religious or extremely loving, and the same is true of the fundamentalist sectors of Islam."

We get a sense of the complexity of the situation if we think of Orthodox Judaism as Jewish fundamentalism, a case which can easily be made. Orthodox Judaism encompasses a wide range of sects, including many classes of Hasidim such as the Lubovitchers, a kind of Jewish equivalent of Christian Evangelicals. (Although Jews don't generally seek to convert non-Jews to Judaism, Lubovitchers actively solicit converts to Orthodoxy from among non-Orthodox Jews.) But if we regard the Orthodox as Jewish fundamentalists, Hixon said, "the problem is that many of the Orthodox rabbis have the richest mystical teaching at their disposal. So we have to become a little more refined in our distinctions."

Hixon believes that many of the favorable aspects of our society derive from the people who describe themselves as fundamentalist Christians. "They may just take on the problem of homelessness and do something about it at a certain point, even though they're traditionally connected with Republicans and people who don't want to spend money on social programs. All that can change in an instant, because religious consciousness and spiritual energies are very creative and powerful and can realign political issues. A good example is the dropping of the Wall between the two Germanies, bloodlessly and within a period of time which was shockingly brief. A kind of spiritual energy brought that Wall down. Although a lot of the dissidents met in churches, it was something outside of formal religion. The spirituality inside people was manifesting itself, as it was in the case of Dr. King's various marches. We mustn't try to identify religion with only its institutional function. It's much vaster than that, and it's ultimately inside the human heart." If we complain that people are institutionalizing religion, and yet identify religion with the institution, he argues, we are in complicity. Whereas if we see religion as "something that belongs to all the people and permeates all hearts spontaneously, we begin to see a very different picture. We don't see the picture that an atheist or agnostic scholar of history would see. We see the planet as a living, sacred world, where people are operating out of spiritual motivation, no matter what they call it."

The Nation of Islam (which the members of the Black Muslim community call the First Movement), and black separatism generally, according to Hixon, "is considered a huge mistake, absolutely not Islamic. They by and large hold that the son of Elijah Muhammad, whose name is Warithuddin Muhammad, presided over a bloodless revolution, with the exception of the martyring of Malcolm X. Aside from Minister Louis Farrakhan, who heads a small sliver of the Black Muslim movement, the present members of the movement, all followers of the son of Elijah Muhammad, are strict Sunni Muslims, with no black separatist aspirations whatsoever. The fact that the Nation of Islam was a mistake is being proclaimed by Muslims, not by scholars from the outside. So here's a case of a tradition purifying itself and making critical judgments about itself. This development was one of the great miracles of cultural evolution in this country." (Indeed, as black scholars are beginning to point out, it was the positive influence of orthodox Islam on Malcolm X, especially his discovery in Africa that Islam tolerates no form of racial discrimination, that was leading him away from the separatist politics of Elijah Muhammad before he was killed.)

Meanwhile, Islam is entering America from many Muslim countries, varying the population of this nation's mosques. Over a million Muslims of different cultural backgrounds have immigrated, and at least a million more grew up here in Black, Caucasian, or Asian communities. "They're all building mosques and marrying at a great rate," Hixon said, "but there is a unique intimacy between Islam and the African-American community in the United States. We have to deepen our understanding of what this means." Hixon wonders whether a lot of the original slaves who came from Africa were from Islamic backgrounds, and whether that has any bearing, but acknowledged that the African-American community is very religious across the board, Christian or Muslim. "There seems to be a spiritual gift among these people, so it's a little difficult to analyze precisely what's going on."

Hixon contravenes the assumption that fluency in Arabic is a prerequisite for Islam. He considers himself a Muslim but is not at all fluent in Arabic, knowing only enough to read the Koran and to pray. "A new Islamic civilization is definitely manifesting, and English is the lingua franca," he said, "because only twenty percent of Muslims in the world speak Arabic as their native language. The only way that a Muslim from Africa and a Muslim from Southeast Asia—and Southeast Asia has the largest concentration of Muslims in the world—can communicate is in English. Arabic is now the language only of the prayers and of chanting Koran."

Nor does he agree with the premise that Islam is not respected and accepted in this country, arguing that the Muslims who are building mosques and dealing with other businessmen and with the community are receiving cooperation from neighboring Christians and Jews. He has seen Muslims learning from the various Jewish organizations which have grown up over the years to protect Jewish values from being overrun in the larger Christian culture. "Muslims are forming their own organizations patterned on Jewish ones to protect Islam as a minority religion," he said. "Yet this country is very liberal, very friendly. Things may be different in rural parts of the South or among Christian fundamentalists, but in general, Muslims have found the United States a very congenial, open place to develop their culture."

Part of the reason for that is the secular nature of American culture. If you have the money to build a mosque, everyone is happy because jobs are created and the tax base goes up. "So there's a blessing in our very secularism, insofar as secular culture appears to be a place where pluralistic religious development can take place," he said. In a strictly religious culture, such pluralistic development would be problematical. "This is how we give the secular culture a religious interpretation. We say God produced a secular environment in order that all of his great traditions could grow together."

Hixon admits that religious conflicts often do occur, and acknowledges the irony that religion, which claims to be the source of illumination, is one of the hardest areas on which to shed light. He likens religion to gold. "Gold is the most precious metal substance, and yet all sorts of vicious behavior and strange explosions of egocentricity happen around it. That doesn't mean that we have to say, 'Someone's made a mistake. Gold couldn't be that valuable after all, because look at all the chaos it's causing.' Nor should we say, 'Let's do without religion. It couldn't be that valuable, because of all the problems it causes.' That's poor reasoning."

Despite any conflicts, though, Hixon sees "no indication that Islam and Christianity are disappearing. They happen to be the two largest spiritual communities on the planet, each with about a billion members, and they're also the two most quickly growing communities. So, in the modern world, in which science and politics were presumably going to take over and run things rationally and pragmatically, Islam and Christianity are vastly increasing in numbers rather than withering away."

Hixon's figures are actually understated. With an overall population of more than 1.5 billion, Christianity is still a force to be reckoned with, its continued growth in South America and Africa more than offsetting attenuation in some European countries. Yet why does it seem that where Christianity and Islam have intersected, from the days of the Crusades to the present, these two great advocates of peace, love, and a merciful God have so relentlessly been at each other's throats? Hixon doesn't see religious opposition as the fundamental issue. He sees "cultural rivalries and national rivalries and ethnic rivalries. They may all be shouting and claiming that it's about religious differences, but it isn't. In Northern Ireland, are Catholics and Protestants fighting about the Trinity, or communion? Is that the source of their differences? Religion has gotten a bad rap from historians as the source of conflict, when, in fact, the opposite may be true. Stalin and Hitler didn't have any religious tradition, and they killed more people in their single generation—many more people—than were killed in religious conflicts since the beginning of humanity. It was precisely the lack of religion which enabled Pol Pot, Stalin, and Hitler to maneuver the way they did. Although religion often becomes a focal point for cultural and ethnic rivalry, it has educated the planet spiritually and has prevented many awful things from happening."

"In other words," I said, "you reject the old saw that more people have been killed in religious wars than in all the other wars combined."

Hixon was emphatic. "Just in our century, many more people have been killed by nonreligious, antireligious leaders, than by any religious wars," he said. "And, of course, I contradict all old saws. Old saws are dull and they're not useful anymore."

Instead, he feels that any conflict between Christianity and Islam may stem more from their relatedness than from their differences. "Judaism and Christianity and Islam are closer than brother or sister traditions," Hixon said, "although each has its own unique integrity. They come from the same roots, and sometimes the closer neighbors are, the more arguments take place between them and the more difficult it is to make peace. You can make peace in some abstract fashion with someone on the other side of the city, but the person living next to you is the hardest person to make peace with." He added that "the unsettling nature of this closeness" may account for why so many Christians have gone to Buddhism and Hinduism for inspiration, "but have not yet found Islam," something which is also largely true of Jewish seekers.

Of course, religious traditions are *supposed* to be unsettling. Part of their function is to unsettle our presuppositions about a self-centered way of life. "Religion does not exist as an opiate, as in the now defunct Marxist viewpoint," Hixon said. "Obviously, religious institutions can oppress people. But religion is meant to be an awakening, revolutionary force. When you encounter another religion, you encounter a whole other set of variants which are designed to wake people up and to unsettle them, but since it's a different set from the one you're used to, it's doubly disconcerting."

One major tenet that links Islam to the Jewish-Christian continuum is belief in an eternal afterlife as opposed to the concept of reincarnation common to most Oriental belief systems. Since Hixon practices both Eastern and Western disciplines, I asked him how he resolves this apparent discrepancy. "Reincarnation and the heavenly journey are two alternative ways of looking at a situation," he said. "It's like the wave theory and the particle theory in understanding the nature of light. Depending on the experimental context you set up, light appears to behave that way. So the particle theory could be the heavenly journey of the soul. The wave theory could be the reincarnation of the soul. But the point is that light is so much more than the way it behaves in certain artificial experimental contexts. In much the same way, a religion always stays open to the fact that it is not ultimately explaining God or reality, but is giving certain guidelines, mainly for spiritual practice, for a form of maturing and evolving as a person."

The enormous differences in these two sets of guidelines regarding the afterlife is one of the "interesting factors" of major religions. "Both teachings have integrity and both are based on experience," Hixon said. "But reality itself is much beyond that. For instance, in Buddhism, reincarnation is part of the sphere of relative truth, not part of absolute Truth. The absolute Truth is that there are no separate individual beings in the first place. And similarly with Islam and Christianity, although the voyage to Paradise is definitely the way things happen, there's a sense that one can go beyond Paradise and merge into the Divine Essence, or have some sort of mystic union with the Essence, in which neither Paradise nor the temporal creation appears. The way to understand it is to see that these are guidelines for spiritual maturing. They represent experiences that people have after death, but they are not necessarily the final teaching or the final truth. They're stages on the way."

The underpinning for the four separate spiritual traditions that Hixon practices is Vedanta, particularly the teachings of Ramakrishna of Bengal, the founder of the Vedanta Society, who died in 1886. "His teachings were that all the religions are true, and they all have the fullness of truth," Hixon said. "For him, they all led to the same point of advanced spiritual evolution." Yet if any of the major traditions can lead to enlightenment or salvation, why follow four? Hixon doesn't feel he needs more than one, because "each one of them would be adequate and total." But he can move "in different environments with some flexibility. That's my particular gift, and a part of my spiritual evolution is to be involved with these four."

As if echoing the sentiments of Basil Pennington and Bernard Glassman, he added, "One of the truths I'm discovering is that Christianity does not have to go to Buddhism to figure out how to meditate. And Buddhism does not have to go to Christianity to figure out how to serve the poor. Each one has its fullness. But given that very tolerant basic principle, there is a lot of interaction between the traditions, and has been throughout history. They don't exist in hermetically sealed chambers. Once again, religious history is a very milky medium in which you can't draw lines easily. But each of the traditions has its own kind of universality. Christianity says, 'The Holy Spirit operates everywhere.' Islam says, 'All the prophets brought the same message.' Buddhism says, 'Human consciousness is all one consciousness, and it can be perfected and enlightened.' There are signs pointing to universality in each of the traditions, and those have helped me to keep a balance. If you ask why I'm doing this, I have to answer that I don't have an agenda or plan. I may be like a scientist who is investigating a subject without any idea that certain technology will come out of his researches. It's science for science's sake, with the implication that, if we find things, people will use them and find more things that will be useful for humanity."

But of the four traditions, Islam is the only one in which Hixon holds a formal teaching position. Under his religious name of Sheikh Nur al-Jerrahi, Hixon has led the community at the mosque Masjid al-Farrah in lower Manhattan since 1980. "When I teach in the mosque and when I teach the Dervishes, I stay with Islam and keep a very firm direction. There my job is not to confuse people or to bring in unnecessary complexities of other traditions, but to illuminate Islam directly. I try to do that, and I have the permission and responsibility to give people initiation into our Halveti-Jerrahi Order of Dervishes, which is an ancient one from Istanbul and from Egypt." It's a unique opportunity, giving him "an indication of what it's like to lead a community and to have spiritual responsibilities, and that gives me a better insight into the phenomenon of religious communities, which is what religion is all about."

Hixon feels that the question of whether Westerners are too materialistic by nature or social training to respond to the spiritual imperatives coming from the East and Middle East has been overstated. "We have to see that Westerners are *very* open to spiritual development," he said. "The teachers I've known who have come here from the East have been extraordinarily moved by Americans. Material affluence is no impediment to spiritual openness and development. In fact, to some extent we can see the emptiness of sheer material affluence, so we're looking for something more, something deeper. Besides, people in cultures such as India often have a tremendous resistance to spiritual development. Spiritual things have been around in their culture from time immemorial, and they're suspicious of them. People in India are more suspicious of gurus than we are in America. Many people there have authentic gurus, but many others in India want nothing but material development."

Asked what *he* does for a living, Hixon said that he had "received a fellowship, a financial inheritance, which gives me an independent

life without having to work in a regular job. It's a fellowship to explore
religious and existential issues, and I'm still trying to figure out who
granted me this fellowship." Part of what he does with his fellowship
is to advise spiritual seekers who want to move on in their development. When people come to him and say they want to go further,
he sometimes asks where they live. "That may sound ridiculous," he
said, but if they live near a spiritual center he knows, he advises them
to go there. "It's like a chessboard, although in this case, it's non-
competitive chess. The checkmate is when the person comes into
relationship with the truth through some direct manner. I give different advice or nonadvice, as the case may be, to different people
under different circumstances, and there's no way I can generalize.
Sometimes I get scared for people getting into mainstream religions,
because I know how dogmatic and narrow those can be. Sometimes
I get scared for people getting involved in small intensive groups,
because I know how alienating those can be from the mainstream
ones, even though there may be more freedom for the individual. It's
a very dangerous field. As Somerset Maugham indicated in the title
of his famous book, taken from the ancient *Upanishads*, the path is as
sharp as a razor's edge." If he tells a Jew to go back to his local
synagogue, for instance, that person may run into a very secular-
minded rabbi who will completely turn him off again, and then it may
take years, if ever, to get back to his native tradition. "The traditions
in which people are born do have a special quality for them," Hixon
said, "and I don't like to see people isolated from that. But I don't
like to see them get so intensely religious that they think the family
is unclean and they forget the values of an agnostic position, which
at least is tolerant of other points of view."

When people ask him for guidance in furthering their spiritual pur-
suits, he is aware that they may have a lot of romantic notions about
spiritual practice which he can't dispel overnight. "They have to live
through that," he said. "But it makes me nervous, too. So I pray for
them and encourage them to remember that they already have inside
them a true longing for and sensibility about truth. They have a tremendous sense of compassion and a willingness to sacrifice their own
interests for the genuine interests of other people. All these things are
what religions exist to remind us of and to intensify. But they don't
exist only in the religions. They already exist in the human heart."

Likewise, he tells them, God is not an ideal, but is "more real than human thinking and perception, more real than the entire creation, more real than the millions of galaxies. We think that science is uncovering reality. When they say they've discovered several million galaxies more, we think that's wonderful. But the simplest religious believer will tell you that God is more real than these millions of galaxies that are being discovered. You don't have to be an intellectual to feel that. Modern science is finding out some wonderful things that are really there—they're not imagining all these galaxies—but this is just the outer skin of reality. Einstein's theories of relativity and of the space-time continuum were brilliant, but they didn't explain why a person would love another person or sacrifice his life for another.

"Some scientific discoveries indicate such an amazing level of intelligence and penetration on the part of the scientist that it does make you think. What kind of being is it that can find one hundred million galaxies when it starts looking around itself? That might give us a little more confidence that the human being is extraordinary. But people found God before they found these hundred million galaxies, and that is as valid a level of knowledge as the scientific knowledge—and possibly more significant. Living in a sea of a hundred million galaxies, which are essentially physical energy, is not as significant a vision as living in the embrace of an Infinite Intelligence. I don't think anyone would say it was."

CHAPTER 17

Barbara Grizzuti Harrison: Witness to Faith

■ ■ ■

And don't ask me about the origins of evil, or about rats and bloated bellies and earthquakes and why He permits them. I don't know. When I was a Witness, I had the answer to all those questions, or thought I did. What I did not have was faith in the ultimate goodness of God. Now I don't have answers; I have faith. "For now we see through a glass, darkly; but then face to face: now I know in part; but then shall I know even as also I am known." I only know that I will know. I know that that leap into belief was not an escape into passivity or resignation or withdrawal from the world; it was the beginning of a truly human struggle to realize God in the world.

—Barbara Grizzuti Harrison, *Visions of Glory*

[Not] until now has there ever been a time in which so many of the prophecies are coming together. There have been times in the past when people thought the end of the world was coming, and so forth, but never anything like this.

—Ronald Reagan, December 1983

■

Every so often, usually when you're least prepared for it, a car comes sweeping up the driveway and two people emerge, either a woman and a man or two women, but rarely two men, and sometimes a child is with them. After the briefest of preliminary chitchat, they get around to asking whether you are familiar with the Bible. When this happens to me and I admit that I have studied it, their interest perks up, somewhat warily. There follows a fairly lengthy period of back-and-forth jousting and Bible quoting, during which they make their usual points about the impending Armageddon, and hence the need to be counted among the saved. During these Biblical skirmishes, I try to get them to explain why their last several predictions of Armageddon have failed to materialize. They have answers to most of my questions, but almost all of them require an absolute belief in the Bible as the only acceptable revelation of Truth. This makes real dialogue difficult at best, and my visitors usually leave after the conversation starts going around in circles. After all, they have more proselytizing to do.

But the truth is that I never know quite how to deal with the visiting Jehovah's Witnesses, members of the only American religion—and it is entirely of domestic origin—to employ the tactics of door-to-door salesmen. In the past I counted them sometimes an amusing diversion, sometimes an irritating invasion of privacy. But until I happened across former Witness Barbara Grizzuti Harrison's sparkling and ruthlessly researched book, *Visions of Glory: A History and a Memory of Jehovah's Witnesses*, I never thought of them in sinister terms. I still can't work up much serious concern, although Harrison cites evidence pointing to their being an especially closed-minded fundamentalist sect, apocalyptic, virulently anti-Catholic (their term for the Church is "the scarlet whore of Babylon"), misogynistic, and racist. They claim that the world will end with the destruction of the wicked at Armageddon in our lifetime (although they have had to change the exact date at least half a dozen times as the appointed days have come and blithely gone), and that only the chosen will survive. However, by standing up to the U.S. government, they have also been instrumental in winning a number of court decisions that bolstered laws regarding freedom of religion and press, and conscientious objection to military service. As Harrison puts it, "It is impossible to speak of the history of civil liberties in this country without speaking of the Witnesses. Whatever their motives, we are very much in their debt."

In her book, Harrison points out that the Witnesses, whose notoriety derives from their refusal to accept blood transfusions, salute the flag, or serve in the Army, and from their aggressive proselytizing, "subject themselves to total conformity in practice, outlook, and belief. To the extent to which they are known . . . they are perceived as rather drab, somewhat eccentric people, and dismissed as an irrelevant joke. Little is known of their motives, their anguish, their glorious surges of communal happiness, and little thought is given to the comment their existence makes on the larger society."

Because, aside from their door-to-door proselytizing, the Witnesses keep a low profile, they do go largely unnoticed. Those who came to my door some time after I had interviewed Barbara Harrison seemed less doctrinaire and closed-minded than the ones she depicted in her book. Two of them told me the Witnesses had undergone a self-critical period during which members who insisted on a specific date for the Apocalypse departed the community. They insisted that theirs is the only authentic interpretation of the Bible, a position as unpliable as the papal infallibility of Roman Catholicism or the Biblical inerrancy of fundamentalist Christians, but they were willing to listen politely to other points of view.

After Harrison converted to Jehovah's Witnesses with her mother while still a child, it took her thirteen years to find her own way out of what she finally came to see as a destructive belief system, and back to the tradition in which she had been born. She considers herself a staunch Roman Catholic, even if, around the time we sat down to talk in her apartment in the Park Slope section of Brooklyn, she was at "a very confused point" in her life. Having just returned from Romania, which had recently deposed the dictator Nicolae Ceausescu, she had witnessed firsthand the devastating effects of his regime. So overwhelmed was she by the sight of thousands of abandoned, AIDS-infected infants in the state hospitals that she felt God was temporarily "distant" from her life.

Her sobering trip to Romania was part of her work as a journalist (an assignment to interview the Romanian Olympic hero Nadia Comineci for *Life* magazine). Among her other writings are the feminist book *Unlearning the Lie: Sexism in School* and a thoughtful string of travel articles and books about her visits to Italy, Eastern Europe, and England. Her apartment was laden with some of the spoils of her journeys, including a collection of colorful French and Italian tiles of all descriptions. In her mid-fifties, with graying hair, Harrison would just as soon talk about her love of Italian hill towns or 1940s film noir as about anything spiritual. Resting briefly from her Romanian jaunt before flying to Hollywood to interview the film director Peter Bogdonovich, Harrison explained that she needs time to empty her mind between trips, and sometimes watches six hours of television at a stretch, mostly old movies, to accomplish that. Even this seemingly harmless activity she traces back to her harrowing days with Jehovah's Witnesses. Yet what is most memorable about her is her abiding good humor. The novelist Robert Stone once said that he thought growing up Catholic enriched one's sense of humor. "At a certain point," he told me, "there's something kind of touching and gallant and funny about the situation of being a kid and having to deal with eternity and all these absurd and monstrous concepts. There's an inherent comic aspect to all that which is inescapable."

Born in 1934 in Coney Island Hospital in Brooklyn, to an Italian immigrant father and a second-generation Italian-American mother, Barbara Grizzuti Harrison remembers very little of her early years as a Catholic, and what she does recall is "double-sided. I associated it with gloom and incense and old ladies in my grandmother's house. On the other hand the romance of it was very real—little communion brides who looked so good and smelled so pretty." But she could not recall having seen her mother go to church. "She was extremely passionate by nature and extremely intelligent," Harrison said of her, "but she didn't seem to know where to go with it." Her father found the Catholic Church "too womanish," whereas he thought the Presbyterian minister was a "regular guy." At her Presbyterian Sunday School, Barbara was told to be so quiet she could hear a pin drop. She remembers "not hearing it. I think my earliest visions of doom came from that experience, because I thought I was the only person who didn't hear the pin drop. But I was evidently very literal-minded. Even today my dreams are very literal."

Talking over those early days in Brooklyn with her brother recently, Harrison decided that the family "wasn't as poor as we thought we were." Her father, who liked the horses, gambled a good deal, but because he belonged to a strong typographical union, he also worked as a printer all through the Depression. "Although we lived in rather straitened circumstances," she said, "that was in part because of my father's gambling and in part because of my mother's incredible frugality, which seems to me so un-Italian. It always seemed significant that I didn't have a middle name. I never knew another baptized Catholic who didn't have one, but my mother was frugal even as to middle names."

In much the same way, religion in the house was "nonexistent," and neither of her parents was a strong presence in those days. "I never saw my mother and father as a couple at all," she said. "I saw them linked later in a terrible symbiotic union. But at that time, nobody seemed to be linked in any way to anybody else in my life, including family members. I had viral pneumonia and a Miss Silver came to the house. Miss Silver was my third-grade teacher, and she had very sibilant esses and was always rustling. She had very chunky Mexican jewelry, which I forever after associated with lesbians—possibly because she was a woman who paid attention to me, and both my mother and father took a very dim view of this. What she told them, as I lay fevered, was that I was very smart, which came to me as great news. I had no idea that this was true. It was the first time that I objectified myself, and it's always a strange experience when you see yourself as a person in the world in relationship to other people. It's the first image I have of myself as somebody other people might talk about and relate to."

Harrison described a kind of religious void accompanying the personal one, to the extent that, when she decided to be confirmed as a Catholic many years later, she had to do research to determine that she had been baptized. "I wasn't sure," she said, "because nobody spoke of it." As for spiritual feelings outside of religious instruction, she could recall only "a sense of something transcendental, but I don't know whether I identified that with God. If anything, it was a sense of something communal, something that held people together, perhaps in part because I felt that my family was so atomized. It seemed to me that I had some kind of dream or vision of people moving together in concert toward something wonderful. We had an illustrated Bible, which my mother burned along with the rest of her past when she became a Jehovah's Witness. In this Bible were drawings with those shafts from the skies that are steps to heaven, and I found that very fetching, but no more so probably than I would have found a Maxfield Parrish drawing. So I don't suppose that was a spiritual experience."

By way of filling the spiritual vacuum, Harrison and her mother soon became inordinately devoted to the apocalyptic teachings of Jehovah's Witnesses. It all began when her father picked up a magazine on a street corner. "He never forgave himself, poor man." The magazine was *The Watchtower*, the Witnesses' perennial publication, and the man from whom her father bought it came to visit shortly thereafter, convincing the Grizzutis to participate in a "home Bible study." What they actually studied was the Witnesses' textbook, *The Truth Shall Make You Free*, along with scriptural corroboration. Although her father's casual curiosity soon wore off and he lost interest in the arguments, Barbara and her mother began devouring the teachings of their instructor, attending meetings at the local Kingdom Hall, the Witnesses' meeting center, and later preaching door to door—all to her father's great chagrin.

Their newfound religious fervor bitterly divided the household, but it continued to grow until, in 1944, at the age of nine, Barbara Harrison became one of Jehovah's Witnesses along with her mother. After her baptism at a national convention of 25,000 Witnesses in Buffalo, New York, by her own account she became an ardent proselytizer, distributing *The Watchtower* and *Awake!* on street corners and from door to door, spending as much as one hundred fifty hours a month in the service of her newly found faith, under the directives of the Watchtower Bible and Tract Society, the legal and corporate arm of Jehovah's Witnesses. In *Visions of Glory*, Harrison writes:

> As I had been immersed in water to symbolize my "dedication to do God's will," I became, also, drenched in the dark blood-poetry of a religion whose adherents drew joy from the prospect of the imminent end of the world. I preached sweet doom; I believed that Armageddon would come in my lifetime, with a great shaking and rending and tearing of unbelieving flesh, with unsanctified babies swimming in blood, torrents of blood. I believed also that after the slaughter Jehovah had arranged for His enemies at Armageddon, this quintessentially masculine God—vengeful in battle and benevolent to survivors—would turn the earth into an Eden for true believers.
>
> Coincidentally with my conversion, I got my first period. We used to sing this hymn: "Here is He who comes from Eden/All His raiments stained with blood." My raiments were stained with blood too. But the blood of the Son of Man was purifying, redemptive, cleansing, sacrificial. Mine was proof of having inherited the curse placed upon

the seductress Eve. Mine was filthy. I examined my discharges with horror and fascination, as if the secret of life—or a harbinger of death—were to be found in that dull, mysterious effluence.

Trying to locate the underlying causes for her mother's swift conversion, Harrison writes of the Witnesses' curious appeal: "For women whose experience has taught them that all human relationships are treacherous and capricious and frighteningly volatile, an escape from the confusions of the world into the certainties of a fundamentalist religion provides the illusion of safety, and of rest." She proposes that her mother, who had been the product of an unhappy and often violent marriage, probably found herself in a similar situation in her own marriage. Unable to "love either her family or the world," Harrison conjectures, her mother chose a religion: "She chose 'spiritual brothers and sisters'—who told her, as her family had, that the world was *other* and evil, alien, and cruel. She found shelter. She waited for God to smash the wicked world. All her longing was for the future; all her love was for a jealous, devouring God who promised her rest."

As for why she herself converted, Harrison chooses to believe that "the motives of that little girl who pledged her life to God are necessarily obscure to me. My childhood has been fed into the devouring maw of psychoanalysis, but the leap into belief (or into fancy) is still unsusceptible of analysis, still mysterious." She wonders "how much of an element of will a nine-year-old could have. And, of course, there was my beautiful mother. She was the most important reality in my life. All else aside, I think I would have been swept away by her."

For whatever reason Barbara decided to join, she is clear as to why she stayed. "From my point of view it was nifty—at first," she told me, "because suddenly people were paying attention to me. My parents were extremely self-absorbed, although I don't know exactly what the focus of their absorption was, and I was absolutely starved for any kind of attention at all. And I loved the terrible, dark poetry in the eschatology and the imminence of Armageddon, full of images of blood and water. It made me feel singular because I had possession of this wonderful dark knowledge. But it certainly was a double-edged sword, because very soon it made me feel like a freak, both within and without the community of Jehovah's Witnesses. I felt set apart in both places. For obvious reasons I was cut off from people my own age and those members of my family who were not Jehovah's Witnesses, which was almost everybody else. And for less obvious reasons I was cut off from the Witnesses. Part of that was that I took seriously everything they said, whereas other kids my age did not. I mean, I was a jerk."

The Witnesses thought Barbara was strange to some extent because she was a precocious child. But at school she was set apart from her classmates, mostly in negative ways for the things she couldn't do. "I couldn't salute the flag. I couldn't celebrate holidays or birthdays. I was also driven to proselytize—although I found it hateful and it gave me great pain—and that made me very odd." The rationale for the Witnesses' refusal to salute the flag or recite the Pledge of Allegiance is the Biblical admonition in the Second Commandment not to bow down to any graven image. They believe that "you don't give your allegiance to a flag, you give it to God." This among other interpretations of Scripture led them to challenge a number of laws relating to the First and Fourteenth amendments, winning over one hundred fifty State Supreme Court cases and thirty Supreme Court cases in the process.

Barbara found "something intensely romantic" in the Witnesses' roles as perennial outsiders. "For one thing, they built up a sort of hagiography and mythology about all the male Witnesses who were in prison for not having joined the armed services. I didn't know them because I became a Witness after they'd gone, but I invented them in my mind. And we all waited for their return. It was very exciting, and I kept falling in love with them." What she remembers best from this period are more of the details that set her apart from her schoolmates. During wartime, schoolchildren were expected to join in the war effort by collecting tin foil or making balls of rubber bands, giving money to the Red Cross, and praying for the Allies. "I couldn't do any of that," she said. "It sounds self-indulgent to complain about that now, but anything that sets you so dramatically apart from everybody else is pretty horrible. Because I couldn't salute the flag or stand up for the national anthem, I felt physically the cynosure of all eyes. It was quite dreadful, and I hated that."

Although Harrison credits the Witnesses' success in standing up to the government over freedom of religion and press, she hardly finds them anti-authoritarian. "They rejected one authority only because they chose to cleave to another more obscure one," she said, adding that the Witnesses she knew personally and with whom she worked were often both tyrannical to those below them, mainly women, and slavish to those in authority over them. "Also, it was a time when everything was the occasion for guilt. I didn't know whether I was supposed to go to the movies, for instance. It was similar to deciding, if you lived in India as I have, whether to give to beggars. First you decide to give to the cute ones. And then you decide that that's not very good, so you give to nobody, or to everybody. I was making decisions when I was nine years old that I would go to certain movies but not others. I was my own Legion of Decency, and I must say that the other Witness kids my age didn't seem to be going through all this."

The constant weighing of guilt, which may sound familiar to Americans raised in strict Roman Catholic or observant Jewish households, "having always to establish my being good and always failing," as she put it, carried over into Harrison's life long after she had left the Witnesses behind. "I realized some years ago that I'd spent years convincing my children that I was good," she said. "And they didn't need any convincing. It was not an issue for them. But I spent years asking people to forgive me for something like lying in bed for an hour, and I made up huge stories about why I was doing it. I never took anything easy."

What was even worse to her mind, though, was a censoring of fantasies and thoughts. "I didn't allow myself to fantasize. But I was a child, and I went off the rails with that. Even now I speak of it as if it were something bad. I did fantasize, but I thought it was a wicked thing to do. So I was always in a position of having delicious, wonderful fantasies and then censoring them and feeling terribly guilty about them and about my dreams. I ended up seeing myself as a sort of obnoxious little midget, insisting on my superiority both to myself and, implicitly, to others, because I went from door to door and said, 'You're living wrong. I, a nine-year-old, will tell you how to live.' But, on the other hand, I felt totally worthless, with no way to live up to anything that was expected of me."

In addition to the religion itself being "stringent and loveless," Harrison is convinced that her mother was legally insane. "And the religion nicely accommodated her madness, so it was a mess," she said.

"The delight my mother took in the imminent destruction of human-kind is the sort of thing that lands you in the booby hatch unless you have some vehicle for it. She had a fear of the outside world, a sense of menace that she perceived in inanimate objects until she appro-priated them to herself. I can remember her shopping and fingering clothes as though they were going to get her. Everything was part of the Devil's world until it became part of her immediate world. By the time I was in my early teens, she was totally detached from reality. She hadn't read a book or a publication other than the prescribed religious ones, and did not until she died, forty years later."

Saying that, Harrison thought of enclosed orders of nuns. The irony for her is that, far from being shut off physically from the world, her mother was an "extremely beautiful woman who removed herself emotionally and mentally, but moved in the world and was perceived by others to be a rather ripe, luscious, beautiful woman. She was only nineteen years older than me, and had a coat with an ocelot collar and wore a black snood—one of those nets into which women stuffed their hair in the forties. The Witnesses weren't enclosed. The whole trick for us was to be, as they said, 'in the world but not of it.' That's a neat trick. I later thought the people who really exemplified that were the ones who worked at Mary House, or the Catholic Workers who were in the world as much as they could be—in the dirt and suffering and grit—but not of it in that they exercised Christian values. But the Witnesses had a very different notion of what they meant: to divorce yourself entirely from any worldly structures and from the common endeavor insofar as the common endeavor could be located. And in those days it could. The common endeavor was World War II."

Harrison was at pains to make clear that there were among this sect she ultimately found so inhospitable many members "who were in-deed conscientious and fun and loving and good people. It's very easy for me to see them as all villainous, and they weren't. But in some ways they reminded me very much of immigrant Italian families, the sort who would extend love and warmth—but if you stepped one inch out of the boundary, forget it. If you said the wrong thing or had the wrong friend or doubted what Uncle Pat said, it was all over. And that was perhaps more intensely true for women. Both with the Wit-nesses and my family, there was an 'official story.' The 'story' was designed to protect you, to keep you from asking questions, and to afford some way to deal with the world. But if you questioned the story or stepped out of the frame, then it was all over. And it didn't matter how small the detail was."

As an example of the Witnesses' "official story," Harrison recalled their habit of dividing people into either "sheep" or "goats," depending on whether they showed an interest in becoming Witnesses or not. "Can you imagine thinking of people that way? We had little charts when we went from door to door and we would mark each person 'sheep' or 'goat.' We would also somewhat more pragmatically write 'I' for interested, 'NI' for not interested, 'O' for opposed, or 'NH' for not home. There wasn't supposed to be a category of people called good but not interested. Those people didn't exist. Yet almost immediately I found a category of people who extended what I could not but interpret as love to this poor wild child of nine, sometimes with my younger brother four years old, poor thing, going from door to door. It was as much love as I was getting from within the family and the religion, and they weren't the least bit interested in the religion. They were interested in me, and in my brother, and they were kind. I simply could not believe that God was going to destroy them, and that was a major departure from the story. My inability to lock them into the story as it was told, in fact, eventually led to my leaving. It took years, but that was it."

Jehovah's Witnesses are one of a number of apocalyptic sects that were founded before the end of the nineteenth century. As conceived under the original name of Zion's Watch Tower Bible and Tract Society by a Pittsburgh haberdasher named Charles Taze Russell, its distinctive element was not merely the destruction of the damned (unbelievers) in Armageddon but also the elevation to heaven of the 144,000 elect as predicted in the Book of Revelation, to rule over the remaining faithful who would live eternally on a perfected earth. According to Harrison, the Witnesses base many of their predictions on the Book of Daniel, as do other apocalyptic movements. In it, the prophet foresees the destruction of Babylon if idolatry is not forsaken. It also contains "a lot of beasts with a lot of heads. Starting with the Communist countries, the world was going to rise against the scarlet whore of Babylon, the Catholic Church, destroy her and drink her blood—and it doesn't take a genius to figure out how much misogyny underlies all that. Then everybody would jump on that bandwagon until all of worldly religion was destroyed and God would step in to save his people. The earth was going to be scoured clean after Armageddon in our lifetime. It always seems such an astonishing thing to me that there were Witnesses in 1944 who didn't have their teeth filled because they were waiting for Armageddon to come. Why bother to spend money on the dentist? People didn't buy houses."

The bones of the multitudinous dead would then be buried or picked clean by the birds, according to the Witnesses' very graphic description. "After the evil had their eyes plucked out by birds with mighty beaks, we would all live in a land of flowers and peace. Nobody's imagination covered what would happen after that, by the way." When she asked what one was supposed to do if one lived forever, Harrison was told, " 'Think of all the things there are to learn. You can learn about seashells.' For millions and billions of years. You wouldn't have to find a cure for cancer, after all, because that would be gratuitous." (When I once asked a similar question of a pair of visiting Witnesses, I was told that I could study all about insects. "For a million years?" I asked. "Why not?" was the reply.)

If the Witnesses exhibit an especially virulent strain of apocalyptic fundamentalism, they are by no means alone in their beliefs about a kind of perennial "end time." Robert Lifton and Charles Strozier have stated that among an estimated 50 million fundamentalist Christians in America, most share a belief that the world may come to an end in their lifetime. As recently as March 1990, a group called the Church Universal and Triumphant, led by the spiritualist Elizabeth Clare Prophet, began gathering near their extensive system of underground bomb shelters in Paradise Valley, Montana, in anticipation of a possible Armageddon induced by nuclear warfare. The "dangerous period" was to occur around April 23, but when nothing serious eventuated, the church members from around the world dispersed, asserting that their prayers had contributed to the lessening of tensions. As the end of this millennium nears, we can probably expect to see the rise of still more millenarian groups predicting a destructive climax to the twentieth century.

Why the Witnesses survived out of all the millennialist groups that sprang up in the late 1800s is a mystery to Harrison, other than that, "For some reason, this one evolved. It's a good example of social

Darwinism." The Witnesses have had only three presidents since Russell's death in 1916, when Joseph Franklin Rutherford took over and later gave the Watch Tower Bible and Tract Society the name Jehovah's Witnesses (1931), from a Scripture in Isaiah. He was followed by Nathan Knorr and the present leader, Frederick William Franz, who rules over the approximately 4 million Witnesses worldwide. Their growth is all the stranger in light of the fact that numerous predictions of the end of the world—which they first prophesied for 1914, then 1918, 1920, 1925, 1941, and 1975—have turned out to be so irrefragably off the mark. Witnesses to whom I put that question explained that these were approximations, that "it seemed that mankind had been on Earth for six thousand years," in fulfillment of the Biblical prophecy. Their calculations may have been off, they said, but the end was still near, even if they now declined to put a date on it.

Harrison does see a certain "prescience" in millennial groups. "They seem to spring up at times when Apocalypse appears either desirable or inevitable. But the Witnesses had it wrong, because according to their scenario, the world would turn against the Catholic Church, which was always a major villain, and it would all start with the Communist countries. Well, I seem to have noticed that the Communist world isn't headed in that direction at all. I'm sure that's thrown a spanner in the works. But I absolutely trust the Witnesses to find a way to cover their flanks. Some scholar of millennial groups has said that three is the highest number of dates they can set for the end of the world before their followers say, 'Are you nuts?' But this group goes on and on. They're an exception to that rule."

Her own doubts about the group were accelerated when, at fifteen, she fell in love with a high school English teacher. "It's always an English teacher," she said, smiling. "Have you noticed that? When was the last time somebody fell in love with a science teacher? Anyway, his name was Arnold Horowitz, and it's easy for me when I'm not angry at God, which at the moment I am, to think of his being placed in my way. I do believe that in some way God broods through all the events in the world, both large and small. One doesn't know how, but he's there. Miss Silver had told my parents I was smart. That was very dangerous. Arnold told my parents I was good. That was much more dangerous. But for me, it was redemptive. I saw re-

demption in the shape of a Jewish atheist who wanted for me everything my religion forbade. He wanted me to go to college, which I
wasn't allowed to do. So I could not imagine God destroying him,
and that put me in the position of being more compassionate than
God, or having better judgment than God. And it suddenly occurred
to me that maybe I did."

It was another departure from the official story, and drove a wedge
in her attachment to the sect. Then, when she was nineteen, she spent
the summer working in a cannery run by the Witnesses. Her decision
was based on what she calls "my version of *The Nun's Story*. I didn't
seem to be doing too well living in the world and not being of it, so
I thought I should be working full time at the Witnesses' headquarters,
which was indeed a consuming life. Every minute of your time was
accounted for there. And your trial was to go to Staten Island and
work in a cannery under a little tyrant woman who insisted that she'd
gotten pregnant without selfishness, which I understand to mean
without sex." After passing the test of the cannery, Harrison was
chosen to work at the headquarters building, where she served as
housekeeper for the newest male recruits, cleaning fifteen rooms a
day, vacuuming, dusting, washing floors, and scrubbing baths. "It
wasn't even meant as a lesson in humility because they didn't think
that women needed humbling" she said. "It was very clear to them
that this was what women were for, to clean rooms."

Her movement out of the fold was further quickened when, after
a couple of years of cleaning, she graduated to proofreader in the print
shop. The new job was challenging in ways she hadn't imagined. "I
was told that I had to be careful to be subordinate to men," she said.
"So if I said to put a comma in, and the man said to take the comma
out, it became a battle. I started having St. Paul read to me over
commas. I remember once allowing Khrushchev's name to be spelled
four different ways in one single column of print." That she was
suddenly living away from home, among 450 people, roughly 425 of
whom were men, was further disorienting. The dozen or so young
women living at the headquarters were "very much sought after with
a kind of ambiguous sexuality, because we weren't allowed to do very
much but we also weren't forbidden. It wasn't clear what we were
allowed to do. Nothing was clear. They had a ship that we often danced
on, throwing beer cans off the side—not very ecologically sound."

One day while Harrison was working in the proofreading room, a storm rose outside, "one of those storms that comes on very suddenly. The sky got black, and the guy I was working with, whom I couldn't abide, said, 'Oh, God, isn't this wonderful? Maybe it's Armageddon!' I was filled with terror, thinking that I wasn't ready and the world wasn't ready. I said, 'I don't *want* Armageddon to come.' Later I was called on the carpet to explain my not wishing this to be God's chosen day."

While falling away from the Witnesses, Harrison secretly read Salinger and Camus, and continued seeing Arnold Horowitz. She called this "my double life, but it got to be too much. The easy way to say it is that I saw too much hypocrisy. The real thing is that it was a culmination of years and years of saying, 'God can't kill all these people. What is all this nonsense about? Why are *we* so special? Why are *we* so good?' I wasn't doing well at my job, nor was I doing what I was supposed to do—going from door to door, I don't know how many hours a week, while cleaning rooms and proofreading. Perhaps as a result of all that, to this day I need huge periods of time in which I apparently do nothing, and maybe, in fact, do nothing. And then something comes from that. It's the only way I can function. The thing about the kind of regimen the Witnesses kept us on is that you don't have time for the unconscious to play in any way. You don't have much time for vice, but you also don't have any time for creativity. There are no spaces for anything to happen, no dark for anything to grow in. You wake up exhausted and you go to bed exhausted." And then, in Barbara's case, you have what approximates a nervous breakdown. Toward the end, she couldn't walk upstairs to preach. "And then I couldn't walk downstairs, and then I couldn't walk across a subway platform. And then my voice wouldn't come out."

If ever in her life she thought she might go crazy, this was the time. She felt totally alone. "Arnold was useless," she said. "When I said I wanted to leave, he said, 'Now you'll be like everybody else.' Since I wanted to hear, 'Will you marry me?' those words were not thrilling. I was walking three feet above the ground, by which I don't mean I was in ecstasy. I mean I was not rooted. I was frightened every single minute. The future was bleak and uncharted, and all I kept thinking was, What is this going to do to my mother? I didn't know what to do, so I waited for events to overtake me. I couldn't just wake up one morning and say 'I'm through.' And so events overtook me. Eventually I left, but then the weaning away was hard."

Her sudden desire to leap over boundaries found its expression in a racial way, as it had as a child. "For example," she said, "we lived in Jamaica for a while, and I used to touch black people and tell them they were beautiful. Then I was given a Black Sambo doll and told never to touch black people again." Before she left the Witnesses, Harrison had acquired the habit of slipping off in the night to Birdland, the famous Manhattan jazz club, returning to her room "smelling of smoke and praying that my roommate wouldn't notice. She'd be on her knees praying and I would be adrift in some Count Basie dream." At the time, she had a crush on Basie's vocalist Big Joe Williams. When she left the Witnesses, jazz was her first resort. She went to the legendary Harlem nightspot called Minton's Playhouse on 128th Street and promptly fell in love with the drummer. He was married, but she carried on an affair with him for several years. "It was love at first sight," she said, "a phenomenon in which I'm bound to believe since I experienced it. It was one look and that was that. Of course, the music was part of it. There's something very witty about the drums, and God knows I needed wit in my life. I needed wit and explosion and heat. It was all there."

Although she was one of the few white women in that particular scene, she was "protected" because she wasn't considered a groupie. "It was clear to everybody that I had one relationship and that I wasn't fooling around in any sense," she said. There she met Louis Armstrong, and became friendly with Billie Holiday. One night at Minton's, while the drummer she was in love with was playing his set, a "very angry guy" came up and asked her if she knew who the Mau Mau were. "I was twenty-two and working as a secretary at Macmillan," she said. "What did I know? I said, 'Yeah, they're terrorists.' Whoa! That began my education in radical black politics. And while he was giving me a dressing down, I heard a voice from behind my shoulder say, 'You leave her alone. She's a woman, so she's a nigger. She can be raped.' And that was Billie Holiday. This was before the women's movement, before that was a general perception, and very close to the time of her death. I loved her immensely for that. We weren't friends for long, but I did deeply love her. I hadn't stopped to think of women's position much before then, but it certainly opened a door that made it possible for me to entertain ideas of feminism."

Among other imprints that Harrison's early experience with Jehovah's Witnesses had left on her was a paradoxical yearning. For although, in retrospect, she considered what the Witnesses were doing to be "insanity" and "organized wickedness," it also created "a hunger and a thirst that the religion couldn't possibly satisfy, because of its triviality and rigidity and doctrinaire nature. That hunger was eventually satisfied by Catholicism."

As she was tottering on the brink of leaving the Witnesses, Harrison went to see an optometrist in Greenwich Village. She didn't know why she went to the Village, a place she had never been, and couldn't remember the name of the doctor, who is no longer there. He took an inordinately long time examining her eyes and finally said, "I don't know who you are or what you're doing in your life. But whatever you're doing, you'll have to stop. I've never seen anyone so rigidly controlled or under so much strain. You're seeing things that aren't there, and you're not seeing things that *are* there. You may last six days or six weeks or six months, but you're heading for a breakdown, and it won't be pretty when it comes." Then he added prophetically, "I sometimes have to tell priests to take six months off. I'm telling you to take the rest of your life off, if you want to live." It was all she needed to hear.

After leaving the Witnesses, Harrison felt that spiritually "there was nothing. I don't believe that's ever actually the case, but it felt that way to me. I had to spend many more years in rebellion, at least in the sense that to acquire ideas was a form of rebellion to me. I hadn't been allowed to have ideas before that. Ideas, lovers, an apartment, a job—all those things were acts of rebellion. I had some good years, some very happy years. Those were the days in the Village when people sat around asking one another if they had the right to be happy. Can you imagine?"

During this time, she took writing classes at the New School and worked as a secretary at Macmillan. She saw the drummer, whom she calls only Grass, over the next few years, and during that time she had a number of psychic experiences of the sort known as precognition. "I always knew when Grass was in town," she said, "and

I would always present myself there, much to his disapproval. Various other women also were there because he'd told them to be there. He was not what you'd call monogamous, even in adultery. And I always knew when my brother, who was involved in gang wars, was hurt, and I would present myself at home. The last time I had an experience—this is not susceptible of proof, but I know it's true—was in a taxi. When these things happen, they don't hit you with the force of an earthquake. They just lightly brush your mind. I thought, Oh dear, we're going to run a red light, and we're going to hit a boy on a bike. And we did exactly that. At that time the nearest thing that approximated a prayer was my saying, 'Dear God, I don't want to have this anymore.' And thereafter I did not. Whether those experiences form part of the spiritual puzzle, I don't know."

She ended her affair with the married musician with mixed feelings. On the one hand, she felt, it was entirely good. "I say this now as a Catholic. It was sex outside of marriage, it was adulterous, and it was good—for me. It was sexually liberating, and thrilling, and good. But your unconscious doesn't let you get away with stuff like that very easily. My guilt caught up with me, and I married somebody I didn't love sexually very much, or at all. He seemed plausible in many ways. He was politically active in a way that was attractive to me. We used to march around women's prisons with lilacs and demonstrate against apartheid."

Her husband worked with an American relief agency, and two years after her marriage their son was born in Libya, on an American Air Force base. The birth of her first child was accompanied by a feeling that "this is all I'm ever going to have, and it isn't enough. That was terrifying. I did not love my husband, but the actual birth of my child, whom I adore, was an occasion of great joy. It's thwarting when there's no place for that joy to go. I always saw it as if I were in a box and there was a lid on the box, and I couldn't get out of it. I wanted to praise, but I didn't know who or how."

Her daughter was born eleven months later in India. Not long after, they were traveling in South Central India, near Hyderabad, when Barbara asked to stop by an abandoned temple that was no longer used for worship, "in a grove of holy trees with monkeys leaping around. I went into that temple and I had a sense of presence as strong as any I've ever had, which absolutely terrified me. It was neither

benign nor malignant, it just was. I had stayed away from any manifestation of Indian religion. I was involved in matters of the heart
and living on a day-to-day basis, like how you get the diapers clean,
and how you get the snakes out of the garden. But something happened at that temple. The Indians have a wonderful word, *darshan*,
which means a glimpse of the god within. I think now of that feeling
in the temple as being one of those things that permitted me later to
understand that I was not what I thought I was, and that the universe
was constructed differently from the way I thought."

The family then moved to Guatemala, the first time, she said, that
she had been in "so declaratively a Catholic country. I found myself
making the sign of the cross whenever I passed churches. I have no
idea why I did it, and I don't know what that gesture meant at the
time. I just did it. Somehow it's a gesture that satisfies me intensely
even now. If you ever fly in a plane in Mexico that encounters turbulence, you'll see more ways of making the sign of the cross than
you thought were possible. I still cross myself on takeoff and landing."

She felt "at home" in Guatemala, which she described as "one of
the most physically beautiful countries in the world," but by the time
they returned to New York, Harrison knew her marriage was over.
Her son, Josh, had been diagnosed as having leukemia, which at that
time was a death sentence for a child (it turned out to be a misdi-
agnosis). "My husband said that he was going to pray, and I wanted
to kill him," she recalled. "He was an unreligious Protestant and
cynical, in a glib way, about religion. I thought, You don't ask promises
from God when you're in extremity. You never asked him anything
before, how dare you ask him now? I did not pray at that time, and
I was damned if I was going to."

Nonetheless, she had glimpses of something spiritual "working in
the dark," although the first signs of real light did not appear until
several years after her divorce. She met and lived with an Irish immigrant named Paul Kelly. He had been an Olympic runner, and she
described him as "enormous and funny. He was an alcoholic, and he
used to sing hymns. He hated the Church with a passion, and this
found expression in very witty anecdotes which I asked him to repeat
endlessly. But I also asked him to say Catholic prayers for me, because
he had a beautiful voice, and I liked the rhythm of them very much.
I loved the Hail Mary."

After a year and a half of living together, she kicked him out "because he was a drunk." When he died of acute alcoholism at forty-five, she felt "the most intense, corrosive hatred I've ever felt. I felt it even before he died. Although I asked him to leave, I felt abandoned because he preferred alcohol to me. I didn't know what to do with this anger, which colored everything and was crippling, like a disease—it *was* a disease—so I prayed, quite angrily. I said, 'God, I don't know if you're there or not. I doubt very much you are, but I don't know what else to do with this rage, and I want to give it away.' This seems too easy, but the next morning I woke up and it was gone. I concluded from that that God had removed the pain, the anger. I could have come to several other conclusions, but that was the one I came to. I also concluded that it entailed obligation."

Harrison spent that summer at the MacDowell writers' colony, going to concerts with her friend Loudon Wainwright, Jr., the author, who later died of cancer of the stomach. "He used to call it Puritan Quaker chic," she said. "We'd go to wonderful white clapboard churches and hear wonderful music and see women in quilted long skirts do square dances. I was ecstatic that summer. Naturally I thought I was in love with Loudon at the time, but now I think I was falling in love with God. And it was a true love affair. All the music seemed religious to me, and a lot of it was—Bach, for instance. I wanted very much to go somewhere with it, so one day back in New York I walked off the street and into St. Patrick's Cathedral. I went into the rectory and said, 'I want to take religious instruction.' And it was given to me rather halfheartedly, I must say, by the priest."

Looking back at the MacDowell Colony, Harrison was impressed by how, just when she was thinking about Catholicism, it seemed to her that God placed so many Catholics in her path, "and, as it happened, intellectual Catholics. Maybe he thought that was what I needed at the time, but there they all were. I never have been back to MacDowell, surrounded by people who wanted to go to church on Sunday morning. It was only that one summer when I was on my way, and they're all friends of mine still."

The time was the mid-seventies, following the Second Vatican Council's liberalizing influence on laity and clergy. So, when Harrison told the priest in St. Patrick's that she did not plan to bring up her children Catholic, which she now regrets, he told her that she could show them by example. "Since my example isn't all that great, I'm not sure that was a good formula," she said. "I was also pro abortion then, and I said that I couldn't be anything other. The priest said that was all right. I think he was wrong, and I was wrong. But those were the two things that I saw as obstacles to my becoming a communicant." She has since gone through permutations of her feelings on the abortion issue, saying now that she is "glad the Church is anti-abortion."

She doesn't consider herself a convert to Catholicism, since she had already been baptized as a child. "Graham Greene says that baptism is like a vaccination," she said. "It always takes. Maybe that's true, but I felt that I needed some formal way of doing this. My religious instructor at St. Patrick's suggested I go to a church in the Village which was well known for its emphasis on social action and feeding the poor. He said it was hard enough to be Catholic without going to your neighborhood parish, and he was right. This is a continuing problem in my life. I'm tired of shopping for churches. I love it in Italy where I just pop into the nearest church and understand about half of what I'm hearing and all of the mass, but in this country I have a very hard time. And I despise myself for it, because there's a way in which I think the most heroic Catholics are those who go to their parishes and just do it." Still, she insists on feeling nourished by more than just the mass. "It doesn't have to be beautiful," she said. "I don't expect a Caravaggio in Brooklyn, and I don't mind plaster saints if there's honesty and lack of pretension. But it's offensive to me if it's overtly sexist or reactionary, or when I'm expected to embrace all that seems foreign to me in the modern world. I don't like it when priests get fancy. When they start comparing Bette Davis's performance to something in the Gospels, it drives me crazy. And if you think I pulled that example out of the air, you're very much mistaken."

But aside from these shortcomings, she credits the Church with providing several important gifts in her life, even when she has felt most disaffected. For one thing, it "provides a vehicle for praise. Another is that I love the swing of the liturgical year, its going from dark to light. Insofar as anything can reconcile me to death, which I consider outrageous, that does, because it culminates in Easter and the Resurrection. The third thing is that for me it's the only viable philosophy, and what makes it viable is the Incarnation. If there were no Incarnation, then it would all be worthless. Without the idea of a God who became human, the Catholic Church is nothing, worse than nothing, a terrible fraud. Those are the reasons I'm Catholic."

Yet her experience of the horrors of Romania is still vivid enough to add to her doubts. "One's own pain is relatively easy to bear," she said. "One can always see the lineage and chronology of pain. I've seldom felt, Why me? I've always seen my complicity to some extent in my own pain. The pain that is harder to bear, not for reasons of goodness but because one doesn't have insight into it, is the terrible pain and suffering of others. When people in my immediate world whom I love tremendously are in pain, I just say their names to God. I don't think God needs to be filled in with a lot of information. I hate those prayers on television that keep telling God what he did: 'Dear God, who created the earth and on the seventh day rested.' Presumably God doesn't have to be reminded of that. What was St. Augustine's prayer? 'My Lord and My God.' It's a very good prayer, and it fits in very nicely with breathing when you're on an airplane and scared to death."

For whatever reason, the suffering she witnessed in Romania overwhelmed her ability to see God's hand in it. "I'm still trying to sort out why it affected me more even than anything I saw in India," she said. "At first I had to consider the possibility that I was racist. I asked my daughter, 'Is it just that it's happening to Europeans?' But somehow in India—and I don't say this cavalierly—suffering seems almost ordained. The heat is a central fact of life. People have suffered for thousands and thousands of years and have almost accommodated themselves to it. I don't say they should, and I don't say it's good, but there it is. It seems ultimately to be a result of the environment. In Romania, human suffering was the work largely of one man. You could look around and say, 'This did not have to be.' That's one reason it seemed so atrocious that human evil could so overwhelm human good. The other thing was that so much of the pain devolved upon children."

The practice of giving transfusions to newborns with unscreened blood made matters worse; of the more than 130,000 Romanian orphans and unwanted children, at least 2,500 are infected with the HIV virus. "Just as the world was ready to adopt these beautiful Romanian children, now no one wants them," Harrison said. "And this cruelty unfortunately dovetails with one of the nightmare things about the Church, its inability to come to terms in a healthy way with human sexuality and contraception." As a result, Harrison is personally sending condoms into Romania. "It may seem like a foolish thing to do," she said, "but it's the only thing I can think of besides sending in reading matter for people who've been deprived. God seems absent, and the Church seems to me entirely wrong. How dare Cardinal O'Connor prescribe for people in this degree of human suffering? I almost begin to feel as if I'm back in the world of Jehovah's Witnesses where there's no compassion. How can one say this suffering is for something? One can say that about one's own suffering. You must put your own suffering to use, because you're going to suffer anyway. But one doesn't wish to say that about hundreds of thousands of children. That's obscene."

Harrison's faith has been affected by other seemingly unspiritual concerns. She referred to the words of the mass, coming just after the Eucharist, which tell the faithful to be free from all anxiety. "I used to think, 'Easy for you to say, God,' because for years I had what I later discovered was a severe panic disorder," she said. "In practical terms, that means that I was extremely hypochondriacal because I was tuned to my body's aches and pains. This time last year I might have been talking to you as I am now, with an appearance of ease, but I would have been feeling like a person hanging onto a mountain ledge with her fingernails. I was terrified, and terribly agoraphobic. I often had to make a phone call and have people help me cross the street." Harrison's condition is now thought to be biochemical in origin, "probably abetted by childhood traumas, of which I had my share." A psychopharmacologist prescribed Prozac, the now popular antidepressant, and she has not had a severe anxiety attack since she started taking it.

"What's interesting to me about this is that we act as if we have free will," Harrison said. "How else can we act? But the biochemical origin of so many of our ills does seem to work against that idea. This doesn't discourage me from believing in God's grace, which I feel has been operative in my life. But it is setting me off in directions that I've just begun to explore. For all I know, the fact that I'm Catholic is biochemical in origin, and I'm quite serious about that. That's why the theory of the anonymous Christian, the person who serves God without knowing he or she is doing it, is so valuable."

Since Harrison discovered that her brain cortex was "dripping something into my body that was making it impossible for me to cross a piazza, it has become increasingly difficult to be judgmental about people, except for those who are themselves judgmental, like the Church. But all of us are probably going to think a lot now about biochemistry and what that says about the soul. Unless God works for the psychopharmacologists, the mass did not free me from anxiety to go forth and serve the Lord."

When I brought up the subject of private devotional life and practices such as meditation, Harrison had an unusual response. Admitting she doesn't have as rich a prayer life as she should, and acknowledging a real difference between meditation and prayer, she said that there is a way in which she understands levitation, and a time in which all doubts go away. "It's when I swim. I'm not sure how this is married to spirituality, but it is. I have the odd ability to float standing up, without treading water. The water comes up to my collarbone, and I simply don't think. It's very disorienting to people watching me, who say, 'But I thought this was the deep end of the pool.' I bliss out, and I can do that for hours, which I often do, and go into some sort of fugue state. I also float on my back for hours, and have fallen asleep doing that. I have to have people around to wake me up. This resting on the water is closely allied to my feeling about God. I haven't gone any further with it in my own mind, and I don't particularly want to, because I love what I do in the water."

For Harrison, the waters are maternal. "And though I think of God as male, and cannot bring myself to say 'she,' yet there's something about resting on the waters which is like—I can't say going back to Mommy, because my mother was hardly restful. Maybe it is the maternal element of God I'm experiencing there. It is heaven to me to be able to relinquish everything—physical pain and cerebration. My favorite place to do this is a pool in the circular hill town of Luccignano in Tuscany. It's a sweet, small town, with a garden which I love very much where people have huge lunches. And it's one of those very Italian gardens where there's no discrimination, where gladiolas grow next to dandelions. I always think it's like memory, which doesn't have any hierarchy. There's a family pool, and the proprietor lets me and my friend swim there. It's surrounded by roses which for some reason smell of cinnamon, and by three churches, so I feel as though I'm floating in fragrance and church bells."

She referred to a book in which Iris Murdoch used an outdoor hot spring pool where people go for regeneration and renewal. "I'm sure she derived her inspiration from one in Budapest, which is quite remarkable," she said. "When I was there, it was freezing. Everybody was wearing fur, but in the middle of all this fur were hot pools where people sat naked, playing chess for hours. So there is a reason why images of water have to do with renewal and regeneration. Maybe that's as close as I ever get to a very quiet unity with God and prayer. And this may sound ludicrous, but I also empty my mind by watching television. That again puts me in a fugue state in which I'm just not letting my mind work."

Although she believes "the essential fact of human history to be that God became man," Barbara Harrison also believes that "an atheist can be an agent of salvation, and can certainly be saved. I believe that a conscientious Muslim or Hindu is partaking of the Truth and indeed knows truth that I don't know. It remains true, however, that in some real way I see the Roman Catholic tradition as the repository, because it is the one that said to us that God became man, which is thrilling to me. When I pray for the happiness and salvation of my children, I'm not thinking about Zen Buddhism. But do I for a minute think that God excludes from his love and mercy anybody who isn't Roman Catholic? Absolutely not. I would cease being Roman Catholic if I were obliged to believe that. That's why I ceased being a Jehovah's Witness. Do I believe in the goodness of non-Catholics? It doesn't require an answer. Do other religious disciplines have potential for salvation? Yes. I also believe that I will see Arnold Horowitz in heaven. By loving me, he made it possible for me to love God."

As for the specific beliefs of some of those religions, she does have problems with, for instance, reincarnation. "Woody Allen said in one movie that he didn't want to believe in reincarnation because that meant he'd have to see the Ice Capades again," she said. "Do we remember past lives? I hate that idea—unless you're Shirley MacLaine and can afford to spend the rest of your life figuring out who you were the last time. I haven't begun to deal with that yet. It's one of those things I look forward to doing, like reading St. John of the Cross, which I'll never do.

"Catholicism is the way in which God was revealed to me, and I'm rather stubborn about it. I certainly don't believe that unless you confess Jesus Christ to be your savior, you're shit out of luck, to use a phrase from the world of jazz. But if I were to decide out of some perverse intellectual or trendy reason to become a Buddhist tomorrow, I would probably be damned, because something else has been revealed to me. That doesn't mean that I might not decide at some time that I want to learn more, but the reasons should be pretty good. And I don't think I should ever forget what I know. When one of the kinder Witnesses I knew died, a woman called Marguerite, I immediately thought, Oh, well, I'll see Mike—we all called her Mike—in heaven. That was the first time I allowed into my consciousness the idea that these people who made my life so damn miserable, and who are so reprehensible in so many ways, also have a call on the Truth. So if I can feel that about them, it's unlikely that I won't feel that about anyone else."

CHAPTER 18

Robert Schwartz:
A Born-Again Christian Jew

. . .

The religious mind is something entirely different from the mind that
believes in religion. You cannot be religious and yet be a Hindu, a
Muslim, a Christian, a Buddhist. A religious mind does not seek at all,
it cannot experiment with truth. Truth is not something dictated by
your pleasure or pain, or by your conditioning as a Hindu or whatever
religion you belong to. The religious mind is a state of mind in which
there is no fear and therefore no belief whatsoever but only *what is—
what actually is.*

—J. Krishnamurti, *Freedom from the Known*

.

Charles B. Strozier, the co-director of the Center on Violence and
Human Survival at John Jay College, has made an extensive study of
Christian fundamentalism, and estimates that there are at least 50
million fundamentalists in this country, in addition to many million
more born-again Christians. (That figure corroborates Andrew M.
Greeley's 1989 study, *Religious Change in America*, in which the Catholic priest and sociologist puts the number of "fundamentalist/evan-
gelicals" at one fifth of the population.) In a paper prepared for the
Center, Strozier noted, "The most distinguishing characteristic of fundamentalism today is that it is no longer at the fringe of the culture,
as it has been historically, but at its center." Those are sobering words
for observers who may have thought they could write off the fun-

damentalist phenomenon in America as a marginal group set mainly in the South.

Differences do exist between the designations of fundamentalist and born-again Christian, although the distinctions are often blurred. Simply put, all fundamentalists have been born again—which is to say they have gone through a conversion experience in which they accepted Jesus Christ as their personal savior—but not all born-again Christians are fundamentalists. Apart from the experience of having been reborn, fundamentalists stress inerrancy or literal interpretation of the Bible, and are usually apocalyptic—they believe that the end of the world, and the Second Coming of Christ, is imminent, a belief Strozier feels is reinforced by the realities of the nuclear age. Many fundamentalists—especially those who refer to themselves as such, with a capital F, like the Southern Baptists—also tend to be rigidly conservative in their politics (Southern Baptist fundamentalists are mostly white), and unemotional in their practice. Jerry Falwell, who rose to fame as founder of the since disbanded Moral Majority, is a quintessentially fundamentalist Baptist minister. The appellation "born-again" applied to Christians means only that they have taken Christ as their personal savior. Born-again Christians may be Fundamentalists, but they may also be Pentecostalists or Evangelicals or unaffiliated—Falwell is born again, but so are Pat Robertson, Oral Roberts, Jim Bakker, and Jimmy Swaggart.

Part of the objection Jim Bakker's followers raised against Jerry Falwell's taking over the PTL during that much-publicized scandal—in which Bakker was accused, and finally convicted, of pocketing millions of dollars in contributions—was that Falwell's dour fundamentalist style did not jibe with Bakker and the PTL congregation's more emotional, Evangelical one. Evangelical, Pentecostalist, or charismatic prayer meetings are likely to include hand clapping, spontaneous prayer and testimony, speaking in tongues, healing by laying on of hands, and upraised arms accompanied by shouts of "Praise the Lord!" (from which the initials PTL were derived). Many fundamentalist Baptists, who don't believe in tongues, for instance, are put off by that kind of exuberance. It may also be helpful to keep in mind the major parallel between Christian fundamentalism and Islamic and Jewish fundamentalism—a conscious return to fundamental principles and beliefs that, of necessity, requires a certain intolerance of those who practice "modernized" or less rigorous forms of the same religion.

Almost from the start of working on this book, I was undecided as to whether to include a fundamentalist or born-again Christian. The born-again experience clearly falls within the category of spiritual transformation, yet some inner feeling made me suspicious of the group as a whole. My lumping all "born agains" together should have tipped me off to my own prejudice, but I was sure my instincts were right. I associated born-again Christians in this country not only with the Moral Majority's religious intolerance (fundamentalists have a reputation for being anti-Semitic as well as anti-Catholic, a prejudice which Charismatic Catholics who have come in contact with them have verified), but also with the narrowness of their views on political issues from abortion and prayer in schools to having fundamentalist historical perspectives such as creationism written into public school textbooks. Like many Americans who had recoiled from the highly moralistic fire-and-brimstone preachments of the televangelists, I felt a certain vindication when first Jim and Tammy Faye Bakker and then Jimmy Swaggart were publicly defrocked for engaging in what appeared to be the most flagrantly hypocritical activities. (In Swaggart's case, revelations of his dalliance with a prostitute in a New Orleans motel room, followed by his televised lachrymose remorse, cast serious doubt on his integrity as one who had preached loudly against the evils of the flesh.) As the comedian Jay Leno put it at the time, "There are some good side effects to the Bakker thing and the Swaggart thing. Even people who are atheists are starting to say, 'Hey, maybe there *is* a God.'"

Surely the fact that any number of Eastern teachers to whose writings or belief systems I was more favorably disposed have been accused or found guilty of flagrant transgressions should have given me some perspective on this issue. But for whatever subjective reasons, I put off the question of interviewing anyone who had been "born again." I rationalized this by saying that my book was about people whose transformations had opened them up to the spiritual realm rather than sealed them off in a world of intolerance and parochialism. I did get the name of a woman in New Jersey from a niece who had herself been born again at sixteen. I wrote the woman's name and phone number down in three places and did my best to ignore them all. All the time I felt vaguely guilty, caught between a sense of obligation to be fair and representative, and an urge to follow my instinct and forget about it.

Then one evening, not long before the filing deadline for income-tax returns, I went with my wife Margery to see our accountant. We were filing joint returns for the first time, and we expected a long and complicated session since we are both self-employed and had brought along piles of paperwork. Compared to the fast pace of my previous tax accountant in Manhattan, the new one worked at a leisurely rate in his office in a lovely old stone house in Kingston, New York. A friendly, intelligent man, with a narrow face, bushy mustache, soft brown eyes, and dark hair combed straight back, Robert Schwartz had impressed us on previous occasions as honest, efficient, and good-humored. He enjoyed talking about personal matters—his passion for running the marathon, for instance—as much as about amortization and depreciation. But no matter how much I tried to focus on what we were doing, I found my eyes aimlessly investigating details of the antique fireplace grille and the convoluted molding that ran around ceiling and floor, painted a tasteful shade of dark gray. I marveled at its intricacies, its way of folding in on itself, and wondered about the bygone craftsmen who must have found delight in such gratuitous elaboration. About an hour into our session, though, I was called away from my reveries when the accountant finished with my wife's income and came to me.

I had already told him I wrote books for a living, and he wanted to know what kind of books. My usual answer is to say "nonfiction," and let it go at that. But for reasons I can't explain—maybe it was the look of genuine interest in his eyes, or the way he put down his pencil and stopped what he was doing as if encouraging us to take a break from our labors—I gave him a detailed rundown of each of several books I'd had published, ending with a thorough description of this book. Schwartz began probing me with questions about the format of my new book, the experiences I'd had researching it and whether they had changed me. He wanted to know if I had found a religious practice as a result of my investigations. I was beginning to feel like one of my own subjects. Finally he leaned back in his chair and looked straight at me. "It's interesting that you're writing a book about spiritual transformation," he said, "because I've had such an experience myself. It's not a long story, and I haven't told many people, but if you'd like to hear it I wouldn't mind telling you. Do you have time, or are you in a hurry?"

Margery and I exchanged glances. As it happened, we were the last appointment of his day and had the office to ourselves. We couldn't think of anything else we had to do (although when we emerged some hours later, we realized that we had both forgotten other appointments). I could see from the look on Robert Schwartz's face that he had a story he was burning to tell, and something about the intensity of that gaze told me it might just be a good one. He was, minus the cigar, the white suit, and the rattan furniture, the picture of a Joseph Conrad narrator preparing to launch into one of those long, absorbing tales of adventure, sin, and redemption which I had grown up reading in the dim-lit basement of my home. My wife and I nodded eagerly and put down our note pads and papers. "We'd love to hear your story," I said.

He gave us a look at once candid and searching. "I'm a born-again Christian Jew," he said. Immediately I felt my prejudices rising, native curiosity at odds with a horror of being trapped in the same room with someone who believes God actually created the universe in six working days. "My experience happened about eight years ago when my daughter Lacy was five years old, around the Christmas season of 1983," Schwartz began as the light slowly turned a deeper blue outside. "I had fallen into a period of great gloom, although I was doing very well at the time, making a lot of money. I had a wife and a daughter and a successful business. I was also smoking grass and using cocaine, but all of this had failed to fill the void I was feeling, and, in fact, only succeeded in casting me deeper into my despondency."

At this point I stopped him and asked him to backtrack a little, to begin before the experience he wanted to talk about, so that we would have some context in which to place it. "Actually, the beginning of my experience happened long before that," he said. "I had begun to feel the emptiness of the absence of God in my life, an absence that had been evolving over a long period of time. And the more effort I put into finding a sense of fulfillment from other things, the more God's absence became apparent."

Schwartz had been raised in New York City, "a New York Jew,

which is a type of Jew culturally different from all others," and had grown up in Brooklyn, going through the bar mitzvah procedures but never feeling anything spiritually moving in that teaching or experience. "I grew up believing that God was a very distant concept who forced us to behave under a code of honor that gave some order to the world," he said, "but that wasn't enough for me. I knew there had to be more. There had to be a relationship. At the time I didn't know that was necessary, but I knew that a lot more was needed besides a code of rule books.

"Over the years before this event, I explored other areas to find my fulfillment, as most of us do at one time or another, experimenting with this and that. For a while they seemed like the answers, but as time went by they proved to be empty promises. Yet by all the standards of our culture, I had everything going for me. I was a successful accountant. I had a wife I loved, a healthy and wonderful family. I had a lovely home in the country. So I should have been at peace, but I wasn't. I felt great unrest in my soul and didn't know how to find that peace. I expected that to be a condition that I would have to live with. The more I searched for other outlets, the more I felt the unrest in my soul. I didn't think in terms of looking for God or finding answers or truths. I didn't think they were possible. I never had any real exposure to Christians or deeply believing Jews or, for that matter, to teachers of any religion. I was not a seeker. I did not see myself going to the mountaintop. So I just plodded through life feeling that this was as far as anyone could go. I experimented with drugs for a while. Pot and cocaine, the usual. That experience left me with a double feeling—a feeling of pleasure and heightened awareness, and at the same time a sense of the evilness of them."

Just how much the drugs had distorted his values became clear to Schwartz one day when a friend took him shopping for a birthday present for the friend's son. They were looking at bicycles, and his friend found one that he thought his son would love, but he decided not to buy the bike because the price was too high. Schwartz realized then that he or his friend would have spent that amount on an evening's cocaine without a second thought. "I knew something was wrong here," he concluded.

He was at another friend's house one night when cocaine was brought out after dinner. The man's daughter came in the room with her friends, and he quickly hid the drugs and yelled, "Get out of here, you can't come in here now! You know you don't belong in here!" Again Schwartz sensed something greatly out of place. "At least that much truth reached me," he said. Although he was able to keep his drug use to only a recreational pastime, and said it never got in the way of his work, he did see many clients lose their businesses and wealth through drugs. "I didn't need to hit rock bottom to be saved," he continued. "Everybody has the conception that the person who gets saved is the drunk lying in the gutter, and so it's easily explainable: When you're lying in the gutter and this news comes along, it's gotta sound good because what else have you? Well, I wasn't the drunk lying in the gutter, but just the absence of God in my life was the spiritual equivalent of that. I had no ethics. I moved along on what seemed good and felt good."

Then one night an unexplained event occurred in his home in Krumville, New York. "We had a nice little country house, a comfortable place in the Catskills," he said. "Lacy was five and seemed a well-adjusted child, but that night she woke up absolutely terrorized, screaming with terrible pain and fear. My wife Peggy and I jumped out of bed and found her cowering in the corner of the bathroom floor, seeming to be having a nightmare, although she was awake. She was pointing at visions and things she saw that frightened her terribly. She didn't see us, she just saw these things. The closer we approached, the more fearful she became. It was horrible because we couldn't help this person that we loved most. After a few minutes, she blacked out and fell into a sleeplike trance, and when we woke her up, she had no recollection of what had happened. We put her to bed, and although we were quite shaken by it, we felt it was a normal child's nightmare and it would pass. We figured it was just a stage she was going through, and left it at that."

But the same thing happened the following night and most nights thereafter. "It reached a point where we would wait until we could hear her steps upstairs over our bedroom, knowing that she was walking in a trance and that it would be an absolute horror for us to find her in this state. She was horribly pained by what she saw and felt, and we couldn't comfort her. On the contrary, she was frightened by us. As we approached her she would actually recoil with fear, and then black out in a trance once again. Being a twentieth-century person, I felt that this was something we could get medical science to explain and treat, something she would grow through. But it troubled me more deeply than that. It filled me with a sense of unrest that just wouldn't leave, the same kind of unrest I felt with the drug use.

"At about the same time, I began to experience a presence of Satan. Now, what does that mean? I didn't see him with my eyes, or hear him talk to me. I just felt a sense of doom, of negativism. Not a sense of depression, because that comes from within, but a sense of doom that came from outside. I had never given much thought to Satan. He was that comical character we see in the movies or in cartoons. I never studied the subject or had much interest in it. But suddenly, I was preoccupied with the influence that Satan was having in the world. At the time, though, I wasn't relating it at all to what was happening in the house."

I asked Schwartz how the concept of Satan had entered his consciousness, since it is not one he might have picked up in a Jewish household. "Satan was not a being in my experience, it's true" he said. "We all saw *The Exorcist*, of course. That movie was very painful and unsettling for me to watch. But I was actually living it, which was far more frightening because at least you can always leave the movie theater. I felt a sense of Satan in my life with such absolute sureness that I thought I was losing my mind. My mind was saying, This is not what rational people think. And yet my spirit was saying, This is reality: See it and be moved by it.

"I went along functioning quite well for the two or three months that this went on, but it was tormenting me greatly. Lacy continued to have the same experience, and it bothered us so much that I knew I had to do something about it. Each time I awakened her and asked her if she remembered what she'd seen, she said no. One Friday morning we were having breakfast, and I asked her once again if she remembered what she'd seen, if she remembered her dream. And she said to me, 'Daddy, it wasn't a dream. It was real.' A chill ran through me because I felt for the first time that what was happening was not dreamlike, but something she could actually distinguish as different from dreams. I was very agitated and didn't know what to do."

Schwartz had a business appointment in New Paltz that morning, and since his family doctor was there, he decided to consult the doctor for a scientific explanation. But the doctor was busy with builders renovating his office, and when Schwartz told him briefly of the problem, the doctor put him off, suggesting he call the following week for an appointment. "I don't fault him for that," Schwartz said, "but it was a clear sign that the door was closed. I felt hopeless and empty. While driving back to work in Kingston I had a revelation—I use that word to distinguish it from an idea—that I should seek counsel with a friend named Johnny Walker. Walker had been a client of mine for years. He's a Christian, but at the time I didn't know or care much about his spiritual foundation. I just knew that he was a special person, that whenever he visited me in the office he would direct the conversation more to spiritual matters than to business. He prayed with me sometimes, and whenever we had a business matter to decide he would suggest we pray about it, which is extraordinary for a businessman. But I went along, and I always felt lighter when he left my office. I didn't know quite why, but I knew he was special, and so it occurred to me to visit Johnny Walker and seek counsel with him.

"He's a very successful maverick, an ornery, headstrong old codger who was fortunate enough to have the New York State Thruway built through his farm. Now he owns a gas station, which is where I thought I might find him. Whenever you're looking for John, you can't make an appointment or get him into your office, but when you have to see him on a matter that has to be answered tomorrow, suddenly there he is. That day he wasn't at his gas station, so I left word and decided to go back to work. As I was driving back, I had to wait for a traffic light on Washington Avenue. It's a long light, and by this time my mind was starting to shift from this crazy idea of seeking counsel with an uneducated farmer back to business. Who do I have to see? Who do I have to call? As I sat there at the traffic light, I saw Johnny Walker drive by in his rusty old blue pickup truck, and I was shaken by that coincidence. I wasn't yet tuned in to believe it was a signal or a sign, but it certainly was a coincidence. While the light stayed red, I was deciding whether to turn down Hurley Avenue and try to find him or to drive back to the office. Time seemed to stretch out, and the longer I sat there, the more it seemed I should drive back to the office because it was unlikely I would find him. But when the light turned green, I did something that was very unlike me. I turned the wheel, or somebody turned it for me, and I drove to where I might find Johnny Walker.

"I was beginning to think I was really losing my mind now, chasing a truck on the hope that John might give me some answers to my daughter's nightmares. I didn't know what was going on inwardly, but I drove about a mile and a half and I found John on the side of the road, working on a bulldozer that had been sitting on some lot for years. I thought it was amazing that I had caught him so easily. Not yet recognizing the significance of that, I told him, 'John, I have to talk to you. Please, can you give me some time?' He said, 'Sure, Bob.' He hadn't had lunch and neither had I, so we went over to the Dietz Stadium Diner and sat in a booth. I was unable to eat lunch as I told him what was happening with Lacy, and what I was feeling. I told him this Satan consciousness had overcome me.

"Rather than being shocked or calling me a fool, he spoke with words that rang true in my heart but sounded foolish to my ears. He told me that God has dominion over all things, and he was allowing Satan to do this to get my attention, because this is when he's calling me. I didn't know what all these things meant, but while he was talking a great struggle was going on within me that I didn't understand then, but which I now understand. I was being drawn between two forces, and I knew I had to make a decision. Figuratively, I felt I was at a train station with baggage, lots of old stuffed baggage, and I had to get on the train and leave everything on the platform. I guess the baggage was the things I treasured most: my physical belongings, my wealth, my drugs, my sense of control, all the things I'd grown to worship, in a way. You could call it idolatry. I didn't know this at the time, I just knew that I was going through torment. I was being called and I knew I was going, but I also had to make a decision.

"John spoke on and on, and his voice kind of faded in the background. If it were a movie, you would hear his voice and you would see the struggle going through my mind. We barely ate our lunch, and John told me, 'Bob, when you go home tonight, you put your daughter to bed and you pray with her. Ask that the evil, demonic forces in your house be removed.' All this sounded crazy to me, but I was willing to do anything by this point. And John spoke so truthfully that it really touched me."

They left the diner and drove back to the bulldozer, and after sitting in the car for a while, John suggested they pray together. Schwartz felt he stood at the crossroads as Walker asked at the end of his prayer, "Bob, are you ready?"

"He never said for what," Schwartz said, "but God made me know that I had to take a step of faith. I could see myself standing on the edge of a cliff and looking down, and God saying, 'Jump, Bob. I'll catch you.' I'm saying, 'Fine, show me your hands and I'll jump,' and God is saying, 'Jump, I'll catch you, and then you'll see my hands.' It was a tough thing to do, to take a step of faith and be willing to give up all I had."

Here Schwartz mentioned the passage in the Gospel of Matthew about the young man who asks Christ what he must do to have eternal life. Christ tells him to keep the Commandments, and when the man says that he always has, Christ tells him to go and sell everything he has and give the money to the poor, "and thou shalt have treasure in heaven, and come follow me." But when the young man heard that, the Scripture goes, "he went away sorrowful, for he had great possessions." Then Christ delivers the famous line that "it is easier for a camel to go through the eye of a needle than for a rich man to enter into the kingdom of God." Schwartz felt that Christ was speaking figuratively about possessions. "He doesn't mean give them away and live as a homeless person," he said. "He means stand ready. I knew I had to give up everything figuratively and put God first. So I jumped. I said, 'John, I'm ready.' John said some words and I felt the hand of God touch me. I felt cleansed and renewed. I felt the presence of God in my life. I felt the knowledge that Jesus Christ is the Messiah, the Savior provided for the sinfulness of man. And I also felt I was the only Jew in the world who knew this."

Tears welled in Schwartz's eyes as he told this part of the story. "Whatever that meant, it was okay, because this proof was absolute. As I cried, I felt God's love poured out on me. It makes me cry thinking about it. I knew life would never be the same, and I knew that this was Truth. It wasn't deduced, it wasn't something I read or studied or taught myself or was indoctrinated about. God himself called me."

He left that moment feeling very light, then returned to the office, tended to a few things, and went on to meet a friend for an afternoon run. As excited as he was, Schwartz didn't know how to talk about his experience, so he kept it to himself. He decided not to share it even with his wife, because their relationship wasn't going well at the time. "If I came home and said to my Jewish wife from New York, 'Honey, I found Jesus,' I think I would have been thrown out," he said. "In retrospect, I know God tempered me from saying that. It wasn't my own decision, because I've learned that God's timing is perfect and mine stinks. The more I listen and follow God's timing, the better off my life is in the long run. I did take Lacy and put her to bed that night, and as I did most nights, I asked her to bring one of her favorite bedtime books so I could read her a bedtime story. While she was doing that, I was praying: 'O God, how can I bring you to my daughter? I've never spoken about you.' They're pretty sophisticated, these five-year-olds. What do you say? 'Oh, by the way, I forgot to mention there's a Creator of this world and He loves you— it just kind of slipped my mind'? Since I didn't know God myself, how could I bring Him to anybody? I thought that I might not be able to follow John's advice and might go through the night and not say a word to her."

It was around Christmas time, and Lacy came back to bed with the Children's Passover Haggadah, a book she hadn't ever asked him to read her. "A chill ran through my body," he said. "I knew that I did not have control, that there were forces going on that were not of my design. When I read her the book, she asked, 'Daddy, who is God?' I said a few words, and then I said, 'Let's pray.' I don't know what I said or how I said it. I was never much good at praying, at least not like those evangelists, anyhow. I said some simple words and she looked up at me with her little innocent brown eyes and she put her hands on her heart. She said, 'Daddy, I feel God in me.' How unusual for a child to say that! Children somehow speak the truth that adults find so hard to say. I knew that this was the end of her torment and what I now know was her demonic possession. I went downstairs feeling very calm. Peggy later said to me, 'You seem awfully relaxed. Aren't you worried that she's going to get up again?' I said, 'No, it's over.' Peggy was puzzled by my answer. But I knew it was over, and it was."

Schwartz sat back in his chair a moment, as if resting from the weight of his own narrative. In fact, it did feel harrowing. It's one thing to watch someone "testify" on television before a room full of believers, quite another to listen across a desk, feeling the emotion behind the words. Then he leaned forward again. "That sounds like the end of the story," he said, "but it really is the beginning, because from that time I began to read God's word and piece together how God planned the world. I began to do strange things, like going to visit people in the hospital, something that wasn't me. I learned that John Walker's wife Doris was in the hospital with cancer, so I went to see her. I walked in and she said, 'Oh, Bob, I'm so glad you've been saved. We've been praying for you for a long time.' I said, 'Oh, is that what *saved* means?' I knew so little about the lingo. No matter what else anybody can say about what happened to me, they can't say that I was convinced by self-suggestion. I had no idea. Religion and faith was the last thing of any interest to me. I said, 'Is that what it means, Doris? But I'm Jewish.' She said, 'Bob, you've just been fulfilled. We're grafted into your tree. It's truly a Jewish blessing to know the fullness of God's experience. That doesn't end at the Old Testament; it ends at the end of the New Testament. The Old Testament teaches the hopelessness of man to reach God, and the New Testament teaches the provision.' She made me feel better, but I still thought I was the only Jew in the world who had found Jesus."

Several months later, Schwartz happened to notice the Christian bumper sticker of a client who was a computer specialist. Schwartz broached the subject in conversation one day and the client told him of a Jewish friend who also was saved. "Now I knew there were at least two of us," Schwartz said with a smile, "so I called up this fellow, who was a principal of a Christian school, and introduced myself. We became friends, and I began to see that there was a strong movement of revelation to the Jewish people of the truth that we've been kept from knowing all these generations, and I found comfort in that. I still didn't tell Peggy, though. Every week I would ask God, 'Now?' God would say, 'Wait.' I didn't audibly hear him. I just felt a sense that the timing was wrong, so I waited about a year. She knew something was up, though. Suddenly we were going to strange houses for dinner, and these Jewish friends she was meeting were teaching in Christian schools."

When Schwartz finally told his wife, she cried, not in sympathy or joy but because it was against everything she had been taught, even though her Judaism was primarily cultural. But to his mind, she did say something that proved that God's timing was perfect. She said, "I don't know what's happened to you, but I like you a lot better now than I did a year ago."

By this point in the story we'd been sitting in his office almost three hours. It had grown dark outside, and quiet except for the occasional hum of a passing automobile. Our tax papers still lay in front of us. Somehow we managed to finish up the work we'd come there to do, and headed out into the night feeling exhilarated. Robert Schwartz had hardly changed my mind about born-again Christianity, but he had succeeded in humanizing it. I still disagreed with many of the theological tenets of Christian fundamentalism, and almost all of its political ones, but I would never again be able quite so blithely to think of such Christians as a faceless mass of slavering book-burners. My questions about the involuted philosophy and perpetual moralizing of the born-again movement could wait for another day. In that moment, at least, I was able to feel a closer connection to a person, and by extension a group of people, who a few hours before had seemed like a force to be dreaded and shunned.

The time for asking questions came just a few weeks later, at Robert Schwartz's home in Woodstock, one of those spanking new contemporary houses that often look at odds with the old woods where they are set down like prefabricated gazebos beloved of certain suburban gardeners. And yet it fits the character of a man who is neat and precise in his work and appearance, perhaps reflecting a sense of order in his new life—not unlike the pride felt by some of the Buddhists I had met about the spareness and simple order of their zendos. Even the firewood logs in Schwartz's backyard were stacked as lovingly and precisely as gold bullion in a bank vault. The interior of the house, where his family was finishing dinner, looked just as meticulously groomed as we walked through to settle into the glassed-in sun deck facing a front yard newly ploughed and awaiting the spring plantings. There, dressed in a neat sweat suit and running shoes, Schwartz seemed more relaxed but no less intent than he had in his office. We took up where he had left off, and set to filling in some of the blanks in that long narrative.

For the record, Schwartz considers himself a fundamentalist, although he is uncomfortable with labels. "I hate to think I could be called *anything*," he said. "I couldn't tell you how the fundamentalist viewpoint differs from the Evangelical viewpoint. It never really interested me, and I haven't found the need for it in doing God's work in my life."

Robert Schwartz was born in 1943 in Philadelphia, the younger of two sons, to a Jewish immigrant father and a second-generation Jewish mother. The family moved to New York when he was about five, living in the Bronx for a couple of years and then in Brooklyn, where he spent the next twenty years growing up in the Jewish neighborhood of Flatbush and Church avenues. His father was a waiter who worked seven days a week until he died. Robert was sixteen then, and his mother was forced to work as a bookkeeper to support the family. The household was fairly poor, and Robert worked from high school through college to help out. He had a good deal of freedom—a lack of direction, actually—being raised in a Judaism that was mostly cultural. "Judaism is an interesting religion," he said. "It has different levels of formality and observation: Reform, Conservative, and Orthodox. Although we went to a Conservative temple, we actually practiced more on the Reform level, probably the most widespread configuration of Judaism in the U.S. My mother lit candles on Friday night, we went to temple on the High Holy Days, Yom Kippur and Rosh Hashannah, we had our Passover dinner, and that was about the extent of it. I never quite connected the whole experience, but that was what we were expected to do, and the neighborhood seemed to do it. As far as I knew, the whole world was Brooklyn, and the whole world celebrated Passover. I didn't know much else was going on."

That provincial aura stayed with Robert as he went to Erasmus Hall High School and Brooklyn College. His grades weren't good enough to get him into day school there, so he worked full time and went to college at night for two semesters, then matriculated to day school. Not having any clear idea of what he wanted to be in life, he decided to go through the curriculum index alphabetically, and accounting was the first subject listed. He tried it and has stuck with it since. By Schwartz's own admission, he did well at accounting without studying much. While in night school he had worked as a mail clerk for an accounting firm and was favorably impressed with the offices of the partners. "That smelled wealth," he said, "everything about it. I liked the respect they had and the pin-striped suits they wore. I asked them,

'How do you get to do what you guys do?' They said, 'You become a CPA.' I liked that, and it became my first and only choice. It's an advantage in any career to start as early as possible."

Not considered a likely candidate by his fellow students, Schwartz nonetheless passed the exam to become a Certified Public Accountant on his first try after graduating from college. He worked in midtown Manhattan, lived at home in Brooklyn, and married his summer camp sweetheart, Peggy Glasgold, whom he had known for many years from the neighborhood. They moved to Queens and rented an apartment in Rego Park, Forest Hills. Peggy worked for the New York City Department of Parks as a "parkie," overseeing the operation of one of New York's many small inner-city parks. But Schwartz knew that the city couldn't work for him. "I had to get out, so I answered an ad from an accounting firm in Newburgh looking for a partner," he said. "At this time we were building our house in Krumville, so we made an arrangement whereby I was to phase in as the third partner." He left his city job, moved up to the country, and commuted daily from Krumville to Newburgh, a trip of about an hour each way. Six months later, Schwartz decided to leave that firm and open his own office in Kingston. After about a year and a half, he had developed enough clientele that Peggy was able to leave her job and move up.

What, then, happened to this all-American Dream progression? How did it evolve into the drug lifestyle he had earlier described? To begin with, Schwartz feels that he had never stopped being "a good person." He also believes that the odyssey he went on "was part of God's perfect timing and plan." And yet the energy he and his wife were expending to build their house and his accounting practice, to notch out a comfortable life, had no further outlet. There were no large projects to consume their spirit and give them a sense of purpose. He felt, he said, like "a captain without a ship," needing to find something that would once again give him that motivation. And so he began to seek out worldly ways. "Don't get me wrong," he added quickly. "I didn't hang out in bars and drink incessantly. I didn't do cocaine before business meetings. But the emptiness of everything struck me. In a way, I can see now that it's almost a blessing to be poor, because at least you live in hope that richness will provide you with fulfillment. What happened to me and many of my clients who have attained success over the years, many far more so than I, is that we have come to see what a dead-end street that is. Actually, in the long run perhaps it's good to have attained material success, because then you're driven to find the real answers in life."

But having achieved everything that he had put his energies into attaining made him see how empty those things were. "I always need a project," he said. "I'm always working on something, moving or building something around the house or in my office. That doesn't displace my need for God. God said, 'Put me first and all things will be given to you.' But I do drift away at times and get consumed. The secular world is very powerful, an outgrowth of Satan's power and deception, and appeals very much to our senses. But I know that the only source of peace is God's presence. That's one of the reasons I need to live in the country and run so many miles a day. God's presence is more apparent in this environment. Not that you can't find God in New York City, as Simon and Garfunkel once said, but the distractions are far greater. The world shouts at you; God whispers. So you have to be listening."

Several things struck me about Robert Schwartz's retelling of his life. One is the similarity between his account and those of people who have experienced Eastern or New Age transformations: the sense that nothing is a coincidence, that what seem like accidents reveal, in retrospect, the hand of God or some spiritual energy at work. His story about not wanting to make the leap of faith until he could see God's hands waiting to catch him reminds me of Paul Lowe's parable about the man hanging from a cliff who, when he hears the voice of God telling him to let go, asks if he can have a second opinion. Finally there is the power of prayer. I have little doubt that what Schwartz described as his daughter's healing was the direct result of his praying for guidance. Furthermore, I don't believe these similarities are merely chance, but rather that they reflect a pattern in the process of spiritual transformation so powerful that it can transcend surface differences as apparently disparate as Christian fundamentalism and Oriental spirituality.

Not everything Schwartz said that day fit into the standard born-again scenario, either. For instance, an event that occurred one night while he was sleeping, a few years before he was saved, sounds more like a New Age anecdote than a Christian one. "As best I can describe it, I had a mind-body experience," he said. "If that sounds crazy, it was crazy to me, too. I didn't take it as routine at the time, but in the middle of my sleep I felt an essence of me, a spiritual essence, leave my body. It left my body long enough that I was awakened, was aware this was going on, and later felt the reunion of the two. That reunion was so incredibly wonderful that it felt euphoric—not just knowing what was going on, but the absolute elation of having my spirit and body reunited. The experience shook me so that it dwelt in my mind for several weeks after, completely unexplained, because it was not drug-induced. I didn't share this with everybody because it was pretty bizarre to me. I'm a rational person by our Western, twentieth-century standards, and I didn't accept this without question. But I knew that there was a dimension to me I had never known before, because I never thought that there was a spiritual essence, and I left it at that."

A marathoner by avocation, Schwartz runs forty-five to seventy miles a week. Although he says he doesn't win any races, he does take pride in having run uninjured for twenty-five years. But a knee problem recently threatened to force him to give up the sport. It got progressively worse over a period of weeks until he was having dif-ficulty walking up steps. Schwartz, who said that he prays "for God to cure my cold or get rid of a headache, and sometimes he does and sometimes he doesn't," was lying in bed one Saturday afternoon, resting the knee. He was watching a television program about unex-plained physical phenomena on the Discovery Channel. One story involved someone with an incurable disease who had been healed through hypnosis, another profiled a girl who, while sitting in church during a sermon about the Crucifixion, received the stigmata. Her hands and feet began to bleed, along with her forehead where the crown of thorns would have been placed on Christ's head. Neither story dealt with faith healing but with the influence of the mind over the body.

As Schwartz was watching the show, his knee in great pain, he felt God say to him, "I want to heal your knee." It didn't come in words, but in a feeling. "I was at peace and open and accepting," Schwartz said, "which is a place I'm not at much these days. I said, 'God, please heal my knee.' And I felt a tingling sensation in my right leg, my right arm, up and down my whole right side, like when your leg falls asleep and you get up. I felt God say, 'Don't move it, don't move it.' I was saying, 'I want to move it, I'm dying to try it.' But God said, 'Don't move it,' and then the tingling left. God said, 'Move it.' I lifted my knee and the pain was totally gone. Some might call it mental suggestion. I guess secular humanism can find rational explanations for every miracle. But I knew God healed my knee, and I went out and ran a race on Sunday, and finished eighth in a field of one hundred thirteen. I won a trophy and I biked thirty-three miles home from Hunter Mountain after the race. I really put God to the test.''

About a year later, Schwartz re-encountered a former client, Paul Butterfield, the white blues harmonica player and singer who had been a cult favorite during the sixties and seventies. Butterfield had come to Schwartz for some financial help while living in Woodstock, and had drifted out of sight soon after. Schwartz hadn't seen him for several years, until one day when he was boarding a bus in Kingston, bound for New York City. It was about seven in the morning when he noticed a grungy, desperate-looking person who seemed vaguely familiar. "Then I realized it was Paul Butterfield," Schwartz recalled. "I prayed he wouldn't come over and talk to me. I got on the bus and took a seat, hoping he wouldn't recognize me. He came down the aisle, sat next to me, and said, 'Bob, how are you doing?' So there I was facing two hours of riding next to a derelict soul. Then I felt God tell me what needed to be done. 'Paul,' I said, 'what have you been doing? You look awful.' "

Butterfield went on to tell how he had become a drug addict and a desperate street person, someone who stole to support his habit. Schwartz knew he had to hear about Jesus. "He had to know that there is a power that can save him," he said. "So I spoke to him, and something bizarre happened. Every time I spoke and told him what Jesus wanted for him in his life, his head would drop and he would collapse in his seat. When I finished, his head would rise and he'd go on to tell me how troubled he was, how much he needed to hear this, how he was driven and possessed by drugs. Then I would start again and tell him how Satan had control of his life, and he would pass out again. I don't mean just close his eyes and meditate on what I was saying. He would physically collapse in his seat.''

Schwartz thought of the Scripture in which Christ said, "Inasmuch as you have done it to one of the least of these my brethren, you have done it to me.'' To his mind, Butterfield was the least of the least. The whole way down, they spoke. When they got to Port Authority, Butterfield said he wanted to hear more. Schwartz had a string of appointments lined up for the day, but promised to call later. He had scheduled as many meetings as he could for his day in the city, but after his first meeting, when he called ahead to confirm, each of his appointments had to cancel for one reason or another. By then it was one o'clock, and he decided to call Butterfield and go visit him in Greenwich Village. There he found Paul living in relative squalor in an unfurnished flat, the apartment of a drug addict. "He wanted so badly to hear what I had to say," Schwartz related. "He also wanted the twenty bucks that he asked me to lend him, which I did. Then he pulled out a poem he had written, and read it to me. It expressed so well the heart of a tormented person. He lived in blackness, and he needed and wanted to be released from the prison he was in. I did everything I could. I poured out my spiritual essence, feeling drained by the end of the day, and then I left. I wrote to him and called him a few times since, and then we lost contact."

The next thing Schwartz heard of him was when he read in the paper a few years later that Butterfield had died of a drug overdose. "I still have his poem in my office," he said, "and I read it now and then. We each have our choice, and I guess God wasn't his. I don't know what this means to his eternal status, but I didn't do much good in my work with him."

Like a large number of born-again Christians, Schwartz finds the greatest comfort in worshipping by himself. "I don't go into some deep corner and go through a ritual," he said. "It may be a short prayer while I'm running in the morning, or as I leave the office after hearing some bad news about a friend who's sick or a client who's in the hospital. There's no regular scheduling." But he puts great stock in spreading the word of God through one-to-one meetings, such as the one that had taken place between us in his office. "God makes me feel that the best thing I can do during tax season," he said, "is to be of gentle temper and good disposition and have people say to me, 'Under all this stress you really seemed relaxed,' so that I might someday tell them where my source of peace comes from. I know God has given me my office to share his word with others. And when I leave the day feeling like I've done two hundred tax returns, even if I might not have gotten even one done because I spent half the day talking to people, I feel more accomplished. I know that's how God measures my productivity. I don't need confirmation every day, just once in a while. I once said to Johnny Walker, 'John, nothing's happening lately. I haven't been witnessing. What's going on?' He said, 'God wants you to be like a carpenter. Sometimes you're just picking up nails and sawing lumber, and other times you're putting it together. Now, just pick up nails.'

"Whether I'm persecuted for it or not, whether I lose friends or win disfavor, my truth is to share with you that until you accept Jesus as your personal messiah and are born again, you're not acceptable to God and you stand to pay the punishment, the wrath that God has promised for all in the Bible. This message seems like an easy one to accept. All you have to do is say a few words and you can go on with life. You don't have to wear robes or chant mantras or anything. But it's something that the human heart won't do. Until our eyes are open, we don't recognize the need for Jesus. No one is going to take Jesus on as their personal savior unless they feel and see the need for it. You have to come to God with a broken and contrite heart.

"After all, we make mistakes driving cars, otherwise there wouldn't be insurance companies. We make mistakes skiing. We go out without an umbrella and it rains. Why couldn't we also make a mistake about this? But if you go out without an umbrella and it rains, all you get is a wet head. Here we're talking about eternity. Is there a tiny, infinitesimal possibility that this is true? If it is, let that mustard seed of faith grow. Pray. Ask God. I've never met somebody who has asked God who hasn't gotten an answer. Don't be so bold and in charge not at least to ask. But if you ask from the heart, you'd better be ready, because you're going to get answered. And your life will never be the same."

In tone and substance, if not in actual language, what Schwartz was saying is not so different from what Paul Lowe said to me, or Bernard Glassman, or Father Hopko. In discussing New Age religions, for instance, Hopko said that he sometimes worries about "the people who never get into any one tradition deeply enough to get to the point where they're broken. As Thomas Merton said about Simone Weil, at some point you learn that the real reason you come here is to get your heart broken, but you've got to be into it long enough to have that wounded heart and to have that breakthrough. You don't have many breakthroughs without having a few breakdowns, and that's all orchestrated by the hands of God."

Hopko is concerned that too many people read books, such as the one I told him I was writing, and then think "that they can just jump in and have *experiences*, but not *the experience* of reality, for which you dearly pay with your blood. It takes time and it takes obedience and it takes direction and it takes counsel. It's an inscrutable mystery, but there is a sense in which you've got to pay the price. The Old Fathers said, 'Give blood, get Spirit.' You've got to be smashed and restructured, to use Jeremiah's image. The vessel has to be broken and then God has to reshape it and fill it to his purposes. I don't know much about anything except my own religious tradition, but from what I hear, just in meetings and from reading, you find that principle in every single one."

Although Robert Schwartz's language sometimes makes me feel uncomfortable, I can still write him off as a sincere but zealous missionary of fundamentalism. Father Hopko makes me feel just as uncomfortable at times, but given my Catholic background, it's harder for me to write him off completely. A priest and an intellectual, with a deep commitment to one tradition and at least a passing knowledge of several others, living in both the inner world of meditation and study and the outer world of family, he is not easily pigeonholed. Yet how different, finally, are his words from Robert Schwartz's? Schwartz might not consider Hopko saved, and Hopko might have difficulty with Schwartz's fundamentalism, yet they seem to be speaking the same language.

Where Schwartz most clearly parts company from a Father Hopko or Bernie Glassman is in the arena of religious toleration. Unlike Hopko or Glassman, Schwartz is adamant that people cannot reach salvation outside of his belief system. But given an infinitely merciful God, why are some people saved and others not even given the opportunity? What about the world's Muslims, I asked, who probably live a more stringently moral life than most Christians. Their religion forbids drinking, gambling, and usury, and commands them, as a matter of dogma, to give money to the poor. The first part of Schwartz's answer was that the non-Christian religions are primarily religions of works. They teach that through sacrifice, abstention, and good deeds, one can obtain a relationship with God. "But Christianity in its absolute and purest sense is a religion of grace," he said. "God does it all. There's no favor that man can win. All the mantras, all the fasting, all the good deeds can't bring you any closer to God and Christianity. Grace is unmerited Love, and God has to be given all the credit. Even when an unsaved person becomes saved, it's not that he or she was ready; what faith that person has come to have is a gift from God. So when I speak of my faith, it's my faith as it was given me. I take credit for nothing. All I know is that after I was saved, as much as I might have been distracted, I wanted to do good things. It was like a geyser. When you hold down one spring of water, it pops up somewhere else. And I think it comes in one package: faith and then works, not the other way around."

Schwartz is not alone among fundamentalists in his way of belief. John Wimber, the evangelist and pastor of Vineyard Christian Fellowship in Anaheim, California, writes in his book *Power Evangelism*, "We think that the key for maturity and power is to be 'good.' We then focus on our behavior, but our behavior never meets the high standards of Christ's righteousness." By concentrating on his own behavior for years, Wimber was in constant turmoil because his behavior was never good enough. "Then one day, sixteen years ago, I fell to my knees and asked God to help me. He responded, 'Since you can do nothing without me, how much help do you want?' Then he said, 'The issue is not being good, it is being God's. Just come to me, and I'll provide goodness for you.' . . . He told me that I needed to begin to listen to his voice rather than try to distill the Christian life down to a set of rules and principles." Wimber began to listen for God's voice during his prayer and Scripture readings. Now, he writes, "I no longer try to be good; instead I am only concerned with doing God's bidding: what he commands, I do. . . . Following his commands does not leave much time for sin."

That is only part of the issue, though (and sidesteps the fact that most Christian sects believe in a combination of faith and works). Schwartz still hadn't addressed the issue of those people who never received the gospel because they live in parts of the world in which Christianity is not known. "That's a tough one, and I'm not sure exactly where I stand on it," Schwartz said. "My feeling is that, in the absence of knowing Jesus, the faithfulness of the individual is the criterion which makes him acceptable. Once the message is proclaimed, however, it serves one of two purposes, either to save or convict. Unfortunately, most of my friends and loved ones have heard the message one time or another, and if they're not in, my heart goes out to them, because I feel they're excluded. Excluded is a poor term, but that's the consequence of it all."

Does that mean that Mother Teresa, who as a Catholic would not be considered saved by most fundamentalists, might end up in hell if she hasn't taken Jesus as her personal savior? "Maybe," he said. "I don't know her heart's inclination. But if she hasn't, then yes, she will be eternally damned. See, God doesn't change his mind. From the very beginning, God hates sin. He made it known, and told the Jews what was necessary to live sinless lives. If you read the four hundred or so requirements to live the sinless life [in the Old Testament], you find that if you are fortunate enough to keep all of those rules, you may still fail on the state of your heart, because your feelings can't be controlled. In other words, we might be able to avoid eating fish and dairy, and we might be able to observe when necessary, but those are outward actions. Sinfulness is an outgrowth of man's evil heart, and that's something we cannot control. As I understand it, if Mother Teresa sinned once, she's separated from God. The Bible also says that we're born in a sinful state. We are descendants of the first sinner, Adam, so our heritage is sinful. Even if from the date of birth we've led a good, holy life, we're convicted at birth."

But according to Mother Teresa's religious convictions, the sacrament of Baptism would have cleansed her soul of Original Sin. Schwartz's response is that, in any case, Catholicism doesn't preclude one from being born again. "We use these labels to pigeonhole people in a way that becomes counterproductive," he said. "I believe a lot of Catholics, in their hearts, are born again. Not everybody is fortunate enough to have the theatrics that happened to me. Many times it's a subtle change, a change of heart. It's an inward feeling, a kind of knowledge, a peacefulness that comes when you have a relationship with God. You might be a Catholic, you might be a Jew, you might be anything, provided that you've seen yourself as a sinner in need of a messiah, and you've taken on Jesus as your personal savior."

To Schwartz, being both born again and a member of an institutional religion presents a problem. In the case of Catholicism, for example, the institution "shares the divine authority of Jesus. Whereas the born-again Christian believes unequivocally that there is no shared authority." Schwartz knows Catholics who say they have experienced a born-again revelation while continuing to practice Catholicism, although he also says that "a true born-again saved person who calls himself a Catholic could not accept the legitimacy of the Pope." That would appear to leave out the movement within the Church of Charismatic Catholics whose members have accepted Jesus as their personal savior but also accept the authority of the Pope.

Nonetheless, Schwartz's relatively generous interpretation of the born-again theology didn't sound much like the vindictive variety propounded by radio and television evangelists, and I told him so. He insisted that the majority of believers he had met have come to be born again through an unspectacular evolutionary process, but that the media has misdirected the public's view of them through sensationalism. Schwartz had enjoyed the teachings of Jimmy Swaggart, and was shaken when he fell from grace. But then he felt great peace about it because, in retrospect, he realized that he had been focusing too much on Swaggart. "I don't have much time in the day to relate to God, and instead of using it for that, I was using the time to follow the teachings of Swaggart," he said. "So what seemed very hurtful at first evolved into a blessing in my case. I won't stand in judgment of him, but in my own experience it was good that he fell from his place of authority, because he was becoming an authority in my life, and there should be only one authority. I hope many have had that same experience."

Clearly, the linchpin of Schwartz's belief system is that you are better off coming to God on your own. He has an abiding distrust of religious institutions and of any religious authority outside of Jesus and the Bible. "The more I see an organization or sect grow to power, the more my heart tells me that it's something I should look away from," he said. "I guess God knew he wouldn't get me into a church or temple no matter how hard he tried, so he had to work it his way. Other people are more accepting of institutional bodies and teachings, but I'm not easily influenced. If somebody had been hammering on me right along, not only would I not have been convinced, but I probably would have been greatly turned off. How you get there and at what speed doesn't matter. It's being there that counts, realizing that it's the work of God and not man."

Over the past eight years, Schwartz's daily practice of religion has varied quite a bit. He has "tried it all," having some good moments in public worship, and feeling flat and empty at other times. Often he was embarrassed by the practices he encountered in church. "I enjoy being alone a great deal," he said, "and I feel threatened in the presence of institutions, whether they're large corporations or churches." He has gone to Christian Fellowship meetings and to Jews for Jesus functions and weekend retreats. He belongs to the Woodstock Jewish Congregation, where his daughter will be bat-mitzvahed, but he has also received considerable flak from the head of the Congregation for his Christian beliefs. "Jesus's truth gets a reaction that no other political, sexual, humanistic viewpoint would get," he said. "Even if you don't believe that Jesus is your personal messiah, you have to recognize that something about this person brings a reaction that nothing else does. So I don't go to the Woodstock Jewish Congregation on a regular basis. For a while I felt maybe I should be more of a demonstrator about my cause. But then I look at the gentle nature of Jesus and I think that his work is best served on a one-to-one basis rather than a confrontational one."

Since Schwartz considers himself a fundamentalist, I asked if he agreed with the political positions taken by fundamentalists in recent years. "I'm not an activist about it," he replied, "but I do agree with them. I feel that the absence of prayer in school and the separateness of Church and State has accounted for the level of moral degradation that our country is reaching, and will ultimately bring the demise of the United States as a leader in the world, which we're seeing already. I'm not out marching and picketing, but when given the opportunity I'll share my view. I'm very much anti-abortion, but I don't feel that God will use political forces to solve the problems of the world. They have to run their course, and I think that sharing one on one and speaking from the heart is the most effective way for a point to get across. I don't think God respects nationalities or political subdivisions, so I don't feel there's much mileage to get out of picketing in front of abortion clinics. It might even be counterproductive. Will lives be saved? Perhaps. But will sentiments be changed? Probably not. Those people seem to feel that there's a political solution for a problem in the heart of man. I feel that man's heart is inherently evil and that laws won't change the nature of that. Each individual has to undergo a spiritual rebirth for the hope of this world. And we can't legislate goodness."

His view on Satanism is that its greatest danger comes from those who deny the existence of Satan and "don't recognize Satan as a real force for evil in the world. Satanism as a practice captures a very small number of people. Most damage is done by the deception that Satan doesn't exist in twentieth-century civilization, because you don't fight an enemy when you don't think you have one. That's his first battlefront. The second is to take the gospel message and distort it so that people think they have a relationship with God, whereas they're being misled and kept from the truth in slight and subtle ways. Those are the distorted modifications of true Christianity as we see it today in, for example, Roman Catholicism. Many of the world religions are simply the gospel message twisted slightly enough that you don't really have to follow it to get in, and that keeps people from the truth. Even Buddhism accepts Jesus as just another teacher. So Satan does have a real force, but in ways that aren't in the media today." To his way of thinking, the media focus on teenage Satan worship, Satanic ritual, and suicide misses the point. "That's a very minor battlefront which comes with the territory."

Along with their anti-Catholicism, fundamentalists are known to have a high incidence of anti-Semitism. Many apocalyptic fundamentalists do support the State of Israel because of their belief that the "ingathering" of the Jews is a prerequisite for Armageddon, but their attitude toward individual Jews is less tolerant. As a Jew, how does Schwartz feel about this? "Jesus said a true prophet is without honor in his own home," he replied. "The Supreme Court of Israel just proclaimed that a Jew who believes in Jesus is not a Jew. Every Jew in the world is guaranteed citizenship in Israel, but Jewish Christians are theoretically without a home. I've never felt comfortable in fundamentalist church services, nor in many organized places of worship, and now I've lost my citizenship in Israel. Many fundamentalists might be anti-Semitic, but my view is that the believer who truly follows the word of God has a heart for the Jewish people. I've met many who do, so I know that's true. I won't stand in judgment of people or groups, but I do say there is some spiritual dysfunction even among the saved. It doesn't make them any less saved or less acceptable to God. Once you become saved, you are assured of your eternal salvation, but it doesn't mean you're always going to do the right thing. Sometimes it takes a lifetime to find out what that is."

So Mother Teresa, with her selfless devotion to the poor, might not make it to heaven, but some wife-beating bigot who happened to be "born again" would get in? Such an absolute belief system doesn't allow for very much leeway. "I have come to believe there is an absolute Truth, a part of our own perceptions," Schwartz said. "There is an absolute good that is unchanging and eternal and applies to every human being. At some point during many people's lives, if they keep searching, they will find it. God wants us all, not part. He doesn't want to fit in a place in our life. He wants to be our life, and that's why it's so difficult for us to bring ourselves to ask to see Truth, because then we're denying that we have control. But I guarantee you this, I have yet to meet a saved person who has said they didn't like being saved, or wished they were back unsaved. With the good and the bad, the persecution, the suffering, the sacrifice, and whatever comes with it, being saved is so wonderful that you never want the old life anymore."

As for Armageddon, Robert Schwartz is certain that we are in the last day. "I feel that Jesus will return," he said. "I saw a cute bumper sticker that said, 'Jesus is coming soon, and boy, is he pissed.' Jesus isn't coming to carry out a vendetta, but to save and call home those who need to be in the presence of God. But keep an open heart and ask for direction. All the books in the world, all the teaching of man, won't take you as far as a good answered prayer."

EPILOGUE

Personal Effects

■   ■   ■

Whatever gets you thru your life 'salright, 'salright
Do it wrong or do it right 'salright, 'salright . . .
Whatever gets you to the light 'salright, 'salright
Out the blue or out of sight 'salright, 'salright
—John Lennon, "Whatever Gets You Thru the Night"

■

Immersing myself in the study and exploration of modes of spirituality has made it almost inevitable that some of the teachings and behavior I observed would have a bearing on my own life. Not to have been affected would have been peculiar, considering that I undertook this project out of a deep personal interest in what role the spiritual could play in my life. Still, the ways in which I was influenced by my researches were fortuitous, and I could not have imagined beforehand what they would be. From my late teens until my late thirties, I had pretty much abandoned the whole idea of religion. Then a little over six years ago, I began spontaneously re-examining my experience of Catholicism. My curiosity about what my upbringing had done to me, and about my subsequent need to get away from Catholicism, led me to write *Once a Catholic*, a book in which I discussed with some well-known current and former Catholics the imprint that our Catholic training had left on us. That got me thinking about the implications of belief. My discovery, for instance, that some artists and intellectuals I admired had kept their faith, and valued their religious practice enough to work their way through the tortuous paradoxes that Church dogma represents for any freethinking person, caused me to question why I had abandoned my own faith so readily.

But no matter how deeply I cross-examined myself, I never came up with a simple answer to the question of why I left the Church, nor could I bring myself to embrace it again. Two insights did, however, become clear to me. The first was that the religion I had quit around the age of eighteen had little in common with the most fervent moments of my childhood devotion as I recalled them. It had, instead, become a hopeless tangle of moral and legalistic regulations devoid of sustenance or savor. The other insight gradually took the form of a question: If not Catholicism, what about something else, something that did connect to that child's urge to reverence that had been suppressed by the punitive dictates of Church doctrine?

In that frame of mind it happened that, before I began work on this book, I undertook a course of study in a spiritual discipline completely unfamiliar to me, Eckankar—a course that started by accident when I accompanied my wife to a meeting. I later discovered that Eckankar is generally looked down upon as too simplistic by members of more established religious traditions. I found its teachings more confusing than oversimplified, although the practices, including the contemplation described earlier, and a year-long course in dream work, were beneficial in subtle but noticeable ways.

Although Eckankar, also called "the Ancient Science of Soul Travel," was founded in the sixties by the late Paul Twitchell, a Kentuckian, it claims to be "the most ancient religious philosophy known to man." Twitchell wrote that he received instruction in the art of Soul Travel, or extended out-of-body experiences, from his older sister when he was three years old, and subsequently studied with the Sikh master, Sudar Singh of Allahabad, India (about whom little is known), and, on the "inner plane," with an adept named Rebazar Tarzs, a Tibetan master whose physical existence is not recorded anywhere outside of Eckankar. (The inner plane is a nebulously defined psychospiritual state somewhere between trance and conscious dreaming in which it is presumably possible to contact and be taught by highly evolved souls.) Through a lifetime of Soul Travel, Twitchell charted a number of trips to invisible worlds which he described in his many books as a series of distinct planes situated above the visible one.

Eckankar's theology holds that throughout history, a Living Eck

Master has always been physically present somewhere on the earth. The first-century Greek philosopher and ascetic Apollonius of Tyana, the thirteenth-century Sufi mystic Shams-i-Tabriz, and his student Jalaluddin Rumi are said to have been Eck Masters, and the tenth-century Buddhist saint Milarepa, a student of Eckankar. Following Twitchell's death in 1971, the leadership passed to a man named Darwin Gross, and subsequently to the current Living Eck Master, Harold Klemp, an unassuming-looking man who grew up on a farm in Wisconsin.

For all Twitchell and Klemp's talk of timelessness, much of the terminology of Eckankar appears to be borrowed from Hindu, Buddhist, Sufi and other religious traditions, with their meanings slightly altered. Its clearest connection is with an international Hindu offshoot called Radhasoami, which developed toward the end of the last century and spread to America early in this century. The spiritual ideas of Eckankar combine elements of Eastern practices with a kind of Christian love ethic, all shaped around the practice of Soul Travel. None of that is particularly surprising, given the theory that Eckankar is the current manifestation of a universal religion that has gone through many reincarnations, appearing in different strategic locales whenever the need has been greatest. (This notion itself appears in the Hindu holy book, the *Bhagavad Gita*, in which Krishna, an incarnation of Brahman, says, "When goodness grows weak, when evil increases, I make myself a body. In every age I come back to deliver the holy, to destroy the sin of the sinner, to establish righteousness.") It would, of course, be hard to argue with the idea that the West needs a spiritual direction right now. I'm not sure that Eckankar is it, although I couldn't prove otherwise, and it did serve as a valuable introduction to alternative spiritual practice for me.

During the year that I attended Eck meetings, called Satsangs, I performed the prescribed spiritual exercises and kept a dream journal. At no other time in my life, including years of standard psychotherapy, have I had such plentiful dreams, remembered in vivid detail, many in full color and often taking place in otherworldly settings. I noticed changes in my personality, too subtle to explain at any length, but impossible either to overlook or to ascribe to accident. In my first Satsangs, our Arahata or teacher, a bright and personable but self-effacing young woman named Ellen Kieve, instructed us to "open the heart center." At the time, I had no knowledge of the spiritual-energetic body centers or chakras, but the mere suggestion to begin by opening our hearts—to God, to each other, to love—was helpful and meaningful. At other times I found the work frustrating and maddeningly imprecise. (For instance, the instructions for meditation were open-ended and vague, but this may have been a blessing in disguise since it did not saddle me with the notion that there is only one proper method for meditation.) The regional seminars that bring together Eckists for discussions and artistic expressions of their belief could be cloying. And, on a purely aesthetic level, I loathed some of the phraseology, which spoke inelegantly of "spiritual unfoldment" or the "attitude of gratitude." But if nothing else, my experiences with Eckankar made me comfortable with traditions other than mainstream Christianity, and gave me a glimpse of the benefits and difficulties that can come from doing any intensive inner work. I still feel a strong attraction to some of the people I met in Eckankar, more than to the practice itself. And I still remember some of those dreams.

In the further course of research, partly to get a feel for the territory and partly to find out which disciplines and techniques might work for me, I encountered quite a few different teachers and systems. I chanted and meditated with Swami Muktananda's co-successor Nityananda, took instruction in Zen meditation at a mountain monastery, attended prayer groups that combined evangelistic Christian fervor with Eastern mysticism, put myself in the hands of New Age healers, bodyworkers, and spiritual counselors, and went to hear some of the living spiritual masters who still teach in America, such as Swami Satchidananda and Pir Vilayat Inayat Khan. Although my contact with most of them was little more than superficial, I always felt that I had learned something of value, even if the something was that a particular tradition or teacher held no appeal for me.

My encounters with spiritual teachers during the next couple of years were hardly extraordinary, but on at least a couple of occasions they gave me some inkling of what the people I'd been interviewing were talking about. The first of any note occurred when my wife and I took a weeklong summer retreat to study the Healing Tao as taught by Mantak Chia, a Thai master of Taoism and Tai Chi Chuan. The retreat was held in a center near Big Indian, New York, that had once been owned by an American spiritual guide named Rudi (Albert Rudolph, who had served as Da Kalki's first teacher). It was a ramshackle place with Spartan accommodations and an abundance of Hindu stone sculptures—Rudi had been an art importer as well as guru. The participants of the retreat made up a curious cross section of humanity, skewed to the arts and the upper middle class as these gatherings often are. We had a machinist who worked for NASA, a potter, a rock musician, a molecular biologist, textile artist, concert pianist, stonecutter, massage therapist, acupuncturist, architect, child psychologist, sign painter and apprentice, journalist, art gallery owner, civil engineer, travel agent, sculptor, and cartoonist, among others, and several more women than men. They had come from all across America and Canada, and as far away as Puerto Rico, France, West Germany, and Switzerland.

The first two days of the retreat were a succession of discomforts, disappointments, and long lectures in a hot lecture hall rendered more trying by Chia's accent and delivery, which took some getting used to. (It was also a source of humor for us and several jaded workshopgoers we met, as Chia turned Methodists into Mentholists, Seventh Day Adventists into Seventh Avenists, and a Taoist exercise called the Six Healing Sounds into the Sickly Sow.) And we spent several excruciating hours each day trying to learn Tai Chi, a Chinese martial art form that was taught in muscle-numbing slow motion. By the third day, Margery and I were ready to forgo the rest of the week—for which we had paid $700 apiece including the minimal room and board—but decided to give it one more day. We muddled through the morning's Tai Chi and meditation and the usual breakfast of gruel-like porridge, granola, and hot bread with Skippy Peanut Butter (Chia's few concessions to American culture were supremely mystifying, like the cans of Lysol spray disinfectant in the otherwise barren bathrooms, or the giant jars of processed, sugared Skippy as part of a holistic breakfast). Then we gathered in the meditation hall for the next two-and-a-half-hour session.

During the lecture, Chia analyzed the guru-student relationship from a perspective I hadn't heard before. His theory is that traditional spiritual masters seek to tune their students to their own frequency by means of mantras, a mala or necklace with the guru's picture on it, diet, control of their sex lives, and other methods. "He upgrades your energy by refining it," Chia said, "but then he wants you to give the energy back to him." The guru teaches his students to focus their energy on him, even after his death, by praying to and meditating on his image. The guru draws on that energy as from a bank account or an electric generator, and in return may help his devotees with insights and inspiration, or by raising their level of consciousness. Chia likened this to the feudal arrangement between medieval lord and serfs: when it was good it was very good, but too often it invited corruption. The disciples who are closest to the master usually receive the biggest return of energy, and that closeness can sometimes be won with sex or money rather than through spiritual attainment. Chia's system would be different, he told us. He would teach us to develop our own energy through the practice of a Taoist form of meditation, and would not make us reliant on him as guru.

That sounded appealing. The key to Chia's system, as elaborated in his *Taoist Secrets of Love* and other books, emphasized the conservation of sexual energy, not through continence but by retaining seminal fluids during sexual intercourse. He taught specific techniques, both mental and physical, for accomplishing this feat, not very different in essence from those of Tantric Yoga. This "dual cultivation," as he called it, could also be practiced by oneself ("individual cultivation") as a way of rechanneling one's sexual energy without dissipating it through ejaculation. The conserved energy could then be set in motion through a series of energy centers in a circuit called the Microcosmic Orbit (similar to the flow of energy up the spine during Kundalini).

I experimented with his techniques over the following months and found them remarkably useful, if rather difficult to master. But was there a spiritual aspect to all this absorption in sexuality? For Chia, the body is supremely spiritual; meditation techniques are methods of "moving energy" reminiscent of Vicki Mullen and Bob Tobey's conception. Chia contended that most of the ecstatic states reached by Hindu, Buddhist, Taoist, and Christian mystics were actually orgastic in nature, but that the mystics kept this secret to themselves, mainly for fear of arousing the ire of the relatively narrow communities in which they lived. But neither in Chia's books nor in his lectures is there any mention of a relationship with God as we might understand it. He talks about the Universal Force, which he conceives of as a kind of electromagnetic pull exerted by the North Star, but that is as close as he comes to any overriding concept of a Supreme Being.

Then again, I had learned that in the spiritual realm, verbalized conceptions may not count for as much as the actual techniques and how they work for those who use them—to paraphrase John Lennon's song, whatever gets you through the dark night of the soul. What strikes me as most misleading about certain spiritual teachings is the idea that only one path works for everyone. Krishnamurti may have been closest to the truth when he said there is no path, and that every path leads to God. In any event, Chia promised that after the lecture he would transmit some of his own energy to us during a meditation that would incorporate the mental aspects of his techniques. (He was always scrupulously careful not to encourage outward displays of sexual arousal. For all Chia's talk of orgastic sex, he preaches and claims to practice strict monogamy, for practical rather than moral reasons.)

The meditation was much more illuminating than the lecture. Nothing discernible happened, aside from an unusually strong but fleeting sexual feeling in the perineal region, and a slight tingling or numbing along the chin, as if it had been brushed with novocaine. But when it was over, I had two distinct sensations. For once, the time had flown by; the hour-long meditation seemed to take only a few minutes. And when we emerged from the hall, I felt euphoric, as if I had taken a mild mood-elevating drug. I floated along, wondering if I was the only one feeling this way, but Margery reported much the same response. For the first time in three days we were upbeat and uncomplaining. When we got to our room, I looked out the window at the surrounding mountains sheathed in mist and felt I finally understood why people went on these retreats, or why they entered ashrams and never wanted to leave. Margery turned to me and said, "Why don't we come back next week, too?"

It sounded like a good idea. Books, baseball, movies, restaurants, money, achievement—all seemed as pointless as they had ever been painted by religious teachers and writers. The feeling didn't last long, though. A few hours later, after lunch and a long, leisurely walk, we were back on the grass being confounded by a new Tai Chi form and some Iron Shirt exercises that were living up to their name. The afternoon lecture, which had been heralded as a discussion of Taoist sexuality, was a question-and-answer filler session. But the impression from the morning remained real and vivid, enough from which to infer a world of possibilities.

By the time the week was up, unfortunately, we had serious misgivings about Chia, if not about his teachings or techniques. There was finally something too self-satisfied about the man, too egotistical, to qualify him as a genuine spiritual master. I resolved to continue to work with the meditations and practices and keep my eyes open for a more suitable teacher. I also decided not to interview Chia or any of his students, as I couldn't find a single disciple during the week who I felt would be a reliable and engaging subject, and that in itself told me something.

I might, of course, have been wrong about all that. In this area a very fine line can be drawn between healthy skepticism and the fear of being taken for a ride, a basic distrust of anyone who asks you too emphatically to suspend your disbelief. And yet, as Ram Dass admitted in the *Common Boundary* article previously cited, you could characterize all of the confusing array of spiritual techniques as traps of a sort. "For a method to work," he said, "you must become entrapped. For the method to complete its work, it must self-destruct. That includes teachers, techniques, and all of it. Otherwise one gets left with being a good meditator or a good devotee. The process is complete when you've gone beyond the method itself. But you have to be entrapped for it to work. You can't dilettante your way through. You better get sucked in."

So far, at least, not getting sucked in had been my mode of operation in this area. In the further course of doing research, I did come across a teacher who impressed me as having both his heart and head in the right places. Lex Hixon, with his four different disciplines, was a figure who appealed to me in a number of ways. But since Islam was not a path I wanted to pursue, I saw him only a couple of times. The second time was when I went to hear him teach at his mosque Masjid al-Farrah, located in the Tribeca district of Manhattan. I did this with some trepidation, however, because as strong a connection as I felt with Hixon, I still carried an essential wariness of Muslims. Hixon is an American WASP with no foreign demeanor at all, but what other images of Islam did I have? Besides Muhammad Ali, the only Muslims I knew much about at the time were Louis Farrakhan and the Ayatollah Khomeini.

The location of Hixon's mosque on West Broadway had a curious resonance for me. It was in a downtown area just below SoHo that not many years previously had been the locale for a string of after-hours clubs that served drinks and live rock-'n'-roll until dawn, during a time and in a milieu in which it was unthinkable to stay home at night any more often than was absolutely necessary. As a music writer and editor for an arts-based weekly newspaper, I had to cover that scene as part of my beat, although I suspect my involvement in it was enthusiastic beyond any merely professional sense of thoroughness. That was also a search of sorts, but one whose object was not always so potentially uplifting as my current one. So I could taste the irony as I walked down those same half-deserted streets and up to the nondescript mosque, an unmarked brown storefront equipped with a buzzer and intercom whose presence were obviated by the open door.

Once inside, I found a vestibule for removing one's shoes—a traditional requirement for entry to a mosque—and a large rack for storing them. The downstairs area resembled a long, unfurnished loft with a coffered tin ceiling and exposed brick walls, commonplace in that part of town. Persian carpets covered the floor, and two large structures of polished wood stood on either side of the far end of the mosque, one resembling a pulpit, the other a large niche or doorway with Arabic writing inlaid above it in mother-of-pearl. (I later learned that the pulpit is called a minbar and has seven steps representing seven levels of consciousness, a kind of Jacob's ladder to heaven. It is used only on Friday for the noon prayer, at which time the Imam of the mosque ascends the stairs and gives a sermon. The prayer niche, which faces east toward Mecca, is called a mithrab). On the walls hung large circular ornaments filled with more Arabic calligraphies containing either Koranic verses, Divine names, or the names of revered Islamic caliphs, in line with the Muslim law forbidding the worship of pictures or statues.

A trio of black youngsters played noisily on the carpets while a black man in Muslim garb sat against the wall at the far end, studying two large volumes. The only other person in the room was a young woman who seemed lost in meditation. I noticed several people walking up and down a staircase at the rear of the vestibule, and after waiting in vain for something to happen, I wandered upstairs to see what was going on. The upstairs was a less formal arrangement, consisting of several long couches covered with colorful Turkish kilims, a kitchen area, and an office. Several men in turbans or kaffiyehs sat smoking cigarettes and chatting amiably on one of the couches. The mother of the three children I'd seen playing was admonishing her youngest boy, now happily barefoot, to "get downstairs and get your socks back on." The people seemed friendly enough, but I felt out of place, and after staring at the floor a while, I retreated downstairs to wait.

The young woman nodded to me, so I asked her if Lex Hixon would be coming. He would, she said, but not for another hour, so I used the time to ask questions. She told me she had been born in Israel of nonreligious Jewish parents, but hadn't "come alive" until she'd embraced Islam some years ago. I asked if that hadn't been a difficult thing, given her Jewish background. "Not at all," she said, not quite getting my intent. "Islam is an easy religion, especially compared to Judaism. You have to pray five times a day, but they're short prayers. And you have to fast during Ramadan." During Ramadan, she informed me, devout Muslims fast strictly from sunrise to sunset. I wondered if that part was hard on her, but she had it all worked out. Beginning at sundown she ate as much as she could, staying up most of the night and going to sleep just before dawn. Then she slept until two in the afternoon, minimizing the period of fasting. This nonetheless upset her habits enough to create a certain "lightness," reconfiguring her way of seeing things and altering her consciousness, something she recommended highly. But when I probed deeper into the internal transformation that accompanied her conversion to Islam, she said it was impossible to describe such a thing, that words would be meaningless.

By then, Hixon had arrived. He greeted us, resplendent in a light green floor-length robe, and made his way upstairs. The Israeli woman told me I should go up, since the teaching that precedes each service would begin. When I walked in, Hixon was counseling the black woman on a personal matter, then moved on to general religious instruction. Over the next hour, congregants trickled in and exchanged embraces with Hixon, a mixture of local whites and African Americans, and immigrants from Lebanon, Turkey, Egypt, Afghanistan, and other parts of the Islamic world. The man sitting next to Hixon resembled a young Allen Ginsberg as he read from a religious text to which Hixon provided commentary. The principal activities in the room, aside from this, seemed to be drinking tea and smoking cigarettes. As I sat on the floor, a young man served me a cardboard cup of very hot Tetley's tea, and while I was blowing on it, I became aware of Lex's voice directed at me. "The man sipping his tea," he said. "Do I know you from somewhere?"

I was caught off guard, not realizing that he hadn't recognized me when he came in. Our interview had taken place only two weeks before, and we'd spent that entire afternoon and evening talking and eating dinner together. "Yes," I answered slowly. "I met you in your house."

The room, which had been respectfully silent, broke into loud laughter. They were having a laugh at their sheikh's expense, probably at the idea that this man of wisdom had only a vague recollection of someone who had been a guest in his own home. The laughter put me at ease, and Hixon proceeded to tell them about our interview and then asked me to explain the book I was writing. When I did, the Lebanese man sitting next to me said that he wanted to write a similar book. He later told me that he would also like to make a documentary film on the subject, although he admitted that he was neither writer nor filmmaker—he just liked the idea.

Talking about my work, I mentioned something I'd read in Hixon's book *Coming Home*. At the end of it, he suggests techniques for meditation, including the use of a visual image which he calls an *ishtadeva*, "the chosen ideal or guiding Divinity of our contemplation. Any traditional manifestation of the Divine can become our ishtadeva: Shiva, Allah, Christ, Krishna, Buddha, Yahweh, or one of the myriad forms of the Goddess, such as Kali, Tara, or Mary." As I first read that passage, I had begun to see again the picture of the Sacred Heart of Jesus that had hung over my bed as a child. Subsequently, I told the members of the mosque, I incorporated the image into my meditations. Assuming that ethnic Muslims might have only vague ideas of Catholic iconography, I explained what the picture looked like: Christ with his exposed heart emanating flames, burning with love for humanity.

Hixon interrupted my description. "That's pure Sufism," he said, delighted. "A heart on fire with love!" Just then the lyrics to an old devotional song that we used to sing in church came to mind, and I recited them: "To Jesus, heart all burning, with fervent love for men. . . ." The congregation seemed moved by this discovery of an imagistic link between Catholicism and Islam. Lex found further connections, as in the Sufi mystic Mansur al-Hallaj's "I am the Truth," and Christ's "I am the Way, the Truth, and the Life." ("This is why you could say that Sufism is the bridge between Christianity and Islam," he later told me.) As the evening wore on and I listened to the devotional reading, to Hixon's commentary on it, and to the words exchanged by members of the community, I began to sense how deep that link is. The connection exists on the surface but also at the heart, since Islam, too, is a religion of prayer and fasting and almsgiving, of souls condemned to hellfire or rewarded with Paradise, but it is above all a religion of Love, of an all-merciful God. Throughout the Koran, the words "God is forgiving and merciful" echo like a refrain. In Hixon's instruction that evening, he returned again and again to the image of the heart on fire with love, weaving it deftly through the hour.

Downstairs in the mosque, the lights had been dimmed for prayer, which was conducted in Arabic and Turkish. For the first time the group was separated by gender according to Islamic tradition, the men in diagonal rows facing the wooden niche, the women huddled in back. A man went around pouring rosewater into the hands of worshippers for the traditional ablutions, and it felt cool and refreshing rubbed on my hands and face. The formal prayers and prostrations were followed by the zhikr, a combination of dance, prayer, and chanting that is said to generate a hypnotic effect. The words were in English about half the time now, and the result of the chanting, linking arms, and swaying in rhythm was exhilarating in a way that reminded me of black church services I had witnessed years before. After the zhikr ended, members shook hands and embraced, kissing each other on both cheeks. I felt comfortable joining them. In fact, I was made to feel like a friend among these people who moments ago had been total strangers.

Later that night, it occurred to me that the more religions and the more spiritual cultures in which I participated, if only for a few hours, the less foreign the world would appear. Before that service, few places on earth would have felt more alien to me than an Islamic mosque. (One in Teheran or Islamabad or Baghdad might still feel that way, of course, but for political rather than religious reasons.) I returned home feeling buoyant and opened in some subtle way in my heart. I thought of Ellen Kieve talking about the heart center, and of the image of the Sacred Heart on fire with love, and for the first time they seemed to form a coherent picture.

Looking back on that night, I can see the heart beginning to reclaim the role that reason had usurped in my life. It is a slow process. Just about everyone I talked to said it would be. For one thing, the voice of the heart is harder to hear, since the head is usually making so much noise. In any event, the process is embryonic, and the end is nowhere in sight.

ANNOTATED
BIBLIOGRAPHY

. ■ .

A young man who wishes to remain a sound atheist cannot be too careful of his reading.

—C. S. Lewis

■

Allison, Audle. *Meditation: Ancient Teachings of the Masters.* Oklahoma City: Lotus Center, 1975.
A basic handbook from an unsung American teacher.

———. *Basic Meditation.* Oklahoma City: Lotus Center, 1981 (cassette).
More of the same, but somewhat expanded to include Allison's engaging blend of Christian beliefs and Eastern techniques, including the proposition that Christ was a master meditator as documented in the Gospels.

Arberry, A. J. *Sufism: An Account of the Mystics of Islam.* London: Allen & Unwin, 1950.
Scholarly to the point of abstruseness, but mercifully compact.

Bartholomew. *"I Come as a Brother": A Remembrance of Illusions.* Taos, N.M.: High Mesa Press, 1986.
One of the best of the "channeled" books, it contains remarkably sensible advice and wisdom that is more accessible than books by many corporeal teachers.

Bennett, J. G. *Gurdjieff: A Very Great Enigma.* York Beach, Me.: Samuel Weiser, 1973.
Somewhat specialized, but does a good job imparting the flavor of the geographic, ethnic, and spiritual sources out of which Gurdjieff developed

his unique system. Recommended companion reading for any of Gurd-jieff's books.

Benson, Herbert, M.D. *The Relaxation Response*. New York: William Morrow, 1975.
A simple, nonsectarian approach to meditation for absolute beginners, complete with scientific verification.

Besant, Annie, and C. W. Leadbeater. *Thought-Forms*. Wheaton, Ill.: Theosophical Publishing House, 1969.
Originally published in 1901, this work by two clairvoyants can be seen as another precursor of the current New Age, or simply as a study of the shapes and colors of auras produced by different kinds of mental and emotional states, visible to the authors.

Brother Lawrence. *The Practice of the Presence of God*. White Plains, N.Y.: Peter Pauper Press, 1963.
Perhaps the ultimate guidebook to the spirituality of everyday life, written in the seventeenth century by an unlearned former footman and soldier turned Discalced Carmelite lay brother.

Campbell, Joseph. *The Hero with a Thousand Faces*. Princeton, N.J.: Princeton University Press, 1949.
Brilliant discussion of, among other things, figures of religious history and myth as archetypes for our own lives. Campbell is much more enjoyable without the self-serving interruptions of a television interviewer.

Capra, Fritjof. *Uncommon Wisdom: Conversations with Remarkable People*. New York: Simon & Schuster, 1988.
A look inside Capra's process of creating his influential books *The Tao of Physics* and *The Turning Point*, it details lengthy intellectual collaborations with some of the modern greats of physics and psychology, and shows an appreciation for the spiritual underpinnings of both disciplines.

Chia, Mantak, with Michael Winn. *Taoist Secrets of Love: Cultivating Male Sexual Energy*. Sante Fe, N.M.: Aurora Press, 1984.
————, and Maneewan Chia. *Healing Love Through the Tao: Cultivating Female Sexual Energy*. Huntington, N.Y.: Healing Tao Books, 1986.
The theory and practice behind Chia's approach to increasing spiritual and physical vitality through conserving seminal fluids.

Cowan, Paul. *An Orphan in History: Retrieving a Jewish Legacy.* Garden City, N.Y.: Doubleday, 1982.
For an agnostic Jewish journalist, tracking down his ethnic and religious roots turns into more of a mystery than he, or we, might have imagined, and is never less than intriguing.

————, with Rachel Cowan. *Mixed Blessings: Marriages Between Jews and Christians.* Garden City, N.Y.: Doubleday, 1987.
A how-to book for couples contemplating or involved in religiously mixed marriages, from people who have counseled many such couples based on their own experiences.

Cox, Harvey. *Turning East: The Promise and Peril of the New Orientalism.* New York: Simon & Schuster, 1979.
A Baptist theologian investigates Eastern religious practice among Americans. Cox's distinctive eye illuminates things a little differently.

Da Love-Ananda [Da Kalki]. *The Knee of Listening: The Early Life and Radical Spiritual Teachings of Franklin Jones.* San Rafael, Calif.: Dawn Horse Press, 1973.
A standard among recent spiritual autobiographies, clearly and unsentimentally written by one of our most highly regarded teachers. The first half is personal experience, the second is complex but exhaustive how-to.

Dürckheim, Karlfried Graf. *Zen and Us,* translated by Vincent Nash. New York: E. P. Dutton, 1987.
The Zen master of the Black Forest, who knew Klee and Kandinsky as well as Heidegger and D. T. Suzuki, shows simply and eloquently how Zen can function for Westerners.

Evans-Wentz, W. Y., ed. *The Tibetan Book of the Dead.* 3rd edn. London: Oxford University Press, 1957.
Ancient Buddhist text traces the experience of life between death and rebirth, purportedly based on the experiences of yogis who had total recall. Fascinating on any level, this edition has Jung's original "Psychological Commentary."

Gallagher, Fr. Chuck, S. J. *The Marriage Encounter: As I Have Loved You.* Garden City, N.Y.: Doubleday, 1975.
The founder of the Marriage Encounter movement in America writes

about his experiences in clear language, although this is not so much a manual as a record of his impressions.

Gallup, George, Jr., and Jim Castelli. *The People's Religion: American Faith in the 90's*. New York: Macmillan, 1989.
Exhaustive research drawn from Gallup Polls and other studies shows America to be more consistently concerned with religion than previously believed. Although the focus of religion, and the general perception of its popularity, shifts from decade to decade, its underlying pull on American life has not abated.

Gibb, H. A. R. *Mohammedanism: An Historical Survey*. London: Oxford University Press, 1970.
Somewhat dated and written by a non-Muslim, but with great understanding and succinctness.

Gilman, Richard. *Faith, Sex, Mystery: A Memoir*. New York: Simon & Schuster, 1986.
Honest and at times startling account of one man's journey from agnostic Judaism to belief in Roman Catholicism and back again.

Gordon, James S. *The Golden Guru: The Strange Journey of Bhagwan Shree Rajneesh*. Lexington, Mass.: Stephen Greene Press, 1987.
Well-documented view of life at Rajneesh's Indian ashram and Oregon commune by someone who participated but never became a full-time follower. Gordon appears to have been genuinely moved by the Bhagwan's teachings but repulsed by the greed, paranoia, and megalomania of his lieutenants, and tries to make the case that Rajneesh was responsible for their excesses.

Griffiths, Bede, O.S.B. *The Golden String*. New York: P. J. Kenedy & Sons, 1954.
Bede's account of his spiritual journey from disillusioned orthodox believer to unorthodox Benedictine monk, with many perceptive insights along the way.

Guinness, Alec. *Blessings in Disguise*. New York: Alfred A. Knopf, 1985.
A witty and literate life of the renowned British actor and the role that his faith played in his long acting career.

Gurdjieff, George I. *Meetings with Remarkable Men*. New York: E. P. Dutton, 1969.

A classic story of spiritual coming of age by one of the remarkable men of twentieth-century religious practice.

Harrison, Barbara Grizzuti. *Visions of Glory: A History and a Memory of Jehovah's Witnesses.* New York: Simon & Schuster, 1978.
By turns angry, funny, and moving, this exhaustive and splendidly written survey of an apocalyptic sect and the author's thirteen-year sojourn in it is rife with detailed information about the Witnesses, possibly more than most readers are looking for.

Hixon, Lex. *Heart of the Koran.* Wheaton, Ill.: Theosophical Publishing House, 1988.
Meditations on key passages from the holy book of Islam by a contemporary American Sufi sheikh successfully deliver the flavor and fire of the Muslim spirit.

————. *Coming Home: The Experience of Enlightenment in Sacred Traditions.* Los Angeles: Jeremy Tarcher, 1989.
Heidegger, Krishnamurti, Ramakrishna, Ramana Maharshi, Plotinus, St. Paul, Zen, Hasidism, Sufism, Vedanta, and the *I Ching*, all explored in one book, a staple of modern spiritual writing.

Huxley, Aldous. *The Perennial Philosophy.* New York: Harper & Row, 1944.
A treasurehouse of source material from all the major spiritual traditions—in the form of quotations taken from the various holy books and the writings of many saints and mystics—strung together by Huxley's syncretistic narrative. Makes a great starting point for readings in the mystical or unitive experience of God.

James, William. *The Varieties of Religious Experience: A Study in Human Nature.* New York: Modern Library, 1936 (first published 1902).
The classic examination, in exhaustive detail, of the psychology of belief, from conversion to mysticism. Over five hundred pages, James's brilliant intellect and elegant writing style make the book a pleasure to read.

Johnston, William, ed. *The Cloud of Unknowing and The Book of Privy Counseling.* Garden City, N.Y.: Image Books, 1973.
An acknowledged masterpiece of the Christian mystical tradition, coupled with a later, less well known work by the same anonymous author. Both are practical guides to meditation.

Juhan, Deane. *Job's Body: A Handbook for Bodywork.* Barrytown, N.Y.:
    Station Hill Press, 1987.
A highly recommended but also highly technical work on many areas
concerning therapeutic manipulation of the body.

Jung, Carl G. *Psychology and the East,* translated by R. F. C. Hull. Princeton,
    N.J.: Princeton University Press, 1977.
An excellent collection of Jung's commentaries, forewords, and essays
concerning Buddhist, Taoist, and Hindu spirituality.

Kandinsky, Wassily. *Concerning the Spiritual in Art,* translated by
    M. T. H. Sadler. New York: Dover, 1977 (first published 1914).
Like Scriabin, Klee, Mondrian, and other early twentieth-century artists,
Kandinsky was influenced by Madame Blavatsky's explorations of Hindu
and Buddhist teachings. His descriptions of spiritual principles at play in
his and his contemporaries' work expand the conventional notion of what
spirituality is.

Kennedy, Eugene. *Tomorrow's Catholics/Yesterday's Church: The Two Cul-
    tures of American Catholicism.* New York: Harper & Row, 1988.
A former priest and one of the most astute commentators on the American
Catholic scene, Kennedy here evaluates the Church's lagging response to
its faithful.

Khan, Pir Vilayat Inayat. *Introducing Spirituality into Counseling and Ther-
    apy.* Lebanon Springs, N.Y.: Omega Press, 1982.
It may have been designed for therapists, but this book reads like a
practical spiritual guide for lay people as well.

Klemp, Harold. *The Wind of Change.* Minneapolis: Eckankar, 1980.
An accessible, down-to-earth introduction to the basic premises of Eckankar through the autobiographical experiences of its present leader.

―――. *Soul Travelers of the Far Country.* Minneapolis: Eckankar, 1987.
More stories tying Klemp's exploits on the road to becoming the Living
Eck Master to the principles of Eckankar. Folksy.

Koontz, Ty, ed. *The Holy Jumping-Off Place: An Introduction to the Way of
    the Heart Revealed by Heart-Master Da Love-Ananda (Avadhoota Da Free
    John).* San Rafael, Calif.: Dawn Horse Press, 1987.

Just what it says, a good introduction to Da's way of seeing things, with excerpts from his many books and commentary by some of his followers.

Kopp, Joseph P. *Teilhard de Chardin: A New Synthesis of Evolution*. Glen Rock, N.J.: Paulist Press, 1964.
A concise survey of the key points of Teilhard's thinking.

The Koran, translated by N. J. Dawood. 5th rev. edn. New York: Viking/ Penguin, 1990.
This edition conveniently numbers the *suras*, or verses, and provides a comprehensive index for the general reader unfamiliar with Islam.

Krishna, Gopi. *Kundalini: The Evolutionary Energy in Man*. Boston: Shambhala, 1985.
A reissue of Krishna's definitive 1967 Kundalini autobiography, in which he describes in fine detail the actual physical and psychological effects of the experience, saving for the final chapter any ruminations on its spiritual implications.

Krishnamurti, J. *The First and Last Freedom*. New York: Harper & Row, 1954.
————. *Freedom from the Known*. New York: Harper & Row, 1969.
Maybe the most intensely gripping experience in all spiritual literature is Krishnamurti at his best, represented by either of these two great books. Reading these lectures with full concentration is like holding a live wire to your frontal lobe.

Krishnamurti, U. G. *Mind Is a Myth: Disquieting Conversations with the Man Called U.G.* Goa, India: Dinesh Publications, 1988.
If J. Krishnamurti is a live wire, reading U. G. (no relation) is equivalent to shorting out your brain circuitry altogether. This book is as hard to find as it is hard to take, and clearly not for the faint of spirit or for anyone seeking comfort and reassurance.

Kushner, Harold. *Who Needs God*. New York: Summit, 1989.
Using the Psalms as a guide, this Natick, Massachusetts, rabbi gives a commonsensical explanation of the value of traditional religion that avoids hokiness and the other common pitfalls of "inspirational" books. Should appeal to both Christians and Jews.

Larson, Bob. *Larson's Book of Cults*. Wheaton, Ill.: Tyndale House, 1989.
A fundamentalist radio evangelist whose openness to beliefs other than born-again Christianity is nil, Larson is nevertheless extremely thorough in his rundown of the basic tenets of dozens of belief systems, from Astara to Zen. If you can get past his hostile slant (or laugh at it), this is a worthwhile source book.

Lester, Julius. *Lovesong: Becoming a Jew*. New York: Henry Holt, 1988.
Highly recommended story of a black author's journey from his childhood as son of a Southern Methodist minister to atheist to Reform Jew.

Lewis, Samuel L. *Sufi Vision and Initiation: Meetings with Remarkable Beings*. San Francisco: Sufi Islamia/Prophecy Publications, 1986.
Excerpts from the largely unpublished writings of one of the earliest influential figures in American Zen and Sufi practice. Sufi Sam, as he was sometimes known, shows surprisingly fresh perceptions of these two disciplines.

Lings, Martin. *Muhammad: His Life Based on the Earliest Sources*. Rochester, Vt.: Inner Traditions International, 1983.
Considered by many Islamic scholars to be the best biography of the Prophet to date, written from within the Islamic tradition and based on Arabic sources from the eighth and ninth centuries.

London, Jack. *The Star Rover*. New York: Macmillan, 1915.
Fictionalized rendering of the story of turn-of-the-century outlaw Ed Morrell, whose confinement in a prison straitjacket reportedly led him to develop the ability to leave his body and relive past lives. Intriguing premise, and the storytelling is pure London.

Lowe, Paul G. *The Experiment Is Over*. New York: Roximillion Publications, 1989.
Lowe's only book is a series of interviews conducted by various disciples, on subjects ranging from sexuality, relationships, marriage and children to business to healing, AIDS, and death.

Luzzatto, Moshe Chayim. *The Way of God and An Essay on Fundamentals*, translated and annotated by Aryeh Kaplan. Jerusalem: Feldheim, 1983.
Not recommended for beginners, this book gives a fairly complete workup

(in Hebrew and English) of the beliefs of mystical Judaism by a renowned eighteenth-century Italian rabbi. Available at stores dealing in Judaica.

Maharishi Mahesh Yogi. *Science of Being and Art of Living: Transcendental Meditation.* New York: New American Library, 1968.
The theoretical underpinnings of TM explained in excruciating detail can make slow reading, but it is a requisite for anyone interested in this form of meditation.

Matthiessen, Peter. *Nine-Headed Dragon River: Zen Journals 1969–1982.* Boston: Shambhala, 1987.
This Westerner's journey into Eastern spiritual discovery is helped immensely by Matthiessen's first-rate skills as a writer. Includes details of his studies and travels with a number of prominent Zen teachers in America and Japan.

Merton, Thomas, *The Seven Storey Mountain.* New York: Harcourt Brace Jovanovich, 1948.
Probably the quintessential spiritual autobiography of the modern West, it traces Merton's development from brilliant but disillusioned young intellectual to Catholic convert to Trappist monk, all in clean, spare, perfect prose.

———. *Contemplative Prayer.* Garden City, N.Y.: Image Books, 1971.
Written for clergy, but with the lay person also in mind. More theory than practice.

Muktananda, Swami. *Play of Consciousness.* South Fallsburg, N.Y.: SYDA Foundation, 1978.
Opens a window into the intensive spiritual training of an Indian holy man, freighted with much unfamiliar lingo but well worth the effort. Features moving and often dazzling stories of advanced meditation wonders, and a useful glossary of key names and terms.

———. *The Perfect Relationship: The Guru and the Disciple,* translated by Swami Chidvilasananda. South Fallsburg, N.Y.: SYDA Foundation, 1980.
Somewhat more abstruse than *Play of Consciousness* but rich in helpful insights about a relationship with which many Westerners have difficulty.

Murthy, T. S. Anantha. *The Life and Teachings of Sri Ramana Maharshi.* Clearlake, Calif.: Dawn Horse Press, 1990.

Written by a longtime devotee, this biography of Ramana shows him to be not merely a teacher and sage but someone the Christian West would regard as a saint. (Forewords and afterwords by Da Love-Ananda and disciples, whose publishing house brought out this book, identify Da's link to Ramana.)

Natu, Bal, ed. *Showers of Grace: Avatar Meher Baba*. Ahmednagar, India: Meher Nazar Books, 1984.
People who knew the Indian mystic and teacher Meher Baba recall him in anecdotal fashion.

Needleman, Jacob. *Lost Christianity: A Journey of Rediscovery*. New York: Harper & Row, 1980.
Absorbing story of a philosophical search for an "intermediate" Christianity, somewhere between the mystical and the mundane.

———. *The New Religions*. New York: Crossroad, 1987.
This survey of some Eastern traditions and teachers come West, especially Zen and Tibetan Buddhism, TM, Subud, Meher Baba, and Krishnamurti, provides a useful overview of the field. Originally published in 1970, it deserves a fully updated version.

Occhiogrosso, Peter. *Once a Catholic: Prominent Catholics and Ex-Catholics Reveal the Influence of the Church on Their Lives and Works*. New York: Ballantine, 1989.
Oral history with an emphasis on the interplay of spiritual training and everyday life. See especially the interviews with Robert Stone, George Carlin, Patricia Heidt, Maura Moynihan, and Enrique Fernandez.

Orr, Leonard, and Sondra Ray. *Rebirthing in the New Age*. Berkeley, Calif.: Celestial Arts, 1977.
Firsthand descriptions of the origins of this method of reliving the birth process, written by its developers.

Pagels, Elaine. *The Gnostic Gospels*. New York: Random House, 1979.
Scholarly but highly readable and deeply intriguing account of the early Christian heretics known as Gnostics, based on their long-lost writings, gives insights into many possibilities the established Christian Church left behind in favor of orthodoxy.

Parrinder, Geoffrey. *The Wisdom of the Early Buddhists*. New York: New Directions, 1977.

Illustrative scenes from the life of the Buddha taken from some of the oldest Buddhist texts. Brief and literate.

Peale, Norman Vincent. *The Power of Positive Thinking*. New York: Prentice-Hall, 1952.
A classic of its kind, it may now seem dated and oddly materialistic. But the basics are there, along with many foreshadowings of New Age thought.

Pennington, M. Basil, O.C.S.O. *Centering Prayer: Renewing an Ancient Christian Prayer Form*. New York: Image Books, 1982.
Modern approach to meditative prayer that incorporates elements of Eastern philosophy in a solidly Christian base, it should provide useful practical advice for Catholics and other Christians looking to reconnect with their traditions.

Rajneesh, Bhagwan Shree. *Tantra, Spirituality & Sex*. Rajneeshpuram, Ore.: Rajneesh Foundation International, 1977.
Whatever Rajneesh's reputation, his writings are rarely less than brilliant. This short book is extremely valuable for anyone wrestling with the role of sex in spirituality.

————. *The Mustard Seed: Discourses on the Sayings of Jesus from the Gospel According to Thomas*. New York: Harper & Row, 1978.
Rajneesh applies his highly unorthodox mind to one of the great Gnostic Gospels.

Ram Dass. *Be Here Now*. Boulder, Colo.: Hanuman Foundation, 1978.
The first section is recommended for its colorful stories of the Harvard professor and LSD advocate's spiritual transformation. The rest is pot luck.

————, and Paul Gorman. *How Can I Help? Stories and Reflections on Service*. New York: Alfred A. Knopf, 1985.
Ram Dass, whose primary vehicle for realizing liberation is service, and Gorman, the WBAI-FM talk host, have assembled a practical handbook for helpers and healers, combining first-person anecdotes with their own acquired wisdom.

Reps, Paul. *Zen Flesh, Zen Bones: A Collection of Zen and Pre-Zen Writings*. New York: Anchor Books, 1961.

Perhaps the best introduction to Zen through actual stories and anecdotes, with no theorizing or preaching. Contains many classic Zen tales in whittled-down language.

Rumi, Jelaluddin. *The Ruins of the Heart*, translated by Edmund Helminski. Putney, Vt.: Threshold, 1981.
————. *Unseen Rain*, translated by John Moyne and Coleman Barks. Putney, Vt.: Threshold, 1986.
Among the better and more accessible introductions to the lovely and mystical lyric poetry of this Sufi saint.

Sannella, Lee, M.D. *The Kundalini Experience: Psychosis or Transcendence?* Lower Lake, Calif.: Integral Publishing, 1987.
A sympathetic survey by a psychiatrist who is also a spiritual practitioner familiar with different religious traditions and able to make the relevant connections.

Satya Bharti, Ma. *Drunk on the Divine: An Account of Life in the Ashram of Bhagwan Shree Rajneesh*. New York: Grove Press, 1981.
Written by a disciple during Rajneesh's years in India, it is not as uncritical as you might expect, devotion often disarming judgment. What it lacks in objectivity it makes up for in graphic descriptions of what actually went on inside those controversial encounter groups.

Schuon, Frithjof. *Understanding Islam*. Baltimore: Penguin, 1972.
Almost universally regarded as one of the best books on Islam. Written from the Sufi point of view, but not easy reading.

The Secret Teachings of Jesus: Four Gospels, translated and edited by Marvin W. Meyer. New York: Random House, 1984.
Delving into these long-lost alternative Gospels can be provocative, yielding Eastern-hued pearls. It can also be confusing, and Meyer's lengthy annotations are indispensable.

Shah, Idries. *The Sufis*. New York: Doubleday, 1964.
Probably the most popular book on Sufism, loaded with information and anecdotes, although its historical accuracy has been questioned by some insiders. Still a good starting point.

Spalding, Baird T. *Life and Teaching of the Masters of the Far East*. 5 vols. Marina Del Rey, Calif.: DeVorss & Co., 1964.
Life among the Ascended Masters. If you can keep your mind open to

the possible truth of these accounts, you may be astonished. If not, it reads like a fascinating science fiction travelogue. (Film rights were recently acquired by a prominent actor.)

Steindl-Rast, Brother David. *Gratefulness, the Heart of Prayer: An Approach to Life in Fullness.* Ramsey, N.J.: Paulist Press, 1984.
A Catholic monk with an Eastern orientation explores the spiritual value of gratitude in its many ramifications.

Stevens, Jay. *Storming Heaven: LSD and the American Dream.* New York: Harper & Row, 1987.
Fun with psychedelics through the eyes of its earliest experimenters, including Huxley, Leary, Alpert, Kesey, et al. The function of LSD and other drugs as introductions to spirituality is implied rather than explored in depth.

Suzuki, Daisetsu Taitaro. *Mysticism: Christian and Buddhist.* London: Allen & Unwin, 1957.
Zen's foremost scholar draws some useful parallels and contrasts between two great wisdom traditions with much in common.

Suzuki, Shunryu. *Zen Mind, Beginner's Mind.* Tokyo: Weatherhill, 1970.
A landmark book considered an essential text by many beginning students of Buddhism. Not a survey of Zen but a concise guidebook to the underlying principles of meditation and practice.

Sweeney, Terrance A. *God &.* Minneapolis: Winston Press, 1985.
Delightful, brief interviews with some unlikely figures about their relationship with God, including Frank Capra, Ray Bradbury, Martin Sheen, and Jerzy Kosinski. Sweeney was since bounced from the Jesuits under dubious circumstances.

Trungpa, Chögyam, as told to Esmé Cramer Roberts. *Born in Tibet.* Boston: Shambhala, 1966.
Highly detailed revelations of the training of a Tibetan lama and his subsequent escape from the Communist occupation make this a most unusual spiritual autobiography.

Trungpa, Chögyam. *Meditation in Action.* Boston: Shambhala, 1969.
Recommended for non-Buddhists and anyone seeking valuable advice on the relationship of meditation to active life.

———. *Cutting Through Spiritual Materialism*. Boston: Shambhala, 1987.
An essential text on the dangers of treating spiritual development like one more growth industry, it is also laden with illustrative stories from the history of Tibetan Buddhism.

Twitchell, Paul. *Eckankar: The Key to Secret Worlds*. Minneapolis: Eckankar, 1969.
Intriguing but often hard to follow limning of the inner realms of consciousness and the invisible worlds discovered by this modern Soul Traveler.

———. *Letters to a Chela*. Minneapolis: Eckankar, 1980.
A lucid exploration of world religions, from the viewpoint of a master of Eckankar.

Tworkov, Helen. *Zen in America: Profiles of Five Teachers*. San Francisco: North Point Press, 1989.
Delineates some of the transformations in classic Japanese Zen that have taken place in American Zen monasteries and communities.

Uhlein, Gabriele. *Meditations with Hildegard of Bingen*. Santa Fe, N.M.: Bear & Co., 1983.
All-too-brief excerpts from the work of a great female mystic, the twelfth-century Bavarian nun whose writings have modern, ecologically conscious overtones.

Wakefield, Dan. *Returning: A Spiritual Journey*. New York: Doubleday, 1988.
A Protestant first loses his faith, then loses his way in Hollywood. Falling into drink, drugs, and despair, in that order, he later comes to an entirely different appreciation of his Christianity.

Ward, Benedicta, S. L. G. *The Desert Christian: Sayings of the Desert Fathers*. New York: Macmillan, 1980.
Startling tales of early Christian ascetics that make for enlightening and often disturbing reading. Best in short doses.

Ware, Archimandrite Kallistos. *The Orthodox Way*. Crestwood, N.Y.: St. Vladimir's Seminary Press, 1986.
Excellent survey of the Eastern Orthodox Christian world view.

Washington, Jerome. *A Bright Spot in the Yard: Notes and Stories from a Prison Journal.* Trumansberg, N.Y.: The Crossing Press, 1981.
Revealing sketches and short stories on prison life from a Buddhist perspective.

Wason, Katherine. *The Living Master.* Punjab, India: Radhasoami Satsang Beas, 1966.
An obscure, hard-to-find book recounting the author's study under a Sikh master of the Radhasoami tradition with many similarities to the basic teachings of Eckankar.

White, John, ed. *The Highest State of Consciousness.* Garden City, N.Y.: Anchor Books, 1972.
————. *What Is Enlightenment? Exploring the Goal of the Spiritual Path.* New York: St. Martin's Press, 1985.
Both books collect excerpts from the work of outstanding figures in spirituality and psychology, but the first is out of print. The passages are brief and tantalizing, best used as guides to further reading in these fields.

Wimber, John, with Kevin Springer. *Power Evangelism.* San Francisco: Harper & Row, 1986.
Followers of Eastern and New Age religions are not the only ones who claim or believe in special powers, as this book by a Christian evangelist proves. The title refers to presenting the gospel with "a demonstration of God's power through signs and wonders," and Wimber has the stories to back that up.

Woolger, Roger J. *Other Lives, Other Selves: A Jungian Psychotherapist Discovers Past Lives.* New York: Doubleday, 1987.
Belief in the principles of reincarnation is not a prerequisite for this utterly intriguing book. At times it reads like a mystery novel, replete with case histories and explanations that are far from stereotypical past-life fantasies.

ARTICLES

Berger, Joseph. "Religious Surge by 'Baby Boomers' Is Found." *The New York Times,* November 19, 1986.

Butler, Katy. "Encountering the Shadow in Buddhist America." *Common Boundary* (May–June 1990).

Gleick, James. "Science on the Track of God." *The New York Times Magazine,* January 4, 1987.

Jakobson, Cathryn. "The New Orthodox." *New York* magazine, November 17, 1986.

Lifton, Robert Jay, and Charles B. Strozier. "Waiting for Armageddon." *The New York Times Book Review*, August 12, 1990.

Miller, Patrick D. "In the Spirit of Philosophy: An Interview with Jacob Needleman." *Free Spirit* (Fall–Winter, 1989–90).

Rushdie, Salman, "In Good Faith: A Pen Against the Sword." *Newsweek,* February 12, 1990.

Sanders, Joanne. "Why Spiritual Groups Go Awry." *Common Boundary* (May–June 1990).

Stein, Benjamin J. "Hollywood: God Is Nigh." *Newsweek*, December 12, 1988.

Stevens, Jay. "Good Vibrations." *Utne Reader* (November–December 1990).

Strozier, Charles B., and Ayla Kohn. "The Paradoxical Image of Jews in the Minds of Christian Fundamentalists." *Journal of Distress* (March 1991).

Wakefield, Dan. "Spreading the Gospel at Harvard." *New York Times Magazine*, May 22, 1988.

•

Most of the living teachers referred to in this book can be reached by writing them in care of the publishers of their most recent book. Information about Brother Charles's meditation tapes is available from M.S.H. Association, Route 1, Box 192–B, Faber, Va. 22938. Vicki Mullen and Robert Tobey can be reached at P. O. Box 624, Salisbury, Conn. 06068. Daniel Castro's address is 109 West San Francisco St., Santa Fe, N.M. 87501. Bernard Glassman's address is c/o Greyston Family Inn, 114 Woodworth Ave., Yonkers, N.Y. 10701. Shya and Ariel Kane's mailing address is 175 Fifth Ave., Suite 2418, New York, N.Y. 10010. Although retired from public speaking, Paul Lowe accepts letters c/o Roximillion Publications, 1202 Lexington Ave., Suite 325, New York, N.Y. 10028.

INDEX

■   ■   ■

Page numbers in **boldface** refer to definitions of terms.